SERIES ON
ECONOMIC DEVELOPMENT
AND GROWTH VOL. 3

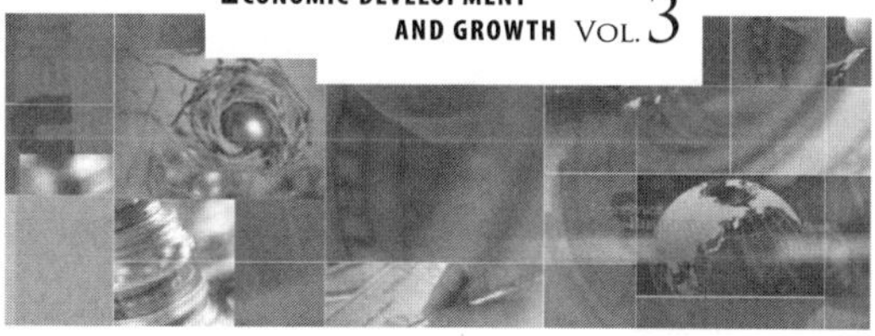

INDUSTRIAL DEVELOPMENT IN EAST ASIA

A COMPARATIVE LOOK AT JAPAN, KOREA, TAIWAN, AND SINGAPORE

Series on Economic Development and Growth **(ISSN: 1793-3668)**

Published

Vol. 1 Globalisation and Economic Growth in China
edited by Yang Yao & Linda Yueh

Vol. 2 Elderly Entrepreneurship in an Aging U.S. Economy
It's Never Too Late
by Ting Zhang

Vol. 3 Industrial Development in East Asia
A Comparative Look at Japan, Korea, Taiwan, and Singapore
(With CD-ROM)
by K. Ali Akkemik

SERIES ON
ECONOMIC DEVELOPMENT
AND GROWTH VOL. 3

INDUSTRIAL DEVELOPMENT IN EAST ASIA

A COMPARATIVE LOOK AT JAPAN, KOREA, TAIWAN, AND SINGAPORE

K Ali Akkemik

Baskent University, Turkey

World Scientific

NEW JERSEY • LONDON • SINGAPORE • BEIJING • SHANGHAI • HONG KONG • TAIPEI • CHENNAI

Published by

World Scientific Publishing Co. Pte. Ltd.
5 Toh Tuck Link, Singapore 596224
USA office: 27 Warren Street, Suite 401-402, Hackensack, NJ 07601
UK office: 57 Shelton Street, Covent Garden, London WC2H 9HE

Library of Congress Cataloging-in-Publication Data
Akkemik, K. Ali (Kucik Ali), 1976-
Industrial development in East Asia : a comparative look at Japan, Korea, Taiwan, and Singapore / by K. Ali Akkemik.
p. cm. -- (Series on economic development and growth, ISSN 1793-3668 ; v. 3)
Includes bibliographical references and index.
ISBN-13: 978-981-283-279-5
ISBN-10: 981-283-279-3
1. Industrial policy--East Asia. 2. Industrialization--East Asia. I. Title.
HD3616.E183.A45 2008
338.095--dc22

2008040321

British Library Cataloguing-in-Publication Data
A catalogue record for this book is available from the British Library.

Printed in Singapore by World Scientific Printers

PREFACE

This book revisits the puzzle of whether government intervention in industrial development in East Asia led to welfare improvement. For this purpose, four well-studied East Asian countries, Japan, Korea, Singapore, and Taiwan, are taken. The specific features of these late-industrializing countries make up a heterogeneous group. Among the four, Singapore deserves special attention as its government has maintained interventions in product and factor markets to date whereas the other three have reduced government activism largely during the last one and a half decades. A common characteristic of these economies is that all of them exercised industrial policies of some sort during the course of industrialization. The book reassesses the impact and consequences of such activist policies of the governments.

One of the most important conclusions of this book with regards to industrial policies in Singapore is that industrial policy in Singapore has contributed to positive growth and productivity increases especially after 1990. This finding clearly contrasts earlier findings in the literature. I have always been suspicious and critical of the validity of the findings of some highly influential studies for Singapore which found zero productivity growth. It seems quite unlikely for such a rapidly growing economy. Several recent studies also found similar results for improved TFP growth after 1985. The argument of this book is such that pragmatic attitude of the government and its industrial policies had a positive role in this. Another striking finding is that interventions of the governments in Japan, Korea, and Singapore did not result in welfare losses.

The reader may find that the book is heavy on quantitative analyses and their detailed discussions. The techniques used in the analyses are standard ones. However, it was necessary to provide the details about productivity analysis as it is highly data-intensive and data construction process closely follows the technical details. The methodology is based on a detailed and very careful process of data construction. There is no doubt that data accuracy is highly important in productivity analysis. These data are also presented in the appendix at the end of the book.

With regard to contribution of the book to the literature, it can be a used as a resource material for economists interested in East Asian industrial policies and for those in similar professions. It provides a case study in quantitative policy analysis using standard techniques. One of the anonymous reviewers of the earliest draft of this book recommended to use the book as a teaching material at graduate level if provided with the database and the model in an attachment. Following this recommendation, the database and the model are provided in a CD-ROM for the readers. However, the reader should be reminded that the model has been built using General Algebraic Modeling System (GAMS) software, distributed by GAMS Development Corporation based in Washington, D.C. The demo (beta) version of this software does not allow the running of long models. Therefore, the licensed version of the software is needed. The programming code of the model can also be viewed with a standard text editor.

Part of this book is based on my doctoral dissertation submitted to Nagoya University, Graduate School of International Development in Japan. I am grateful to a number of people who encouraged me during my research. First and foremost, I wish to express deepest gratitude to Prof. Hiroshi Osada, Prof. Mitsuo Ezaki, and Prof. Shigeru Otsubo at Nagoya University for their guidance and encouragement during my research. I benefited a lot from Prof. Osada's suggestions and long discussions with him as well as thought-provoking questions by students at his seminar class. I benefited from fruitful discussions with Prof. Ezaki and Prof. Otsubo, especially on modeling part. The general equilibrium model in this book is different from the one I used in the dissertation. The current model includes more sectors and is different in equation specifications and special features regarding the behavior of economic agents. I am grateful to the Ministry of Education, Culture, Sports, Science, and Technology (*Monbukagakusho*) in Japan for the generous financial support during my graduate study.

Sincere thanks and deep appreciation are extended to Delfin Go at the World Bank for sending me the programming code for his model, to Assoc. Prof. Mahinda Siriwardana at the University of New England in Armidale (Australia) for sending me his papers, and to Dr Paul Norman at the University of Manchester for his support in iterative proportional fitting technique. Last, but not the least, further thanks go to the staff of Singapore Department of Statistics for their timely response to my data inquiries.

Parts of this research were presented in academic conferences held in Middle East Technical University (Turkey) and Nihon Fukushi University (Japan). Comments, in particular, by Professors Shoichi Itoh and Toru Yanagihara are greatly acknowledged. Finally, I would like to thank four reviewers of the *Economic Development and Growth Series* and the series editor, Dr Linda Yueh, for their insightful comments and critiques. Dr Yueh of Oxford University made very important suggestions on the earlier drafts of the book. Comments by four anonymous reviewers helped me add new perspectives. Special thanks and praise are due to Juliet Lee of World Scientific for her great effort during the editing stage of the book. I am fortunate to have worked with such a nice editor. She made me fully enjoy my first experience in writing a book. The editing team checked every word and corrected even the smallest mistakes. They did an excellent work and I feel indebted to them.

On a different note, I would like to thank fellow researchers and friends at GSID. Further gratitude goes to Prof. Aysit Tansel at METU and Prof. Mete Tuncoku at Canakkale Onsekiz Mart University, my teachers during my undergraduate years at METU, for their support and encouragement before and during my studies in Japan. I have accumulated many debts to a long list of friends for their intellectual and personal support. David Gregory, Noriko Kanazawa, Poh Wei-Leong (for his assistance during my field work in Singapore), Dr Emre Saraoglu, and Semih Sunkar deserve special recognition. I am especially indebted to my "two families" for their encouragement and forbearance during my six-year-long study in Japan. My parents in Turkey always gave me the courage I needed especially during times when I was in distress living in a foreign country. I received great spiritual support from my two sisters, Esen and Latife. Many thanks are due to my in-laws, the Nakanishis, in Hachioji, Tokyo, who always encouraged me during my study, hosted me in their home, and treated me like their own son. Delicious dishes of my mother-in-law, Emiko (*okasan*), have been the most important fuel of my research. Grandma Yukiko (*obachan*) and my sister-in-law (Miho) provided me personal encouragement and made my life in Japan more enjoyable. I learned a lot from them, especially from my father-in-law (*otosan*), Osamu.

My wife, Tomomi, has always been there when I desperately needed support. I started my doctoral study soon after we got married. She has been a great wife to me and a wonderful mother to our son, Mert Shouei. She deserves more than half of the credits for this book. Mert was born six months before I received my doctoral degree. During the stressful final months of my research where everything surely goes wrong and it takes a lot time to fix the errors, watching his smiling cute face was enough for me to forget about all the trouble and gave me an extra power in completing my research.

In the development economics discipline, there are many theories but not enough facts. This book is intended to deal with a special topic for which theories are contentious. I hope that this book meets the expectations of people in the field and those who have supported and encouraged me.

Ankara, September 2008

CONTENTS

ACRONYMS

CES	Constant elasticity of substitution
CET	Constant elasticity of transformation
CGE	Computable general equilibrium model
CHE	Chemicals industry
CON	Consulting services
CPF	Central Provident Fund
CSC	Committee on Singapore's Competitiveness
DEC	Declining manufacturing industries (transport equipment and oil refining)
EDB	Economic Development Board
EDU	Education services
ELE	Electrical and electronic machinery industry
ENV	Engineering and environment services
EPC	Economic Planning Council
EPZ	Export processing zone
ERC	Economic Review Committee
FDI	Foreign direct investment
FIN	Financial and business services industries
GAMS	General Algebraic Modeling System
IFPRI	International Food Policy Research Institute
IIP	Index of industrial production
ILO	International Labor Office
INF	Info-communications services
IPI	Import price index
IT	Information technologies
LEFS	Local Enterprises Financial Scheme

LETAS	Local Enterprises Technical Assistance Scheme
LIUP	Local Industry Upgrading Program
MAN	Other manufacturing industries
MAS	Monetary Authority of Singapore
MNCs	Multinational corporations
MTI	Ministry of Trade and Industry
NCB	National Computer Board
NIEs	Newly industrializing economies
NSTB	National Science and Technology Board
NWC	National Wages Council
OTH	Other sectors (construction, other services, agriculture, and utilities)
PRE	Precision equipment industry
PSB	Productivity and Standards Board
PSDC	Public Sector Divestment Committee
SAM	Social accounting matrix
SDF	Skills Development Fund
SEP	Strategic Economic Plan
SMEs	Small and medium-sized enterprises
SMPI	Singapore Manufactured Products Price Index
SOEs	State-owned enterprises
SPRING	Standards, Productivity, and Innovation Board
TFP	Total factor productivity

CHAPTER 1

INTRODUCTION

1.1. Economic Development in East Asia

The role of government in the East Asian economic development has been one of the most controversial issues in development economics. Much has been said and written about this topic. Most of the researchers praised the macroeconomic stability established in these economies as well as high savings rates, high rates of human and physical capital accumulation, and the active role of the government in monitoring development. Four countries in East Asia have received the largest portion of the attention: Japan, Korea, Singapore, and Taiwan. Common characteristics of industrial development in these economies, such as the incentives designed for selected firms, provision of public goods, superior infrastructure, education, etc., are emphasized in most of the studies related to industrial development in East Asia. Although it is true that governments in these countries engaged actively in industrial development, there are great diversities among them with regards to the implementation of policies. The goal in Korea, Singapore, and Taiwan was the same, altering the industrial structure for further economic development through interventions in factor and product markets. However, the ways this was realized were diverse.

A critical issue is the extent and quality of government intervention as well as its nature. Many studies have characterized the state in Japan, Taiwan, and Korea as "developmentalist." They were developmentalist in the sense that they mobilized domestic and, when necessary, foreign resources for the development of the industries that were necessary for economic development. On the other hand, Singapore government, cannot be described as developmentalist, but rather as "pragmatist." One important aspect of government intervention in Singapore is its bias towards the foreign content in the domestic economy.

Table 1.1. Sectoral Shares in GDP at Current Market Prices in Japan, Korea, Singapore, and Taiwan.

	1960	1970	1975	1980	1985	1990	1995	2000	2005
Japan									
Primary sectors	9.0	5.0	4.5	3.2	2.6	2.1	1.7	2.0	1.6
Industry	43.0	32.9	31.2	31.1	30.4	30.7	29.4	34.6	29.7
Manufacturing	16.5	25.8	22.5	22.0	22.1	21.1	19.1	23.8	21.0
Services	48.0	36.3	41.8	43.7	44.9	46.1	49.8	63.4	68.7
Korea									
Primary sectors	36.9	26.9	24.5	14.2	12.6	8.5	6.2	4.6	3.0
Manufacturing	14.0	20.5	25.3	26.1	29.2	28.8	29.4	31.5	25.3
Industry	15.9	22.4	27.5	37.8	40.9	43.1	43.2	42.7	35.8
Services	47.4	50.7	48.0	48.1	46.5	48.4	50.6	52.7	61.1
Singapore									
Primary sectors	3.4	2.3	1.9	1.1	0.9	0.4	0.2	0.1	0.1
Industry	11.6	20.4	24.1	28.5	23.3	27.1	24.8	26.5	32.2
Manufacturing	19.0	30.3	33.5	36.0	36.0	34.4	33.5	34.3	26.5
Services	77.6	67.4	64.6	62.9	63.1	65.2	66.3	65.6	67.7
Taiwan									
Primary sectors	28.7[a]	15.5	12.8	7.8	5.9	4.2	2.4	2.1	1.7
Industry	29.5[a]	41.3	45.9	51.4	50.1	41.2	37.5	32.3	25.0
Manufacturing	22.3[a]	29.2	30.9	36.0	37.6	33.3	27.9	26.3	21.9
Services	41.8[a]	41.2	41.3	43.0	44.0	54.6	60.1	65.6	73.3

[a] These data are for the year 1961.

Sources: ADB *Key Indicators* (various years), DGBAS (2001), IMF *International Financial Statistics* (various years), Li (1988), and World Bank *World Development Report* (various years).

Table 1.1 shows that the sectoral structure of output has changed considerably in Korea, Taiwan, and Singapore from 1960 until the 1990s. The share of primary sectors decreased gradually while the share of industry (i.e., manufacturing, mining, and energy), especially the manufacturing sector, increased remarkably within two decades. This happened at a time when Japanese sectoral structure of output reached maturity in the 1970s and when Hong Kong started to deindustrialize (see Table 1.2). During this transformation, these countries were implementing what we call today

Table 1.2. Percentage Share of Manufacturing in GDP at Current Market Prices in Asia.

	1960	1970	1975	1980	1985	1990	1995	2000	2005
Korea	14.0	20.5	25.3	26.1	29.2	28.8	29.4	31.5	25.3
Singapore	19.0	30.3	33.5	36.0	36.0	34.4	33.5	34.3	26.5
Taiwan	22.3	29.2	30.9	36.0	37.6	33.3	27.9	26.3	21.9
Hong Kong	30.0	27.4	21.5	21.9	22.1	17.6	8.3	5.1	3.3
Indonesia	8.3	8.8	8.9	11.6	16.4	20.7	24.1	26.0	30.5
Malaysia	6.3	12.7	17.5	9.4	19.8	24.2	26.4	34.3	30.5
Thailand	13.0	16.2	18.1	24.2	21.9	27.2	28.4	33.4	39.1

Sources: ADB Key Indicators (various years), IMF International Financial Statistics (various years), Li (1988); for Taiwan: *Quarterly National Income Statistics in Taiwan Area, the Republic of China*, Directorate General of Budget, Accounting and Statistics, Executive Yuan, Republic of China.

"industrial policies." The recent upwards surge of the share of services in these countries can be attributed to the maturity achieved. In Korea, the decline in the share of agriculture has been accompanied with an increase in the share of industry above 40 percent of GDP. These data are enough to see that the East Asian economies realized a remarkable industrial progress.

The experiences of the East Asian latecomer countries were later replicated by a new generation of latecomers in Southeast Asia, i.e., Indonesia, Thailand, and Malaysia (Table 1.2). This new industrialization current started two decades after the start of the first one in Taiwan, Singapore, and Korea, but its motives and policy instruments were different. While first-generation latecomers industrialized in an era that tolerated protectionism for developing countries in trade, the second-generation latecomers did not face such a favorable global trading system. Instead they benefited largely from massive amounts of foreign direct investment that relocated to these countries to exploit low wages. Foreign investment flew into these countries mainly for exporting.

1.2. The Role of Government in East Asia

Rapid economic development of Japan, succeeded with a delay by the newly industrializing economies (NIEs) of East Asia (Korea, Singapore, and Taiwan), also called the "late-industrializing economies," or "Asian latecomers" in short, attracted the attention of many researchers. The NIEs recorded very high growth rates with rapid industrialization within three decades starting from the early 1960s. Rapid industrialization was made possible by industrial policies of the governments that were designed to change the industrial structure away from primary economic activities (e.g., agriculture and textiles manufacturing) towards advanced industries that ensure further growth of the economy with an ultimate aim of enhancing the welfare of the nation. This required a shift of available productive resources for this purpose. As a result, the three resource-poor latecomers of Asia (Korea, Singapore, and Taiwan) realized rapid changes in the industrial composition of production away from traditional light industries (e.g., textiles and food) toward heavy and chemical industries. Thus, the discussion about the concept of "industrial policy" focuses on the roles of government and market mechanism in industrial development (Amsden, 1989; Wade, 1990, pp. 8–33; Chang, 2000; Pack, 2000).

There are conflicting views about the role of government in industrialization in East Asian experience. Anglo-Saxon economists showed no interest in industrial policies at the beginning because they believed in the supremacy of neoclassical prescriptions (Itoh *et al.*, 1988). But industrial policies were already being discussed by Japanese economists in the 1960s and 1970s. Western economists recognized the industrial policies as a new approach towards economic development in the late 1970s and early 1980s.

The pros and cons of industrial policies can be categorized into three groups. At the beginning, mainstream economists portrayed industrial policies of the NIEs as a new perspective on development placing them in between central planning and the free market economy. They argued that planners cannot fully acquire information required for efficient resource allocation and the market mechanism can do this efficiently. These so-called "neoclassical" economists place the market at the center and confine the role of government to maintaining macroeconomic stability, provision of infrastructure and public goods, improving the institutions in markets to enhance development, and redistributing generated wealth (Krueger, 1980). In the neoclassical view, resource allocation is performed by the market itself. The comparative advantage of a country is determined by resource endowments of the country and resource allocation is based on this, i.e., resources are shifted to the sectors that produce the goods for which the country holds comparative advantages. Finally, the proponents of the neoclassical view suggest that free trade leads to efficient allocation of resources. This is because free trade determines the relative prices of traded goods. In short, according to the neoclassicals, market forces, not government intervention, lead to efficient resource allocation based on price signals.

At the other extreme, there are arguments emphasizing the role of government and market failures. The neoclassicals claim that market provides a mechanism for coordination of economic activities and they see market failures as an exception. Counter arguments, on the other hand, stress the role of government in correcting market failures in coordination. One such argument is the so-called "developmental state" (Johnson, 1982). The proponents of this argument point out the importance of a centralized state in institution-building to facilitate further growth. However, as Wade (1990, p. 26) argues, these arguments are descriptive rather than analytic and say little about industrial policies and their impact on industrial development. It is rather those arguments by the so-called "Revisionists" that offered the theoretical underpinnings for the evaluation of the role of government in industrial development (e.g., Amsden, 1989; Wade, 1990, 1992). The revisionists argue that the main reasons for success of industrial policies in the East Asian economies are productive investments that made up a large portion (as large as 40–50 percent) of GDP and high degree of export orientation. They argue that such high investment levels could not be achieved without government intervention. The distribution of incentives and subsidies was used as an effective tool for resource allocation. To put differently, resource allocation was not left to the market but was rather controlled by the central governing body. In fact, these governments were generally of authoritarian nature. However, although they established public firms to engage in production activities, they relied primarily on private firms for the success of their industrial policies and did not systematically aim at substituting private firms by public companies.

Furthermore, some empirical studies emphasize the irrelevance of the neoclassical comparative advantage theory and stress that technology transfer, learning, and government entrepreneurship were important factors behind the success of industrial policies (Amsden, 1989; Wade, 1990). They argue that Asian latecomers created comparative advantages via extensive government intervention in industrialization. This means that the industries whose development was deemed necessary for industrialization (e.g., steel, chemicals, machinery, oil refining, and shipbuilding) were nurtured by governments. This is because these industries required large-scale investments and the governments acknowledged that private firms could not afford such a big drive and took the initiative. At their infant stages, these industries were protected by the government and by the time they achieved competitive position, they were opened up to international competition.

In between these two extremes, there are other arguments which try to incorporate these two extremes in search for a mid-way explanation. Two of these are the "market-friendly approach" developed by the World Bank (1993) and the "market-enhancing approach" developed by Aoki (1998). The former tries to compromise neoclassical arguments with the revisionists' findings. The fact that government intervention cannot be ignored led the World Bank report (East Asia Miracle) in 1993 to conclude that the rapid industrialization in East Asian countries was facilitated by industrial policies. But the World Bank's study emphasizes the "market-friendliness" of governments rather than extensive use of the government to manipulate national comparative advantages. Market-enhancing approach, on the other hand, points to complementarities between government and private firms in economic activities and the role of government in coordination.

All these arguments try to explain the sources of rapid growth from different perspectives. All but the neoclassical one emphasize the positive role of the governments' industrial policies during the early stages of development. In Chapter 2, the concept of industrial policy will be explained under the light of the experiences of Japan, Korea, Singapore, and Taiwan.

1.3. Objectives and Methodology

This book analyzes the effects of industrial policies in Japan, Korea, Singapore, and Taiwan on productivity, sectoral resource allocation, economic growth, and welfare. For this purpose two quantitative techniques are used, a supply-side partial equilibrium analysis of productivity and a computable general equilibrium (CGE) analysis.

The first tool used is the translog production function to estimate total factor productivity (TFP) growth. The translog production approach follows the conventional growth accounting method where TFP growth is computed as a residual by deducting the weighted growth rates of production factors from real output growth. It integrates qualitative changes in production factors into productivity estimation. As a result, the resulting residual is free of improvements in factor quality and is a better measure for disembodied technical change although it includes various other factors as well. TFP growth is then decomposed into intra-industry productivity growth and resource reallocation components. While the former relates to TFP growth resulting from within individual industries, the latter refers to the effect of intersectoral reallocations of capital and labor on aggregate TFP growth. The effects of the changes in the industrial composition of factors stimulated by industrial policies can be captured by the second component. In addition to TFP growth, a similar analysis for labor productivity is also conducted to examine the impact of the reallocation of labor across industries.

The second tool is a Walrasian applied CGE model. The results from two existing models for Japan and Korea are used. For Singapore, however, a model had to be built. For this purpose, first, a social accounting matrix (SAM) for the year 1995 is prepared. Then, a CGE model for the Singapore economy is constructed. The CGE model incorporates the macroeconomic structure of the economy with individual transactions of economic actors, i.e., government, households, enterprises, and the rest of the world. Unlike the partial equilibrium analyses where only the supply-side is considered, the CGE model combines both supply- and demand-side of the economy. The functional forms of the relations between economic actors and production and consumption decisions of producers and consumers capture the effects of certain policy changes on the economy through linkages within domestic agents in the economy and between the domestic economy and the rest of the world. The CGE model also exhibits some country-specific features of the Singapore economy: (i) imports and domestic goods are imperfect substitutes; (ii) the dependency on imports are very high especially for inputs; (iii) total trade accounts for more than twice the gross domestic product (GDP); (iv) government owns capital and earns profit from its investments, both domestic and abroad; and (v) all goods and services are treated as tradables. The model follows the standard neo-classical class of CGE models as presented in Dervis *et al.* (1982).

The CGE model, which is designed as a multi-sector dynamic model, quantifies the effects of internal and external macroeconomic shocks and major changes in policies on the economy as well as individual sectors. The effects of these shocks on the economy are analyzed via policy experiments.

Much has been written about the role of industrial policies in East Asia. In light of the existing literature, it is expected to find from empirical analyses that the industrial policies are expected to have a favorable impact on aggregate productivity and economic growth as well as national welfare. The analyses in this book address this important issue using quantitative methods.

1.4. Organization of the Book

The remainder of the book is organized as follows: Chapter 2 presents an overview of the concept of industrial policies in East Asia with experiences of Japan, Korea, Singapore, and Taiwan. The theoretical underpinnings of the industrial policy concept are discussed in detail. Chapter 3 sketches the industrial policies of Singapore in an historical context. The recent changes in industrial policies are especially distinguished. The differences and similarities between the industrial policies of Singapore and other three East Asian countries (Japan, Korea, and Taiwan) are discussed in Chapter 4.

Chapters 5 through 7 analyze productivity growth and its sources and draw policy implications from them. Chapter 5 investigates labor productivity and the impact of inter-sectoral reallocations of labor on aggregate labor productivity growth. Chapter 6 computes aggregate and industry-level TFP growth rates and then analyzes the impacts of the inter-sectoral reallocations of labor and capital on TFP growth. Productivity analyses are also enriched in Chapter 7 with international comparisons of Singapore with the other East Asian economies and developing countries of other parts of the world.

CGE analyses are presented in Chapters 8 and 9. Chapter 8 constructs the Singapore CGE model and presents its mathematical formulations. Policy simulation experiments are presented in Chapter 9. In addition, Chapter 9 also outlines the policy simulations with regard to industrial policies in Japan and Korea. Finally, Chapter 10 concludes with final remarks and policy discussions.

CHAPTER 2

INDUSTRIAL POLICIES IN JAPAN, KOREA, AND TAIWAN

This chapter presents specific features of industrial policies in East Asia.[1] In the past, three East Asian economies, Taiwan, Korea, and Singapore, and forerunning Japan, adopted industrial policies for industrial development and recorded extraordinarily high growth rates with rapid industrialization. Here the aim is not to defend industrial policies or government intervention, but rather to provide theoretical explanations to sketch the nature of industrial policies in East Asia. The industrial policies implemented from the late 1940s to the early 1970s in Japan and from the 1960s to the 1990s in Korea and Taiwan make up the largest part of this chapter, while Chapter 3 presents a comparative look at industrial policies in Singapore.[2]

2.1. Industrial Policy: Definition and Theoretical Underpinnings

The concept of "industrial policy" was born in Japan during the early postwar period to describe the interventionist industrial development policies of the government. The experience of Japan was emulated by Korea, Singapore, and Taiwan with a delay of two decades.

---

[1]There are a number of critical evaluations of industrial policies. See, for instance, Pack (1988, 2000), Chang (2000), Amsden (2001), and Noland and Pack (2005).

[2]Primary sources used for country experiences, apart from World Bank (1993) are as follows: *Japan*: Johnson (1982), Shinohara (1982), Itoh *et al.* (1988), Inoue *et al.* (1993), and Kato *et al.* (1994). *Korea*: Jones and Sakong (1980), Amsden (1989), Kang (1989), Leipziger and Petri (1993), SaKong (1993), Stern *et al.* (1995), Lee and Lee (1996), Shin (1996), Lee (1998), Park (1999), Chang (2000), and Ranis (2000). *Taiwan*: Li (1976, 1988), Inoue *et al.* (1993), Myers (1990), Wade (1990), Hong (1997), Meaney (1994), Ranis (2000), and Smith (2000).

Macroeconomic policies are well-defined policies but the same is not true for industrial policies. As pointed out by Wade (1990, p. 30), what distinguishes the industrial policies (in East Asia) from macroeconomic policies in general is that macroeconomic policies are designed to affect aggregate demand. They may have various indirect effects on various industries, but these are not intended directly. Industrial policies are designed to influence investment and production decisions in selected national industries. The term "industrial policy" gained a general meaning today, implying all sorts of state policies for the development of specific industries.

According to Itoh *et al.* (1988), a comprehensive definition of industrial policy can be made as follows: "a set of policies designed for the development of selected industries to increase the welfare of the country and to achieve dynamic comparative advantages for the these industries by use of state apparatus in resource allocation."

This definition encounters five points:

(i) industrial policies are designed for selected industries,
(ii) industrial policy is not a single policy but a combination of various policies,
(iii) industrial policy is concerned with government intervention,
(iv) industrial policy targets resource allocation (most possibly due to market failures),
(v) industrial policy aims to create dynamic comparative advantages for targeted industries.

The second point will be explained in detail under the light of East Asian country experiences in Section 2.3. The third and fourth points were discussed earlier. Therefore, in this section the focus will be on the first, fourth, and fifth points.

Industrial policies are designed to nurture selected industries. The governments select these industries on the basis of their importance for future growth. For instance, Japanese government put priority on the iron and steel industries in the late 1940s and the early 1950s because the outputs of these industries were important inputs for other heavy industries whose development the Japanese government considered very important for rapid growth of the economy. Similarly, the Korean government nurtured heavy and chemical industries in the 1950s in order to establish the future industrial base. Upon selection, winner industries are generally protected and heavily subsidized at first. Once they achieve a competitive position, they are opened to foreign competition. This process is called the creation of "dynamic comparative advantages."

The involvement of government in industrialization process is often credited to "market failure" arguments, which state that the governments in backward economies can allocate investments and resources better than the market. The reasoning goes as follows. During the initial stages of industrial development, there is a necessity to undertake large-scale investment projects which are by their nature complementary. The so-called "Big Push" argument introduced in 1943 by Rosenstein-Rodan[3] argues that there are positive externalities resulting from the spillovers among complementary investments. In addition, scale economies require large-scale investments in small economies where domestic demand is not sufficient and therefore new investments involve high risks. When nurturing an industry or a group of industries, the government needs to consider both demand and supply sides (Itoh *et al.*, 1991, p. 32). Industries to be promoted are determined by high income elasticities on the demand side and high productivity potential or prospects for technological advances on the supply side. Heavy and chemical industries seem to be the most appropriate candidates from this perspective. The Big Push argument contends that it is possible with a large-scale industrialization drive for the linkages among industries to create new markets and the risk of insufficient demand is lessened.

Rosenstein-Rodan argued that individual investment decisions lead to non-optimum allocation of resources because the investor maximizes private (not social) net marginal product, externalities are not exploited sufficiently, and capital markets are imperfect. He contended that markets work efficiently in allocating consumer goods, but they do not function efficiently in allocating investment and capital, and hence resource allocation in the economy is not efficient. During the early stages of industrial development, lack of sufficient capital and entrepreneurship are common problems. In consequence, governments take the initiative and an active position in coordinating investments or they engage directly in production activities.

During these early stages, the governments generally protect the "infant" industries by establishing strong trade barriers and providing massive

---

[3]Cited from Meier (1984).

subsidies. Considering that the investments made are large scale, this helps the established industries attain economies of scale. There are two ways to establish and develop these industries (Itoh *et al.*, 1991, p. 52). One way is the direct provision of production subsidies that enables the newly established industry enjoy product prices that exceed average cost and hence enable the expansion of production. Another way is to impose strong temporary restrictions on the imports of products produced by the established industries that helps expand the production. This is a workable option only if domestic demand is sufficiently high since large domestic demand leads to economies of scale. When production reaches a sufficient level that allows the established industry to stand on its own feet, import protection can be removed. From the supply side, these arguments justify the use of government intervention and infant industry protection. On the other hand, higher prices lead to set-up costs, i.e., a social cost on the domestic consumers in the form of higher prices.

Note that infant industries exhibit the characteristics of externalities and dynamic economies of scale (i.e., improvement in cost conditions over time through learning by doing and investment in technology development) (Itoh *et al.*, 1991, p. 81). It was argued earlier that the establishment and development of these industries require government intervention and protection by the government. Thus, the government undertakes, fully or largely, the establishment costs of the infant industry development. In the case of East Asian latecomers, initially, the capital-intensive heavy and chemical industries were the industries that demonstrated the characteristics of dynamic economies of scale. Later on, when the industrial structure matured towards these industries, the industries that require technological sophistication emerged as infant industries. Governments protected infant industries until they gained international competitiveness and later turned to overseas markets for further expansion of these industries. One reason is almost full exploitation of the expansion opportunities of domestic production under protection that is met by domestic demand. When economies of scale are achieved, and domestic demand is fully exploited, the governments in the East Asian latecomers adopted an export-oriented strategy and international trade became an integral part of industrial policies. Attainment of economies of scale and expansion of production led to productivity gains and allowed domestic industries to compete with foreign counterparts.

When the opportunities of industrialization associated with exploitation of domestic demand exhausted and therefore, the governments turned to overseas markets, they faced the problem of competitiveness. At the beginning, they enjoyed lower wage rates compared to industrialized countries. However, this gave them a competitive edge only in the exports of labor-intensive products (e.g., textiles). As put forward by Amsden (2001), lower wages may prove inadequate against industrialized countries' higher productivity levels, and hence latecomers could not industrialize simply by specializing in low-technology industries. Even in such industries, productivity would be the determining factor in competitiveness. Then the latecomers faced a trade-off between maintaining low wages and raising productivity through technological improvements. They recognized the large gap in skills and productivity between them and industrialized countries and established an institutional mechanism to promote technological and innovative capabilities of their national industries, and the labor force employed in these industries.

2.2. The Objectives of Industrial Policy

Industrial policies primarily address welfare improvement. The most important objective of industrial policies is achieving economic growth by way of industrialization. This translates into the desire to alter the industrial structure towards industries with high-growth potential, most notably heavy and chemical industries.

Bhattacharya and Linn (1988) list employment creation, national economic independence, export development, and technological development as objectives of industrial policy. Achieving national economic independence is rather a political objective. Creation of employment opportunities results, in general, from the increasing demand for labor due to rapid growth of certain manufacturing industries. In other words, it is a consequence rather than an end.

2.3. Instruments of Industrial Policy

There are multiple instruments to achieve the targets of industrial policies. Major instruments of industrial policies in the East Asian latecomers are discussed in the following sections.

2.3.1. *Competition policy*

One crucial feature of industrial policies is the allocation of resources by the hands of the government. The neoclassical argument asserts that competition for profits by firms leads to efficient allocation of resources. The Asian latecomers, on the other hand, generally did not leave resource allocation entirely up to competition among firms. The primary aim of the governments was to catch up with advanced industrial nations. For this purpose, the East Asian governments disciplined and controlled private firms. In the case of Japan, for instance, competition was highly regulated and in many cases replaced by cooperation during the first two decades in the post-war era (Itoh *et al.*, 1991, p. 144; Okazaki and Okuno-Fujiwara, 1999).[4]

When there are increasing returns and decreasing marginal costs, markets are expected to fail (Wolf, 1988). In this case, if a single producer can achieve the lowest cost, then market mechanism leads to monopoly. Under such a circumstance, government intervention in the form of state ownership of natural monopoly or anti-monopoly measures may be helpful in remedying this type of a market failure. The governments in Asian latecomers except that of Taiwan promoted an oligopolistic competition market structure where market entry and exit were controlled centrally.[5] This oligopolistic market consisted of large domestic firms. In Japan, oligopolistic competitive markets were dominated by the so-called *keiretsu* groupings which had close relations with the economic bureaucracy (Shin, 1996, pp. 95–102). Even after the liberalization movements of the 1960s, Japanese government maintained its strong ties with local businesses. With liberalization, the policy of the government shifted from protection of domestic firms to making them internationally competitive. For this purpose, the government stimulated mergers and acquisitions among domestic firms, production adjustments, and price adjustments (Kuchiki, 2003; Johnson, 1982). This policy strengthened the existing oligopolistic structure of Japanese industries. In Korea, from 1960 onwards

[4]The government realized this by rationing and licensing foreign exchange, imposing production quotas, allocating available funds, and sparing large amounts of funds for licensing to introduce foreign capital (Itoh *et al.*, 1991, p. 177).

[5]The degree of controls was the weakest in Taiwan. Taiwanese government promoted a competitive environment from which a large number of small and medium sized firms benefited.

the government promoted large conglomerates, named *chaebol*. After 1980, there was substantial liberalization. A competition law was enforced and most markets were deregulated. Despite the commitment of the government to remove the discriminative bias in the allocation of incentives and the allocation of public funds towards the *chaebol*, the vested interests of these large firms had already become an obstacle against fair trade practices. In Taiwan, on the other hand, the government relied mainly on private firms for industrial development and a large number of small- and medium-sized enterprises (SMEs) gained importance from the 1960s and they were supported by the government with financial incentives. Wade (1990, p. 270) argues that the Taiwanese government was concerned with preventing large-scale capital from acquiring enough autonomy to shape the regime unlike in Korea where large-scale capital were kept under control and disciplined in order to achieve the national targets of the industrialization plans.

The high level of autonomy the economic bureaucracy enjoyed gave the governments the power to distribute generated rents among the cooperating firms. Rent creation took the form of rationing foreign exchange in the existence of foreign exchange restrictions and controls, creating production quotas for firms, awarding rationed exports to countries that impose quotas, priority allocation of funds to those firms conforming to industrial policies, and so on. This was reinforced with the creation of a strong relationship between the government and the business sector. Such strong relations gave the government the power to discipline the activity of the big businesses in Korea. Under such circumstances, there is a risk that favored firms seek favoring and permanence of such rent creation for themselves (Itoh *et al.*, 1991, p. 177). This may give rise to policy failures because politicians may cooperate in preserving the vested interests of the favored businesses. Rent creation was successfully applied in Taiwan and Korea as evident in the rationing of foreign exchange and production quotas during the early periods of industrial policies in Japan, allocation of American import quotas in Taiwan, and allocation of directed credits in Korea (Cho, 1998; Itoh *et al.*, 1991, pp. 177–178).[6] Governments allocated financial and tax-related incentives according to performance criteria designated by the governments.

[6] Bond and equity markets were of minor importance in financing investments in Korea and Taiwan.

In Korea, for instance, directed credits were provided on the basis of realized exports and conformity with the export targets set by the government.

2.3.2. *Trade policy*

It is argued that exports contribute to expansion of productive capacity through receipts of foreign exchange needed to import capital and intermediate goods and foreign technologies. This, in turn, may facilitate technical efficiency gains and improvements in productivity (Hobday, 1995). Various studies link the contribution of trade policies to the success of industrial policies in East Asia, economies of scale, and spillover effects. In general, trade policies in the Asian latecomers served for purposes other than creating revenues for the government, mainly to create dynamic comparative advantages. In earlier stages, infant industries were temporarily protected behind high tariffs but this protection was later eased and largely removed when these industries gained competitiveness. These industries enjoyed also low-tariff rates in the imports of raw materials and intermediate inputs.

It is well known that Japanese government established very high protective barriers in order to promote newly established capital-intensive industries (e.g., electronics, machinery, oil refining, and so on) in the postwar period until large-scale liberalization in the 1960s although non-tariff barriers were maintained for a long time. During the liberalization in the 1960s, some strategic industries such as automobiles and electrical appliances and small and medium industries such as food processing were still being protected heavily by high effective rates of protection (Osada, 1993). Trade policies of Korea and Taiwan were implemented in line with export-oriented development policies, whereas Japanese government relied more on investments rather than export promotion after the 1960s. Korea and Taiwan protected traditional industries (food and textiles) in the 1950s behind high tariffs with an import-substitution strategy. Export promotion started in the late 1950s in Taiwan and in the early 1960s in Korea. Korean government supported and promoted labor-intensive export industries in the 1960s with financial and tax incentives. Taiwanese government initially promoted light industries as export industries by providing tax incentives and low-cost financing. From the late 1960s, Taiwanese government established export processing zones where foreign firms could export their entire output.

Table 2.1. Degree of Import Liberalization in Korea (1966–1985).

Unit (percentage)	1966	1970	1975	1980	1985
All manufacturing industries	37.5	47.7	52.6	66.8	79.8
Light industries	33.7	38.2	43.7	62.3	76.8
Heavy and chemical industries	44.5	62.5	61.2	70.5	81.7

Source: World Bank (1993, p. 297).

Export-orientation in both Korea and Taiwan did not immediately result in free trade although these economies were highly open in terms of the volume of trade as a percentage of national income. Selected export industries in Korea were protected heavily during the early stages of industrialization drive. As Table 2.1 presents, the degree of import liberalization taking into account tariff and non-tariff barriers for Korean manufacturing industries was very low until the 1980s. In Taiwan, the protectionist stance of the government was similar to the Korean government, but there was a gradual liberalization of imports from the early 1960s. Exchange controls were abolished in the early 1960s.

2.3.3. *Tax and financial sector policies*

The Asian latecomers provided various tax incentives and intervened in financial markets in order to provide necessary capital at low cost for investments in targeted industries. Investments in the early stages were capital-intensive and required massive amounts of capital. Tax incentives allowed domestic firms to raise funds internally for their investments. These incentives include, among others, accelerated depreciation, very low or zero import taxes for capital goods, and exemption from corporate tax for a certain period of time. Government's direction of funds in financial markets in favor of promoted industries provided enough capital for expansion of output and exports. Tax and financial incentives provided to firms in the Asian latecomers and Japan took the following forms:

(i) establishment of development banks and long-term credit banks to provide long-term capital, at the expense of the discouragement of the development of bond markets;

(ii) moderate repression of interest rates (therefore avoiding financial repression); and
(iii) provision of directed credits (i.e., policy loans) to exporting firms.

Japanese government introduced a number of finance schemes for large investment projects undertaken during reconstruction and development in the aftermath of the World War II, as part of the *keisha seisan houshiki* policy (i.e., priority production system). This policy was designed in the second half of the 1940s to build infrastructure and to promote priority industries such as iron, steel, and shipbuilding the development of which were deemed necessary for further growth of national industries. Under this policy, various tax and financial incentives were established and prices of important inputs such as coal and steel were set and controlled by the economic bureaucracy. A policy of rationalization followed this policy in the first half of the 1950s. In order to raise funds for these efforts, loans from the Japan Development Bank were utilized and tax exemptions were provided. Japanese firms later on benefited from the so-called "main bank system," where a group of firms that have tight and strong business dealings with each other gather around a private bank and capital is circulated within the group for new investments (Teranishi, 2002).

During the import-substitution period in the 1950s, the allocation of import quotas, foreign exchange allocation, and import restriction were the main sources of economic rent in Korea. However, the allocation of this rent was discretionary. From the 1960s on, Korean government extended large amounts of credits to promote exports and to support exporters. The government spared substantial amounts of low-interest loans for its Heavy and Chemical Industries Drive in the 1970s, which aimed at the promotion of heavy and chemical industries (i.e., iron, steel, electronics, shipbuilding, automotive, electronics, chemicals, and machinery) in order to attain self-sufficiency in industrial production. Combined with tax privileges, these credits favored the *chaebol*. These credits, coming mainly from the National Investment Fund and the Bank of Korea, were far cheaper than other available credits. This created a large difference in the cost of borrowing between privileged firms and other borrowers. Even in the mid-1980s, policy loans made up around half of outstanding loans in Korea (World Bank, 1993, p. 281). The *chaebol* effectively assumed control over assets and this led to increasing concentration ratios in Korean industries. These credits went mostly to exporters. Cho (1998) argues that the government established a government–industry–bank coinsurance scheme to protect industrial firms from unexpected circumstances. This is similar to the main-bank argument in the Japanese case. In Korea, the government was able to manage risks by credit intervention and Cho argues that this saved Korea from being exposed to severe crises.

Finally, the Taiwanese government provided tax incentives to promote exports. Low-cost financing was another important feature of financing. As in Korea, low-cost credits were valuable sources for exporting firms, mainly SMEs, in Taiwan. Export performance was the main criterion to ensure the continuity of low-interest credits. This created a contest among a large number of firms for the credits. Banks were required to allocate a certain portion of their loans to SMEs.

It is important to note that the importance of directed credits was reduced largely with the deregulation of financial markets during the 1980s in Taiwan and Korea. Although various studies have praised the policy loans for facilitating export expansion, some others such as Bhattacharya and Linn (1988) and Hellman *et al.* (1998) argued that the direction of credits by the government resulted in significant moral hazard in banks' investment choices. It is because the banks possess less information on the quality of investment projects. They argue that the government, which needs considerably large information for an efficient allocation of resources, has even less information than banks. As a result, they claim that it is difficult for the governments to maximize social returns through resource allocation.

2.3.4. *Labor market policies*

Governments in the Asian latecomers enjoyed industrial relations relatively favorable to industrial development. This was realized by the use of authoritative state power in Korea, where labor movements were deliberately avoided by the government until the 1980s. Japan and Taiwan, on the other hand, enjoyed robust labor–management relations. Japanese government benefited from important institutional innovations from the early 1950s such as life-time employment system, seniority-based wage system, and enterprise-based unions.

Investment in education and labor training is another important component of labor market policies. For continuous growth, there is a need to maintain high productivity growth rates. Formal and informal manpower development methods are used extensively by the governments for this purpose. Formal education system enables skills upgrading of future labor and in-house training upgrades skills of the existing labor force. Governments in the three Asian latecomers invested heavily in national education systems and achieved a high level of success in this area. In-house (on-the-job) training of labor is out of the scope of this study, but it should be noted that governments provided technical and financial assistance to private firms for this purpose.

2.3.5. *Technology policies*

One distinctive feature of the early stages of development in the Asian latecomers is their reliance on *learning* rather than *innovation*. They aimed to narrow the gap in technological capabilities between themselves and industrialized countries. Catching-up initially required technology absorption via substantial purchases of foreign technology. However, the competitive pressure from newly emerging developing economies led the Asian latecomers to consider technology development and technological upgrading of local firms seriously. In addition, as pointed out by Stiglitz (1989), to the extent that technological change (i.e., learning) is localized, productivity increases for the types of production processes used in advanced economies will have limited spillover effects in the developing latecomer economies. For these reasons, with the involvement of the governments, national technology development institutes were established. A weak research and development base would have left the East Asian latecomers dependent on foreign technology transfers but these economies were successful in developing an innovation base during the course of industrial development.

Technology policies aimed at technical advances in order to improve the skills of the workforce and to improve production processes, which eventually impact on competitiveness. Governments had three roles in technology development: (i) provision of necessary infrastructure and fiscal incentives to facilitate technological progress, (ii) establishment of public research and development institutions and joint research projects in collaboration with the private sector and disseminating produced technologies to private firms, and (iii) creating a favorable environment for technology transfer from foreign firms to local firms. Direct involvement of government is justified on the ground that new investment in research and development is associated with a high degree of uncertainty and there is a minimum scale for research and development activities. These reasons may lead to under-investment in such activities by private firms.[7] The product of technology development policies, i.e., knowledge generated, is also considered as "public good" by the government. Both Korean and Taiwanese governments established public research institutions and science parks for technological infrastructure development.[8] The institutions in Taiwan not only conducted joint research projects, but also engaged in manufacturing production. The government encouraged joint ventures between public and private firms in the 1980s, e.g., the Taiwanese Semiconductor Manufacturing Company which was established in 1986. From the late 1980s, the focus was on high-technology industries and technology transfer to SMEs. Firms undertaking research and development activities were also provided a wide range of incentives such as provision of capital, technical support, low-interest loans, tax incentives and deductions, and tariff exemption for intermediate goods (Wu and Tseng, 1998). On the other hand, public research and development institutions in Korea not only engaged in joint research activities with private firms, but also provided high-level training to technicians in private firms (Hong, 1997). Korean government facilitated large-scale research and development projects in collaboration with private firms from the mid-1970s in high-technology industries (e.g., electronics, biotechnology, and informatics). Amsden (1991) names the governmental efforts in Taiwan, Singapore, and Korea to subsidize research and development projects and to shift the productive capabilities of the economy towards higher value-added and more technology-intensive activities as "neo-import-substitution." It is also important to note that while the Korean government turned to improve the innovative capabilities of the large *chaebol*, the Taiwanese government

[7] In the high-technology industries, the life-cycle of products is so short that the firm is forced to be productive. This means that, the firms must manufacture the product in a short time and in the least costly way so that it can develop a new product before the potential competitors start threatening. Under such circumstances, research and development supports and subsidies are highly useful for such firms (Wu and Tseng, 1998).

[8] Examples of such public research institutions are Korean Electronics of Telecommunications Research Institute, Korean Institute of Electronics Technology, Korean Institute of Science and Technology, Taiwan Industrial Technology Research Institute, and Electronics Support Services Organization in Taiwan.

turned to upgrade the technology in a number of SMEs on a priority basis. Taiwanese government made extensive use of foreign capital for technology transfers to the SMEs (Wu and Tseng, 1998). Finally, the positive role of science parks in developing innovative capacities of domestic firms in Korea and Taiwan needs to be mentioned.

Various studies have emphasized that technology and trade policies have created dynamic gains for the East Asian latecomers. Technology absorption through trade with superior foreign firms facilitates technological innovation for domestic firms. Pack (2001) argued that the need for domestic firms to meet export requirements served as a mechanism to transfer and locally utilize foreign knowledge. Urata (2001) argued that an FDI-trade nexus emerged in East Asia after the 1980s. He found that the regional production and trade networks created by the multinational companies (MNCs) affected the division of labor though the regional production networks they formed.

On the other side, skeptics such as Amsden (1991) argued that Korea and Taiwan had to intervene in the export industries to compete with superior firms in industrialized countries and offset the problem of higher productivity achieved by the foreign firms. Amsden gives an example from the textiles industry. Therefore, these firms had to be deliberately subsidized and prices had to be gotten wrong.

2.3.6. *Foreign investment policies*

The modern industrialization process of the East Asian latecomers relied on learning (i.e., first adapting and then diffusing the new technologies) and technology transfer. In other words, assimilation of foreign technologies was an essential component of industrial policies. During infant industry protection stage, these economies started off with the assembly of simple consumer products. In the export orientation phase, technology transfer for product improvement gained importance. Finally, during the transition to knowledge-economy, technology creation became more important and national technology development plans were initiated.

The industrialization experiences of the East Asian latecomers almost perfectly suit the "flying-geese" and "product life-cycle" models. By the mid-1970s, domestic firms in these economies had already learned the manufacturing processes of a large number of products that were developed in the West and Japan. During the 1980s, there was a rapid growth in the production and exports of technology-intensive manufactures in Korea, Singapore, and Taiwan. In the 1990s, they shifted a part of their productive resources to the newly developing information technologies, i.e., complex software, semiconductors, telecommunications, etc., though they still needed to catch-up with the industrialized countries in many of such areas.

Although all the Asian latecomers transferred foreign technologies extensively, governments' approaches towards foreign investment differed across countries. Japan and Korea were generally hostile to foreign investment but both Korea (despite its hostility) and Taiwan made much use of foreign capital during the course of industrialization. Technology transfer was mainly realized through joint ventures with the foreign companies, licensing, original equipment manufacturing (OEM) and own design manufacturing (ODM), and informal channels (e.g., hiring of foreign engineers, dispatching local engineers for training, return of trained nationals from abroad, etc.). The governments intervened in foreign investments and technology transfer too. The government in Japan preferred internal fundraising for industrial development to foreign investment. The main bank system and the cross-shareholding system served for this purpose.

Korea received substantial aid from the United States amounting annually up to 15 percent of its GDP until the mid-1960s. At the beginning, this aid was used for light industries, such as textiles, and the entry of foreign capital into heavy and chemical industries was banned (Amsden, 1989, p. 76). Korea resembles Japan in that internal fundraising was encouraged and promoted by the government. The *chaebol* received massive amounts of subsidies and incentives for this purpose. However, Korean government made extensive use of foreign capital as well, despite strict controls. The government approached foreign capital as a source for technology transfer and allowed foreign investment mainly in those areas where production know-how lacked, such as electronics (Amsden, 1989, pp. 232–233). Korea imported foreign technologies mostly in the form of technology licensing, technology transfer agreements with the foreign companies, capital goods imports, and reverse engineering. In many areas foreign investors were required to train Korean employees (Kim and Ma, 1998). Foreign investment was under strict government control and 100 percent foreign ownership was not allowed in order to force foreign investors to go into joint ventures with local firms. Korea was successful in diffusing imported technologies to domestic firms and this paved the way for Korea to establish an innovative technological base.

Taiwan received economic aid from the United States until the mid-1960s. With the termination of this aid, the government established EPZs, first in Kaohsiung in 1966 and followed by new ones within a few years, to attract foreign capital (Li, 1988, pp. 92–100). Foreign technologies were attracted through the incentives established for the foreign firms in the EPZs. Taiwan is the pioneer country in the world in EPZs where local and foreign firms participate in export activities. EPZs had superior infrastructure facilities and the sale of finished products in the domestic market was strictly prohibited. Foreign investors were provided 100 percent ownership, generous reductions in local content requirements, and tax reductions. EPZs helped promote Taiwan's exports in high-value-added manufacturing products and facilitated technology transfer. Taiwanese government also sought to attract foreign capital for the purpose of technology transfer, mostly in areas where local firms lacked entrepreneurial capacity.

2.4. Summary and Conclusion

Industrial policies in the Asian latecomers initially aimed at protection of infant industries. However, with the exception of Japan, this policy reached its limit due to small sizes of domestic markets and governments adopted an export-oriented strategy and turned to building international competitiveness of promoted industries.

Large-scale investments undertaken by both private and public firms and export promotion helped promoted industries become competitive and the general-purpose industrial policies became more vision-oriented. The primary target of industrial policies became technology development for which combinations of measures to attract foreign investment and to stimulate private sector efforts for technology development activities go along with government action.

The Asian latecomers enjoyed an international economic system that tolerated interventionist development policies until the mid-1970s. They were able to penetrate into expanding markets of advanced countries. However, this expansion came to a halt with slowing growth rates in advanced countries after the oil shocks in the 1970s. There was a move towards freer trade and capital movements after the late 1970s with demands from developed countries to deregulate and liberalize the distorted domestic markets. Subsequently, tolerance towards industrial policies of the Asian latecomers was replaced by strong criticism.

Under these circumstances, industrial policies in the East Asian latecomers adapted to the changing economic environment. There were significant changes in Japanese industrial policies from the late 1970s due to trade frictions with the United States especially in automobiles and some high-technology products. Japan undertook wide-scale deregulation of its markets from the mid-1980s. But, it had already established itself as an advanced economy by the 1970s and its strong industrial base and technological capabilities had made its industries highly competitive.

In the case of Korea and Taiwan, the same pressure was experienced with a delay after Japan. New international agreements[9] on trade and investment restricted the implementation of industrial policies. Both countries also faced trade frictions in some high-technology products in which they had mass production capabilities. Both countries established comparative advantages in heavy, chemical, and technology-intensive industries by the end of the 1980s. But, both governments responded positively to the demands of abandoning developmentalist policies and undertook large-scale deregulation and left a very large stake in domestic industries to private firms.[10]

---

[9]Although WTO allows for some protective measures and some instruments of industrial policies, their uses are conditional (such as remedying the balance-of-payments problems) and do not necessarily take into consideration the need for a country to industrialize.

[10]Developmentalist industrial policies were abandoned in Korea with the change of the government in 1980. Private sector investment was encouraged and directed credits were largely reduced. Labor movements were allowed and the pressure on wages was eased.

CHAPTER 3

INDUSTRIAL POLICIES IN SINGAPORE

3.1. Singapore Economy at a Glance

Industrial development and economic growth in Singapore is a success story. Being a small island of only about 700 km^2 and having a population of only four million in the 2000 census, Singapore was the world's 13th largest exporter in 2006. According to the International Monetary Fund (IMF) statistics, nominal per capita GDP in Singapore was USD 29,917 in 2006 and this put Singapore in the 24th rank out of the 179 countries, and this was a little higher than the European Union average (USD 29,476). In purchasing-power-parity (PPP) terms, it was USD 32867 and Singapore's rank was 17th, surpassing Japan, Germany, Italy, France, Taiwan, and the European Union average. In 1965, when Singapore gained independence, its per capita GDP was 54 percent as large as Japan's per capita GDP and only 14 percent as large as that of the United States. In nominal terms, Singapore's per capita GDP was still 50 percent of Japan's per capita GDP in 1990 but GDP reached 87 percent in 2006. Most remarkably, it reached 54 percent of US per capita GDP in 1990 and 70 percent in 2006. In addition, a comparison of Japan with other group of countries shows that per capita GDP growth has been much higher in Singapore (Table 3.1).

At the heart of this successful transformation is the industrial policies of the government, which facilitated continuous industrial upgrading and restructuring. Over time, the government emphasized the need for Singapore to promote manufacturing and financial business services. Accordingly, the shares of these activities in GDP grew remarkably (Table 3.2). This was not associated with substantial shifts of employment to the manufacturing sector. In the case of the financial business services sector, a general tendency for its share in total employment is observed throughout its development path from the 1970s (Table 3.3). The government has always maintained its heavy presence in the economy and intervened extensively in

Table 3.1. Per Capita Percentage Growth Rates, Annual Compound Averages for 1960–2000.

	1960–1969	1970–1979	1980–1989	1990–1999
Singapore	6.9	7.6	5.3	4.5
Low-income countries	1.7	0.7	1.9	2.2
Middle-income countries	4.7	3.1	0.9	1.2
High-income countries	4.3	2.8	2.2	1.8

Source: World Bank, *World Development Indicators*, various issues.

Table 3.2. Sectoral Structure of GDP in Singapore (Percent).

	1959–1965	1966–1978	1979–1985	1986–1997	1998–2002
Agriculture	3.5	2.2	1.0	0.2	0.1
Mining	0.2	0.2	0.3	0.1	0.1
Manufacturing	10.4	21.5	26.6	25.6	25.7
Utilities (electricity, water, and gas)	2.4	2.2	1.8	1.7	1.6
Construction	3.4	6.5	8.5	6.7	6.2
Wholesale and retail trade, hotels, restaurants	33.3	26.5	18.3	17.5	17.2
Transport and communication services	13.3	11.2	12.7	11.8	11.1
Financial and business services	16.1	17.1	21.4	26.0	27.3
Other services sectors	17.4	12.5	9.5	10.4	10.8

Source: See Section 5.1.1.

the markets. However, it did so by the market-based economy principle and never resorted to central planning as in a command economy. To illustrate, Singapore has recently been ranked among the top ranks of list of countries for being one of the most business-friendly economies.

Table 3.3. Sectoral Structure of Total Employment (Percentage Shares).

	1959–1965	1966–1978	1979–1985	1986–1997	1998–2002
Agriculture	0.7	1.2	1.1	0.4	0.3
Mining	0.6	0.3	0.2	0.1	0.1
Manufacturing	19.0	25.8	24.7	23.3	18.2
Utilities (electricity, water, and gas)	3.1	2.4	0.8	0.5	0.5
Construction	6.6	5.3	7.2	7.7	6.7
Wholesale and retail trade, hotels, restaurants	6.0	21.2	23.8	23.4	21.7
Transport and communication services	13.7	10.3	11.7	10.7	11.1
Financial and business services	13.4	7.8	8.3	11.7	16.9
Other services sectors	36.9	25.7	22.2	22.2	24.6

Source: See Section 5.1.1.

Unlike many other contemporary developing countries, Singapore lacked natural resources or an agricultural base but the long-run vision of the government enabled specialization at the high-end manufacturing products and the transformation of the country into a free port of manufactures. Industrial policies in the 1960s and 1970s emphasized taking-off through development of the industries using cheap labor and low- and medium-level technology, substantial increases in exports, and attracting massive foreign investment. Accordingly, the shares of labor-intensive export industries, such food manufactures, occupied a high share of total manufacturing value-added and employment (see Tables 3.4 and 3.5).

In the late 1970s, this strategy was replaced with large-scale restructuring that aimed at promoting higher value-added generation, but eventually this strategy led the economy to a deep recession in 1985. Since then, the government introduced new initiatives such as gradual liberalization of

Table 3.4. Industrial Composition of Manufacturing Value-Added (Percentage Shares).

	1959–1965	1966–1978	1979–1985	1986–1997	1998–2002
Food, beverages, and tobacco	24.4	11.7	6.0	4.9	3.1
Textiles	0.4	2.3	1.3	0.5	0.2
Wearing apparel	1.7	3.2	3.5	2.0	0.5
Leather products	1.0	0.3	0.2	0.1	0.1
Wood products	5.2	4.5	1.8	0.4	0.2
Furniture	1.2	0.8	1.1	0.8	0.4
Paper products	0.9	1.1	1.4	1.6	0.9
Printing and publishing	12.2	4.9	4.2	5.0	3.8
Industrial chemicals	2.7	4.8	6.4	11.4	22.2
Oil refining and petrochemicals	7.7	17.2	14.5	7.1	5.7
Rubber and plastic products	12.7	5.1	3	3.2	2.7
Non-metallic minerals	6.6	3.7	3.3	2.0	1.4
Iron, steel, and non-ferrous metals	1.9	2.4	1.7	1.1	0.3
Fabricated metal products	6.7	5.5	6.4	7.0	5.5
Basic machinery	3.3	5.4	9.1	5.5	5.9
Electrical and electronic machinery and equipment	3.5	11.9	21.3	35.5	35.2
Precision equipment	0.3	1.3	1.6	2.1	3.4
Transport equipment	6.1	11.9	11.4	8.4	7.6
Others	1.3	1.8	1.6	1.2	0.8

Note: Sources of data are explained in Section 5.1.1.

Table 3.5. Industrial Structure of Manufacturing Employment (Percentage Shares).

	1959–1965	1966–1978	1979–1985	1986–1997	1998–2002
Food, beverages, and tobacco	18.4	9.3	5.0	4.1	4.5
Textiles	2.3	4.9	2.3	0.8	0.4
Wearing apparel	4.6	10.5	10.4	6.8	2.4
Leather products	1.5	0.6	0.4	0.2	0.2
Wood products	7.9	6.7	2.7	0.7	0.5
Furniture	1.4	1.4	2.4	2.0	1.5
Paper products	1.4	1.9	1.5	1.4	1.3
Printing and publishing	11	5.3	4.7	4.8	5.2
Industrial chemicals	4.2	2.8	2.5	3.1	4.9
Oil refining and petrochemicals	1.2	1.4	1.3	1.0	0.9
Rubber and plastic products	15	6.4	4.2	4.8	6.0
Non-metallic minerals	7.2	3.3	2.2	1.8	1.7
Iron, steel, and non-ferrous metals	1.6	1.4	0.8	0.7	0.4
Fabricated metal products	6.6	6.3	7.2	8.6	10.8
Basic machinery	3.7	5.1	7.7	8.0	11.1
Electrical and electronic machinery and equipment	3.3	15.4	30.4	38.8	32.4
Precision equipment	0.3	2.0	2.4	2.4	2.8
Transport equipment	6.4	11.1	9.7	8.2	11.4
Others	2.2	4.3	2.2	1.7	1.7

Note: Sources of data are explained in Section 5.1.1.

the labor market, promotion of an external economy, and promotion of the long-ignored local firms, among others. A large-scale restructuring in the economy has been under way, especially in the manufacturing sector, with a strong emphasis on allocating productive resources towards promising technology-intensive operations. The aim is to maintain high growth rates. Productivity enhancement has become a major concern for policymakers and upgrading of production activities was strongly encouraged.

Two features of the economy are important to understand the transformation path which the Singapore economy and its industries are following. First, Singapore's local industries are dominated by large foreign multinational companies. Singapore has long been dependent on foreign direct investment for industrial development. Second, external trade has been vitally important. The small island's economy is highly dependent on imports of resources and intermediate inputs and exports of its products. Due to high dependence on foreign trade, changes in external markets have strong influences on the domestic economy. The dependence on trade also forces Singapore to remain competitive. In order to maintain its competitive position, especially, against the new tier of upcoming industrializing countries in Asia, productivity has been a major concern for the government and a strong commitment to enhancing productivity on the island has been visible since the early 1980s.

A deep recession struck the economy in 1985 and the industrial policies underwent a serious review. To revitalize the economy and achieve industrial diversification, especially since the beginning of the 1990s, the government became more involved with productivity, upgrading production technology, and technology transfer. Starting from the 1970s, the shares of upstream manufacturing industries in total manufacturing value-added especially that of electrical and electronic machinery and equipment and chemicals industries rose to high levels (Table 3.4). A large portion of manufacturing labor was employed in the electrical and electronic machinery and equipment industry. Recently, the government has committed itself to the development of promising high-technology manufacturing and engineering fields.

This study is motivated by the changing industrial policies of the government during the end of the 1980s and the beginning of the 1990s. Some earlier studies on Singapore's economic performance in the post-recession period (e.g., Young, 1992; Kim and Lau, 1994) found non-existent productivity growth, while some others found that productivity improved in the post-1985 era. A large part of other studies that evaluate the post-recession industrial policies and their specific features are descriptive rather than analytic. This book aims to measure the impact of industrial policies of the government and the changes in these policies which took two decades ago on the economic performance of Singapore. A principal objective of this book is to quantitatively analyze the effects of those changes on productivity, resource allocation, sectoral performance, economic growth, and economic welfare in Singapore.

3.2. Singapore's Industrial Policies: A Historical Perspective

Singapore economy took start under British colonization in the 19th century as an entrepôt where the primary products of Southeast Asia were traded. A short import-substitute industrialization period under the Malaya Federation was followed after independence in 1965 by export-oriented policies of the government with an open-door policy for foreign investment. The government emphasized turning Singapore into a free port where manufactures are traded and went on to build manufacturing industries according to industrial policies. It closely monitored resource allocation and introduced substantial amounts of foreign investment to build the manufacturing base.

The year 1985 marks a demarcation in Singapore's industrial policies. Prior to the recession in 1985, the emphasis was mainly on the attraction of foreign investment, technology absorption, and infrastructure development despite restructuring efforts during the late 1970s and the early 1980s. After the 1985 recession, especially after 1990, the government's industrialization vision evolved with new initiatives and the integration of the opportunities brought about by globalization into industrial policies, in order to turn Singapore into what the government calls a "total business center." In the following sections, these issues are elaborated in detail with reference to Singapore's economic development history.

3.2.1. *Industrial policies before 1985*

When Singapore gained self-government in 1959, the government decided to promote industrialization in an attempt to diversify economic activities from traditional services of an entrepôt economy (Hughes, 1969).

From 1959 to independence in 1965, Singapore implemented the import-substitution policies of the Malaya Federation, to which it belonged to. The governors of the time expected to exploit an anticipated large Malayan domestic market. However, such expectations did not materialize.

After separation from Malaysia in 1965, the government adopted free trade and export-oriented strategy to develop labor-intensive industries. At the time of independence, Singapore economy was heavily dependent on traditional trading activities and the biggest problem for the government was critically high unemployment rate (see Table 3.6). The task of implementing

Table 3.6. Main Economic Indicators (1965–2003).

	GDP Growth (%)	GDP per capita ($US)	Trade/ GDP (%)	X (bln S$)	M (bln S$)	CAB (mln S$)	ER (US/S)	LPGR (%)	Unem. (%)
1965	7.5	512	230.4	1.0	1.3	NA	3.060	—	NA
1966	10.8	561	223.9	1.1	1.3	NA	3.080	9.1	8.9
1967	12.2	619	210.7	1.1	1.4	NA	3.090	7.3	NA
1968	13.6	701	208.0	1.3	1.7	NA	3.080	8.7	7.3
1969	13.6	803	218.8	1.5	2.0	NA	3.090	7.8	6.7
1970	13.7	914	211.7	1.6	2.5	NA	3.080	6.3	6.0
1971	12.0	1061	205.0	1.8	2.8	NA	2.900	6.0	4.8
1972	13.4	1354	191.4	2.2	3.4	NA	2.820	8.0	4.7
1973	11.1	1903	208.8	3.6	5.1	NA	2.490	3.3	4.5
1974	6.1	2321	274.1	5.8	8.3	NA	2.310	3.8	3.9
1975	4.1	2505	238.2	5.4	8.1	−584	2.371	2.6	4.5
1976	7.1	2586	263.9	6.6	9.1	−568	2.471	3.1	4.4
1977	7.8	2828	284.4	8.2	10.5	−295	2.439	3.2	3.9
1978	8.5	3332	294.9	10.1	13.0	−452	2.274	2.0	3.6
1979	9.4	3959	337.5	14.2	17.6	−736	2.175	2.7	3.3
1980	9.7	4854	369.8	19.4	24.0	−1563	2.141	4.6	3.5
1981	9.7	5483	349.5	21.0	27.6	−1469	2.113	5.9	2.9
1982	7.1	5769	320.5	20.8	28.2	−1276	2.140	3.8	2.6
1983	8.5	6484	287.6	21.8	28.2	−584	2.114	3.6	3.2
1984	8.3	6872	280.8	24.1	28.7	−354	2.133	11.3	2.7
1985	−1.4	6466	277.5	22.8	26.2	58	2.200	4.0	4.1
1986	2.1	6570	267.3	22.4	25.5	374	2.177	6.3	6.5
1987	9.8	7404	297.4	28.6	32.5	−109	2.106	4.8	4.0
1988	11.5	8900	328.1	39.2	43.8	1937	2.012	5.0	3.3
1989	10.0	10275	313.2	44.6	49.6	2964	1.950	4.8	2.2
1990	9.2	12110	306.5	52.6	60.6	3122	1.813	3.4	2.0

(Continued)

Table 3.6. (*Continued*)

	GDP Growth (%)	GDP per capita ($US)	Trade/ GDP (%)	X (bln S$)	M (bln S$)	CAB (mln S$)	ER (US/S)	LPGR (%)	Unem. (%)
1991	6.6	13773	289.6	58.9	66.0	4880	1.728	1.9	1.9
1992	6.3	15427	271.9	63.4	72.1	5915	1.629	2.9	2.1
1993	11.7	17601	272.6	73.9	85.0	4211	1.616	9.1	2.0
1994	11.6	20660	273.2	96.7	102.4	11400	1.527	6.4	2.0
1995	8.1	23806	289.0	118.1	124.2	14900	1.417	3.3	1.9
1996	7.8	25122	278.0	124.6	130.9	12822	1.410	1.4	2.1
1997	8.3	25156	269.9	124.4	131.7	18123	1.485	2.3	1.8
1998	−1.4	20886	258.0	108.5	101.4	18544	1.674	−2.8	2.4
1999	7.2	20850	277.3	114.2	110.7	15185	1.695	7.4	3.6
2000	10.0	23052	298.0	137.5	134.1	13281	1.724	5.9	3.5
2001	−2.3	20816	280.0	121.2	115.5	16138	1.792	−5.4	2.8
2002	4.0	21162	277.5	124.7	116.0	18692	1.791	3.6	4.3
2003	2.9	22061	298.5	143.6	127.4	49106	1.742	2.3	4.5
2004	8.8	25342	346.5	198.6	173.5	21543	1.690	10.7	4.4
2005	6.6	26879	368.5	229.8	200.2	28605	1.664	5.5	4.2
2006	7.9	29473	386.0	271.6	238.5	36290	1.588	−2.2	3.4

Note: CAB: current account balance; ER: average exchange rate; M-X: merchandise imports–exports; LPGR: labor productivity (GDP at 1990 prices per worker) growth rate; Unem: unemployment rate; NA: not available; S$: Singapore dollar; $US: US Dollar.

Sources: *ADB Key Indicators*, *Yearbook of Statistics*, and UN Comtrade Statistics Database.

industrial policies was given to the Economic Development Board (EDB)[1] which was established in 1961 as a statutory board[2] (Table 3.7).

[1]Three offshoots of EDB that were born in the reorganization of EDB in 1968 played major roles in industrial policies in Singapore. Housing and Development Board (HDB) was responsible for the provision of housing for citizens; Jurong Town Corporation (JTC) was responsible for the development and planning of industrial estates in Jurong area; and the Development Bank of Singapore (DBS) was responsible for the provision of long-term loans for industrialization.

[2]Statutory board is an autonomous government agency whose staff is made up of civil servants, businessmen, professionals, and trade union officials. Although they are responsible to the related ministries for their business operations, they are responsible to the government to a lesser degree compared to other governmental departments. They enjoy a high level of flexibility in their activities and raise their funds mostly from their business activities. They enjoy a high degree of autonomy in management and business- and finance-related operations.

Table 3.7. Major Statutory Boards.

Name of the Statutory Board	Year Established	Main Tasks Assigned
Agency for Science, Technology and Research	1990	Promoting science and technology development
Central Provident Fund Board	1955	Enabling secure retirement for citizens
Civil Aviation Authority	1985	Regulation and promotion of air transport
Economic Development Board	1961	Promoting industrial development
Housing and Development Board	1968	Providing affordable housing for citizens
Infocomm Development Authority	1999	Promotion of infocomm technologies
Inland Revenue Authority	1947	Assessing, collecting, and enforcing tax payments
International Enterprise Singapore	1983	Helping Singapore-based firms internationalize
Institute of Technical Education	1992	Promoting industry-based training and providing post-secondary technical education
Intellectual Property Office	1937	Infrastructure provision for intellectual property rights
Jurong Town Corporation	1968	Promoting industrial estates
Maritime and Port Authority	1996	Promoting Singapore port
Monetary Authority of Singapore	1971	Conducting monetary policy and issuing currency
Public Transport Council	1987	Public transport
Science Centre Board	1977	Promoting the dissemination of knowledge in science and technology
Sentosa Development Corporation	1968	Promotion of Sentosa island
Singapore Workforce Development Agency	2003	Enhancing the competitiveness of employees

(*Continued*)

Table 3.7. (*Continued*)

Name of the Statutory Board	Year Established	Main Tasks Assigned
Singapore Standards, Productivity and Innovation Board	1996	Improving productivity and providing assistance to SMEs
Urban Redevelopment Authority	1974	City planning

Notes: Statutory boards are not limited with the above list; there are many others, including polytechnics, national university, national library, arts and council boards, etc.
Source: Internet websites of each statutory board in the list.

To overcome the shortage of capital for industrialization, the government did not refrain from establishing public enterprises.[3] Two of the most important of these were International Trading Company (Intraco), whose responsibility was the promotion of exports and undertaking raw materials purchases for local industries, and Neptune Orient Line (NOL), a shipping company. The government was also able to raise enough funds for public investments through its budget surplus, surpluses of major statutory boards,[4] and increasing amount of private savings accumulating in the Central Provident Fund (CPF) (Lim *et al.*, 1988, pp. 223–231, 362–370). CPF was established in 1955 as a social security scheme where both employees and employers contribute at predetermined percentages of the wage bill. Figure 3.1 shows the CPF contribution rates over time in Singapore. Until 1985, there was a rising trend in CPF contribution rates.

During the early years of industrialization, policies were based on the recommendations of the United Nations Industrial Survey Mission (Hughes, 1969). The mission group prepared the State of Singapore Development Plan[5] (1961–1964) which stressed the need for industrialization to provide

[3]These enterprises enjoyed monopoly or near-monopoly power but were allowed to go bankrupt and their performance was assessed on commercial criteria (Wong *et al.*, 1998).
[4]These include Housing Development Board (HDB), Jurong Town Corporation (JTC), Port of Singapore Authority (PSA), Public Utilities Board (PUB), Sentosa Development Corporation (SDC), Urban Redevelopment Authority (URA), and Singapore Telecom.
[5]Lim *et al.* (1988, p. 66) report that "...the government had only one formal development plan (1961–1964, extended to 1965)... Second Development Plan for 1966–1970 was never published or implemented." They argue that government had little faith in economic planning and continuity of a cohesive leadership that makes all the vital economic policies made planning unnecessary.

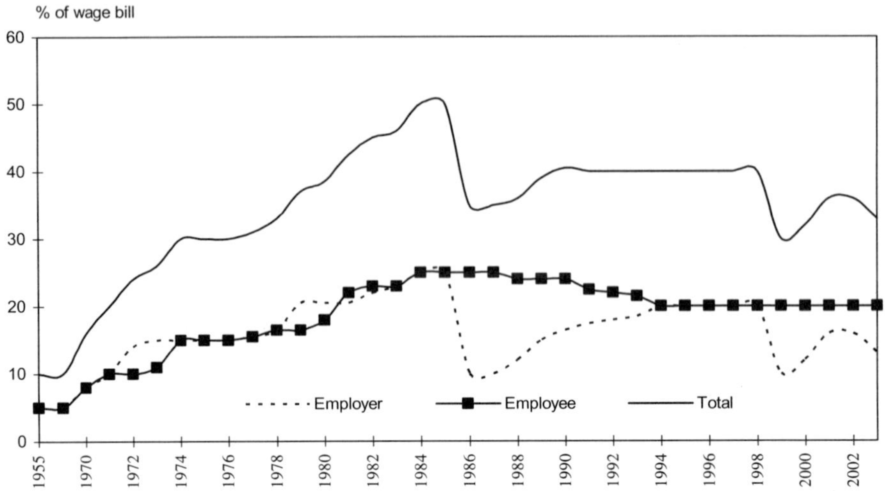

Fig. 3.1. Average CPF Contribution Rates (1955–2003).
Sources: Pebbles and Wilson (2002, p. 90, Table 4.7) and various annual issues of *CPF Annual Report*.

employment opportunities for the expanding labor force at the time. The drawback of British military forces[6] in Singapore from 1966 was a major economic shock during the first years of independence. The plan foresaw attracting foreign investment and technology due to the lack of local industrial expertise, and hence turning Singapore into an attractive location for foreign investors. Accordingly, the government emphasized the promotion of labor-intensive manufacturing exports, such as shipbuilding, textiles, clothing, footwear, and leather industries (Rodan, 1998). On the other hand, the small economy of Singapore was traditionally dependent on trade. Total volume of trade (exports plus imports) stood at more than 200 percent of GDP in 1965 (see Table 3.6). The government expressed the initial necessity to transform Singapore into a free port for manufactures, which required penetration into overseas markets since the domestic market was extremely small to stimulate such a drive. In addition, the government emphasized that local Chinese entrepreneurs who specialized mainly in trade and commerce-related services and processing of a few primary products lacked

[6]Goh (1976) reports that the British bases provided employment to roughly one-seventh of the total workforce at the time and contributed to 15 percent of the GDP.

the necessary capital and entrepreneurship and turned its attention away from local entrepreneurs to foreign companies (Chia, 1971). Foreign companies were assumed to possess advanced managerial techniques, better technologies, and ready access to overseas markets. Consequently, the government established a number of incentives (e.g., complementary finance and tax incentives) and plans to build superior infrastructure facilities to attract foreign investment.

The government was already engaging in manufacturing in 1965. During import-substitution era, the government established a shipyard in Jurong and built some industries including ceramics, polymer, sugar, textiles, and storage (Rodan, 1989, pp. 77–78) due to its optimistic expectations from the merger with Malaysia which would allow Singapore to reach the large Malayan market. The government maintained its strong position after separation from Malaysia in 1965.

Export orientation after 1965 was deemed as necessary to offset increasing import requirements and to enable manufacturers to achieve scale economies. Export promotion measures included tax concessions to exporters, encouragement of foreign investment in export industries, and search for new export markets. With institutional changes after 1967, promising local and foreign companies were granted the "pioneer status"[7] and tax exemption for 5 years. In order to establish sound industrial relations, the government exerted pressure on trade unions and denounced any strikes or other forms of industrial actions as illegal unless approved.

These measures bore the desired effect on foreign investment. Substantial amount of manufacturing FDI flew into Singapore, accounting for more than 70 percent of manufacturing investment (see Figure 3.2 and Table 3.9). Young (1992, p. 24) notes that the pioneer status was originally introduced in 1959 but failed to attract much foreign investment until 1968 because it was not until 1968 that the government expanded its own financial participation. Foreign investors enjoyed a number of assistance schemes in

[7]Pioneer status was awarded to any enterprise, local or foreign, that introduces new technologies and advanced skills. An enterprise with a pioneer status is entitled to some benefits such as exemption of profits from corporate income tax for a certain period. Generally, this period was confined to 5–10 years. In 2004, the maximum period of tax exemption was increased to 15 years. In the past, pioneer status was granted mostly to firms engaging in high-technology activities such as information technologies (IT), IT engineering, computers, and related services.

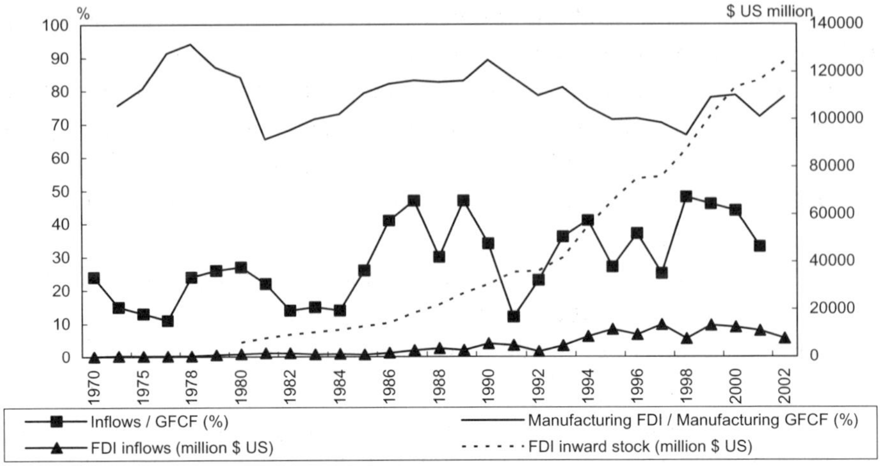

Fig. 3.2. Inbound FDI in Singapore manufacturing (1970–2002).
Note: FDI data are investment commitments by foreigners and GFCF is gross fixed capital formation.
Sources: Yearbook of Statistics (various years), ADB Key Indicators (various years), UNCTAD.

terms of financial support (see Table 3.8 for a list of these schemes). Early FDI chose to exploit lower wages and superior infrastructure facilities. Main recipients of FDI were oil refining industry, due to Singapore's strategic location as a distribution center in Southeast Asia, and electrical machinery industry which required labor-intensive assembly production. Foreign firms soon dominated the manufacturing sector by employing more than half of manufacturing labor and generating two-thirds of manufacturing value-added (see Table 3.9). Young (1992) argues that the rate of return was much higher for foreign capital than domestic capital even during the early 1980s.

Owing to the dominance of foreign firms, an interesting dual economic structure emerged in the manufacturing sector. On the one hand, there were large foreign firms and public enterprises engaging in technologically advanced manufacturing activities, and on the other hand, there were small local businesses that use less capital and operate with lower levels of technology. The performance of local companies in terms of productivity level and share in total output and investment deteriorated *vis-à-vis* foreign companies (see Table 3.9). Lee (1987) argues that public investments undertaken to increase capital intensity and large inflows of foreign investment crowded

Table 3.8. Major Assistance Schemes for Private Enterprises (for both MNCs and SMEs).

Type	Agency	Type of the Scheme	Main Incentives
Tax incentives	EDB, TDB	Pioneer status	Tax-free status for 5–10 years for companies introducing new technologies
		Post-pioneer status	Corporate tax rate down from 26 percent (as of 1997) to 10 percent for up to 10 years
		Development and expansion incentive	Corporate tax rate of 10 percent for up to 10 years
		Venture capital incentive	Offsetting of the loss on the sale of shares against other taxable income
		Investment allowance system	Up to 50 percent can be used towards fixed investment in R&D
Computerization	NCB	Requirements assessment service	Identifying information technology needs of SMEs
		Local enterprise computerization program	Awarding of grants to promote computerization
National automation plan	EDB, NSTB, SPRING	Automation feasibility study	Identifying the potential areas of automation
		Automation leasing scheme	Low-cost financing for investments in automation equipment
Corporate strategy	EDB, SPRING	Total business plan	Encouraging local enterprises to draw up total business plans in such areas as market development technology transfer diversification and business collaboration

(*Continued*)

Table 3.8. (*Continued*)

Type	Agency	Type of the Scheme	Main Incentives
		Product development assistance scheme	Grants to encourage locally owned firms to acquire new processes and development capabilities
		Enterprise collaboration forum	Bringing together local enterprises and holding monthly meeting to explore business collaboration opportunities
Franchise development	EDB, SPRING	Franchise development assistance scheme	Expansion of successful businesses through franchising
Research and development	EDB, NSTB	Double deduction	Expenditures on R&D (excluding depreciation) counted as tax-deductible double expense (twice the amount spent on R&D) thus saving on taxation R&D reserve up to 20 percent of taxable income can be set aside as R&D reserve and is exempt of tax if spent within 3 years
		Product development assistance scheme (PDAS)	Matching grants for product development
		New technology initiatives	Cash grants for worker training between 30 and 90 percent of allowable costs
		Venture fund	Equity investment by EDB (amounting to 1.3 billion Singapore dollars) in new technology companies in Singapore and overseas
		Research and development assistance scheme	Established in 1980 to promote medium to long-term research projects

(*Continued*)

Table 3.8. (*Continued*)

Type	Agency	Type of the Scheme	Main Incentives
		Innovation development scheme	Funding of up to 50 percent of the cost of new product or service development incurred by companies
		Local enterprise financial scheme	Subsidized interest rate for mechanization in local companies
		Local industry upgrading program	Upgrading of local firms to enable them to supply components to MNCs
		Small industries technical assistance scheme	Small amount of fund to assist in computerization of local firms (name was later changed to local enterprises technical assistance scheme (LETAS))
		National Science and Technology Plan	Implemented during the period 1996–2000
		Technopreneurship 21 Initiative	Promotion of the development of Singapore as a knowledge-based technopreneurial hub
		ISO 9000 certification scheme	Effective quality control
Land	JTC	Land provision	Developing and managing industrial estates
		Science park	Research activities
Human resource development	EDB, DAS, SPRING	Skills Development Fund (SDF)	Finance for training needs of the employees
		Design upgrading skills development	Support for industry upgrading

Acronyms: EDB: Economic Development Board; TDB: Trade Development Board; SPRING: Standards, Productivity and Innovation Board; NCB: National Computer Board; JTC: Jurong Town Corporation; DAS: Design Advisory Service; NSTB: National Science and Technology Board.

Sources: SICC (2003) and Lee and Low (1990, pp. 230–234).

Table 3.9. Domestic and Foreign Companies in Singapore Manufacturing.

	Share in the Number of Firms (%)		Share in Output (%)		Average Firm Size (million S$)		Share in Total Investment (%)	
Year	Domestic	Foreign	Domestic	Foreign	Domestic	Foreign	Domestic	Foreign
1968	88.3	11.7	53.9	46.1	NA	NA	57.5	42.5
1975	78.0	22.0	28.7	71.3	2.1	20.4	14.2	85.8
1978	78.3	21.7	28.5	71.5	2.4	22.0	5.8	94.2
1980	75.1	24.9	26.3	73.7	3.3	27.9	15.9	84.1
1983	79.0	21.0	28.5	71.5	3.7	35.0	28.5	71.5
1985	79.0	21.0	29.7	70.3	4.1	36.7	20.7	79.3
1988	77.4	22.6	25.0	75.0	5.0	51.8	17.4	82.6
1990	76.6	23.4	24.1	75.9	6.1	62.5	10.8	89.2
1992	78.2	21.8	25.8	74.2	6.5	67.1	21.7	78.3
1995	78.7	21.3	23.6	76.4	8.4	101.0	28.7	71.3
1999	79.1	20.9	22.2	77.8	9.5	126.9	22.2	77.8
2001	79.5	20.5	21.5	78.5	8.9	131.1	29.8	70.2

Notes: S$ stands for Singapore dollar and NA stands for not available. Local companies include both SMEs and large local companies. Average firm size refers to average output per firm.
Source: Report on the census of industrial production (various years).

out local entrepreneurs[8] and led to the ignorance of local entrepreneurs.[9] Lim *et al.* (1988) argue that the absorption of potential entrepreneurs, i.e., talented graduates, by public enterprises is one reason for the decline of local firms.

Early development policies during the first decade of independence brought about two-digit growth rates (see Table 3.6). However, rapid growth exerted an upward pressure on wages and full employment was achieved by the early 1970s; unemployment rate declined to 3–4 percent. Labor demand fell short of labor supply and an inflow of foreign labor started. Foreign labor inflow and encouragement of female labor participation helped ease the upward pressure on wages (Lim *et al.*, 1988). As a response to changing labor market conditions, the government started to regulate wages to prevent them from rising rapidly and set up the National Wages Council (NWC)[10] in 1972 with which it effectively controlled labor unions and annual wage rises. NWC formulated the guidelines for wage increases which were not mandatory but were generally followed[11] and helped the government in maintaining a sound industrial order. NWC guidelines were an essential component of industrial policies until the mid-1980s. Table 3.10 presents annual recommendations of wage increases by NWC until 1986. The percentage of employees benefiting from NWC wage recommendations or receiving equivalent, averaged above 90 percent after the late 1970s (Lee, 1987).

---

[8]It is argued that during early years of entrepôt development, local capitalists preferred commerce and trade-related activities. With the government's interest in attracting foreign firms led to ignorance of local capitalists in industrialization, although it was not desired explicitly by the government (Deyo, 1981, p. 63).

[9]It is argued that a large entrepreneurial base lacked in manufacturing in the past as entrepreneurs were accustomed to quick returns and were not used to long gestation periods for investments that manufacturing requires. Due to small size of the domestic economy, domestic entrepreneurs could not pass the learning costs to domestic consumers, and highly skilled labor that could be employed as potential entrepreneurs are attracted by the public sector and MNCs (Lim *et al.*, 1988, pp. 268–269).

[10]NWC was a tri-partite body, consisting of representatives from the government, trade unions, and employers. The chairman was independent of the three parties.

[11]Since all the three parties, public sector, trade unions, and employers, were actively engaged in NWC wage recommendations, naturally, they followed their own recommendations.

Table 3.10. NWC Recommendations for Wage Increases (1972–1985).

Year	% Increase	Additional Increase	Year	% Increase	Additional Increase
1972	8.0	—	1979	7.0	(+ S$32)
1973	9.0	—	1980	7.5	(+ S$33) + (3.0%)
1974	10.0	(+ S$40)	1981	6–10	(+ S$32) + (2.0%)
1975	6.0	—	1982	2.5–6.5	(+ S$18.50)
1976	7.0	—	1983	2–6	(+ S$10)
1977	6.0	—	1984	4–8	(+ S$27)
1978	6.0	(+ S$12)	1985	3–7%	—

Note: Figures in brackets refer to additional lump-sum increases in wages included in the guidelines.
Source: Lee (1987, p. 178).

High-wage policy (1979–1985): Fearing that the manufacturing sector could be caught in low-wage trap, the government changed its wage policies in 1979 (Wong *et al.*, 1998). Increasing competitive pressure for labor-intensive manufactures from the neighboring Southeast Asian countries and rising protectionism in Europe and the United States against low-cost export manufactures from Asia after the first oil shock led the government to revise its industrial policy (Rodan, 1989, pp. 136–141). Industrialization strategy was changed towards stimulation of high value-added activities, which are generally less sensitive to trade barriers (e.g., electronics and telecommunications equipment, precision engineering, chemicals, etc.). For this purpose, the government announced a "high-wage policy" in 1979 for a 3-year period. This policy is sometimes called "corrective wage policy" because it was believed that the pressure on wages to maintain low production costs led to a distortion in the value of labor in Singapore. NWC recommended large wage increases and employer contribution to CPF was immediately increased by 4 percentage points (see Table 3.10 and Figure 3.1). In addition, Skills Development Fund (SDF) was established for skill upgrading of employees. Both employers (4 percent of wage bill) and employees (2 percent of the wage) were required to contribute to SDF.[12] Various schemes to enhance

[12]Later on, only the payments to SDF by employees were abandoned and only employers paid for those underpaid workers whose monthly income was below a limit.

labor productivity were also put in place. These changes aimed at restructuring towards high-productivity and high value-added activities.

During the period 1979–1981, wage bills increased by 50 percent. The aim of this restructuring effort was to discourage labor-intensive manufacturing. Rises in wage costs were expected to reduce dependency on labor.[13] After 1981, wage increases were moderated (Table 3.10).

1985 Recession: Economic growth rate declined to about −1 percent in 1985 (see Table 3.6). Manufacturing growth rate also slowed down. These are generally attributed to rising wage costs due to high-wage policy. However, it would be misleading to assert that high-wage policy is the sole reason behind the 1985 recession. There are some other factors that led to the recession: some major industries such as oil refining, shipbuilding, and ship-repairing were growing at low rates in the early 1980s due to declining external demand; and there was an oversupply in the booming construction sector where the boom was supported by the government (Lim *et al.*, 1988; MTI, 1986, pp. 38–46). Declining international competitiveness and rising operating costs, especially labor costs, required a reappraisal of industrial policies.

3.2.2. *Industrial policies after the recession*

Industrial policies underwent significant changes after the 1985 recession. The government recognized the exhaustion of the opportunities brought about by rapid industrialization. Increasing integration of global commodity and financial markets was also acknowledged. Newly developing countries of Asia also started to compete in labor-intensive manufactures. These changes in the external economic environment led the government to revise its industrial policies and consider the promotion of industries with higher value-added such as electronics, chemicals, biotechnology, and precision equipment. New initiatives were put in place to improve the technological capabilities of firms. These were undertaken in collaboration with local and foreign firms, labor unions, and academic institutions. Milestones of the industrial policies following the reconstruction efforts of after the recession are explained below.

---

[13] These efforts later came to be known as the "Second Industrial Revolution."

The Economic Committee (1985): As a response to the recession, the government gathered representatives from different circles under the "Economic Committee" to detect the causes of the recession and to formulate a prescription to revive the economy.[14] The report of the committee recognized the importance of the manufacturing sector but also stressed the importance of financial and communication services for sustained growth (MTI, 1986, pp. 141–143). It was emphasized that Singapore could develop as a "total business center" via the integration of several high value-added manufacturing activities with financial and communication services to make Singapore a promising mediator for foreign investors looking for investment opportunities in the Southeast Asian region (Rodan, 1989, pp. 190–191).

With changing comparative advantages, the government allocated large amounts of resources to promote skill- and knowledge-intensive manufacturing activities as recommended by the Economic Committee. The committee's report highlighted three big problems of the economy: the decline of some important industries (shipbuilding and oil refining), declining international competitiveness, and inability of local companies to follow the government's industrial restructuring efforts (Rodan, 1989, p. 192). Accordingly, the government placed more emphasis on the development of local enterprises (MTI, 1986, pp. 134–138), partially due to rising voice of local entrepreneurs who were affected adversely from the recession. The committee also recommended the government to divest and privatize some public firms, but although some action was taken, the government did not show any explicit commitment for this purpose (MTI, 1986, p. 71). Finally, the committee emphasized the need to promote productivity by enhancing product design and development, investing in technology, training of labor, and creating a productivity-conscious workforce (MTI, 1986, pp. 123–126). These measures are explained in depth in Chapter 4.

Apart from these long-run measures, the report also recommended some short-run cost-cutting measures to enhance competitiveness. Following

[14] Singapore government occasionally gathered committees to draw guidelines for policies as a response to changes in the economic environment. These committees consisted of representatives from the government, academics, domestic and foreign businesses, and labor unions. The government prefers flexible and changing policies in order to adapt or react to changes in the global economy.

these recommendations, employer contributions to CPF were reduced from 25 to 10 percent (see Figure 3.1), wage levels were frozen for a 2-year period, and both corporate (from 40 to 30 percent) and personal income tax rates were reduced. These measures proved to be successful; by 1988 Singapore was back on its high-growth track (see Table 3.6). In the labor market, most of the restrictions were removed after 1986 and a flexible wage system was introduced so that firms could pass some of the shocks of a recession to wage earners. Accordingly, NWC wage increase guidelines lost their functionality.

The Next Lap and the Strategic Economic Plan (1991): The government prepared the Strategic Economic Plan (SEP) to draw strategies for Singapore for the 1990s to achieve the status of a developed nation. In this plan, long-run strategies to maintain international competitiveness were strongly emphasized. Key strategies for growth include the improvement of human resources, establishing an external wing for the economy, improving domestic resource efficiency, improving the so-called "soft-infrastructure" (i.e., technological infrastructure, an institutional structure which supports innovation, and a system that encourages cooperation between government, labor, and business), attraction of foreign talent, and encouragement of the internationalization of Singapore companies via overseas investments (EPC, 1991, pp. 5–9).

The Next Lap, the official development program of Goh Chok Tong, who took office from the long-serving Prime Minister Lee Kuan Yew in 1990, also set industry-specific plans for the year 2000 (Wong 1996b). *Manufacturing 2000* targeted sustaining of the manufacturing sector's share in GDP at 25 percent (which was achieved); *Regionalization 2000* aimed to build an external economy for growth; *National Technology Plan* aimed at boosting Singapore's innovative capacity; *IT 2000* targeted turning Singapore into an "intelligent island"; *Local Enterprises 2000* targeted enhancing productivity in SMEs; and *Co-Investment Program* aimed at building and extending relations between MNCs and SMEs in order to exploit the external economies arising from their subcontracting relations.

Majority of the targets were attained by the year 2000. Singapore became competitive in the production of certain manufacturing products, mainly in electronics, computers, and precision engineering industries. The share of manufacturing in GDP was maintained at one-fourth level, electronics industry alone accounting for half of the manufacturing output. However, the goal of increasing the share of research and development expenditures in GDP to 2 percent could not be attained. In addition, manufacturing sector was still heavily dominated by large foreign firms. They accounted for over two-thirds of total manufacturing investment and value-added generation (Table 3.9). Significant institutional changes also took place in this period.

While EDB retained its position as the main implementing agency in industrial policies, new institutions were set up to assist EDB and the existing ones were restructured and given new tasks in industrial policies.[15]

Asian Financial Crisis and the Committee on Singapore's Competitiveness (1998): The Asian financial crisis in 1997–98 hit Singapore hardly due to financial ties of local banks and portfolio investments and outward FDI by local firms in the region. Growth rate declined from 8.6 percent in 1997 to −0.9 percent in 1998; unemployment rate doubled from 1.8 percent in 1997 to 3.6 percent in 1999; and the Singapore dollar fell from 1.4 to 1.7 against the US dollar from 1996 to 1999 (see Table 3.6). The slump in world markets for high-technology products, mainly electronics, in the mid-1990s had already put Singapore into trouble (CSC, 1998). In May 1997, a little before the Asian crisis, the government set up the Committee on Singapore's Competitiveness (CSC) to identify problem areas and to search ways to increase competitiveness over the next 10 years.

The report of CSC acknowledged the principles of SEP such as the importance of manufacturing and services sectors, strengthening of domestic SMEs, developing human and intellectual capital, leveraging science, technology and innovation, optimizing resource management, and enhancing the role of the government as business facilitator. The committee drew two essential sets of recommendations to improve competitiveness through cost-cutting measures both in the short- and the long-run (MTI, 1998, pp. 3–5). Short-run measures stressed the need to ease the bitter effects of Asian financial crisis and maintaining investor confidence.

[15]Productivity and Standards Board was established in 1996 to assist local firms in labor training and to enhance productivity. Trade Development Board (TDB) was restructured in 2002 as International Enterprise Singapore. The Development Bank of Singapore (DBS) and business undertakings of the government-run Post Office Savings Bank, the largest banking entity, were merged into a dominant financial unit in the local capital market.

Long-run measures emphasized developing Singapore into an advanced and globally competitive economy with manufacturing and financial services as twin engines of growth. Attraction of FDI was also deemed necessary especially in high-technology industries, by way of public investments to enhance infrastructural facilities to be the best in the world and by increasing technological capabilities of domestic firms. For this purpose, research and development grants, tax and other incentives were continued (Table 3.8).

Slump in global markets and the Economic Review Committee (2003): The revival after the Asian financial crisis lasted only for 2 years and for three consecutive years (2001–2003) the economy recorded low growth rates due to the slump in the global export markets of Singapore, mainly global electronic markets. As a response, the government established the Economic Review Committee (ERC) in December 2001 to review the development strategy and reformulate it for restructuring. The report of the committee which was published recognized the achievement of the developed nation status[16] and the drastic changes in the external environment with the integration of China into the world economy (MTI, 2003, pp. 8–15). The report emphasized the need for Singapore to restructure further and build on its own strengths. To realize this, six major areas were addressed:

(i) expansion of external ties via multilateral trade relations;
(ii) enhancing competitiveness by reducing direct taxes, shifting toward indirect taxes, and competitive pricing of infrastructure and production factors;
(iii) promotion of twin engines, i.e., key manufacturing clusters (i.e., electronics, chemicals, biomedical sciences, and engineering) and financial services;
(vi) enhancing manpower by training and welcoming foreign talent;
(v) promoting local firms, including SMEs and government-linked companies, by rationalizing, upgrading, and expanding into the external economy; and

[16]By the 1990s, per capita GDP level of Singapore passed the levels of some developed countries and it was raised to the rank of "developed country" by international economic institutions.

(vi) restructuring to upgrade skills even at the cost of structural unemployment.

Following these policy changes recommended by the ERC, Singapore recovered from the recession. The favorable conditions in the world economy helped the economy grow by 7.8 percent in average during 2004–2006. The government is expecting an annual average growth rate of between 4 and 6 percent for the next 10 years after 2007.

3.3. Characteristics of Industrial Policies in Singapore

The success of Singapore's industrial policies is generally attributed to effective and successful integration of the tasks of various government agencies. At the center of the decision-making and policymaking lies the EDB. The blueprints of various sub-policies of the official industrial policies are prepared by the economic bureaucrats in the Ministry of Trade and Industry (MTI) but are actually implemented in by EDB bureaucrats and officers.

Since its foundation in 1961, EDB coordinated and monitored activities of various government agencies, which were established to carry on industrial policies. These agencies include, among others, Trade Development Board (later restructured as International Enterprise Singapore), Jurong Town Corporation, National Science and Technology Board (later renamed to Agency for Science, Technology and Research) and Productivity and Standards Board (later restructured as Standards, Productivity, and Innovation Board).

EDB and collaborating agencies operate as statutory boards. EDB has successfully enabled and monitored the attraction of foreign investment into Singapore. It is also important to note that most incentives and support schemes for both local and foreign companies were administered directly by the EDB, i.e., it was the primary financier of industrial policies, which allocated investible funds to the promoted industries. These funds were provided by financial institutions and the government (mostly from the savings that accumulated in CPF). In the following sections, main features of sub-policies under Singapore's industrial policies in the post-1985 era are elaborated.

3.3.1. *Labor market policy*

Labor market has been an area where the involvement of the government has been the most extensive.[17] Its involvement in the labor market has evolved through three stages, 1965–1978 (early post-independence rapid growth years), 1979–1985 (economic restructuring), and after 1985. In the first period (1965–1978), the immediate problems to solve for the government were high unemployment rate (above 10 percent) and ensuring continuous economic growth. The government's responses to these challenges were twofold. One was the promotion of export-oriented labor-intensive industries (especially, textiles industry and the assembly-based electrical machinery and appliances industry) as part of the export-oriented development strategy. The other response was the use of abundant unskilled labor for this purpose. The economy grew rapidly in this period and the problem of unemployment was solved through this process. Unemployment rate, which stood at 9 percent in 1966, was brought down to 4 percent by 1973, bringing the economy to a point where full employment is achieved. Labor, then, became scarce in some fast-growing sectors and the government sought to increase the female labor-force participation rate and allowed imports of unskilled foreign labor, mainly from Malaysia. The signs of tight labor market conditions led the government to revise its labor market policy. Consequently, the NWC was established in 1972 in order to bring wage settlement and labor-management relations under control. NWC was given the authority to recommend on annual wage increases, which were later closely followed by the both public and private firms. In the early 1970s, NWC opted for wage restraint (i.e., wage increases lower than the increase in consumer prices) where real wages were put under pressure in order to cushion the destructive effects of the oil shocks that could bring in high inflation to the country. Until the second half of the 1970s the growth rate of the real wages generally fell below that of labor productivity (see Figure 3.3).

The government changed its policy of promoting labor-intensive industries in favor of higher value-added activities in the late-1970s. This came with a restructuring plan in which the labor market policy played a major role. In 1979, the government initiated a "high-wage policy" and wages were deliberately increased at high rates through the NWC (see Figure 3.3).

[17]The information in this section is largely extracted from Carling (1995).

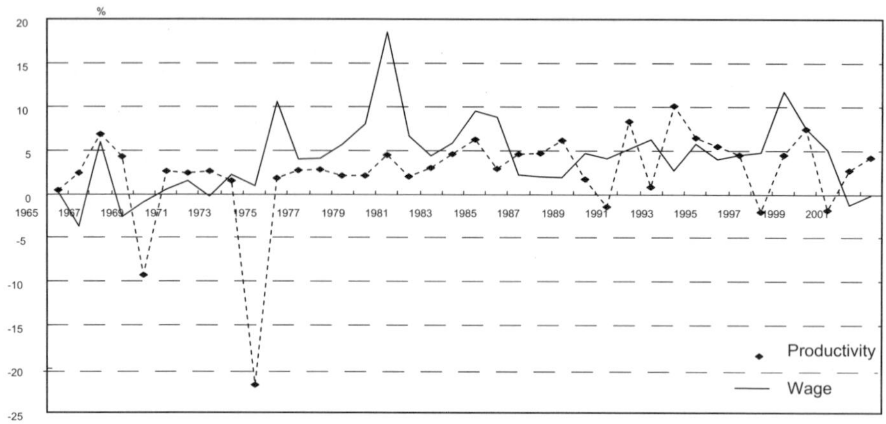

Fig. 3.3. Percentage growth rates of average real wage and labor productivity.
Source: Author's calculations.

This was due to the government's perception that "correcting" the restrained wages and letting them approach to their market-clearing levels would help increase labor costs and reflect labor-scarcity and consequently stimulate the producers to shift to higher value-added activities. The government also put in action some measures to help improve labor skills by establishing the SDF, where both employers and employees contributed equally (2 percent of the wage bill in 1979, which was later increased to 4 percent in 1980). In addition, the government announced additional financial assistance schemes to assist private firms in improving labor skills.

The Economic Committee which was established to investigate the reasons of the recession in 1985 and ways to escape its adverse effects recommended cutting labor costs by reducing the contribution rates of employees and employers to the CPF and freezing of wages for 2 years. These recommendations were soon put in action by the government.

Labor market policies of the government changed largely after the 1985 recession. A sub-committee under NWC recommended in 1986 the introduction of a flexible wage system rather than mandatory announcing of annual wage increases by NWC. This reform was adopted and put in effect from 1987. Flexible wage system divides the wage into three parts: (i) a basic component, (ii) supplement to the wage in the amount of a month's wage or so, which could be adjusted in times of recession, and (iii) a performance bonus which is variable depending on the performance of the workers and the company, i.e., company profits and productivity. The flexible wage system is a move towards the liberalization of the labor market policies of the government. NWC annual wage increases were abandoned from 1987 on and were replaced by qualitative guidelines (i.e., providing recommendations on wage increases taking into account the relation between wages and productivity).

In addition to SDF, the government resumed its policy of assisting the companies to improve labor quality through extensive training and education. Inflow of unskilled labor mainly from Malaysia was allowed to meet the excess demand for such labor. The government also encouraged skilled expatriates to settle in Singapore.

3.3.2. *Investment and tax policy*

The government offered various incentive schemes for both domestic and foreign investors (see Table 3.8). However, foreign investors received a large portion of these incentives. Of these incentives, the most extensively used ones were tax incentives such as tax holidays, tax exemption on profits, double tax deduction for exports, and exemption for various types of withholding taxes. The loss of revenues from these incentives was not a big concern for the government due to its huge revenues from indirect taxes and the large surpluses of statutory boards. These tax incentives are gradually eliminated as firms grew.

3.3.3. *Technology policy*

Absorption of foreign technology was a major concern for the government in the pre-1985 era. But this opportunity was exhausted in the post-1985 era and the government felt the necessity to establish a national innovation system by providing generous incentives to all parties involved, i.e., universities, public and private research and development institutions, and foreign firms. Endogenous technology creation was important as a source to enhance competitiveness and productivity especially after the emergence of low-cost developing countries as competitors for labor-intensive products. It would also help maintain inflows of FDI by making Singapore attractive with its technological infrastructure. EDB has various incentives and financial support schemes to promote techno-entrepreneurship, i.e., promotion of domestic entrepreneurship in high-technology areas. Although technology policies concern all players in the economy, their target for dominantly small local firms is the upgrading of technical capacities and absorption and transfer of technology from large foreign firms.

3.3.4. *Foreign trade policy*

Due to its geographical location and advanced infrastructural facilities, Singapore has developed as a free port and the government has favored a free trade regime to exploit these advantages of the island (Chia, 1985; Rieber, 1996). The free trade regime meant virtually no export or import restrictions or foreign exchange controls. Unlike the other Asian latecomers, nationality of production was not important for Singapore. Singapore has clearly benefited from free trade tradition as it helped maintain high growth rates in trade (see Table 3.6).

Free trade policy is essential for Singapore for various reasons. First, the domestic economy is extremely small and with trade barriers such a small domestic market does not stimulate efficiency in productive activities. Second, very low tariff rates and non-existence of any restrictions on trade helps attract more foreign investors to the island. Third, as Singapore firms are highly dependent on imported inputs for their production, low tariffs are beneficial for them. Since a large part of production is for exports, tariffs on imported inputs will indirectly affect exports and therefore repel foreign investors.

Section 3.3.2 compares free trade policy of Singapore with the selective and strategic trade policies in Japan, Korea, and Taiwan.

3.3.5. *Foreign investment policy*

The government's FDI policy is liberal and manufacturing sector was dominated by foreign firms since the beginning of industrialization. Chia (1985) argues that the main reasons behind the success of FDI policies are liberal incentives, absence of restrictions such as domestic content requirements, and consistency over time. In addition, strategic location of the island, superior infrastructure facilities in transportation, telecommunications, industrial estates, and a well-working administrative framework helped Singapore attract large amounts of FDI.

EDB is the responsible agency for FDI policies. EDB introduced the concept of "one-stop investment" after the 1985 recession. This refers to administration of incentives and various support schemes (see Table 3.8 for a list of some of these incentives) for the foreign investors willing to invest in targeted industries through a one-stop agency (EDB) with minimal bureaucratic costs. Reducing the costs for foreign investors in this way clearly gives Singapore a competitive advantage in attracting foreign investment.[18]

In the post-1985 era, the government aimed to attract FDI by improving the level of productivity and innovative capacity (Chia, 1997).

After long years of rapid growth and rapid accumulation of capital, returns to capital declined to a large extent in the post-1985 era.[19] Coupled with the emergence of new rivals for FDI such as China, the opportunity to attract more FDI seems to be less than before (Pang, 2000; Wong, 2001). Accordingly, the government responded to this challenge with an attempt to attract more foreign firms to set up their regional headquarters in Singapore expand their production in growing areas of Southeast Asia (Tan, 1999).

3.3.6. *Regionalization*

Building a so-called "external economy" was included in industrial policies after 1985. It is argued that the government of Singapore is the most active one as an entrepreneur in promoting regionalization. Building an external economy is considered as a method of facilitating further development of the economy.[20] In this respect, of great importance is the Sijori Growth Triangle including Singapore, and the nearby Johor State (Malaysia) and Riau Islands

[18]It is necessary to note that the government does not disclose the information on the amount of subsidies and incentives provided to the MNCs. Most of these support schemes are negotiated at the company level. Typically, EDB deals with foreign investors and offers different concessions to different firms. Due to the lack of such data the costs and benefits of the attraction of FDI are not known well.

[19]Wong (2000) reports that the return on equity in manufacturing sector declined from 22 percent in 1988 to 11.8 percent in 1998. Of critical importance is the decline in the return on equity in electronics manufacturing from 31.5 in 1987 to 16.5 percent in 1998.

[20]One study estimates that the impact of outward FDI in Singapore on economic growth in Singapore is an increase in sustainable GNP growth rate from 6 to 9 percent (Pang, 2000).

(Indonesia).[21] The government anticipates that in the case of drastic declines in foreign investment inflows, this external wing of the economy will partially counterbalance the vulnerability of the economy by relocating low value-added and labor-intensive production to the triangle (Yeung, 1998). In addition, the government expects that the increased linkages between domestic industry clusters and regional development projects to work for the benefit of domestic firms (Wong, 1996a).

The importance of internationalization of production activities by creating an external sector for the economy (regionalization) was documented in Economic Committee's Report in 1986. Promoting an external economy was originally thought as a method to stay competitive when wages were rising and resources were increasingly exhausted. Relocation of low value-added and labor-intensive production to nearby areas that are rich in natural resources and cheap labor became a viable option for Singapore. Later in the Next Lap, *Regionalization 2000 Plan* was one of the major pillars of economic policies. SEP also recognized the importance of the growth triangle and business alliances with the region (EPC, 1991, p. 101). Since the launch of this plan, there was a tremendous increase in Singapore's outward foreign direct investments both in terms of gross amount and as a percentage of GDP. The number of Singaporean and Singapore-based foreign firms investing in regional projects increased through time. These firms include not only domestic private firms that are subsidized and encouraged by the government, but also public companies, statutory boards, and MNCs. The investing firms receive assistance from the government in the form of tax incentives, provision of information about the overseas markets, and establishing of Singaporean schools for the families settling overseas (Wong, 1996b; Campbell *et al.*, 2003). Most of these incentives were provided by the EDB and introduced during the early and mid-1990s. Even from 1996, the EDB started a new incentive scheme and committed itself to taking 70 percent of the risk of overseas ventures involving local companies.

As a result of these developments, cumulative outward FDI from Singapore increased rapidly to reach 21 billion Singapore dollars in 1993, and almost 90 billion Singapore dollars in 2001 (Yearbook of Statistics, various years). However, majority of outward FDI was realized by Singapore-based

[21] Sijori is a derived abbreviation to describe the Singapore–Johor–Riau growth triangle, made by combining the first two initials of each location.

MNCs that relocated labor-intensive operations.[22] A large portion of FDI from Singapore goes to Asia. An interesting point is the reversal of the ownership of outward FDI in Singapore from wholly or majority local-owned companies (slightly above 50 percent of total outward FDI in the 1980s) to wholly or majority foreign-owned companies (slightly above 50 percent of total outward FDI in the 1990s). It is arguably due to the inexperience of local enterprises in shifting their production overseas and the increasing share of outward FDI by Singapore-based MNCs can also be considered as a reaction of MNCs to declining profitability and declining returns to capital in Singapore's manufacturing sector. MNCs aim to relocate their more labor-intensive operations in neighboring countries where cheaper labor is abundant. SOEs are major local-owned companies as investors abroad. Government companies often invest in high-technology companies at the start-up level in the United States.

Singapore emerged as a major investor in Malaysia, Thailand, Myanmar, Vietnam, and Indonesia recently. These investments are of two types (Lim and Fong, 1991, p. 60): manufacturing investments and conglomerate investments in areas like hotels and property (the latter by way of Chinese family connections across countries). A large portion of these investments are in the form of joint ventures with local partners and investors from third-party countries.

Sijori Growth Triangle: The "growth triangle" including Singapore, Johor State in Malaysia, and Riau Islands in Indonesia was an important component of the external wing of the economy. At the beginning, there were economic incentives for Singapore to expand the economy to the growth triangle[23] (Kumar and Yuan, 1991). Increasing cost of doing business in

[22]Not all of these attempts produced favorable outcomes. For example Chiu *et al.* (1997, p. 132) report some failures of the Singapore government in its investments in the form of venture capital in some Silicon Valley high-technology companies that eventually went bankrupt. However, due to the high risks involved in overseas ventures, Singapore government took the lead in this area.

[23]A "growth triangle" is a localized economic cooperation zone which is established to exploit complementarities between geographically close areas of different countries to gain competitiveness in exports (Thant and Tang, 1998). Regional economic cooperation is supplemented with FDI flows. Examples in Asia other than Sijori include Southern China Growth Triangle (made up of Hong Kong, Guandong, and Fujian), Indonesia–Malaysia–Thailand Growth Triangle (including northern Sumatra, northern states of Malaysia, and

Singapore, constraints of limited labor and land, and an appreciation of the Singapore dollar during the late 1980s, which all lead to declining profit margins, put Singapore into a relatively disadvantageous situation against its neighbors. Consequently, relocation of labor-intensive operations into the growth triangle area emerged as an option. The comparative advantages of Johor and Riau were in cheap and abundant land and labor, although labor in Johor was relatively more skilled in comparison to that in Riau (Kumar, 1998). In fact, Singapore companies (both local and foreign) were already moving to Johor in the early 1980s due to economic forces and adding Riau upon government initiatives into the triangle finalized the formation of the growth triangle in 1992.[24]

Majority of the businesses transferred to Johor from Singapore involved textiles and electronic assembly. In the case of Riau, the Singapore government was the direct dealer of investment projects so that companies have to deal with less bureaucracy. Both low value-added manufacturing and services (especially tourism) are established in Riau by Singapore companies. There are spillover effects[25] from the growth triangle to the Singapore economy. For instance, the growth triangle allows some finance and business services firms to achieve economies of scale; the low costs of land and labor allow Singapore firms in Riau and Johor to run on lower costs; and the need for the provision of logistics from Singapore to the growth triangle creates new business opportunities for Singapore firms. Singapore's public companies have also undertaken an industrial park in Batam Island (an island in the Riau Archipelago) with the Indonesian government in 1992.

southern states of Thailand), and East ASEAN Growth Area (including Mindanao in the Philippines, North Sulawesi in Indonesia, and Sandakan in Malaysia).

[24]Although the investment activities were under way in the late 1980s, the official endorsement of the Sijori growth triangle with the admittance of Riau dates to the Fourth ASEAN Summit in 1992 where bilateral and trilateral meetings between the three countries' top officials were realized. The Indonesian side offered 100 percent foreign equity ownership for 5 years to be followed by a minimum 5 percent divestment, quick handling of bureaucratic procedures for investment in Batam, and permission to establish industrial estates for the private sector. The Malaysian side, on the other hand, eased the requirements for foreign investments in Johor in terms of foreign equity ownership and exports, and reductions in corporate tax rates from 50 to 35 percent (Naidu, 1998).

[25]One may expect the growth triangle to lead to a hollowing out of Singapore industries. However, not much research has been done on this issue and it remains yet to be studied and hence will be neglected in this study.

Overall, Singapore is in the center and is the main facilitator of business development in the growth triangle. However, the development of the growth triangle is not free of problems. Especially the increasing labor turnover in Johor for higher wages in Singapore and Singapore's restrictions on the flow of low-skilled labor into Singapore poses a problem in the labor market (Kumar, 1998).

Other efforts: Apart from the Sijori Growth Triangle, overseas investments of Singapore government and private firms in Singapore concentrate in science-park development and setting up of infrastructural facilities in various locations in developing Asian countries, including Batam and Bintan in Indonesia, Bangalore in India, Wuxi and Suzhou in China, and Ho Chi Minh City in Vietnam. The government and private firms investing in these locations go into joint ventures with local partners, and cooperate with local governments for infrastructure planning and project management. The government expects to enhance regional cooperation between Singapore and regional Asian countries by this way. Public companies are very active in overseas investment as well.[26]

Another form of cooperation is the recent formation of ASEAN Free Trade Area (AFTA) (see Rieber (1996) and Tan (1996) for the implications of AFTA for the Singapore economy). This offers Singapore firms new opportunities to expand overseas. The government wants to establish itself as a "one-stop" investment partner where regional projects are leveraged with the experience of EDB (Wong, 2001). In other words, Singapore government aims to promote these regional projects by providing its past experience to foreign investors.

The regionalization effort of local enterprises in Singapore is still in its infant stages. Indigenous firms still suffer from lack of expertise and they are looking for government's support in this area.[27]

---

[26] Chiu *et al.* (1997, p. 132) report some failures of the Singapore government in its investments in the form of venture capital in some Silicon Valley high-technology companies that eventually went bankrupt. However, due to the high risks involved in overseas ventures, Singapore government took the lead in this area as well.

[27] See Campbell *et al.* (2003) for an evaluation of entrepreneurial characteristics of Singaporeans and regionalization efforts.

3.3.7. *Competition policy and promotion of local firms*

Economic dualism that is observable in many economies took a different shape in Singapore. On the one side, there are large, capital-intensive foreign MNCs with superior technologies mainly producing for export markets and on the other side there are domestic enterprises comprising of state-owned enterprises (SOEs) and small indigenous enterprises.[28] Unlike the SOEs, only a few of local private firms are large. Indigenous firms are dominantly small in size (SMEs) and they operate as subcontractors to MNCs and SOEs. From the beginning, the government stressed the need for foreign capital in industrial development. One hundred percent foreign ownership is allowed in almost all industries and few restrictions exist for the recruitment of foreign personnel. SOEs and the companies linked to them operate mainly in "strategic" industries such as shipbuilding and ship-repair.[29]

After the 1985 recession, the government recognized the need to stimulate private entrepreneurship to leverage high dependence on MNCs in manufacturing. This required the government's exit in certain areas where private entrepreneurship was deemed capable of taking on production activities. However, this was not an easy task since most public firms, including statutory boards, were efficiently run and profitable. In 1985, the government announced a privatization program. The Report of the Economic Committee in 1986 documented that the economy had sufficiently matured for the private sector to become the primary engine. Upon the Economic Committee's report, the newly established the Public Sector Divestment Committee (PSDC) was appointed by the government in 1986. This new committee submitted its report in the same year. In its final report, PSDC identified four different types of privatization: partial privatization (transfer

[28]The government names the majority government-owned firms as government-linked companies (GLCs) and avoids using the term "state-owned companies" in its official publications. GLCs operate commercially and therefore they are different from SOEs in many other countries where SOEs suffer from managerial problems, inadequacy, and inefficiency in production. In this book, the term "SOEs" is used for Singapore to mean the entire body of majority and wholly government-owned companies together.

[29]These SOEs and their subsidiary companies were organized under holding companies owned entirely by the government ministries (e.g., Temasek Holdings, MND Holdings, and Sheng-Li Holding). Their services are diverse ranging from shipbuilding and port services to steel and even retail sales. Unfortunately, the data on their production, investment, and profits are not disclosed.

of the shares of a wholly-owned company to the public), further privatization (transfer of the shares of a partially-owned company), effective privatization (passing the dominance, i.e., control, to the private sector), and total privatization (complete sales of the shares a company) (PSDC, 1987, p. 10). The report studied the possibility of privatization in some areas where the government participated in production activities and recommended the sale of shares in 41 public companies out of more than 600, and seven statutory boards, including the telecommunications company (Singapore Telecom), Public Utilities Board (electricity and gas), Civil Aviation Authority (running Changi Airport), Singapore Broadcasting Corporation, Jurong Town Corporation, and Commercial and Industrial Security Corporation, as part of a 10-year divestment plan (PSDC, 1987, pp. 43–49). The public divestment program was instituted under this committee. Some of the companies studied by the PSDC were not recommended for privatization (PSDC, 1987, pp. 87–92). These companies were the ones recommended to be wound up (mainly dormant and storage companies), the ones with foreign government participation (fertilizer, cement, and mining companies), the ones that are single-purpose or those serve-in-house needs (e.g., hotel, real estates, investment holding, engineering, etc.), the ones that have a social mission (e.g., university hospital, bird park, and social facilities), the ones that may not be attractive to investors (mostly petrochemicals manufacturing, real estate companies), and the ones that have a promotional role (e.g., development of mass storage devices and robot leasing).

The report of the PSDC was welcomed by the government and its recommendations were put into effect. The privatization efforts in education, health, public transportation, and public housing have been under way since the mid-1980s. From 1992 on, public offerings of some major statutory boards (Singapore Telecom, Port of Singapore Authority, Public Utilities Board, Civil Aviation Authority, National Computer Board, and Singapore Broadcasting Corporation) were made (SILS, 1995). There were also big moves in the privatization of GLCs in shipbuilding, food, aviation, and properties sectors. Since then, the government undertook privatization of some large public firms operating in the areas of shipbuilding, food, and aviation as well as in education, health, public transportation, and housing (PSDC, 1987, pp. 43–49; SILS, 1995).

It is important to note that the privatization effort in Singapore was initiated by the government and did not aim at any revenue creation for the budget or bailing out or rationalization of any loss-making or inefficient SOEs, two major factors experienced by many developing countries (Krause, 1987; Lim *et al.*, 1988, pp. 68–69). In fact, there has not been any big failure of SOEs in Singapore and it is often argued that they are run efficiently and are evaluated on a commercial basis by the state. In other words, various studies on SOEs lead to a success story hard found in any developing country. The primary driving force for the government for privatization was to stimulate private sector development. The report of the PSDC implicitly emphasized the need to free the government officials from commercial responsibilities and obligations of running government-owned corporations and devote their effort to remaining tasks. The report declared the objectives of the privatization of SOEs as (i) withdrawing from commercial activities which no longer need to be undertaken by the public sector, (ii) adding breadth and depth to the Singapore stock market by the flotation of GLCs and through secondary distribution of government-owned shares, and (iii) avoiding or reducing competition with the private sector (PSDC, 1987, p. 12).

The government did not expect to raise funds from public divestment. As pointed out in the report of PSDC, statutory boards and SOEs make large profits. Therefore, the privatization move cannot be taken as a radical change in government policies. Low (1988) agreeably argues that privatization in Singapore itself reflects government's eclectic and pragmatic approach to economic development.

Privatization in Singapore has some interesting features. The government announced that funds raised from divestment would be reinvested into new activities where the government considers its existence is necessary, such as in biotechnology area (Low, 1988). Asher (1989) indicates that as the government divests its share in well-established industries, the proceeds of divestment are invested in newer areas or activities in the domestic economy as well as abroad. In some cases, divested SOEs are bought by other SOEs. To put differently, public divestment in Singapore does not directly lead to a reduction in the government's stake in the domestic economy. It arguably leads to an expansion and diversification of government's activities. The government justifies its behavior on the ground that it acts as a counterbalance against the heavy dominance of MNCs in the domestic economy. In addition, SILS (1995) reports that during the course of privatization, industrial relations were not given any type of damage and any changes affecting workers or trade unions were resolved and they were in the long-term interests of all parties.

It is also worth noting the government's policy of reviving the local SMEs.[30] The dominance of manufacturing activities by MNCs and public firms led to marginalization of SMEs[31] in product and labor markets (Lee, 1997). Superior production technologies of SOEs and MNCs on the one hand, and the attraction of high skilled labor and best graduates on the other, did not leave much room for SMEs to develop themselves. Local enterprises accounted for only one-fourth of manufacturing output and investment after the late 1980s (see Table 3.9).The privatization efforts of the government partially address the revival of SMEs. The government extended the assistance schemes listed in Table 3.8 to a larger number of SMEs after the 1985 recession (see Table 3.11). It also initiated a planned action to nurture local firms.[32] In the case of Public Sector Divestment Program, Wong *et al.* (1998) argue that, different from the usual practice in other developing countries, privatization in Singapore rather allowed the government to withdraw part

[30]An SME is defined as a business establishment with fixed assets less than 15 million Singapore dollars in the manufacturing sector and with fixed assets less than 15 million Singapore dollars and total employees less than 200 in the services sector.

[31]There are some conditions for SMEs in an economy to be the driving force of economic growth (Kwong, 2001). The first condition is the existence of a sufficiently large domestic economy that can be exploited by domestic entrepreneurs. Singapore obviously lacks such a large domestic market. The second condition is the existence of superior distribution and supplier links and networks for information. In the case of Singapore, the government and MNCs dominate these networks. The third condition is the availability of industrial capital for the development of SMEs. In Singapore, financial institutions have long neglected extending their financial facilities to SMEs and it is recently through government's encouragement of the financial sector that they extend loans to SMEs. The government's assistance for SMEs also became an important source for their development despite complaints from SMEs for insufficiency.

[32]This plan envisaged nurturing of SMEs in four stages (ESCAP, 1995): In the "start-up" and "growth" stages, the plan foresaw provision of tax incentives, business development, and technical upgrading; and in the "expansion" and "going overseas" stages the provision of advanced technical assistance schemes such as computerization, brand development type of business development, and, when the local firm reaches a certain level of development, overseas expansion of production activities.

Table 3.11. Distribution of Financial Assistance to SMEs (1976–1992).

Unit: Million Singapore Dollars	1976–1986	1987	1988	1989	1990	1991	1992
Investment allowance	4.9	24.1	38.0	31.1	78.7	118.6	66.1
Double tax deductions	13.9	9.5	13.2	14.5	11.8	12.0	16.6
LEFS loans	752.0	289.2	254.1	271.2	321.5	355.9	338.7
LETAS loans	2.6	3.0	3.8	5.5	8.2	10.3	22.1
BDS	0.1	0.1	0.1	0.2	0.1	0.1	0.2
PDAS	4.2	0.8	1.8	1.9	1.8	1.6	1.4
MIDAS	2.1	1.5	2.5	3.3	3.3	2.4	4.1
RDAS	1.3	0.5	NA	0.6	7.5	4.4	17.9
SDAS	0.1	0.4	0.3	0.6	1.1	0.4	2.1
SDF	29.3	9.4	9.9	14.2	13.4	12.4	13.7
ALS	NA	NA	NA	31.3	38.0	22.0	9.9

Notes: LEFS: Local Enterprise Finance Scheme; LETAS: Local Enterprise Technical Assistance Scheme; BDS: Business Development Scheme; PDAS: Product Development Assistance Scheme; MIDAS: Market and Investment Development Assistance Scheme; RDAS: Research and Development Assistance Scheme; SDAS: Software Development Assistance Scheme; SDF: Skills Development Fund; ALS: Automation Leasing Scheme; NA: Not applicable.
Source: ESCAP (1995).

of its equity from well-established and mature industries without losing control over them and invest in other areas of economic activities. As Low (1988) puts it, the privatization program demonstrates how pragmatic the Singapore government is in responding to changes in domestic and international environment.

The role of SOEs, MNCs, and local SMEs in industrial policies in the post-1985 era can be summarized as follows. The government relied mostly on MNCs in output, exports, and technology development. SMEs were deemed necessary as subcontractors and therefore their role as major supporters of MNCs was strengthened by the government by reinforcing the links between SMEs and MNCs. One way to do this was to accelerate technology transfer from MNCs to SMEs in specified industries (see the discussion on Local Industry Upgrading Program in the next chapter). In those industries where private entrepreneurship lacked, the government took the initiative and engaged directly in production through SOEs.

3.4. Productivity-Specific Features of Industrial Policies in Singapore

The importance of productivity for an economy is straightforward. Productivity gains are important to ensure long-run growth. Public policies can be used to improve the quality of factor inputs in an economy. The government in Singapore made productivity[33] growth an important target in its industrial policies especially after 1990 in order to maintain desirable economic growth rates.

Tight labor market conditions and the government's desire to maintain high growth rates make productivity even more important for Singapore. Rapid growth resulted in upward surge of wage levels after the mid-1970s. The adverse impact of a general rise in wage levels can be absorbed partially or fully by producers via gains in productivity. This is especially important in some industries such as electronics, chemicals, shipbuilding, and ship-repairing, to which substantial amount of resources were shifted and on which the pressure on wages was stronger. The government did not support ailing industries and encouraged the shift of resources to more productive industries. This issue is discussed later.

In the following sections, the efforts of the government to improve productivity are briefly discussed. Such efforts of the government can be categorized into three distinct types of policies: (i) those aiming at improvements in the quality of labor force, (ii) those aiming at improvements in labor quality in domestic firms by technology transfer and strengthening of their relations with multinational firms, and (iii) those aiming at the creation and development of technologies and then diffusing them to local firms.

[33]There are internal (intra-firm) factors in the form of management techniques that also influence productivity levels such as total quality management and quality circles. Such practices help firms use their resources more efficiently and are integral to the government's productivity enhancement policies. However, these management-side aspects of productivity are out of the scope of this study. What is of main interest here is the policies with regards to productivity.

3.4.1. *Improving the quality of the labor-force*

Of critical importance in the government's policies regarding productivity is its attempt to enhance labor productivity. Due to limitations on the labor supply to expand further and the conditions of tight labor market, improving the skills of existing labor-force is vitally important. A second reason is increasing competition from surrounding Asian economies, i.e., Indonesia, Malaysia, Thailand, for FDI. A more effective way to ensure continuation of FDI is to improve the quality of human resources and physical infrastructure. The importance of the former was repeatedly admitted in the Report of the Economic Committee, SEP, and Next Lap.

What is aimed by productivity enhancement policies is making workers work more efficiently. This can be realized by making best use of resources, not only available labor, but also other resources such as energy, machinery, and other forms of capital. In fact, some features of the government's authoritative labor market policy in the past such as denouncing strikes as illegal and forcing labor to reduce work stoppages to virtually zero level indirectly helped forcefully achieve some of its productivity-related targets since they improve efficiency of labor in use. Direct involvement of the government took the form of allocating loans and subsidies to firms to enhance productivity levels. The most important of these is the SDF, established in 1979. SDF provides funds to finance industrial training programs run jointly by the government and MNCs (Wong, 2001). The funds for SDF are raised by way of contributions from both employees and employers at a predetermined rate of the wage bill of the employee (1 percent after 2002, down from the preceding rate of 2 percent). There are various assistance schemes under SDF, such as Training Assistance Scheme (for skills upgrading), IT Training Assistance Scheme, Skills Certification Plan, Critical Skills Scheme (for training in critical skills in factory automation, advanced manufacturing technologies, robotics, and advanced programming), and Industry Capability Upgrading Plan. All these schemes have been important instruments for the government to achieve its restructuring and productivity targets especially during the 1990s.

Table 3.11 presents government resources utilized for the development of local enterprises in Singapore from 1976 to 1992. A very large part of direct financial assistance provision was under Local Enterprise Finance Scheme (LEFS), which served for the promotion of mechanization to increase productivity. There are also various other schemes established to assist training, research and development, and automation, including Local Enterprise Technical Assistance Scheme (LETAS), which was designed to help local enterprises with the costs incurred in modernizing and upgrading operations.

A major step in the 1990s was the establishment of the Productivity Fund and the Singapore Productivity and Standards Board (PSB)[34] in 1996, in order to encourage and assist industries to raise productivity. PSB also led the National Productivity and Innovation Movement that aimed to enhance productivity and innovation. In addition, Singapore Productivity Movement was launched in 1981 to promote productivity awareness among companies by skills upgrading and educating labor on productivity. As part of this effort, the government has been offering seminars and training programs since the early-1980s through its productivity agency to local firms on intra-firm quality improvement techniques. The number of participants in these courses has been rising steadily since the early 1980s (Yearbook of Statistics, various years).

Overall, the commitment of the government in enhancing productivity is evident in the abovementioned policies. These efforts in improving labor quality are not directly related to formal education system. The education system, on the other hand, helps improve the quality of the labor entering into the labor market in the future. As well documented elsewhere (e.g., World Bank, 1993) the government has also succeeded in this aspect.

3.4.2. *Productivity improvement through MNC – local firm interaction*

As part of its development policy, Singapore government adopted a liberal open-door policy for FDI which later dominated the manufacturing sector. During early stages of industrialization, government decided to introduce foreign capital to promote export oriented industrialization mainly because of the lack of domestic industrial entrepreneurship (Lim *et al.* 1988, p. 252; Huff, 1994). In the post-1985 era, there was not a big change in the government's FDI policy. However, the government recognized the importance

[34]In April 2002, PSB was restructured and turned into Standards, Productivity, and Innovation Board (SPRING).

of developing domestic entrepreneurship to leverage the high dependence on FDI. In addition, a new initiative to turn Singapore into a "total business center" and a hub for high-technology manufacturing, were put in action.

Lim and Pang (1991) argue that there are dynamic linkage effects from MNCs such as the stimulation of production for local suppliers, raising entrepreneurs who work first for MNCs and then establish their own businesses, and skills upgrading (i.e., training of local engineers). However, they also admit that MNCs also attract a large number of local talents and hence crowd out local entrepreneurship. The government has encouraged strengthening of the subcontracting relations between local firms and MNCs. In order to enhance collaboration between them, the Local Industry Upgrading Program (LIUP) was launched in 1986. This program serves for two pillars of industrial policies, upgrading of promising local firms and developing a sound supporting industry base for MNCs. LIUP includes a wide range of financial and technical assistance schemes provided by EDB. By LIUP, the government aims to trespass advanced technical and managerial expertise of MNCs to local enterprises to upgrade their business operations in order to become competitive (ESCAP, 1995; Shen, 2000).

LIUP is a partnership program between MNCs and SMEs. Each participating MNC works under an individual LIUP, coordinated by EDB. The working of LIUP is as follows (Enterprise Promotion Centre, 1991, pp. 67–68): First, a manager for the specific LIUP is selected. Then a partner MNC selects four or five (or more) local enterprises (SMEs) to assist. Once the partnership is built, both sides work on annual work plans that include recommendations of projects for upgrading. Finally, financial assistance is provided by EDB. MNC partners offer training on engineering practices and improvement of production processes. LIUP is a long-term plan; it aims at upgrading and developing local enterprises in three stages. The target during the first phase is to improve operational efficiency such as production planning and inventory control, plant layout, financial and management control techniques, etc. In the second phase, the objective is to introduce and transfer new products or processes to local enterprises. In the final phase, joint product and process R&D with MNC partners is aimed. Labor productivity is not the main target of LIUP but it is one of the intentions of the government in initiating the program.

In 2002, the number of MNC participants was 78 (EISC, 2002). A total of 132 MNCs and 1200 local companies have benefited from LIUP as of 2002 (MTI, Economic Survey of Singapore, 2003). Improvements in operational efficiency (e.g., cost analysis), capability development (process improvement capabilities such as mould design), product development, and environment-related innovations (e.g., energy saving, recycling of materials, etc.) are remarkable. From 1995 on, LIUP has been implemented at the industry-level (e.g., Process Industry LIUP, Marine Group LIUP, and IT LIUP) to support the EDB's move for cluster development (LIUP Centre, 1997).[35] This allows enterprises in the same cluster to pool their resources and develop industry-wide upgrading. Since skills upgrading through training and information management among local and MNC partners using information technologies are two essential thrusts of LIUP, it also helps improve labor productivity. Recently, SPRING has become a participant of LIUP to expand operational efficiency upgrading. LIUP-type plans have also been effectively and actively implemented in Taiwan and Ireland. Both countries terminated those plans during the 1990s as the targets were almost completely achieved (Shen, 2000).

LIUP is only one type of cooperation that the government facilitated for local enterprises. Another possible form of cooperation is between local firms in the form of mergers between firms competing in the same industry (Chong and Goh, 1992). By this way, they can reach economies of scale which they cannot easily attain individually. This means internalization of externalities that arise among local firms by unifying management and entrepreneurship resources. However, the government has shown no interest in this option.

3.4.3. *Indigenous technology development*

Technological improvements allow producers to expand their output without increases in employment. Until the restructuring efforts in the mid-1980s, the major issue in science and technology development in Singapore was technology absorption, whereas with the restructuring, government

[35] Process industry refers to petroleum and petrochemical industries which process petroleum. Process Industry LIUP was formed in January 1995 with 6 MNCs and 60 local enterprises. Marine Group LIUP was formed in March 1996 with the participation of five big shipyards, foreign and local, which later increased to seven, and 54 local subcontractor companies. IT LIUP was initiated in July 1996 with the participation of NCB, 5 IT MNCs, and 60 local companies (LIUP Centre, 1997).

turned to technology creation (Wong, 2001). The changing stance of the government is marked by the establishment of National Computer Board (NCB)[36] in the mid-1990s and the launch of National IT Plan. The effort of the government to enhance technological upgrading and automation in local firms was a means to decrease the costs of coordination (Wong, 2001).

The government fell a little behind some of its targets in technology development. SEP foresaw an increase in research and development expenditures as a share of GDP from less than 1 percent level in 1991 to over 2 percent by 2000 under the plan IT 2000. However, the actual figure achieved as of 2000 was 1.8 percent (see Table 3.12). However, other targets (i.e., increasing the number of engineers and technicians and increasing the share of private sector in research and development expenditures) were largely achieved.

It is argued that the government was too late in initiating research and development activities by use of state power as in Korea and Taiwan, most possibly due to the lack of an effective institutional mechanism for this purpose (Wong, 2001). Successful experiences of Korea and Taiwan in the late 1970s and throughout the 1980s proved that governments can promote research and development activities in IT by establishing public institutions, direct funding of such activities, and providing subsidies to private firms. The government's first serious attempt in Singapore was to launch the 2-billion-Singapore-dollar-budgeted National Technology Plan (1991–1995) and the establishment of National Science and Technology Board (NSTB) in 1991 (Toh, 2002). The plan was later extended until 2000 as National Science and Technology Plan (NSTP). The first plan targeted public research and development activities, whereas the extended second plan additionally included two universities as partners.

In addition, various institutes were established in the 1990s to promote research and development activities, the most important ones being the Institute of Microelectronics (IME) and Data Storage Institute (DSI). As argued in Wong (2001), the gestation period of these investments to promote research and development activities to materialize as commercial activities

[36]NCB was restructured and merged with Telecommunications Authority of Singapore to form a new statutory board named Infocomm Development Authority (IDA) in 1999.

Table 3.12. Research and Development Indicators in Singapore, 1978–2002.

	Gross R&D Expenditure (% of GDP)		R&D Expenditure by Main Sectors (million S$)				Researchers and Engineers Per 10000 Workers
			Private	Higher Education	Government	Public Inst.	
1978	37.8	(0.21)	25.5	8.2	4.1	—	8.4
1981	81.0	(0.26)	44.2	24.3	12.5	—	10.6
1984	214.3	(0.54)	106.7	69.6	38.0	—	18.4
1987	374.0	(0.86)	225.6	95.4	53.7	—	25.3
1990	571.7	(0.85)	309.5	119.7	99.4	43.1	27.7
1991	756.7	(1.01)	442.0	147.1	96.8	70.8	33.6
1992	949.3	(1.19)	577.5	156.0	105.0	110.8	39.8
1993	998.2	(1.07)	618.9	157.3	106.5	115.5	40.5
1994	1175.0	(1.10)	736.2	179.5	142.1	117.2	41.9
1995	1366.6	(1.15)	881.4	193.4	110.4	181.4	47.7
1996	1792.1	(1.38)	1133.4	238.7	166.8	253.2	56.3
1997	2104.6	(1.49)	1314.5	277.7	216.1	296.3	60.2
1998	2492.3	(1.82)	1536.1	305.8	299.8	350.6	65.5
1999	2656.4	(1.90)	1670.9	310.0	304.9	370.6	69.9
2000	3009.5	(1.88)	1866.0	338.3	423.8	381.4	66.1
2001	3232.7	(2.13)	2045.0	367.0	425.1	395.6	72.5
2002	3404.6	(2.19)	2091.3	NA	NA	NA	73.5

Note: NA: Not applicable.
Sources: *Yearbook of Statistics* by Singapore Department of Statistics (various years) and *Economic Survey of Singapore* by Ministry of Trade and Industry (various years).

is long. The government has taken big steps forward to turn Singapore into a knowledge-based economy by mobilizing substantial resources and capital for this purpose.

Finally, it is necessary to evaluate the outcome of national science and technology policies. Table 3.13 presents some data from a report by the statistical office on the balance of payments on services accounts (Singstat, 2003). The figures in Table 3.13 reveal that technology creation in Singapore has not yet achieved a satisfactory level. As of the early 2000s, the earnings of the country from marketing its technology in the form of royalties are very small compared with its outward payments for royalties. The situation

Table 3.13. Technology Balance of Payments in Singapore, 1995–2002 (Unit: Million Singapore Dollar).

	Computer and Information Services		Royalties		Research and Development Services	
	Exports	Imports	Exports	Imports	Exports	Imports
1995	453.1	263.4	119.0	2451.0	75.1	597.0
1996	402.7	145.9	107.1	2844.2	289.2	591.8
1997	346.1	195.1	96.1	2858.9	298.6	798.0
1998	403.7	258.0	97.9	3122.0	164.1	951.3
1999	347.8	306.1	113.3	6504.8	125.9	991.5
2000	332.0	388.2	150.4	6227.7	159.0	1007.0
2001	345.4	403.9	130.7	5409.3	138.1	874.7
2002	334.8	391.4	147.3	6098.4	155.7	986.1

Source: *Singapore Balance of Payments Services Account* (Singstat, 2003, p. 15).

is more or less the same in the case of marketing research and development activities. In short, technology and innovation policies in Singapore have been successful in absorbing and transferring technology but the progress in technology creation has been slow.

CHAPTER 4

A COMPARISON OF INDUSTRIAL POLICIES IN SINGAPORE WITH THOSE IN JAPAN, KOREA, AND TAIWAN

Industrial policies in Japan, Korea, and Taiwan were elaborated in Chapter 2. Industrial policies in Singapore share many features with these three countries, but it has distinctive features as well. Industrial transformation in these countries is evident from the changing industrial composition of value-added in Table 4.1. The shares of heavy and chemical industries improved significantly since the 1960s especially in Korea, Singapore, and Taiwan. In this chapter, distinctive features of industrial policies of these countries are compared.

4.1. Initial Conditions

First, we start with the historical conditions these countries faced at the start of their industrial development. Japan, Korea, and Taiwan started off after destructive wars. Although it was affected by World War II, Singapore faced more favorable conditions. Here, we will separate Japan from the other East Asian latecomers because having started its industrialization in the late 19th century, Japan had already established a large and strong industrial base, so large enough to challenge even the United States to a war, and accumulated technological knowledge. However, the war-torn economy of Japan and its industries had to be reconstructed in the aftermath of the war and industrial policies accelerated this process. We will focus on the experiences of Korea, Taiwan, and Singapore. These countries exhibited differing initial conditions at the start of their industrial development.

First, colonization by Japan in Taiwan and Korea yielded different outcomes. Resources in Korea were exploited to a large degree by the colonial masters, whereas Japanese colonialism in Taiwan did not cause that much

Table 4.1. Changing Industrial Structure in East Asian Economies: Percentage Shares in Manufacturing Value-added.

	Food	Textile-Clothing	Wood	Paper	Chemicals	Oil Refining	Plastic	Mineral	Metals	Metal Products	Basic Machines	Electrical Machines	Transport Equipment	Precision Equipment	Other
Japan															
1960	8.5	10.8	4.1	7.7	11.0	1.4	1.7	4.7	11.6	4.7	10.3	10.3	9.2	1.5	2.5
1970	8.0	8.2	4.5	7.4	10.1	1.1	3.2	4.8	9.6	6.5	11.8	11.9	9.5	1.6	2.0
1975	10.2	8.0	4.5	8.4	8.8	1.5	3.8	5.0	8.0	6.7	11.1	9.8	10.2	1.8	2.1
1980	9.2	6.7	4.1	7.9	8.5	2.2	4.0	5.0	10.1	6.3	10.5	12.2	9.4	2.0	1.8
1985	9.5	5.6	2.8	7.5	8.7	1.2	4.5	4.3	7.5	6.3	11.0	16.3	10.7	2.0	1.9
1990	9.0	4.8	2.9	7.9	9.4	0.6	4.7	4.3	7.0	7.0	11.5	16.8	10.5	1.7	1.8
1995	10.5	3.9	2.6	8.5	10.2	1.1	4.9	4.2	5.9	7.0	10.5	16.7	10.6	1.4	1.8
2000	11.4	2.9	2.2	8.7	10.4	0.6	5.2	3.9	5.5	6.4	10.6	18.2	10.7	1.6	1.8
2005	12.3	0.5	0.9	1.9	8.0	8.0	5.7	0.9	3.3	8.5	4.7	10.8	15.6	12.7	1.4
Korea															
1960	18.3	17.4	6.1	4.5	7.4	16.7	7.2	6.5	5.1	1.9	1.0	4.1	2.3	0.2	1.5
1970	23.6	15.7	3.8	4.6	8.6	8.0	8.9	5.5	4.1	2.2	1.5	6.6	5.0	0.4	1.7
1975	21.2	22.1	2.6	3.9	10.3	8.1	3.4	5.6	4.7	2.3	2.2	7.0	4.0	0.7	1.9
1980	16.6	19.5	1.7	4.4	10.3	5.0	5.2	5.8	7.8	3.3	3.4	8.1	5.9	1.1	1.9
1985	14.4	13.3	1.6	4.7	9.1	4.6	5.5	5.0	8.0	4.2	4.9	12.2	9.4	1.0	2.0
1990	10.7	12.0	1.5	4.7	9.1	3.4	5.8	5.0	7.4	5.2	7.0	15.1	10.3	1.1	1.8
1995	8.4	10.2	0.8	4.9	9.3	3.4	3.9	4.8	6.8	4.7	8.3	20.1	11.1	0.9	2.3
2000	8.3	8.1	0.6	4.9	9.6	3.9	4.1	3.9	6.4	4.1	8.1	22.0	13.2	1.1	1.8
2005	5.8	3.9	0.5	3.1	11.3	1.9	3.4	2.2	2.9	2.8	8.9	38.6	12.4	0.7	1.5

(*Continued*)

Table 4.1. (*Continued*)

	Food	Textile-Clothing	Wood	Paper	Chemicals	Oil Refining	Plastic	Mineral	Metals	Metal Products	Basic Machines	Electrical Machines	Transport Equipment	Precision Equipment	Other
Singapore															
1960	24.4	4.0	5.7	14.8	1.3	4.0	24.0	3.1	1.1	4.9	3.6	3.7	0.3	4.2	0.9
1970	12.0	8.0	6.0	5.3	5.0	17.8	5.8	2.8	1.9	6.1	2.4	10.8	13.5	0.3	2.5
1975	7.0	5.4	3.0	4.6	5.2	17.6	2.8	3.6	1.8	4.9	8.7	13.7	18.0	2.6	1.1
1980	4.9	5.3	3.1	4.3	4.8	17.1	3.1	2.3	1.8	4.9	8.7	23.6	12.4	2.0	1.6
1985	5.1	4.1	2.8	6.6	7.5	7.0	3.3	2.9	1.1	4.9	9.5	28.7	10.3	2.3	3.8
1990	3.6	3.2	1.6	5.8	10.3	8.4	2.7	1.4	1.1	5.3	6.8	38.5	7.5	1.9	1.9
1995	3.1	1.2	0.2	6.2	9.4	4.8	2.9	2.0	0.6	6.2	6.1	47.7	6.4	2.0	1.1
2000	2.1	0.7	0.1	4.4	15.8	4.8	2.4	1.2	0.2	4.5	5.5	49.4	5.2	3.0	0.7
2005	2.1	0.6	0.1	2.9	26.6	9.7	1.8	0.7	0.6	3.9	6.9	32.9	7.6	3.0	0.6
Taiwan															
1960	34.6	9.2	5.9	9.6	14.0	6.1	1.1	8.4	3.1	2.6	3.5	1.0	0.0	0.0	0.9
1970	18.1	12.7	5.5	6.0	19.8	8.7	4.9	5.4	2.8	2.4	6.2	4.8	0.0	0.0	2.8
1975	13.7	15.7	4.1	5.6	15.2	6.7	6.4	4.8	3.5	3.0	10.2	6.6	0.0	0.0	4.5
1980	11.6	17.6	2.5	5.8	12.1	5.3	6.4	4.5	5.2	4.4	9.6	9.2	5.3	0.9	5.8
1985	11.7	16.8	2.4	4.7	11.9	5.2	7.8	4.0	5.7	4.9	9.1	10.2	5.0	1.2	5.6
1990	9.9	12.0	2.0	4.2	11.1	4.9	7.8	4.2	6.8	5.8	11.7	14.9	7.6	1.2	4.7
1995	8.7	8.1	1.3	2.1	10.8	6.7	7.1	4.4	6.9	7.5	7.6	17.4	7.3	1.0	3.1
2000	5.3	7.5	0.8	1.7	8.3	5.1	5.6	2.4	6.8	7.5	7.5	31.4	6.3	0.9	2.8
2005	3.4	4.1	0.8	2.3	10.1	4.4	3.7	2.1	7.4	5.3	5.9	23.8	23.7	1.2	1.7

Source: See Chapter 7.

damage. It is important to note that most of the early economic bureaucrats and political leaders in Korea and Taiwan were trained in Japanese companies and the army. They were familiar with the wartime economic policies of Japan that emphasized resource allocation by the state and industrialization by the use of state power. Singapore, on the other hand, inherited a well-working bureaucracy and the British legal system. Early political leaders in Singapore, who were educated in Britain, adopted the Western way of thinking, which contrasts the Japanese-educated Taiwanese and Korean bureaucrats.

Second, political considerations differed widely. Internal politics in Taiwan and Korea was bounded by national defense and national interests against hostile neighbors (Communist Mainland China against Taiwan and North Korea against South Korea). Nationalistic goals of the country were linked to its economic interests. For long decades, economic development was perceived as a national goal not only to maintain legitimacy of the ruling elite, but also to strengthen the country against hostile neighbors as well. In contrast, Singapore never faced such a hostile behavior from its northern neighbor except a short-lived tension with Malaysia during the separation from the unsuccessful union with Malaya Federation.

Third, the structure and characteristics of domestic markets were different. Korea and Taiwan took a start after the war with domestic economies characterized by the dominance of agriculture. Both countries started their industrial development after substantial land reforms. In addition, there was a huge surplus of labor in both economies. Singapore, on the other hand, was a small island with a virtually non-existing agricultural sector.

Fourth, specialization in Singapore differed from Taiwan and Korea. Both Korea and Taiwan had to start virtually from zero. Korea lost almost all of its industrial facilities and capacity to the North after separation, and it had only a very small manufacturing sector working with extremely poor technology. Although Taiwan inherited some factories constructed by the Japanese during the colonial period, it did not have the knowledge to turn these facilities into productive use as the Japanese technicians working in these industries returned to Japan after the war. Singapore, on the other hand, had a long-established tradition of trading and trade-related facilities such as commerce through its free port. Local Chinese entrepreneurs specialized in trade and related services between the world wars and accumulated large amounts of capital.

4.2. Characteristics of Governments

Similarities among the countries in East Asia that implemented active industrial policies are most visible in the characteristics of the governments. Interventions in markets in each country reflect certain characteristics of the government. A common characteristic of the governments is the autonomy given to the economic bureaucracy. It is necessary to mention that the absence of a powerful industrial interest group or powerful landowners, thanks to land reforms, was a supporting factor behind the autonomy enjoyed by the economic bureaucracy in the East Asian latecomers. Therefore, the pressure from politics on policymaking and economic decision-making of the economic bureaucracy was minimal. Top leaders in these countries supervised the bureaucracy and enabled effective implementation of policies and reforms.[1]

The state in Taiwan effectively played the role of an entrepreneurial state. The ruling political party (*Kuomintang*) saw the development of the economy as a means to maintain its legitimacy. Research institutes, which were established to undertake research on new technologies, were at the same time, manufacturers of some high-technology products as well. Hierarchically organized technocrats in Taiwan enjoyed the autonomy given to them and their expertise was necessary in order for the state to take the lead in promoting new industries. Thus, Taiwan was characterized by a centralized and autonomous system (Hong, 1997, pp. 147–150). It should be

[1] It is important to note here that the economic bureaucrats and policymakers of the 1960s in Korea and Taiwan were brought up in the Japanese schools during Japanese colonization period. During the wartime period (1937–1945), in its territories, the military government in Japan exercised strong controls in the economy and in the allocation of resources across industries. Some studies claim that this was a main reason why the economic bureaucrats were interested in resource allocation by the hand of the state (Stern *et al.*, 1995; Kim, 1997). Even the founders of some large conglomerates and many qualified workers in Korea had experience working in Japanese companies during the colonial period.

noted that the development of the high-technology industries owes greatly to the personal efforts of some high-level government bureaucrats in Taiwan.

Korea followed Taiwan from behind due to unfavorable conditions, the most important one being the Korean War. During the early stages of industrial development, the government centralized the decision-making mechanism and the bureaucrats were given a very high level of autonomy and power during the Park Chung–Hee era (1961–1979). The preceding president, Syngman Rhee, placed priority on politics rather than economic growth. For Park, the priority was on economic growth. He exerted heavy political pressure on the country's big business leaders and forced them to follow his developmentalist policies (Rodrik *et al.*, 1995). In return for their consent, they were rewarded with cheap means of financing their investments they are asked for. Hattori and Sato (1997) argues that due to its backwardness *vis-à-vis* Taiwan, Korea could not take a more relaxed approach as in Taiwan. However, following the assassination of President Park and the takeover by the new military government, orthodox economists dominated the technocracy and reduced state intervention to a large extent. It is argued that bureaucratic competition among government agencies brought about a lack of coordination and cooperation in Korea before the 1980s. Thus, Korea was characterized by a decentralized system with less coordination (Hong, 1997).

The government in Singapore established a system in which the government took the lead virtually in all markets. Business activities were always under government control. The state in Singapore is characterized by a dominant and authoritative party system with a centralized government and strong coordination among its agencies. Although the political system is a multi-party system, the same political party (People's Action Party) led by Lee Kuan Yew has been in power since independence.[2] The political aspect of economic management in Singapore is not of interest here.[3] We

[2]In his well-known article entitled "A socialist economy that works," one of the architects of the economic management system, Goh Keng Swee, argued that the colonial *laissez-faire* policies led Singapore to a dead-end with little economic growth, massive unemployment, and inadequate education. He also claimed that they (i.e., the dominant People's Action Party government in Singapore) had to try a more activist and interventionist approach under a "democratic socialist economic system" (Goh, 1976).

[3]Further details can be found in Haggard (1999). He talks about four rationales of the authoritarian non-liberal regime in Singapore: national security concerns that identifies the

are particularly interested in four characteristics of the government: meritocracy, elitism, pragmatism, and paternalism (Lim *et al.*, 1988, pp. 61–66). Decision-making process is centralized at the top echelons and there is extensive information sharing between the government and other agents in the economy, i.e., local companies and multinational corporations. The government attracts best graduates of the tertiary education institutions and offers competitive salaries to its officials. This is comparable to the experiences of Taiwan and Korea. Hence, a pool of highly intelligent civil servants contribute to an effectively working public decision-making process. On the other hand, there is a well-working bureaucratic structure inherited from the British colonial masters. Paternalist nature of the government is arguably related to the local culture. In fact, it is argued that the Singapore government creates a local culture through its strong emphasis on marriage and the importance of family, and its emphasis on education, i.e., the so-called "Asian values" (Haggard, 1999).

The most important feature of the government in Singapore is its pragmatic nature. One of the government's most important policy issues is long-term social gains from development. Popular support for politics does not seem to have been a major concern for the ruling party that dominated local politics since independence. The pragmatic nature of the government is visible from quick reactions to changes in the economic environment. To find solutions and strategies to challenges faced, the government responded to them by quickly setting up deliberation councils consisting of representatives from every major acting group in the economy (employees, employers, academics, multinational corporations, government, and local businesses). In addition, the recommendations of these deliberation councils were largely followed and employed as major yardsticks for policy implementation and evaluation. Pragmatism and eclecticism can be said to have coexisted and helped economic development in Singapore.

Shaped by the above features, state intervention in Singapore aims at allocating resources according to the government's economic policies. The

ruling party with the nation (e.g., internal fight against communism), "developmentalism" that legitimates single-party rule with materialized gains, maintenance of the ethnic harmony, and the concept of "Asian values" defended by the rulers. He claims that the government not only charted a non-liberal course, but also defended it against Western detractors through an active cultural diplomacy.

government exercises a control on a substantial portion of economic activities through its enterprises and statutory boards. Apart from the provision of traditional duties of a government such as education, infrastructure, and utilities, the government effectively controls almost all land and housing, is a major participant in the capital market; participates directly in manufacturing production in certain industries; affects investment decisions by providing incentives and subsidies; and controls labor. However, the government does not mean everything in Singapore. Singapore's economic policies are a mix of active government policies with market forces. Private sector, consisting of foreign and local firms, works on market principles, and there is competition in factor and goods markets in the domestic economy among the government and private companies.

State intervention in Singapore definitely changed prices, or using the words of Amsden (1989), the government got the prices intentionally wrong. Although the government allowed the running of all the firms in the economy, including those it owned or controlled, on free market principles, determination of the prices in the economy (e.g., wages) which all firms were exposed to were largely affected by the government. The impact of state intervention on the domestic economy in Singapore is a controversial issue. On the one hand, some others such as Lim (1983) assert that intervention produced favorable results such as welfare of the population, job creation for masses, and encouraging private investment. On the other hand, some others including Krugman (1994) argue that overinvestment and forced savings in Singapore did not bring in efficient resource allocation and improvement in investment efficiency.

Overall, it can be argued in light with the real-world practices of the government that state intervention in Singapore was not associated with full control of firms as in Korean industrial policies. Instead, the government adopted what it calls a "free enterprise system."

4.3. Trade Policies

Exports of manufactured products grew rapidly in the East Asian latecomers. There are many reasons for this. First of all, various factors had a positive impact on the exports of manufactures. These include export incentives and trade liberalization in advanced countries, technology transfer, and the use of foreign capital in export activities. Before the oil crises of the 1970s, most of the exported manufactures were light manufactures and consumer goods that did not require high skills. The theoretical explanations of the "product life cycle theory" and the "flying geese theory" can partially explain this phenomenon (Akamatsu, 1962; Vernon, 1966). In this explanation, the product is originally produced in advanced countries first and then the production spreads to other developing countries while being imported. Finally, the product is standardized and the developing countries start to export it to the advanced countries. The changing pattern of comparative advantages in the East Asian latecomers allowed for a rapid rise in the growth of the exports of manufactures. In addition, the distortion of factor prices and factor endowments under industrial policies also facilitated export growth in the East Asian latecomers.

Trade policies were essential components of industrial policies in Japan, Korea, and Taiwan. Associating industrial policies with export-oriented industrialization in East Asia was an effective means to design a reward system under industrial policies that is less subject to moral hazard. Industry and foreign trade were interrelated and connected in an outward-looking growth pattern in these countries. Trade policies were "selective" and "strategic." Singapore, on the other hand, adopted a free trade regime for reasons explained in Section 3.2.4. Only very few non-trade barriers existed in Singapore. Japan, Korea, and Taiwan, on the other hand, exercised certain levels of protection notwithstanding gradual trade liberalization over time.

The focus in and expectations from trade policies are different in Singapore than in Japan, Korea, and Taiwan. Trade policies in Japan, Korea, and Taiwan were "strategic trade policies" because the governments made explicit commitments to nurture the exports of specific industries or firms by extensive subsidization. These industries generally exhibited oligopolistic structures such as electronics, steel, and automobile industries. In these industries, the subsidies provided to exporting firms ensure economies of scale through exports and decreasing marginal costs. In such a case, the profitability of the firm is maintained by the hands of the government. Therefore, the oligopolistic structure prevailed in these industries.

In the case of Singapore, subsidization of exporters for the abovementioned purposes has no significant impact on the firms and also on the economy for some reasons. First of all, export shares of Singapore-origin exports in many industries are very small, except some highly specialized high-technology products such as disk drives and audio cards. Therefore, subsidization of those exports would not help Singapore enhance its share in total exports in the world. A second reason is the firm composition of export industries in Singapore. Unlike the other three countries, most of the exports are realized by foreign companies in Singapore. Therefore, subsizidization of their exports will only help to improve the profits of foreigners which are likely to be expatriated. However, the provision of various fiscal incentives to foreign firms in Singapore has reasons other than the concerns of the government for its trade policy. The government offers special tax and finance treatments to the MNCs for they create employment opportunities for local labor force and production opportunities for domestic firms through subcontracting relations.

4.4. Industrialization Paths

The most common feature of industrial development in Korea, Singapore, and Taiwan is the industrialization path. They followed a similar path in industrialization. All three countries started with import substitution and, facing the limits of their small domestic markets, they soon adopted an export-oriented strategy. These governments created comparative advantages during the course of industrialization by manipulating factor endowments. Their main advantage was the low cost of factors and they exploited this during the export-oriented development era. When a new generation of developing economies (e.g., those in Southeast Asia, such as Indonesia, Malaysia, and Thailand) threatened them in low-cost production, they moved to more capital- and technology-intensive production activities.

In the case of import protection in certain "strategic" industries, in Japan, Korea, and Taiwan, protection was justified by infant-industry arguments. Infant-industry protection was deemed necessary for fostering national industries. While developing by subsidies received from the government and taking advantage of the opportunities in the domestic markets, they needed to be protected from foreign competition as they were in a comparatively disadvantageous position *vis-à-vis* the foreign competitors due to their relatively higher marginal costs. In addition, they found it viable to build economies of scale by expanding production and learning by doing. For these reasons, governments temporarily protected those industries, while the period of protection differed across countries. The subsidies provided to exporting firms included low-interest policy loans, technical assistance, and direct price subsidies in Japan and Korea.

Due to limitations in exploiting the domestic markets through protection, these countries gradually liberalized trade and turned to non-price assistance to exporting firms such as product design and research and development in order to strengthen the competitiveness of the export industries. Export-oriented policies together with assistance to exporting firms for non-price competition has been praised in many studies as the main source of success in these countries in industrial development. Large-scale investments to build capital-intensive industries helped increase capital intensity and export structure changed towards these nurtured capital-intensive industries. Singapore, on the other hand, resorted to free trade from the beginning.

The industrialization paths of the East Asian economies were affected by the investment policies of the governments aiming at the enhancement of economies of scale and investment coordination. For instance, during the Heavy and Chemical Industrialization Drive in Korea (1973–1979), the promoted industries were those the government saw as necessary to increase the self-sufficiency of the country in basic inputs (e.g., iron, steel, petrochemicals, and non-ferrous metals) and the technology-intensive sectors (e.g., shipbuilding, electronics, machinery, and equipment). It should be noted, however, that picking the promising industries is a risky process and there are examples of failure in industry selection in other Asian countries as well, e.g., the nurturing of automotive and aircraft industries in Indonesia and petrochemicals and machinery industries in Malaysia (Yusuf, 2001).

In order to promote the capital-intensive industries, the governments saw the necessity for large-scale investments in these industries to take advantage of scale economies. They encouraged private firms to invest in those areas by providing various investment subsidies, including directed policy credits, and administrative guidance. These were the two main means the governments used in resolving coordination failures in investment (Rodrik *et al.*, 1995). They recognized that such massive investments could not be realized merely through the entrepreneurial skills of local private firms and it was necessary to undertake large-scale investments in the capital- and technology-intensive industries. The governments also engaged in investment and production through public firms, created institutions to facilitate coordination with the private sector, and also established public firms to engage in manufacturing activities in those industries. Most government investments were in areas where investment in new facilities and up-to-date technologies were necessary and the private sector lacked the capital and entrepreneurship to undertake such investments. Finally, after trade liberalization and move to the capital-intensive production phase, the East Asian latecomers largely narrowed the technological gap between them and the advanced countries. Having caught up to a large extent, and in the face of rapid integration of global commodity and financial markets and strong demands by the advanced countries for them to move towards a more market-oriented market economy, they adjusted their industrial policies to diversify economic activities and encouraged private firms to engage in knowledge- and technology-intensive production. For this purpose, they extended various facilities to the development of those industries but this time they were more selective in their industrial policies. The cooperative relations between the governments and industries continued but policy finance was largely reduced in this period.

In Singapore, the path of industrialization is similar in the sense that the industrial structure shifted from light industries to capital-intensive and then to knowledge- and technology-intensive industries. However, due to its small market size, Singapore did not develop heavy industries such as automobile and machinery industries. It specialized mainly in equipment and engineering industries and semiconductors. The only heavy industry on the island is the shipbuilding and ship-repair industry due to its geographical advantages. But, this industry has been on a decline since the 1980s. It is worth noting that although industrial policies target the development of certain manufacturing industries, the development of the financial and business services sector has been important for Singapore. The government paid attention to services development from early years. Services development was deemed supplementary to the development of manufacturing industries. The government developed the concept of a "total business center" and attracted foreign companies by offering them superior services facilities, which made Singapore an attractive location for multinational corporations to establish their regional headquarters. The concept of total business center envisages the positive role the financial and business services sector can play as an engine of growth together with the manufacturing sector. It is necessary to mention here the qualitative characteristics of this policy. Early development of Singapore was based on existing commercial and port services that served the entrepôt economy until the postwar period (Huff, 1994). Industrialization efforts during the early 1960s decreased the importance of the services sector in economic development. However, two major developments led to the recognition of the tertiary sector by the government as a source of further growth. First, the attempt to create and promote an Asian Dollar Market (ADM) in the late 1960s succeeded. ADM grew rapidly and attracted government's attention. Second, industrial development in Singapore opened the way to services development, e.g., the development of the electronics and telecommunications industries led to the building up of superior infrastructure facilities. As a result of these two developments, the government recognized business and financial services sector as one of the "twin engines" of growth for the economy next to the manufacturing sector. The government aims to turn Singapore into a "services hub" in Southeast Asia.

The financial infrastructure of Singapore consists of a banking sector made up of foreign and local banks established originally by wealthy Chinese families who earned large fortunes during the "rubber boom" of the 1920s and 1930s (i.e., United Overseas Bank, Overseas Union Bank, and Overseas Chinese Banking Corporation, being the most influential), stock exchange market, and the ADM (Huff, 1994). The ADM emerged in the late 1960s and grew rapidly. This market operates as an off-shore market where all non-local currencies are exchanged between financial institutions (Regnier, 1987, pp. 122–124). With the abolition of taxes on foreign currencies, Singapore enjoyed a competitive and advantageous position against regional rivals such as Hong Kong and Tokyo. ADM grew rapidly thanks to contributions from oil-producing countries and Western countries. In 1984, the size of the market reached 130 billion US dollars, and to around 500 billion US dollars in 2002, from less than half a billion US dollars in 1970. The rapid development of the ADM is closely related to the integration of global financial markets. The overseas Chinese network also plays a very important role.

After the financial crisis in 1997–1998, the government announced further deregulation measures in the financial service sector when neighboring Malaysia introduced restrictions on capital movements. In an attempt to improve the efficiency in the sector, two large government-controlled banks, the Post Office Savings Bank and Development Bank of Singapore, both of which helped the government ensure high savings rates and provided necessary public funds for its industrialization policy in the past, merged in 2000. In addition, in December 1999, Stock Exchange of Singapore and Singapore International Money Exchange merged and became Singapore Exchange with securities and derivatives operations integrated.

A second objective of the government is to turn Singapore into a trade and business services hub in Southeast Asia. Recently, it is trying to promote trade and business services by promoting information and telecommunications infrastructure services (Wong, 2001; Yue *et al.*, 2001, pp. 60–62). The existence of a well-established information technology infrastructure can be said to be both a cause and a consequence of the development of financial and business services. Singapore obviously has a comparative advantage in trade and business services due to her skilled labor.

4.5. Fiscal Incentives and Policy-Based Finance

In order to establish and maintain a compromise between industrial policies and firms, all four countries (Japan, Korea, Singapore, and Taiwan) used various incentives for those firms undertaking investment projects in the targeted industries. Governments provided tax holidays and various financial assistance schemes to these firms in order to ease the financial burden of investments. Types of incentives demonstrate similarity in almost all four countries. The governments often made use of public financial institutions to allocate the required funds to local businesses engaging in targeted industries.

Japan was the forerunner among the East Asian latecomers. In order to achieve policy targets and coordinate the large scale investments undertaken by public and private firms during the 1950s and the 1960s, the government of Japan provided a wide range of incentives and supporting schemes. The most important of these was policy-based finance (Kato *et al.*, 1994). Public financial institutions such as Japan Development Bank, Small Business Finance Corporation, Shoko Chukin Bank, and People's Finance

Corporation provided easy-to-access funds to these firms. The government also extended its fiscal facilities to support them by offering preferential tax concessions. Special depreciation allowances and tax relief from investments helped these firms avoid some part of initial burden on investments. In addition, the government directly subsidized some firms. This subsidization took the form of interest payment subsidies in the shipping industry. The government also offered funds for rationalization and upgrading as well. In the case of export industries, the government supported exporting firms by offering them technical support and information about overseas markets, lower taxes for their export activities, low-import duties for materials, and extending credits through the Japan Export–Import Bank. However, attributed to the very close relations between banks and private firms, much of the loans used in policy-based finance were provided by banks and other private financial institutions (Table 4.2). The government did not rely on foreign finance for the development of the country's industries and the necessary funds were raised within the firms or firm groupings (*keiretsu*) and by public financial institutions.

In the case of Korea, firms were given the opportunity to borrow from abroad. After 1965, with changing interest rate policies, a negative interest rate margin was introduced to protect domestic firms from increasing costs

Table 4.2. The Proportion of Policy-Based Financing in Loans of All Financial Institutions in Japan (1955–1990).

Unit (percentage)	1955	1960	1965	1970	1975	1980	1985	·1990
Policy-based financial institutions	13.2	11.0	9.6	9.8	10.6	14.1	13.7	11.8
Japan Development Bank	7.5	4.1	2.8	2.2	1.8	1.7	1.6	1.2
Export–Import Bank of Japan	0.0	0.7	1.4	1.9	1.8	1.7	1.2	0.9
Private financial institutions	86.8	89.0	90.4	90.2	89.4	85.9	86.3	88.2

Source: Kato *et al*. (1994, p. 28).

of overborrowing (Cho, 1998). In the 1970s, the government's policy shifted towards financial repression, i.e., the implicit taxation of depositors to subsidize priority industrial sectors. Rent distribution was another effective tool in industrial policies during the 1960s, e.g., export incentives including a multiple exchange rate system, direct cash payments, and easier access to foreign exchange. Credit allocation was linked to the performance of the rent-seekers, rather than political ties. During the Heavy and Chemical Industrialization Drive of the 1970s, various tax incentives were provided to firms undertaking the government-approved investment projects, such as, exemption from corporate taxes for 3 years, 50 percent reduction for the following 2 years, large tariff reductions for imported equipment and raw materials, etc. (Hong, 1997). This drive required a large amount of funds and the government implemented repressive financial policies to provide cheap financing to the investment projects. The banking system was not capable of raising entire funds. The National Investment Fund was established in 1971 to finance long-term investments and the Bank of Korea extended its rediscount facility to support the industrialization drive. On the other hand, credits became more selective in the 1970s whereas they were provided on the basis of export performance regardless of industries that firms operated in. Foreign loans were also used extensively in Korea although they were subject to government approval. As a result of heavy borrowing, the financial structure of Korean firms became highly leveraged and private firms became vulnerable to external and internal shocks. That not many large companies went bankrupt during this period implicitly means that the government was successful in credit intervention and risk management. After 1980, the new president Chun Doo Hwan abolished government supports in the form of preferential credit allocation and tax incentives to specific industries. They were substituted with incentives for research and development, automation, and promotion of infrastructure and human resource development. The government also supported selected high-technology research projects and subsidized them as well, e.g., the dynamic random access memory (DRAM) project in 1986, which was started as a consortium among public research institutes, private semiconductor firms, and universities (Hong, 1997). However, government guidance after 1980 was different from the previous periods in that the government drew the guidelines only rather than pushing for specific targets. In the 1990s, these incentives started to be extended to SMEs too (Laeven, 2002). Finally, to ease the indebtedness problem of private companies the government took several measures in the 1980s and invigorated the stock market, allowed foreign participation in the Korean capital markets, and allowed foreign borrowing by private firms without state repayment guarantees. However, bank credits were still the dominant source of finance (Hong, 1997).

Taiwan also used large sums of funds to support domestic firms and also provided incentives to encourage upgrading of production technologies. However, the Taiwanese government emphasized the need to upgrade the technologies in high-technology industries more and subsidized research and development costs of domestic firms. The government committed itself more to the provision of funds for high-technology investments. High-technology investments in the science parks were rewarded various incentives, such as tax exemption, technical support, low-interest loans, and training of manpower (Tsay, 1995). Especially after the late 1980s, when the joint ventures of public companies established with Taiwanese and American firms in high-technology industries became successful, private firms also entered these industries. For these newcoming firms, the government offered tax deductions and tariff exemption for intermediate goods. Public research institutes such as Electronics Support Services Organization and the Institute of Information Industry helped the private firms by offering technical training. Indigenous firms were also offered generous incentives to upgrade their technologies by going into technology transfer agreements with MNCs. Human resource development by the government and cheap financing provided to domestic firms were the main channels in Taiwan through which the government promoted the growth of indigenous firms.

Singapore's experience exhibit some differences compared to Korea and Taiwan. First of all, Singapore government did not explicitly provide low-interest loans to targeted industries. Local capital market did not allow this. The main source of public investments, however, was the savings of the nation accumulating in the CPF.

4.6. Foreign Elements

The general stance of Japan and Korea to foreign capital was hostile. Japan did not make much use of foreign investment whereas Korea made extensive use of it despite its hostile attitude. Taiwan effectively used foreign investment and realized substantial technology transfer. Singapore, on the other hand, is another story. Foreign capital dominated its industry and was the main source of industrial growth.

As pointed out in Chapter 2, Taiwan introduced foreign capital through the export processing zones (EPZs) it established after the mid-1960s. During the 1960s, American MNCs searching for overseas assembly sites started to invest in East Asia, first in Taiwan and Singapore. Foreign investment in Taiwan came first for labor-intensive manufacturing such as electronic assembly operations. Due to very high wages in Hong Kong, then the most promising East Asian economy, offered Taiwan an opportunity to attract more foreign investment. However, this form of investment did not bring in production technologies to Taiwanese firms. MNCs engaged mainly in assembly and packaging, there were very small linkage effects between assembly and fabrication (Hong, 1997). The government solved this problem by establishing EPZs first in Kaohsiung in 1966 and then in Taichung in 1971. In EPZs all production was exported and both local and foreign firms were engaging in production activities. However, investments were allowed only in designated sectors. This way of gathering local and foreign firms created spillovers and positive externalities.

Korean government also introduced foreign investment from the early 1960s industries where Korean firms lacked the production know-how, e.g., electronics industry. Changes in legislation in the mid-1960s made it easier for foreign investors to establish assembly sites in Korea (Hong, 1997). However, they were subject to strict government approval. During the Heavy and Chemical Industrialization Drive in the 1970s, not many Korean firms were interested in high-technology industries, such as semiconductors. Foreign firms realized a large part of production in these industries. It was only in the 1980s that Korean companies entered these industries and started independent manufacturing. In the 1980s and 1990s, the government encouraged foreign investors to settle in electronics, biotechnology, and informatics industries in Korea and to establish joint ventures with domestic firms. The government emphasized technology transfer in many ways.[4] For instance, in the petrochemicals industry, the government placed

[4] Both Korean and Taiwanese governments realized that contract manufacturing by domestic firms under foreign companies did not increase the technological know-how. Therefore, the enhancement of the technological capabilities of domestic firms emerged as a necessity. Technology creation and diffusion then became a priority for these governments.

great emphasis on the training of Korean employees by foreign investors (Kim and Ma, 1998).

Singapore's manufacturing sector was largely dominated by MNCs and local entrepreneurs were ignored for a long time for reasons explained before. In Korea and Taiwan, as explained above, FDI was used mainly as a source of technology transfer and never tolerated a very strong position for them in the manufacturing sector.

4.7. Business Structures

The sources of growth in the East Asian latecomers differed across counters. In Taiwan, SMEs have been the main source of growth (see Table 4.3), whereas in Korea the large conglomerates (*chaebol*) (see Table 4.4) and in Singapore the MNCs were the main actors in driving economic growth. This phenomenon can be best seen in the high-technology industries. In all three countries, the high-technology industries were introduced by the MNCs. Korea provided substantial amounts of incentives to the MNCs to bring in new technologies and to transfer them to domestic firms and later attempted to create its own high-technology industrial base by supporting domestic firms with public investment and research and development. The cooperation between domestic firms and public agencies proved successful in the 1980s. The same thing happened in Taiwan but the government opted to promote a dynamic pool of SMEs.

The cooperation between SMEs and the MNCs in Taiwan under government guidance helped the SMEs first increase their technological

Table 4.3. SMEs in Taiwan (1966–1991).

	1966	1971	1981	1986	1991
Number of firms	27578	42315	94038	113314	142788
Number of workers	384641	767377	1654113	2092791	2125671
% of total firms	99.5	99.2	99.5	99.6	99.7
% of total workers	65.2	63.9	75.9	76.0	80.7

Note: SME refers to a firm with less than 300 employees.
Sources: Calculated from Liu *et al.* (1993) and Lin (2002).

Table 4.4. Chaebols in Korea.

Shares of chaebols total mining and manufacturing production (%)						
	1980	1983	1987	1991	1994	
Top 5	16.9	22.6	22.0	23.4	24.6	
Top 30	36.0	40.4	37.3	38.8	39.6	
Shares of chaebols in value-added in GNP (%)						
	1977	1981	1985	1990	1994	
Top 10	20.1	20.4	24.1	22.8	26.5	
Top 30	29.1	30.8	33.1	30.0	33.9	
Number of the affiliated companies of chaebols						
	1987	1991	1994		1997	
Chaebols	Top 32	Top 30	Top 30	Top 5	Top 30	Top 5
No. Affiliated companies	509	561	616	210	819	262
Average	15.9	18.7	29.5	42.0	27.3	52.4
The structure of ownership and debts in the top chaebols (%)						
		1991	1993	1995	1996	1997
Share of insiders		47.0	43.4	43.3	44.1	43.0
Shares held by affiliates		32.9	33.1	32.8	33.8	NA
Shares held by owners and families		14.1	10.3	10.5	10.3	NA
Equity to asset ratio		19.8	19.0	19.9	20.5	18.5
Ordinary income to sales ratio		NA	1.0	2.5	0.2	−0.3
Debt-equity ratio		369.8	348.4	348.8	387.8	449.4

Note: NA: not applicable.
Source: Lee *et al*. (2000).

capabilities and later become a source of technological improvement. The government played a different role in Taiwan than in Korea in the development of electronics industry by supporting small rather than large firms (Hattori and Sato, 1997). Tsay (1995) argues that the strength of SMEs in Taiwan lies in their quick reaction to market signals. For instance, during the early stages of development in the electronics industry, SMEs were mainly producing home appliances (e.g., telephones). When they felt that they needed to move to higher value-added production due to changing market conditions (i.e., increasing competition from other low-wage Asian countries), they could soon switch to the production of microcomputers and computer-related products. It is also well known that SMEs in Taiwan have strong network relations with each other and they maintain their competitiveness by specializing only in a small range of products.

In Singapore, on the other hand, local companies lacked the funds necessary for a big leap forward. As explained in Chapter 3, although the government provided adequate incentives for MNCs to establish themselves, not much has been done for a long period (until the 1990s) to enhance the technological capabilities of local firms, which were dominantly SMEs and mainly operating as subcontractors to the MNCs. Nevertheless, the government turned its face to the SMEs during the 1990s and encouraged technology transfer from MNCs to the SMEs. Overall, Singapore was not successful in developing domestic firms although it was successful in facilitating technology absorption for domestic firms.

Another difference is the role of public companies. In Korea and Taiwan, public companies accounted for a significantly large part of production. During the 1960s, public companies in Korea accounted for 15 percent of total value-added in the manufacturing sector and more than 80 percent of total value-added in the financial services sector. They also realized 30 percent of total investments. These companies operated mostly in monopolistic or oligopolistic markets and they were not allowed to go bankrupt. Many of these companies were the government's agents in industrial policies and they contributed largely to the development of the promoted industries. For instance, a public company, Pohang Iron and Steel Company (POSCO), realized remarkable catch-up and modernization in the iron and steel industry (Shin, 1996). It provided basic materials to other industries at low prices although it enjoyed a near-monopoly status.

In the case of public companies, a major difference between Singapore and the other Asian latecomers is that public companies in Singapore were allowed to go bankrupt and were never bailed out. Most public companies were supported heavily by soft budget constraints in the other latecomers, but in Singapore, their performance evaluation was based on commercial criteria and accordingly, they were run efficiently.

4.8. The Influence of International Political Economy

International political economy played a deterministic role in the implementation of industrial policies. Taiwanese state did not experience that much pressure from the United States while Japan and Korea have always had trade frictions with the United States. Japan, Korea, and Taiwan were all under pressure by the United States after the mid-1970s due to worsening American trade balance against these three countries. Although state intervention in Taiwan was of a much higher degree in Taiwan, the United States did not criticize Taiwan as harshly as Korea. It is argued elsewhere that Taiwan's lack of mass productive capacity in the new high-technology industries in the 1970s was one reason for this difference (Li, 1988; Hong, 1997). In Korea, on the other hand, production activities in the new high-technology industries were concentrated in the chaebol which had a large productive capacity and therefore they were the main competitors of American high-technology producers. In addition, another reason why Korea was criticized by the United States was that most of the high-technology industries in Korea were created almost from zero and the government was imposing several controls on foreign investors, such as limits on foreign share in joint ventures and compulsory technology transfer to domestic firms. Due to the mass production capacity installed in chaebol plants, high-technology industries grew rapidly in Korea. In consequence, the United States exerted pressure on Korea especially in semiconductors trade and Korea faced several trade frictions *vis-à-vis* the United States. This came at a time when the United States had similar problems in trade of automobiles and some other technology-intensive products with the Japanese firms (Shinohara, 1982).

Singapore, however, did not face such trade frictions because of its relatively small influence on the worsening trade balance of the United States.

Even though the exports of high-technology products from Singapore to the United States have been increasing since the 1980s, the American firms that were settled in Singapore accounted for a substantial portion of them. Therefore, due to high degree of foreign content in exports, Singapore saved herself from serious trade conflicts with the United States.

In addition to trade frictions, the attitudes of the international financial institutions and the international capital towards industrial policies in East Asia are also of great importance. Both the International Monetary Fund and the World Bank were in favor of the relief of state controls over the economy in developing countries especially after the mid-1970s. At the same time, the MNCs were demanding the opening up of the markets in developing economies because profitability in advanced countries was on the decline. Although they had some common interests with the governments in the East Asian latecomers, especially in technology transfer, their interests opposed with the developmentalist government policies most of the time. International organizations also insisted on more free trade and more free investment and capital movements after the mid-1970s. Parallel to these developments in the international economy, the importance of industrial policies declined due to the pressure from advanced countries. To illustrate this point, Frey *et al.* (1987) conducted a survey on 900 economists in five advanced countries (Austria, France, Germany, Switzerland, and the United States) and found that the belief in the price system and market mechanism was the central aspect of the consensus among economists at around this time. These economists also supported free trade. Japan, Korea, and Taiwan responded to such calls with deregulation of domestic markets. Singapore, on the other hand, chose to retain the heavy presence of the government in the economy and went on to combine free trade with government interventions. As explained in Chapter 3, the government rather acted pragmatically by responding to changes in the global economic conditions.

CHAPTER 5

LABOR PRODUCTIVITY AND LABOR REALLOCATION: THE SINGAPORE CASE

In the first part of the book, a descriptive analysis of the industrial policies in East Asia was provided. In the second part, we will empirically analyze the impact of the changes in industrial policies on the performance of the economy and its sectors. Since industrial policies are involved mainly with the development of certain manufacturing industries, the emphasis will be on manufacturing industries, especially the promoted ones. However, we do not ignore services sectors as the financial and business services sector in Singapore was deemed as an engine of growth by the government. Therefore, a wide range of sectors and industries is selected.

In the empirical analyses, we have used two steps. In the first step, the allocation of resources and their impact on the economy is investigated through an examination of the changes in productivity growth they induced. In the second step, the impacts of policy shocks are examined using a computable general equilibrium model.

The first of these analyses is undertaken in Chapters 5 and 6. While Chapter 5 discusses the impact of labor reallocations and the government's changing labor market policies on labor productivity, Chapter 6 carries it one step further to include TFP growth and reallocation of productive inputs (capital and labor). Special emphasis is placed on specific manufacturing industries promoted under industrial policies.

During the course of industrial development in the East Asian economies, there were changes in both output and input structures. One expects resource allocation to be optimal to maintain international competitiveness. This makes it crucial to investigate the impact of changes in the input and output structures, especially regarding those promoted manufacturing industries. The question to ask is in what direction and magnitude the allocation of resources contributed to the industrial growth and productivity. This question is especially important for policymakers because diversions from optimal structure incur costs not only for the relevant promoted industries, but also for the society as a whole as they influence the growth and development path of the economy. In fact, productivity was emphasized in all reports of the committees in Singapore that were established to draw recommendations to help the economy out of distress in uneasy times. In addition, wage increases are usually linked to increases in productivity.

In this chapter, we start with labor productivity growth with an application on Singapore. The uniqueness of Singapore in East Asia with respect to the style of industrial policies forces us to emphasize its experience and then compare it with the others. A comparison of Singapore with the rest of the East Asia is made in Chapter 7. The performance of the economy is evaluated for different periods characterized by specific industrial policies. The impact of intersectoral reallocations of labor on aggregate labor productivity is investigated by linking it with labor market policies of the government. Previously, Lim and Lee (2002) found that labor productivity accounts for 78 percent of per capita real output growth rate whereas the increase in employment ratio accounts for the remaining 22 percent for the period 1974–1999. The increase in the employment ratio stems largely from increasing labor force participation ratio for female population. Increasing labor force participation rate was important only during the early phases of industrial development. Once the limits to the expansion of labor force are reached, then the only alternative is improving labor productivity. In this respect, transfer of labor across sectors may be an important source of productivity. Labor can be shifted from less productive to more productive industries and this may help in improving the aggregate productivity.[1]

MTI (2001) is another comprehensive study on labor productivity performance of Singapore for the period 1985–2000 with a decomposition analysis using the same methodology employed in this study. It was found that highly open sectors such as manufacturing had high labor productivity growth rates and domestic-oriented services sectors had low growth rates, i.e., those sectors exposed to international competition succeeded in ensuring productivity gains. In addition, it was found that the predominant

[1] In economies with substantially large agricultural sector, a shift of labor from agriculture to manufacturing is an example.

factor in aggregate labor productivity growth in Singapore was labor productivity growth arising from within individual sectors whereas the shifts of labor across sectors made negligibly small contributions.

5.1. Trends in Labor Productivity and Real Wages in Singapore

5.1.1. *Description of data*

It is important to note at the beginning that the analyses are conducted at two levels. First, they are conducted for major sectors of the economy. Second, only the manufacturing sector is taken and the analyses are narrowed down to sub-industries. For these purposes, major economic activities are divided into nine sectors: agriculture, mining, manufacturing, utilities, construction, commerce (i.e., wholesale and retail trade, hotels, and restaurant services), transport and communications services, financial–business services, and other services (i.e., government services, community, personal, and social services, and all other services). Table 5.1 provides a list of these sectors and industries. Nine major sectors are in capitals. The manufacturing sector is divided into 19 industry groups. In total, economic activities are classified into 27 different groups of production activities. Main data sources are listed in Table 5.2.

The standard industrial classification of manufacturing industries in Singapore changed with major revisions in 1969, 1978, 1986, 1990, and 1996. In order to maintain consistency of the data used in the analyses, necessary adjustments were made to reflect the changes in standard industrial classification. Over time, broad groups of industries and their definitions at either the three- or five-digit level have not changed to a large extent. Wherever necessary, abnormal data were corrected using the iterative proportional fitting technique in order to assure consistency in time series data. Detailed information about this technique is available in Norman (1999).

5.1.1.1. *Real value-added*

In general, two measures of output are employed in productivity analyses: gross output and value-added. Value-added is generally preferred to gross output in productivity analyses because it avoids double counting of

Table 5.1. List of Major Sectors and Manufacturing Industries.

AGR	Agriculture, hunting, forestry, and fishing
MIN	Mining and quarrying
MANUF	Manufacturing industries (19 industries)
Food	Food, beverages, and tobacco
Tex	Textiles and textile manufactures
Wear	Wearing apparel except footwear
Leat	Leather, leather products, and footwear
Wood	Wood and wood products except furniture
Furn	Furniture, except metal furniture
Paper	Paper and paper products
Pub	Publishing, printing, and reproduction of recorded media
Chem	Chemicals and chemical products
Petr	Refined petroleum products
Rub	Rubber and plastic products
Non-met	Non-metallic mineral products
Met	Basic metals
Fab-met	Fabricated metal products
Mach	Machinery and equipment
Elec	Electrical machinery, electrical apparatus, electronic products, and electronic components
Prec	Medical, precision instruments, optical instruments, watches, and clocks
Tran	Transport equipment
Oth-man	Other manufacturing industries, recycling of metal and non-metal waste, and scrap
UTIL	Electricity, gas, and water
CONST	Construction
COM	Wholesale trade, retail trade, restaurants, and hotels
TR-COM	Transport, storage, and communication
FIN-BUS	Financial, insurance, real estate, and business services
OTH-SERV	Community, social, and personal services, government services, other services, and activities not defined

Note: The same abbreviations for industries and sectors are used in the tables and figures hereafter.

Table 5.2. Primary Sources of Data.

Employed persons	SYS, RCIP, MoL
Monthly earnings and labor cost	SYS, ILO, RCIP
Weekly working hours	SYS, ILO
GDP deflators	SYS, SNA95
Index of Industrial Production	SYS
Gross fixed capital formation	SYS, RCIP
Fixed capital assets by type (for manufacturing)	RCIP
Output and value-added	SYS, RCIP
Intermediate materials use	SYS, RCIP
Price Index	SYS

Note: SYS: *Singapore Yearbook of Statistics*; ILO: International Labor Organization (ILO), *International Labor Statistics Yearbook*; SNA95: *Singapore System of National Accounts 1995* published by Singstat; RCIP: *Report on the Census of Industrial Production*; MoL: Ministry of Labor annual reports.

intermediate inputs and measures production that accrues to production factors. Gross value-added data for industries at producers' prices are available from manufacturing censuses. For major sectors of the economy, the data on output are obtained from the national accounts statistics. In the national accounts, GDP by economic activity data present the values at factor prices. Sectoral GDP at factor is a convenient proxy for sectoral value-added. Long value-added series for most services sectors are not available from sectoral surveys. In the case of Singapore, surveys of the services sector have been discontinued for some years or published every 2 years. In this case, the most reliable data for services value-added seems to be the figures in national accounts categorized by the type of economic activity. By comparing the data from different sources such as the *United Nations National Accounts Statistics Yearbook*, and the *World Bank World Tables*, the consistency of sectoral data with the national accounts statistics was ensured. No inconsistency was found in the data. Sectoral real value-added data are calculated by normalizing the nominal figures by sectoral GDP deflators with 1990 as the base year. GDP deflators are obtained from national accounts. Starting from 1998, real output figures in the official statistical yearbook are published in constant 1995 dollars. Therefore, price indices were linked in 1998 and the indices after 1998 were converted to constant 1995 prices.

Value-added data for manufacturing industries are obtained from annual manufacturing surveys (*Report on the Census of Industrial Production*). These surveys do not cover all establishments, but cover a very large part of manufacturing production. Real value-added data for manufacturing industries are not readily available from official statistics. The best way to calculate real value-added is the double deflation method, where the deflated value of intermediate inputs is deducted from the deflated value of gross output. In the case of Singapore, output, output deflator, and intermediate input data are available in official statistics. However, the deflators for intermediate inputs are not available. One reason is that local manufacturing industries use large amounts of imported inputs along with domestically produced intermediate inputs. For domestically produced intermediate inputs, *Domestic Supply Price Index* seems to be an appropriate index. However, data on the price levels of imported inputs and the percentage of imported intermediate inputs in total intermediate inputs are not available in official statistics. For these reasons, the double deflation method does not seem to be appropriate for Singapore.

In her pioneering study of productivity in manufacturing industries in Singapore, Tsao (1982) used the indices of industrial production (IIP) to estimate the changes in real value-added growth. These indices are published by the national statistics office. IIP, by definition, measures changes in the level of real output (not value-added) in manufacturing, mining, and utilities sectors and their subdivisions, given a base year. However, Young (1995)[2] warns that the IIP figures reported by the statistical office in Singapore cannot be used even to compute real output in manufacturing industries because a large part of output recorded in official statistics in this index (amounting to 40–50 percent) is non-deflated and hence, reflects only changes in nominal output.[3]

To my knowledge, there is only one study by Koh *et al.* (2001) that attempts to construct industry-specific output and intermediate inputs price indices for Singapore. In that study, the authors estimated price indices by

[2]However, he uses this index to compute real value-added for the manufacturing sector with the reasoning that there are no other alternative price indices to use.

[3]Koh *et al.* (2001, p. 33) reply to Young's such argument on IIP figures as follows: "...we would suggest that those most likely to suffer from this are electronics and shipbuilding and repairing industries, as well as some fabricated metal industries." In this case, price indices need to be constructed separately. However, if their observation is correct, published IIP figures can be utilized for other industries.

utilizing *Singapore Manufactured Price Index* (SMPI) and *Import Price Index*. However, their calculations are only for six time points, namely 1974, 1980, 1985, 1990, 1995, and 1998. The estimations by Koh *et al.* (2001) remain insufficient as it becomes necessary to obtain data on import components of material inputs for each industry in each year but they are available only in the published input–output tables for the years 1973, 1978, 1983, 1988, 1995, and 2000. As a consequence, two methods seem to be the best ways to compute real value-added: using the manufacturing GDP deflator for all manufacturing industries or using industry-specific SMPI as a proxy for wholesale prices in manufacturing industries. Although a general purpose wholesale price index is not available in official statistics, SMPI, which is published in the annual statistical yearbook, reflects the prices of manufactured products and is the best candidate as a price index for its coverage makes it a useful measure to be used as a wholesale price index. Table 5.3 shows that, there are only small differences in the growth rates of real value-added between the real value-added figures for most industries computed by deflating either way, manufacturing GDP deflator or the SMPI. However, SMPI is available only from 1974 and that there are no other price indices to be used as a proxy to normalize nominal value-added. Therefore, it is assumed that the growth rate of real value-added prior to 1974 is equal to the changes in IIP.

5.1.1.2. *Employment*

Employment data for nine major sectors are obtained from *Yearbook of Statistics*, annual reports on labor force and from manufacturing surveys for manufacturing industries. Data from *ILO Labor Statistics Yearbook* are also used to check for consistency and to correct any errors, where only a few abnormalities were found and corrected. Not only employment data included workers who work for pay, but also all persons engaged in the activity of the establishment, including the self-employed.

5.1.1.3. *Working hours*

In order to obtain annual working hour figures per employee, total hours worked (H) are calculated by multiplying weekly working hours by the factor 52, the number of weeks in a year. These data are obtained from *Yearbook of Statistics* and reports on labor force statistics. Annual reports

Table 5.3. Real Value-added Growth Rates Using two Different Price Indices.

Unit	Real Value-added Growth With SMPI (Annual Average) (A)			Real Value-added Growth With GDP Deflator (Annual Average) (B)			Difference Between the Two Rates (A–B)		
(percent)	1965–1985	1986–2002	1965–2002	1965–1985	1986–2002	1965–2002	1965–1985	1986–2002	1965–2002
Food	6.4	2.4	4.6	5.0	0.9	3.2	1.4	1.5	1.4
Tex	13.9	0.5	7.9	11.8	−2.0	5.6	2.1	2.4	2.3
Wear	13.9	−0.5	7.5	11.8	−2.9	5.2	2.1	2.4	2.3
Leat	8.9	8.5	8.7	6.7	6.1	6.4	2.1	2.4	2.3
Wood	4.9	−4.5	0.7	2.8	−4.4	−0.4	2.1	−0.1	1.1
Furn	13.5	−6.7	4.4	11.4	−7.0	3.1	2.1	0.3	1.3
Paper	18.2	1.2	10.6	16.0	0.4	9.0	2.1	0.8	1.6
Pub	10.0	5.0	7.8	7.9	3.8	6.0	2.1	1.2	1.7
Chem	16.8	17.1	17.0	15.6	14.7	15.2	1.3	2.4	1.8
Petr	8.8	7.9	8.4	10.5	4.7	7.9	−1.7	3.2	0.5
Rub	7.3	6.4	6.9	6.0	5.9	6.0	1.3	0.5	1.0
Non-met	9.6	1.7	6.1	7.5	−0.7	3.8	2.1	2.4	2.3
Met	9.5	−1.8	4.4	7.3	−3.9	2.3	2.1	2.1	2.1
Fab-met	11.9	5.6	9.1	10.4	4.6	7.8	1.5	1.0	1.3
Mach	19.4	6.1	13.4	17.9	5.5	12.3	1.5	0.6	1.1
Elec	23.0	11.3	17.8	21.5	6.8	15.0	1.5	4.5	2.8
Prec	21.3	11.0	16.7	19.7	10.1	15.4	1.5	0.9	1.3
Tran	15.2	4.0	10.2	13.7	5.0	9.8	1.5	−1.0	0.4
Oth-man	15.0	3.0	9.6	13.6	1.4	8.1	1.4	1.6	1.5

Source: Author's calculations.

on labor force are published from 1973 on an annual basis, but they were not conducted for some years. These data take into account only the actual working-hours of employees, including overtime but excluding recess.

Employment data cover both employees and the self-employed. Working-hour statistics reflect working hours of employees. Data on working hours are not separated in official statistics for the self-employed and employees. Therefore, it is assumed that working hours for the self-employed are the same as that of employees. For the periods 1970–1973 and 1988–1997, working-hour data for textile, wearing, and leather products were published together under one industry title ("textiles") and hence the same working-hours data were used for these industries. Similarly, for the period 1988–1997, the data for wood and furniture industries were published under the title "wood," paper and publishing industries under the title "paper," and chemicals, petroleum, rubber, and plastics industries under the title "chemicals". Therefore, same working-hours data are used for industries in the same group.

5.1.1.4. *Labor compensation*

In order to calculate labor compensation, the concept of "total remuneration" is adopted. This concept takes into account wages plus all other payments made to workers. Labor remuneration data are obtained from manufacturing censuses, *Yearbook of Statistics* for manufacturing industries, and *ILO Yearbook of Labor Statistics* and *Yearbook of Statistics* for major sectors. An earlier study on income inequality in Singapore by Rao and Ramakrishnan (1980) also provides detailed information on monthly income for the years 1966, 1972, 1973, 1974, and 1975. The data for monthly income are presented in income groups such as 0–199, 200–399 Singapore dollars per month. To compute monthly income of relevant groups, the group means as computed by Rao and Ramakrishnan (1980, p. 19) are employed. For manufacturing industries, remuneration refers to the amount expended by employers to employees for the whole year and thus, includes salaries with bonuses, contributions to Central Provident Fund (CPF) paid by employers, and other benefits, e.g., cost of living allowances, medical benefits, free and subsidized food, and other payments. Total remuneration figures in official statistics refer to the amount withdrawn from CPF for personal use and the allowances for working proprietors and unpaid family workers. Remuneration data exclude all kinds of indirect taxes on labor remuneration.

For all sectors other than manufacturing, remuneration refers to all remuneration received before the deduction of employees' CPF contributions and personal income tax, inclusive of overtime payments and all other monetary payments earned by employees, and NWC recommendations after 1972. It includes annual wage supplement and variable payments and bonuses. These data are based on the payrolls of CPF contributors. To compute real remuneration, nominal remuneration data are deflated by the wholesale price indices for manufacturing industries and GDP deflators for nine major sectors. For those sectors whose wage data are published in the form of hourly wages (until 1985), weekly wages are computed using weekly working-hours data. These are converted into annual wages by multiplying the relevant figures by the factor 52.

In order to adjust for the self-employed in computing total remuneration, it is assumed that they earn wages equivalent to that of employees. Indirect taxes on labor imply a payroll tax of 2 percent, skills development levy payable to SDF (starting from 1979) by equal amounts by both the employee and the employer, and a foreign worker levy for foreign workers to be paid by the employer. Remuneration data exclude these values in reported statistics. These values were added to remuneration data when calculating total labor cost. In doing this, tax rates for each respective year are applied to total wage data uniformly over all employees. However, no adjustment is made for foreign worker levies because detailed data on the number of foreign workers and foreign worker levies paid are not available in official statistics.

5.1.1.5. *Periodization*

The entire period of analysis is separated into subperiods to reflect the evolution of industrial policies. Data were collected for each year between 1959 and 2002. There are five subperiods. The first subperiod covers the import-substitution years (1959–1965). In this period, Singapore was a member state in the Malaya Federation and implemented the import-substitution policies of the federation. The second subperiod (1966–1978) spans early independence and is characterized by rapid industrialization and export expansion policies. Vigorous public investment programs aimed at expanding domestic production capacity in certain manufacturing industries, such as shipbuilding and ship-repair, petroleum, and chemicals, were implemented in this period. From the late 1960s, large amounts of foreign investment were attracted, most notably in petroleum refining, electrical machinery industries, and financial services. This period was also characterized by severe erosion of wage incomes and governmental measures against organized labor. The third subperiod (1979–1985) is characterized by a restructuring effort where deliberate increases in wages took place (Second Industrial Revolution). The fourth subperiod (1986–1997) is marked with return to rapid growth under new initiatives set by the government, such as a planned action to improve productivity, promoting local enterprises, turning the island into a total business center, a services and IT hub, and a regional financial center. The economy grew at an average annual rate of 7.3 percent until the Asian financial crisis in 1997–1998. In the last subperiod (1998–2002), the effects of the Asian crisis were felt due to its long-lasting impacts on the Southeast Asian economies with which Singapore has strong economic relations.

5.1.2. *Trends in labor productivity and real wages*

Two quantitative techniques are utilized in analyzing aggregate labor productivity growth and its sources. First, the connection between labor productivity, patterns of employment, and labor cost is traced. In theory, integration with global markets and outward orientation are expected to benefit an economy as the absorption of foreign technology and productivity gains may facilitate rises in real wages and total employment levels. Industries exhibiting these characteristics, such as electronics, would also serve as the engine of growth for the rest of the economy. Here, the so-called Hodrick–Prescott filter is used to dismantle the cyclical variations in productivity growth and real wages from their respective historical trends. This method disassociates the trend component and helps us to understand better the wage cycle and long-term productivity patterns. On a second level of analysis, a decomposition exercise on the nature and sources of productivity growth within and across the sectors of the economy is conducted. Here, we have extensively used the methodology described in Timmer and Szirmai (2000).

Labor productivity is a partial productivity measure, which is defined as the amount of output per unit of input (Figure 5.1). This can be represented as

$$P_X = \frac{Q}{X}, \tag{5.1}$$

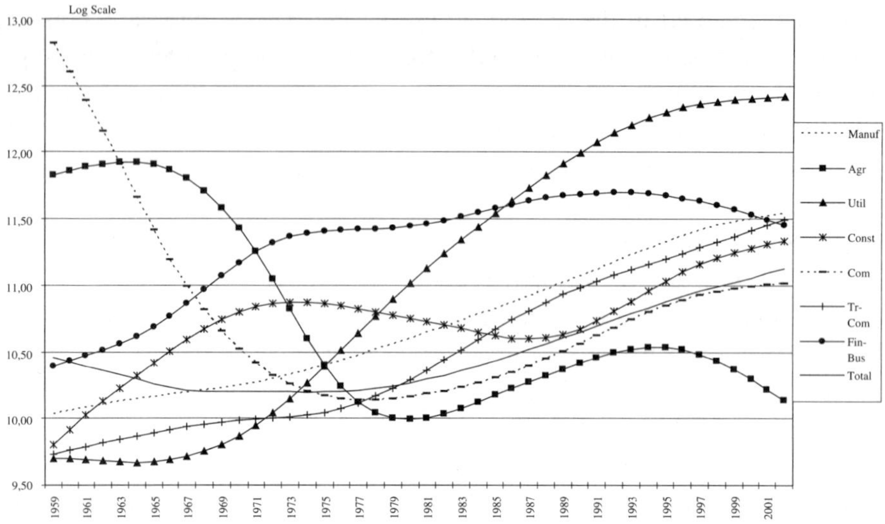

Fig. 5.1. Labor productivity (labor:number of employees) (1959–2002).
Note: The data are smoothed with the Hodrick–Prescott filter.
Source: Author's calculations.

where P_X, Q, X represent productivity, output, and input amounts, respectively. We are rather interested in the growth of productivity, which is calculated as follows:

$$\frac{\Delta P_X}{P_X} = \frac{\Delta Q}{Q} - \frac{\Delta X}{X}, \tag{5.2}$$

where the operator Δ denotes change in a relevant item in a given time period. Equation (5.2) states that the growth rate of productivity of input X equals the difference between the growth rates of output and input X. In the case of labor productivity, X refers to labor input.

In labor productivity analyses, we have used the computed real value-added data for the sectors and manufacturing industries. Labor is represented by both labor hours and number of employees. Consequently, two measures for labor productivity are derived: value-added per worker (Q/L) and per working hour (Q/H). Q, L, and H refer to real output, number of employees, and working hours, respectively.

Labor productivity growth rates for both labor productivity measures at the major sector and industry levels are presented in Tables 5.4 and 5.5.

Table 5.4. Labor Productivity Growth Rates (Labor Input: Number of Employees).

Sectors/ Industries	1959–1965	1966–1978	1979–1985	1959–1985	1965–1985	1986–1997	1998–2002	1986–2002	1959–2002	1965–2002
AGR	0.6	−16.3	9.2	−4.3	−6.5	0.5	−10.1	−2.6	−3.6	−4.8
MIN	6.8	9.3	6.5	8.0	7.1	−2.4	−13.7	−5.7	2.6	1.4
MANUF	3.6	0.0	3.8	2.8	2.3	5.1	6.7	5.5	3.9	3.8
Food	2.4	1.9	4.7	3.0	2.9	2.8	−8.4	−0.5	1.6	1.4
Tex	15.1	4.1	3.8	9.0	2.5	4.8	−1.8	2.9	6.6	2.7
Wear	−2.4	5.0	−1.1	0.2	1.6	2.1	9.2	4.2	1.8	2.7
Leat	−0.9	1.0	3.0	1.1	0.2	5.5	−0.7	3.7	2.1	1.7
Wood	2.4	5.8	−2.1	2.0	2.6	4.8	−5.9	1.6	1.9	2.2
Furn	3.3	−1.8	4.8	2.0	−0.6	2.3	−23.8	−5.4	−0.9	−2.8
Paper	−3.7	3.0	13.3	4.7	7.8	1.8	−8.1	−1.1	2.4	3.8
Pub	−0.8	0.7	5.7	2.1	2.7	5.0	−4.2	2.3	2.2	2.5
Chem	18.0	8.4	5.4	12.4	7.9	4.3	22.6	9.7	11.3	8.7
Petr	14.1	2.6	−5.9	5.9	0.7	5.1	7.0	5.7	5.8	2.9
Rub	9.8	3.5	3.4	4.3	2.5	2.7	−1.0	1.6	3.3	2.1
Non-met	2.9	5.6	−0.5	4.4	3.1	5.3	−10.0	0.8	3.0	2.1

(Continued)

Table 5.4. (*Continued*)

Sectors/ Industries	1959–1965	1966–1978	1979–1985	1959–1985	1965–1985	1986–1997	1998–2002	1986–2002	1959–2002	1965–2002
Met	12.7	6.8	−0.7	6.9	3.6	−0.2	−2.0	−0.7	3.9	1.6
Fab-met	−0.8	1.8	3.0	1.7	2.4	3.0	−2.3	1.5	1.6	2.0
Mach	−0.5	4.3	1.6	2.9	4.8	−1.1	7.7	1.5	2.3	3.3
Elec	0.9	−1.2	8.0	2.5	1.6	5.1	8.0	5.9	3.9	3.5
Prec	1.5	−1.1	7.8	5.2	2.0	4.9	8.8	6.0	5.6	3.8
Tran	3.4	5.3	4.0	4.0	3.7	2.9	−4.0	0.8	2.8	2.4
Oth-man	−0.9	2.6	15.8	5.4	8.2	2.6	−19.0	−3.7	1.8	2.9
UTIL	2.2	10.5	9.1	7.8	9.3	4.5	5.9	4.9	6.7	7.3
CONST	12.4	2.8	1.8	4.1	2.7	5.0	−3.1	2.6	3.5	2.7
COM	−18.7	−4.8	1.0	−7.9	−2.6	6.1	−4.1	3.1	−3.5	0.0
TR-COM	3.4	2.7	7.7	4.1	4.4	4.3	5.5	4.7	4.3	4.5
FIN-BUS	10.1	5.6	4.9	4.4	5.5	0.5	−7.0	−1.7	2.0	2.3
OTH-SERV	6.0	−0.5	2.4	2.6	0.4	4.2	−1.2	2.6	2.6	1.4
Total	−0.8	0.0	3.0	0.3	1.0	4.4	2.9	4.0	1.7	2.3

Source: Author's calculations.

Table 5.5. Labor Productivity Growth Rates (labor Input: Total Labor Hours).

Sectors/ Industries	1959–1965	1966–1978	1979–1985	1959–1985	1965–1985	1986–1997	1998–2002	1986–2002	1959–2002	1965–2002
AGR	6.3	−17.0	9.3	−4.5	−7.1	−0.1	−10.0	−3.0	−3.9	−5.3
MIN	3.3	8.8	8.3	7.4	7.3	−2.7	−13.9	−6.0	2.1	1.3
MANUF	3.1	2.7	4.9	3.4	3.2	4.9	−1.1	3.1	3.3	3.2
Food	3.8	1.4	5.0	2.9	3.3	2.9	−8.8	−0.5	1.5	1.6
Tex	24.0	3.6	4.0	8.4	2.2	4.3	−0.9	2.8	6.2	2.4
Wear	−9.3	4.6	−0.7	−0.1	1.6	1.8	8.4	3.8	1.5	2.6
Leat	−0.6	0.1	3.4	0.8	−0.3	5.2	−1.0	3.4	1.8	1.4
Wood	−1.6	5.1	−1.2	1.9	2.5	4.3	−4.3	1.8	1.8	2.2
Furn	−2.6	2.2	5.7	2.1	−0.8	1.9	−22.9	−5.4	−0.9	−2.8
Paper	−1.3	2.4	13.9	4.6	7.5	1.8	−8.2	−1.2	2.3	3.6
Pub	1.2	0.1	6.3	2.0	2.4	5.0	−4.2	2.3	2.1	2.4
Chem	29.5	7.6	5.7	12.1	7.5	3.9	24.7	10.0	11.3	8.6
Petr	27.1	1.8	−5.6	5.6	0.3	4.7	8.4	5.8	5.7	2.8
Rub	7.8	2.7	3.7	4.1	2.1	2.3	−1.1	1.3	3.0	1.7
Non-met	7.2	4.4	−0.1	3.8	3.0	4.5	−8.0	0.8	2.6	2.0

(*Continued*)

Table 5.5. (*Continued*)

Sectors/ Industries	1959–1965	1966–1978	1979–1985	1959–1985	1965–1985	1986–1997	1998–2002	1986–2002	1959–2002	1965–2002
Met	15.5	6.0	−0.5	6.4	3.3	−0.6	−0.9	−0.7	3.6	1.5
Fab-met	−0.3	1.6	3.2	1.6	2.5	2.4	−2.2	1.1	1.4	1.9
Mach	0.6	4.0	1.5	2.6	4.7	−1.3	8.0	1.5	2.1	3.2
Elec	4.2	−1.2	8.7	2.7	1.9	4.2	8.8	5.5	3.8	3.5
Prec	15.7	−1.8	9.0	5.2	2.1	4.5	9.3	6.0	5.5	3.8
Tran	0.7	5.4	4.2	4.0	3.8	2.8	−3.7	0.9	2.7	2.5
Oth-man	−3.9	3.3	15.9	5.1	8.2	2.3	−20.7	−4.5	1.3	2.5
UTIL	−1.3	11.3	9.4	7.9	9.8	4.5	6.9	5.2	6.8	7.7
CONST	8.6	2.8	1.2	3.7	2.4	4.9	−2.6	2.7	3.3	2.5
COM	−24.8	−4.7	1.3	−7.7	−2.4	6.0	−3.8	3.2	−3.4	0.1
TR-COM	3.0	2.6	9.2	4.5	5.4	4.0	6.1	4.6	4.5	5.0
FIN-BUS	0.9	5.9	5.1	4.5	5.7	0.4	−6.9	−1.7	2.0	2.3
OTH-SERV	9.1	0.1	3.3	3.1	1.0	3.6	−1.0	2.2	2.7	1.6
Total	−2.5	0.1	3.6	0.4	1.3	4.1	3.4	3.9	1.8	2.4

Source: Author's calculations.

Table 5.4 presents the growth of labor productivity measured as output per labor and Table 5.5 presents the growth of labor productivity measured as output per working hour. In these tables, major sectors are denoted by capital letters. The tables show that in long periods (i.e., 1959–1985, 1965–1985, 1986–2002, 1959–2002, 1965–2002) the growth of labor productivity using any of the two measures converge to each other. In short, subperiods (e.g., 1959–1965, 1979–1985), however, they tend to diverge. The remarkable productivity growth performance of the chemicals industry is observable from both tables. This performance was accompanied in some periods by precision equipment and electrical and electronic machinery industries.

In this section, labor productivity and real wages are decomposed into a trend component and to cyclical deviations using the so-called "Hodrick–Prescott filter" developed by Hodrick and Prescott (1997). This idea was borrowed from a study by Voyvoda and Yeldan (1999) on Turkey. The, long-run movements of real wages and productivity can be calculated using this method.

Suppose that series x_t is composed of trend $\tau_t(\{\tau_t\}_{t=1}^{T})$ and cyclical $c_t(\{x_t - \tau_t\}_{t=1}^{T})$ components:

$$x_t = \tau_t + c_t, \tag{5.3}$$

where t denotes time ($t = 1, 2, T$). Hodrick and Prescott (1997) suggest that with the following minimization method, the cyclical component c_t can be isolated from x_t:

$$\min_{\{\tau_t\}_{t=1}^{T}} \left[\sum_{t=1}^{T} (x_t - \tau_t)^2 + \lambda \sum_{t=2}^{T-1} \left[(\tau_{t+1} - \tau_t) - (\tau_t - \tau_{t-1}) \right]^2 \right], \tag{5.4}$$

where λ is the smoothing parameter (also named penalty parameter). The first term in the minimization function (5.4), the sum of the squares of deviations, penalizes the variance of c_t. The second term, the summation of the second differences of the trend component τ_t multiplied by the smoothing parameter λ, places a penalty to the lack of smoothness in τ_t, i.e., a penalty on the variations in the growth rate of the trend component with the degree of penalization directly proportional to the value of the parameter λ chosen. Although Hodrick–Prescott filter is easy to use, selecting an appropriate value for λ is a major drawback. If λ approaches to 0, the trend component is almost equal to the original series, and if diverges to an infinitely large number, a linear trend is obtained. It is recommended to set the value of λ to 100 for annual data in Hodrick and Prescott (1997). Following this tradition, we have set the value of λ to 100.

The results of the calculations are portrayed in Figures 5.1–5.6. In Figures 5.1, 5.3, and 5.5, the long-run trends of average labor productivity and real wages at the sectoral level are presented. Agriculture and mining sectors are ignored in these tables due to their unimportance for the economy. Figures 5.2, 5.4, and 5.6 provide the same figures for major manufacturing industries. All values are smoothed with Hodrick–Prescott filter. For convenience, the values in the figures are presented on a logarithmic scale.

Aggregate labor productivity, defined as real output per unit working hour, declined during the first phase (import-substitution era) and remained almost stable until the late 1970s, when the government initiated a large-scale restructuring to stimulate higher value-added activities via large-scale increases in wages. From then on, average labor productivity has an ever-increasing trend. This needs to be compared with the trend of real wages in Figure 5.5. The trend in real wages is increasing although slightly until the late 1970s and from then on it has an increasing tendency similar to

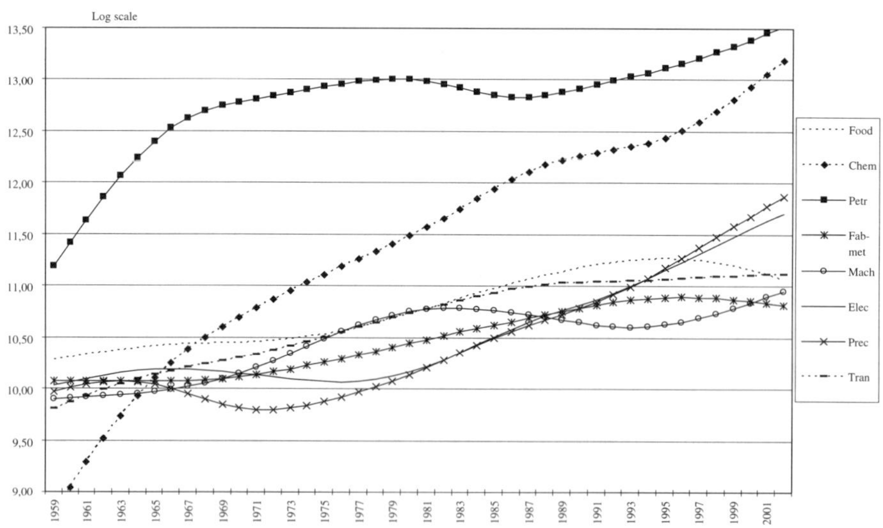

Fig. 5.2. Manufacturing labor productivity (labor:number of employees) (1959–2002).
Note: The data are smoothed with the Hodrick–Prescott filter.
Source: Author's calculations.

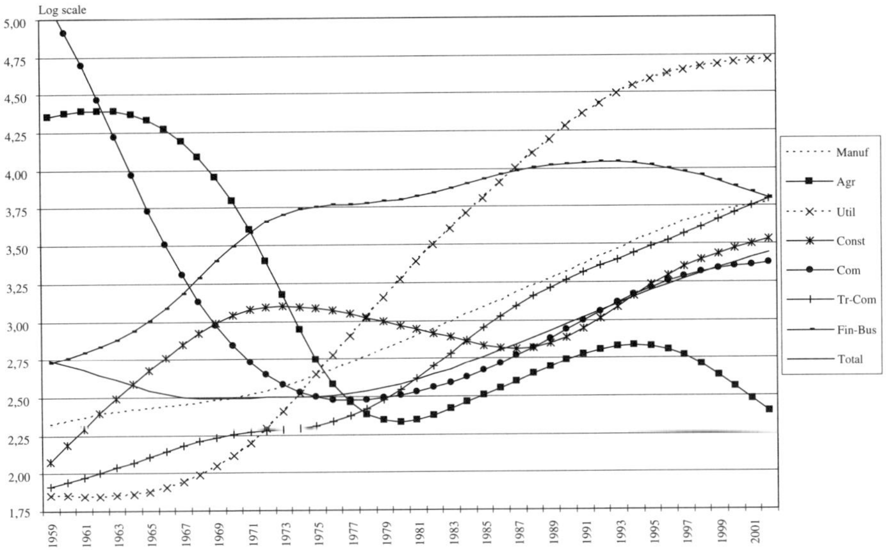

Fig. 5.3. Labor productivity (labor:working hours) (1959–2002).
Note: The data are smoothed with the Hodrick–Prescott filter.
Source: Author's calculations.

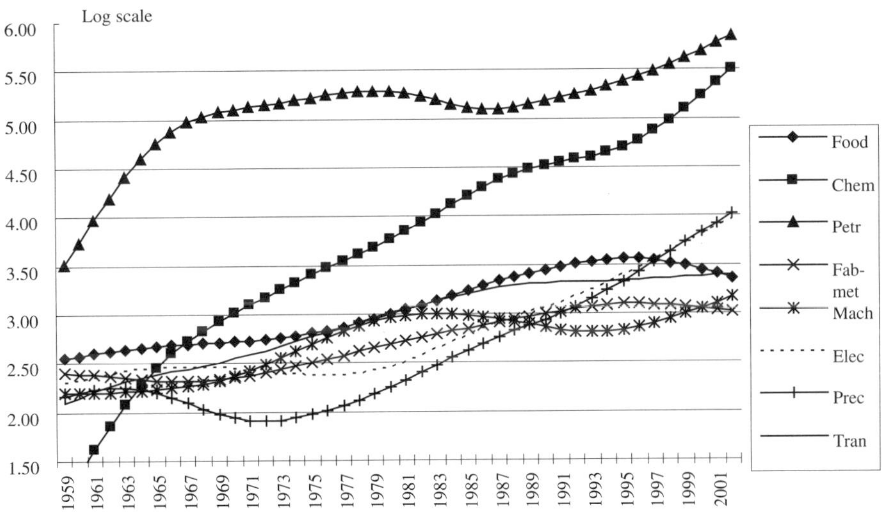

Fig. 5.4. Labor productivity (labor:working hours) growth rates of major manufacturing industries (1959–2002).
Note: The data are smoothed with the Hodrick–Prescott filter.
Source: Author's calculations.

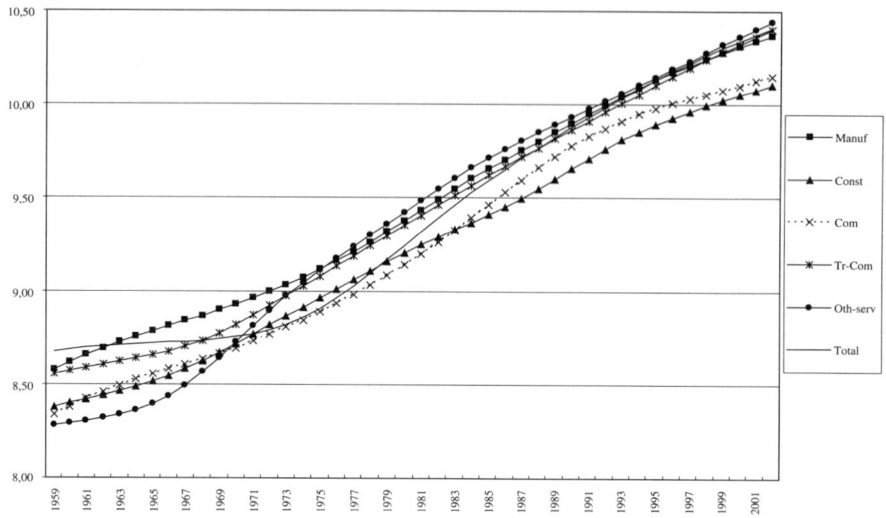

Fig. 5.5. Real labor remuneration levels (1959–2002).
Note: The data are smoothed with the Hodrick–Prescott filter.
Source: Author's calculations.

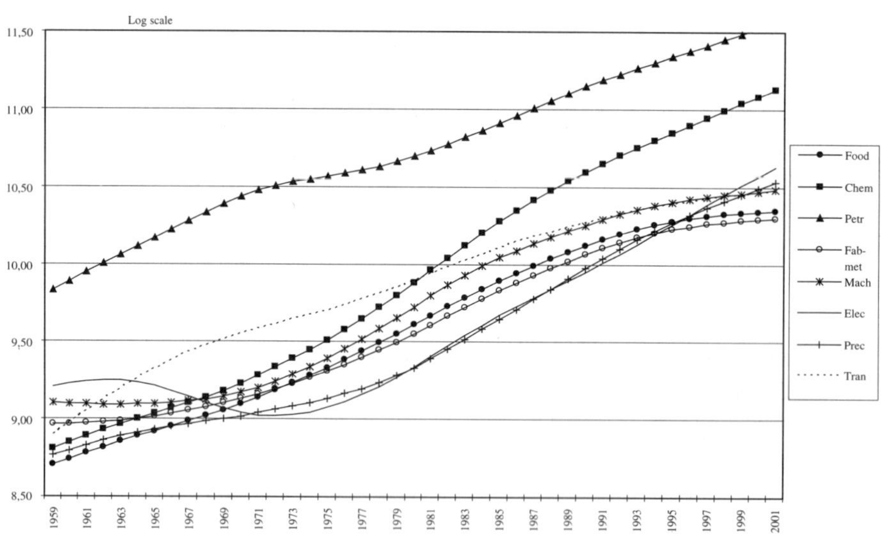

Fig. 5.6. Real labor remuneration levels of major manufacturing industries (1959–2002).
Note: The data are smoothed with the Hodrick–Prescott filter.
Source: Author's calculations.

aggregate productivity growth. Large increases from the late 1970s to the mid-1980s are a result of the high-wage policy. From the mid-1980s on, real wages follow a uniform increasing path with the rate of increase getting gradually lower. As seen in Figure 5.3, value-added per hour worked for the aggregate economy increased at a slowing rate after the mid-1980s. A similar movement can also be observed for the average real wage level in the economy (see Figure 5.5).

If the number of employees is used as the labor input measure, the highest productivity growth rate in the pre-1985 period was recorded by the utilities sector, followed by the services sectors (see Figure 5.1). Primary sectors (mining and agriculture) can be ignored due to their very small shares in employment. For the post-1985 period, the best performer is the manufacturing sector, chemicals, and electrical and electronic appliances industries in particular. Note that electrical and electronic appliances industry increased its share in total employment steadily throughout the entire period, until it remained more or less stable in the late 1990s. Taking total working hours as the relevant labor input measure, there is not much change, but the best performer in the post-1985 becomes the utilities sector and transport and communications services sector exhibits a higher productivity growth rate than the manufacturing sector. Higher productivity levels of the utilities and transport and communications services sectors can be explained by the fact that despite decreases in their both value-added and employment shares, the decline in their employment share was sharp whereas the decline in their value-added share was moderate, hence giving rise to increased productivity levels.

To see the differences between the productivity growth rates across industries better, one should consider international trade as a major economic activity in Singapore. As pointed out by MTI (2001), the degree of competition and openness for each sector is highly important in this respect. The sectors with inferior productivity growth rates (such as services and construction) are, by their nature, producers of less tradable goods and services and are inward-oriented. However, other sectors with high productivity growth performances such as the manufacturing and transport and communications sectors are more open to free trade and hence are subject to competition with foreign rivals, which is a stimulant for upgrading and restructuring.

The trends in real wages reflect the tight labor market conditions in Singapore. The increase in real wages accelerates from the early 1970s when Singapore achieved full employment. It is important to note that real wages increase was slow after the mid-1980s. There seems to be a strong relation between real wages and labor productivity, especially in the manufacturing sector. The initial suppression of wages during the early years of industrialization (until the restructuring efforts of the late-1970s) as represented by relatively little real wage increases in Figures 5.5 and 5.6 was followed by the government's adjustment policies in the labor market to stimulate higher value-added activities and facilitated further increases in real wages. The change in real wage trends to an increasing one from the late 1970s was not accompanied by a rising trend in labor productivity. The trends in productivity rather favored real wage stability or small increases in real wage growth over productivity growth. These findings suggest a weak relation between gains in labor productivity and real wage earnings. Thus, the strong influence of the government in wage determination until the mid-1980s and governmental efforts in improving labor productivity went head-to-head and reinforced each other. Following the restructuring efforts, productivity gains allowed producers to offset production costs brought about by increases in real wages to a large extent.

5.2. The Impact of the Intersectoral Reallocation of Labor on Labor Productivity: Methodology

Structural transformation in Singapore came with changes in labor composition and shifts of labor across sectors. Changes in the composition of production factors may result from different sources. In the case of Singapore, a small open economy heavily dependent on trade, it is possible to argue that one source of these changes is changing demand for its products in world markets. In fact, the purpose of restructuring efforts in Singapore is to respond positively to changing comparative advantages. Certain sectors and industries lead productivity in the island economy. These sectors and industries are those characterized by high learning capabilities. This section investigates the effect of the changes in labor allocation across the sectors of the economy on the ability of output generation by way of productivity growth.

In many countries structural changes coexisted with gains in manufacturing productivity. Some researchers in the past associated structural changes with aggregate productivity growth (e.g., Kaldor, 1963, 1966; Chenery *et al.*, 1986; Syrquin, 1995). Kaldor (1963, 1966) argued that there is often surplus labor in some industries in the manufacturing sector and labor supply in the manufacturing sector is elastic. He asserted that a major source of labor supply in manufacturing is the flow of labor from low- to high-productivity industries and associates aggregate labor productivity growth in manufacturing sector with labor shifts. He also argues that labor shifts across industries increase average manufacturing productivity due to two reasons. First, labor absorbing industry is growing with increasing returns. Second, in the industry that is losing labor, productivity level rises with the withdrawal of labor. Kaldor emphasized increasing returns and externalities in manufacturing. Harberger (1998) further differentiated between what he calls a "mushroom-process" (i.e., innovative activities in a particular industry improve productivity and cause resource shifts from relatively low-productivity activities to itself), and a "yeast-process" (i.e., gains in productivity spreads across industries).[4] Long-run growth is a mix of these two processes.

Now, there is a large literature on the impact of changes in labor composition on productivity for developing as well as developed countries (e.g., Salter, 1960; Syrquin, 1984, 1986; Timmer and Szirmai, 2000). These studies focus on the shifts of labor and capital from primary sectors (e.g., agriculture) to manufacturing and services sectors. They point to the positive contribution of resource reallocation from low-productivity sectors (most likely agriculture and traditional manufacturing industries such as food, wood, and textile manufactures) to sectors and industries that exhibit higher productivity (such as electronics, basic metals, and transport equipment).

In this section, we measure the impact of intersectoral labor shifts to productivity growth using the static shift-share method described in Timmer and Szirmai (2000). This method decomposes productivity growth into productivity growth arising from within sectors and from intersectoral labor shifts and has been used in various studies to analyze the impact of labor

[4] Harberger (1998) describes mushroom and yeast effects as follows: "... yeast causes bread to expand very evenly, like a balloon being filled with air, while mushrooms have the habit of popping up, almost overnight, in a fashion that is not easy to predict."

shifts on labor productivity (e.g., Fagerberg, 2000; Timmer and Szirmai, 2000; Jalava *et al.*, 2002; van Ark and Timmer, 2003).

We start with the following equation:

$$LP_t = \frac{Q_t}{L_t} = \sum_i \frac{Q_{i,t}}{L_{i,t}} \cdot \frac{L_{i,t}}{L_t}, \tag{5.5}$$

where *LP* stands for aggregate labor productivity, *L* for total employment, *Q* for total output in the relevant sector or industry, and the subscript *t* for time. Labor input here is total number of workers. Terms without subscripts refer to the values for the aggregate economy. The term $L_{i,t}/L_t$ in Eq. (5.5) refers to labor share of the sector or industry *i* in total labor and the term $Q_{i,t}/L_{i,t}$ refers to labor productivity for the same industry. Renaming the former as sl_i and the latter as LP_i, Eq. (5.5) can be rewritten as follows:

$$LP = \sum_i LP_i \cdot sl_i. \tag{5.6}$$

Equation (5.6) implies that aggregate labor productivity level is a weighted sum of individual industries or sectors. The weights are the respective shares of industries or sectors in total labor. Changes in labor productivity are defined for any time period [0, 1], where 0 and 1 stand for the beginning and the end years of the period, respectively. Here the analysis is confined into two distinct time periods: pre-1985 (1965–1985) and post-1985 (1985–2003) periods. The analysis starts from 1965 because during the import-substitution period (1959–1965) the limitations on labor and size of the market that affect structural changes are different from the post-1965 years.[5]

The change in labor productivity level can be written simply by subtracting the level of labor productivity at the end of the period (1) from that of the beginning of the period (0):

$$LP_1 - LP_0 = \sum_i LP_{i,1} \cdot sl_{i,1} - \sum_i LP_{i,0} \cdot sl_{i,0}. \tag{5.7}$$

[5]Due to its irrelevance to the present analysis, pre-1965 period is ignored. During 1959–1965, Singapore implemented the import-substitution policy of federal Malaya and economic policies were biased towards exploiting the Malayan market. In 1965, Singapore abandoned import substitution.

Rearranging with some algebraic manipulations and dividing each side by LP_0 to rearrange (5.7) in growth terms, the above decomposition finally takes the following form:[6]

$$\frac{LP_1 - LP_0}{LP_0} = \frac{1}{LP_0}\sum_i (LP_{i,1} - LP_{i,0}) \cdot sl_{i,o} + \frac{1}{LP_0}\sum_i (sl_{i,1} - sl_{i,0}) \times LP_{i,o} + \frac{1}{LP_0}\sum_i (sl_{i,1} - sl_{i,0}) \cdot (LP_{i,1} - LP_{i,0}). \quad (5.8)$$

---

[6]The derivation of (5.8) from (5.7) requires an algebraic manipulation. Since (5.7) holds, $LP_1 - PL_0 = \sum_i LP_{i,1} \cdot sl_{i,1} - \sum_i LP_{i,0} \cdot sl_{i,0}$, then, we get:

$$\begin{aligned} LP_1 - PL_0 &= \sum_i LP_{i,1} \cdot sl_{i,1} - \sum_i LP_{i,0} \cdot sl_{i,0} \\ &= \sum_i LP_{i,1} \cdot sl_{i,1} - \sum_i LP_{i,0} \cdot sl_{i,0} + \sum_i LP_{i,1} \cdot sl_{i,0} \\ &\quad - \sum_i LP_{i,1} \cdot sl_{i,0} + \sum_i LP_{i,0} \cdot sl_{i,1} \\ &\quad - \sum_i LP_{i,0} \cdot sl_{i,1} + \sum_i LP_{i,1} \cdot sl_{i,1} \\ &\quad - \sum_i LP_{i,1} \cdot sl_{i,1} + \sum_i LP_{i,0} \cdot sl_{i,0} - \sum_i LP_{i,0} \cdot sl_{i,0}. \end{aligned}$$

Rearranging the terms, Eq. (5.8) can be obtained as follows:

$$\begin{aligned} LP_1 - PL_0 &= \left(\sum_i LP_{i,1} \cdot sl_{i,0} - \sum_i LP_{i,0} \cdot sl_{i,0}\right) \\ &\quad + \left(\sum_i LP_{i,0} \cdot sl_{i,1} - \sum_i LP_{i,0} \cdot sl_{i,0}\right) \\ &\quad + \left(\sum_i LP_{i,1} \cdot sl_{i,1} - \sum_i LP_{i,1} \cdot sl_{i,0}\right) \\ &\quad + \left(\sum_i LP_{i,0} \cdot sl_{i,0} - \sum_i LP_{i,0} \cdot sl_{i,1}\right) \\ &= \sum_i \left(LP_{i,1} - LP_{i,0}\right) \cdot sl_{i,0} \\ &\quad + \sum_i \left(sl_{i,1} - sl_{i,0}\right) \cdot LP_{i,0} + \sum_i \left(LP_{i,1} - LP_{i,0}\right) \cdot \left(sl_{i,1} - sl_{i,0}\right). \end{aligned}$$

The first term on the right-hand side of Eq. (5.8), which is labor share of the beginning year of the period multiplied by labor productivity change during the period, describes internal productivity growth within individual industries and measures *intra-industry productivity growth*. Sectoral labor shares are used as weights. Therefore, intra-industry effect measures the change in aggregate labor productivity growth that would have resulted if labor shares remained constant over time.

The second term (change in labor share multiplied by the labor productivity of the beginning year of the period) measures labor shift based on the labor productivity level of the beginning of the period. In other words, this effect measures the changes in aggregate labor productivity resulting from the movements of labor across industries with differing productivity levels had the labor productivity levels of individual industries remained constant over time. When the employment shares of industries with high productivity levels rise, this means a reallocation of labor towards industries whose productivity is growing rapidly. Following Timmer and Szirmai (2000), we name this component the *static shift effect*.

The third term, that measures the cross-effect of the changes in labor productivity and labor shares, is the most difficult one to interpret. When the industries whose productivity levels grow rapidly also increase their share of employment, labor is reallocated to industries with rapid growth in productivity. Since it takes into account both labor productivity and labor share changes in the selected period, this term will be named the *dynamic shift effect*, again following Timmer and Szirmai (2000).[7]

The two shift effects measure the impact of structural change on aggregate labor productivity. One can measure the impact of sectoral shifts of labor on the aggregate productivity level in alternative but similar ways as well (Syrquin, 1986). The method adopted here is capable enough to summarize the impacts of labor reallocation on aggregate productivity. Considerably large positive sum of the two shift effects implies a favorable impact on aggregate labor productivity. Note that increases in labor quality reflect not only the improvement in the quality of labor due to in-house training by companies or restructuring within the firms, but also the changes in available

[7] In their analysis of productivity slowdown in the United States, Beebe and Haltmaier (1980) named the intra-industry and shift effects as "rate" and "level" effects, respectively.

capital per labor. Higher capital-labor ratio leads to higher labor productivity level. In turn, the shift effects can be expected to reflect the restructuring efforts of the government starting from 1979 aiming at the reallocation of resources in order to increase capital intensity of local industries. It is important to note that the shift effects are related to average productivity, not marginal product of labor. It is assumed here, for simplicity, that all workers in the same sector have the same productivity, i.e., average productivity remains unchanged by inter-sectoral employment shifts. In addition, labor is assumed to be homogenous.[8] Of interest here is the average productivity growth.

5.3. Empirical Findings

The results of the decomposition exercise are presented in Table 5.6. First, the analysis is conducted for the major sectors and then limited to manufacturing industries to investigate the impact of labor shifts across manufacturing industries on aggregate manufacturing labor productivity. The results indicate that much of the productivity gains resulted from productivity growth within sectors. The contributions of the shift effects to manufacturing productivity before 1985 are large, around 50–60 percent, pointing to substantial gains from labor shifts across manufacturing industries. Here, the results are comparable to a similar study by MTI (2001), which used the same method adopted in this study to measure the effects of sectoral labor shifts on aggregate labor productivity for the period 1985–2000, which largely overlaps with the post-1985 era.

Table 5.7 presents the contributions of major sectors to the sources of productivity growth. Table 5.7 shows that before 1985 much of the intra-industry productivity growth came from the construction and transport and communications sectors. The contributions by manufacturing industries are

[8]Timmer and Szirmai (2000) report some shortcomings of the shift-share method. For example, shift of low-productivity and low-skilled agricultural labor into industry leads to an increase in average productivity in agriculture. In the shift-share analysis, this increase in agricultural labor productivity is included in the intra-industry productivity growth effect, but in fact, it is caused by labor shift, thereby leading to underestimation of shift effects. Productivity levels may depend also on labor quality. If labor shifts to industries with higher productivity due to higher labor skills, shift effects include improved labor quality and result in overestimation of shift effects.

Table 5.6. Decomposition of Aggregate Labor Productivity (1965–2002).

		1965–1978	1979–1985	1986–2002
	Aggregate productivity growth rate (%)	0.0	3.0	3.8
Aggregate economy	Intra-industry productivity (%)	78.7	93.8	135.5
	Static shift effects (%)	83.0	8.5	−22.5
	Dynamic shift effects (%)	−61.7	−2.3	−13.0
	Aggregate productivity growth rate (%)	2.9	4.2	5.2
Manufacturing	Intra-industry productivity (%)	40.2	50.8	115.7
	Static shift effects (%)	62.3	48.9	−10.8
	Dynamic shift effects (%)	−2.5	0.3	−4.9

Source: Author's calculations.

presented in Table 5.8. Within the manufacturing sector, petroleum refining industry is a large contributor. In the post-1985 period, the best performer is the manufacturing sector (in particular, electrical and electronic appliances, chemicals, and petroleum refining industries), followed by the construction, transport and communication, and commerce sectors. Financial and business services sector, however, exhibits a big decline in its contribution with a negative figure.

Shift effects, overall, are negative for the post-1985 period and positive for the preceding period. There is a need to interpret the meaning of the positive and negative shift effects for both periods. Before 1985, the sum of the shift effects are 21.3 (1965–1978) and 6.2 percent (1979–1985) respectively for the aggregate economy and over 50 percent for manufacturing. Dynamic shift effects for major sectors are large only in the period 1965–1978 (Table 5.6). In other periods, they are relatively smaller. For the 1965–1978 period, the largest contributors to the shift effects are the commerce and financial

Table 5.7. Percentage Contributions of Sectors to Aggregate Labor Productivity (1965–2003).

	1965–1978			1979–1985			1986–2002		
	Intra-ind	Stat. sh.	Dyn. sh.	Intra-ind	Stat. sh.	Dyn. sh.	Intra-ind	Stat. sh.	Dyn. sh.
AGR	2.6	7.4	−5.0	2.1	−1.4	−1.1	−0.1	0.8	−0.7
MIN	0.3	1.0	−1.7	−0.6	1.8	0.1	−0.4	−0.5	−0.6
MANUF	1.6	21.6	−5.2	20.5	−20.3	0.4	42.0	−43.3	−2.0
UTIL	19.4	−3.3	−2.2	3.7	−0.4	−0.9	5.0	−2.0	−3.0
CONST	27.3	−31.7	−16.0	10.0	10.7	−2.9	35.4	14.3	−2.7
COM	8.1	42.1	−7.8	0.0	2.0	−0.3	26.3	−11.7	−1.1
TR-COM	15.7	−11.3	−3.1	22.5	1.2	−1.1	28.9	−6.3	−1.4
FIN-BUS	−35.0	80.2	−11.7	26.8	14.7	3.5	−15.7	14.2	−1.4
OTH-SERV	38.7	−23.0	−9.0	8.8	0.1	−0.1	14.1	11.8	−0.2
Total	78.7	83.0	−61.7	93.8	8.5	−2.3	135.5	−22.5	−13.0

Note: Intra-ind: Intra-industry productivity; Stat. sh.: static shift effect; Dyn. Sh.: dynamic shift effect.
Source: Author's calculations.

Table 5.8. Percentage Contributions of Manufacturing Industries to Aggregate Manufacturing Labor Productivity.

	1965–1978			1979–1985			1986–2002		
	Intra-ind	Stat. sh.	Dyn. sh.	Intra-ind	Stat. sh.	Dyn. sh.	Intra-ind	Stat. sh.	Dyn. sh.
Food	−4.4	−36.8	0.3	3.4	−0.3	0.0	−0.9	−0.7	−0.2
Tex	1.5	−12.5	−0.6	−1.9	0.2	0.0	0.2	−0.2	−0.2
Wear	3.4	−10.1	0.0	−2.4	−1.6	0.0	0.5	−1.1	0.5
Leat	−0.3	3.3	0.1	0.0	0.0	0.0	0.1	0.0	0.0
Wood	0.9	−52.5	−1.4	−3.7	2.0	0.0	0.2	−0.3	0.0
Furn	−1.6	−1.5	0.0	0.7	0.4	0.0	−0.8	−0.3	0.0
Paper	1.1	0.1	−0.1	−5.0	1.8	0.0	−0.5	−0.1	0.0
Pub	−1.6	−2.7	0.1	−4.7	−2.1	0.0	2.5	−0.1	−0.5
Chem	9.5	15.1	0.1	−13.0	−1.7	0.0	37.9	2.8	0.6
Petr	19.8	118.7	1.8	49.6	2.8	0.0	16.1	−1.5	−0.7
Rub	4.4	−14.8	−0.3	−2.1	4.4	0.0	0.8	0.3	0.2
Non-met	0.5	−4.8	−1.1	2.2	−5.3	0.1	1.4	0.2	−1.2
Met	−2.2	−41.2	−0.5	0.8	0.3	−0.1	−0.5	−0.3	1.0
Fab-met	−1.3	−6.9	−0.1	−2.2	3.7	−0.1	1.2	0.1	2.2
Mach	2.0	144.6	−0.3	29.6	−8.8	0.0	2.3	−0.5	−0.5
Elec	2.8	−257.8	−0.4	−14.4	27.2	0.0	50.4	−10.2	−0.1
Prec	0.1	−31.8	0.0	0.3	6.8	0.0	4.3	−0.1	−0.2
Tran	7.9	252.3	−0.3	14.7	7.9	0.3	−0.8	1.2	−4.7
Oth-man	−2.4	1.7	0.1	−0.8	11.2	0.1	1.2	0.0	−1.0
Total	40.2	62.3	−2.5	50.8	48.9	0.3	115.7	−10.8	−4.9

Note: Intra-ind; Intra-industry productivity growth, Shift eff: shift effect.
Source: Author's calculations.

and business services sectors. For the period 1979–1985, the largest contributors are construction and financial and business services sectors whereas the contribution of the manufacturing sector runs negative. Before 1985, productivity growth rates of all industries except agriculture, commerce, and financial and business services sectors were larger than the economy average (Table 5.7). Productivity growth rate in the financial and business services sector is negligibly small. The share of this sector in employment also decreased over the period. This gave rise to a largely negative contribution to shift effects by this industry. Overall, the general impact of the shifts of labor across sectors on aggregate labor productivity was positive before 1985.

Among the manufacturing industries, electrical and electronic appliances, petroleum, transport equipment, and basic machinery industries account for a large portion of the shift effects for the pre-1985 era (see Table 5.8). The shifts of labor across manufacturing industries and towards fast-growing industries such as electrical machinery and petroleum refining industries ensured gains from productivity in the rapid growth period (1965–1978). Contributions by traditional industries to the shift effects generally worked in the negative direction. During the restructuring period (1979–1985), shifts of labor towards higher value-added activities (e.g., electronics) impacted positively to aggregate manufacturing labor productivity. Hence, inter-industry labor shifts in the manufacturing sector during the restructuring process facilitated extra productivity gains, i.e., an extra source of labor productivity growth emerged in manufacturing when the government maintained its heavy role in labor allocation and persistent strong control of the labor market.

In the post-1985 era, total shift effects are −35.5 percent for the aggregate economy and −15.7 percent for manufacturing. Dynamic shift effects are negligible and shift effects arise almost entirely from static shift effects (Tables 5.7 and 5.8). This information has an important implication about the shifts of labor. Negative static shift effects arise when those sectors with productivity growth rates higher than the economy average face declining employment shares. In other words, negative static shift effects point to allocation of labor towards industries with lower productivity levels. The employment share of the manufacturing sector, which exhibits the highest productivity growth rate in this period, has declined

Table 5.9. Average Percentage Shares of Sectors and Industries in Total Employment.

	1966–1978	1979–1985	1986–2002
AGR	1.2	1.1	0.4
MIN	0.3	0.2	0.0
UTIL	2.4	0.8	0.5
CONST	5.3	7.2	7.4
COM	21.2	23.8	22.9
TR-COM	10.3	11.7	10.8
FIN-BUS	7.8	8.3	14.2
OTH-SERV	25.7	22.2	22.9
MANUF	25.8	24.7	20.8
Food	9.3	5.0	4.2
Tex	4.9	2.3	0.7
Wear	10.5	10.4	5.5
Leat	0.6	0.4	0.2
Wood	6.7	2.7	0.6
Furn	1.4	2.4	1.8
Paper	1.9	1.5	1.4
Pub	5.3	4.7	4.9
Chem	2.8	2.5	3.6
Petr	1.4	1.3	1.0
Rub	6.4	4.2	5.2
Non-met	3.3	2.2	1.8
Met	1.4	0.8	0.6
Fab-met	6.3	7.2	9.2
Mach	5.1	7.7	8.9
Elec	15.4	30.4	36.8
Prec	2.0	2.4	2.5
Tran	11.1	9.7	9.1
Oth-man	4.3	2.2	1.7

Note: The figures for manufacturing industries refer to their share in the manufacturing sector only.
Source: Author's calculations.

from 24.7 percent in the period 1979–1985 to 20.8 percent in the post-1985 period (Table 5.9). On the other hand, financial and business services sector, whose productivity growth rate was lower than the economy average, has increased its employment share from 1979–1985 to 1986–1997. Among the manufacturing industries, chemicals industry accounts for the largest portion of the positive shift effects after 1985, whereas that of the electrical and electronic appliances and petroleum refining industries account for the large part of the negative shift effects.

These findings beg for interpretation. Negative shift effects after 1985 suggest that throughout the restructuring process some labor was shifted from the relatively more productive manufacturing sector to less productive domestic-oriented sectors and hence were not exposed to international competition. A possible explanation can be found in the exposure of these sectors to international competition. As pointed out in MTI (2001), manufacturing sector is exposed to competition through free trade more than other sectors and this stimulates continuous restructuring, which requires improvements in the quality of labor to enhance international competitiveness. Government efforts such as Productivity Action 21 and SME 21 plans address the low-productivity performance problem of the services sectors and the need to improve their productivity performances (MTI, 2001).

An alternative explanation by MTI (2001) goes as follows: The theoretical explanation that shifts of labor towards sectors with higher productivity levels brings about an extra source of aggregate productivity growth, suggests that more jobs will be created in such sectors and wages will increase. However, this is not happening in Singapore most probably because either shifted labor do not possess the relevant skills required in more productive sectors, or is reluctant to change jobs. This problem points to the need for skills upgrading to induce higher value-added generation, an issue always emphasized in official reports. One of the main targets of the government's labor market policies after 1985 was skills upgrading of the labor in services sectors, which absorb the labor released from the manufacturing sector in the 1990s.

5.4. Labor Productivity and Labor Market Policies: A Policy Discussion

The results of the analysis should be compared with the changing labor market policies of the government.[9] The two periods prior to 1985 (1965–1978 and 1979–1985) where the labor shift effects on aggregate

[9]See Section 3.2.1 for a discussion of the government's labor market policies.

manufacturing productivity are positively large and that of the general economy is positive though small, are characterized by a highly interventionist and strict labor market policy of the government. In the first period (1965–1978), the government mobilized workforce towards labor-intensive industries as part of its export-oriented development strategy. For this purpose, the government adopted a wage restraint policy with strict controls on wage increases in order to maintain cost competitiveness. In the second period (1979–1985), the government's aim of industrial restructuring with the abandonment of the promotion of the labor-intensive manufacturing industries, was associated with the encouragement of the firms to shift their production activities towards higher value-added activities and improve the quality of labor for this purpose. The consequences of these policies that aimed at an allocation of labor towards first labor-intensive export industries and then a restructuring of industries are two-fold. First, there was a substantial shift of labor towards the fast-growing manufacturing sector. Second, the shift of labor across manufacturing industries was towards certain high-performing industries such as the electrical and electronic machinery industry and away from the traditional labor-intensive industries such as textiles. This reallocation of labor brought about a "structural bonus" (Timmer and Szirmai, 2000) for labor productivity, i.e., shifted labor was used in more productive areas, which had a positive impact on manufacturing labor productivity.

After 1985, the impact of the shifts of labor on aggregate labor productivity at both the aggregate economy and manufacturing levels is negative. This means that the shifts of labor worked against aggregate labor productivity. This period is characterized by more liberal labor markets with wage reforms such as the introduction of flexible wage policy and the abandonment of government controls on wage increases. In this period, the government aimed at industrial diversification with an emphasis on financial and business services sector as a new engine of growth together with manufacturing. Due to these adjustments, there was a shift of labor away from the manufacturing sector to services sectors, especially the financial and business services sector. This shift acted as a negative factor for aggregate labor productivity. Similarly, the shifts of labor across manufacturing industries did not provide a "bonus" for aggregate manufacturing labor productivity.

Development economics literature emphasizes the positive role of shifts of labor from less productive areas to more productive areas as a positive factor for productivity growth. This study shows that, prior to 1985, the government could effectively realize such a gain by mobilizing labor. However, a more liberalized labor market and a new target of economic diversification after 1985 led to the shift of labor towards less productive areas and negative gains from productivity.

In conclusion, the most important issue appears to be the reversal of the impacts of the shifts of labor in the post-1985 period. In the liberalized labor market of the post-1985 era, it is possible to expect the labor to move to areas where wage levels are higher. Financial and business services sector, e.g., offers higher wages than manufacturing. Sectoral wage differences largely explain the shifts of labor in a liberalized market. Why such shifts have a negative impact on aggregate labor productivity is a problem to be treated carefully. One possibility is that the labor market is moving towards a point where it will work more efficiently with relief from strong government intervention. That is, the labor market may be moving towards equilibrium. Such a move may bring in negative shift effects since workers will be shifting across sectors in search for better pay for their services. Finally, the general tendency for labor to shift to the third sector when the economy reaches maturity applies also to Singapore.

CHAPTER 6

TOTAL FACTOR PRODUCTIVITY AND RESOURCE REALLOCATION

This chapter broadens the analysis in the previous chapter one step further by taking into account both capital and labor. Chapter 5 used labor productivity as the performance criterion of the economy. In this chapter, TFP is used and first, the method is only applied to Singapore. The results for the other East Asian countries are presented later in Chapter 7. High dependence on imported resources in Singapore especially makes the allocation of resources strategically important. In order to evaluate the impact of the industry-targeting and factor-market distortions induced by industrial policies implemented by the government, there is a need to investigate the impact of resource allocation on TFP growth.

For this purpose, first TFP growth will be estimated and then the impact of resource allocation on TFP growth will be investigated. Here, the emphasis is placed on manufacturing sector for two reasons. First, it was not possible to estimate capital stock figures for the major industries of the Singapore economy due to unavailability of reliable data. Hence, TFP growth could be estimated only for the aggregate economy and individual manufacturing industries. Second, the government's industry targeting favored, in its large part, certain manufacturing industries rather than services sectors, notwithstanding the importance of the financial services sector for the economy and government's economic development policies.

6.1. Measurement of Total Factor Productivity Growth

Theoretically, TFP is assumed to reflect the efficiency of the use of resources used in production. To compute TFP growth, the index number approach as described in Jorgenson *et al.* (1987) and Kuroda (1984) is used in this book. The production function is represented by the so-called transcendental logarithmic production function, or shortly "translog production function," introduced originally by Christensen *et al.* (1973).

The production (value-added) function[1] for any industry i can be written as follows:

$$Q_i = f(K_i, L_i, t) = A_i K_i^b L_i^c, \tag{6.1}$$

where Q_i, K_i, and L_i stand for gross value-added, capital stock and labor, respectively, for any sector i, and t denotes time. The right-hand side terms in Eq. (6.1) are functions of time, t. The coefficients b and c measure the degree of returns to relevant inputs. Under constant returns to scale, b and c sum to unity.

Taking natural logarithm of both sides of Eq. (6.1) and differentiating with respect to time, growth rates can be written as:

$$\frac{d\ln Q_i}{dt} = \frac{dA_i}{dt} + \frac{\partial \ln Q_i}{\partial \ln K_i} \cdot \frac{d\ln K_i}{dt} + \frac{\partial \ln Q_i}{\partial \ln L_t} \cdot \frac{d\ln L_i}{dt}. \tag{6.2}$$

The first term on the right-hand side above (time derivative of A) represents growth rate of TFP. In producer equilibrium under an assumed perfectly competitive market, the elasticity of output with respect to capital and labor equals the value shares of capital and labor in total value-added. Renaming the elasticity terms $\frac{\partial \ln Q_i}{\partial K_i}$ as α_{Ki} and $\frac{\partial \ln Q_i}{\partial L_i}$ as α_{Li}, Eq. (6.2) can be rearranged in growth terms as follows:

$$\frac{\Delta Q_i}{Q_i} = \frac{\Delta A_i}{A_i} + \alpha_{Ki}\frac{\Delta K_i}{K_i} + \alpha_{Li}\frac{\Delta L_i}{L_i}, \tag{6.3}$$

$$\frac{\Delta A}{A} = \frac{\Delta Q}{Q} - \alpha_K\frac{\Delta K}{K} - \alpha_L\frac{\Delta L}{L}, \tag{6.4}$$

---

[1] Translog production function is specified as follows:

$$\ln Q_i = \alpha_{0i} + \alpha_{Ki}\ln K_i + \alpha_{Li}\ln L_i + \frac{1}{2}\beta_{KKi}(\ln K_i)^2 + \beta_{KLi}\ln K_i \cdot \ln L_i$$

$$+ \beta_{KTi}\ln K_i \cdot t + \frac{1}{2}\beta_{LLi}(\ln L_i)^2 + \beta_{LTi}\ln L_i \cdot t + \frac{1}{2}\beta_{TTi}(t)^2.$$

This is a second-order Taylor expansion approximation for the function specified in Eq. (6.1) with all variables in logarithmic form and is conventionally used as the general notation of the translog production function. The parameters denoted by α and β can be estimated using econometric techniques. Mathematically they are derived by taking derivative of the output function with respect to the variables. In this section, rather than estimating the parameters econometrically, we resort to the easier approach and compute the translog index of TFP growth using the constructed translog indices of capital and labor.

$$\frac{\Delta A_i}{A_i} = \frac{\Delta Q_i}{Q_i} - \alpha_{Ki}\frac{\Delta K_i}{K_i} - \alpha_{Li}\frac{\Delta L_i}{L_i}. \tag{6.5}$$

Equation (6.4) formulates TFP growth rate for the aggregate economy and Eq. (6.5) formulates it for individual industries (i). As seen from these equations, TFP growth is calculated as a residual after deducting the weighted growth rates of capital and labor from output growth. It is important to note that the quantities K and Q are in real terms. To estimate TFP growth rate, translog indices of labor and capital are necessary.

6.1.1. *Translog index of labor*

Labor refers to total working hours. As explained in Chapter 5, labor input is composed of six different categories of labor based on gender (i.e., male and female) and education level (i.e., below high-school, high-school, and post-secondary). Following Jorgenson *et al.* (1987, pp. 263–264), in order to quantify the changes in total labor hours, it is assumed that the flow of labor services (L) is proportional to hours worked (H). Thus, for time T,

$$L(T) = c_L \cdot H(T), \tag{6.6}$$

where the constant c_L transforms labor hours into flow of labor services.

It follows from Eq. (6.6) that, for a time period $[T-1, T]$, the growth rate of the amount of labor services emanating from labor of type l is represented by the growth rate of the amount of labor hours for labor of type l:

$$\ln L_l(T) - \ln L_l(T-1) = \ln H_l(T) - \ln H_l(T-1), \tag{6.7}$$

where L_l refers to labor services emanating from labor of type l and H_l refers to working hours for labor of type l. Total annual labor hours are computed as the product of total workers and weekly working hours for an employee multiplied by the factor 52. Due to data unavailability, same weekly hours are assumed for all types of labor in an industry. Denoting total number of employees by N_l, total annual working hours by H_l, and weekly working hours by H_{wl}, total working hours is computed as $H_l = H_{wl}N_l$. Then, the growth rate of total working hours is the sum of the growth rates of the number of workers and of working hours, as follows:

$$\ln H_l(T) - \ln H_l(T-1) = [\ln N_l(T) - \ln N_l(T-1)] \\ + [\ln H_{wl}(T) - \ln H_{wl}(T-1)]. \qquad (6.8)$$

The growth rate of aggregate labor input is defined as a weighted sum of the growth rates of labor inputs of individual industries. Labor services emanating from type l labor (L_l) result from working-hours with a constant c_{Ll}:

$$L_l(T) = c_{Ll} \cdot H_l(T). \qquad (6.9)$$

This constant (c_{Ll}) is different for each type of labor but is constant over time. Since $\ln L = \sum_l \ln L_l$, in continuous time $\frac{d \ln L}{dt} = \sum_l sl_l \frac{d \ln L_l}{dt}$, where sl_l refers to value share of each type (l) of labor in total labor. In discrete time, however, the growth rate of aggregate labor (L) is expressed as the change in the translog index of labor input from period $T-1$ to T as follows:

$$\ln L(T) - \ln L(T-1) = \sum_l sl_l(\ln L_l(T) - \ln L_l(T-1)) \\ = \sum_l sl_l(\ln H_l(T) - \ln H_l(T-1)), \qquad (6.10)$$

where sl_i represents the "Divisia share" of individual industry i in total labor, the arithmetic average of the values of the previous and current periods: $sl_l = \frac{1}{2}(sl_l(T) + sl_l(T-1))$. Note that the terms with no subscripts refer to aggregates. In order to adjust the labor input, the changes in the composition of the workforce are included and a quality index is constructed for labor input. First, total working-hours are defined as an unweighted sum of their components of different types of labor:

$$H(T) = \sum_{l=1}^{m} H_l(T), \qquad (6.11)$$

where l denotes each component of labor. There are six types of labor. As explained in Chapter 5, available statistics in Singapore do not provide detailed working hour data classified by education and sex for individual industries. Therefore, same working hour data have to be used for all categories of labor in an industry.

Recall that working-hours are representative of total labor services (L) emanating from employed labor. Therefore:

$$\begin{aligned}\ln L(T) - \ln L(T-1) &= \sum sl_l[\ln L_l(T) - \ln L_l(T-1)] \\ &= \sum sl_l[\ln H_l(T) - \ln H_l(T-1)]. \qquad (6.12)\end{aligned}$$

Finally, there is a need to incorporate a quality index for labor input in order to capture the changes in the composition of the labor force. The quality of labor (LQ) is defined as:

$$L(T) = LQ(T) \cdot H(T). \qquad (6.13)$$

Then, the growth rate of the quality of labor input is expressed as follows:

$$\begin{aligned}&\ln LQ(T) - \ln LQ(T-1) \\ &\quad = [\ln L(T) - \ln L(T-1)] - [\ln H(T) - \ln H(T-1)] \\ &\quad = \left[\sum sl_l(\ln H_l(T) - \ln H_l(T-1))\right] - [\ln H(T) - \ln H(T-1)]. \qquad (6.14)\end{aligned}$$

Since working-hour data by education or gender characteristics of labor are not available, LQ is calculated for the number of employees, not working-hours:

$$\begin{aligned}\ln LQ(T) - \ln LQ(T-1) &= \left[\sum sl_l(\ln N_l(T) - \ln N_l(T-1))\right] \\ &\quad - [\ln N(T) - \ln N(T-1)]. \qquad (6.15)\end{aligned}$$

Note that the number of total workers equals the sum of the number of each type of labor, i.e., $N(T) = \sum_l N_l(T)$. It follows from Eq. (6.15) that labor quality index remains unchanged if all types of labor grow at the same rate and increases if the types of labor with higher labor services flow grow faster, and vice versa. Finally, the value-share of each type of (l) labor is computed as the ratio of payments to each type of labor (l) to total payments made to entire labor:

$$sl_l = \frac{P_{Ll} \cdot N_l}{\sum_l P_{Ll} \cdot N_l}, \qquad (6.16)$$

where P_{Ll} refers to labor compensation for labor of type l.

The share of labor input in total value-added to be used in the total factor productivity estimations are calculated as the following ratio:

$$sl = \frac{\textit{labor compensation} + \textit{indirect taxes} \text{ on labor}}{\textit{total} \text{ value-added}}. \tag{6.17}$$

Income shares of labor and capital for the manufacturing sector and for the aggregate economy are presented in Figure 6.1. The share of labor for the economy averages 0.53 for the pre-1985 period and 0.46 for the post-1985 period. The averages for the two periods for the manufacturing sector are 0.33 and 0.39, respectively. Among manufacturing industries, the highest labor share belongs to textiles, leather, wood, and furniture industries with labor shares above 0.5 (see Appendix for labor and capital shares in manufacturing industries).

6.1.2. *Translog index of capital*

Capital input (K) consists of four different types of capital assets: (i) building and structures, (ii) plant and equipment, (iii) office equipment,

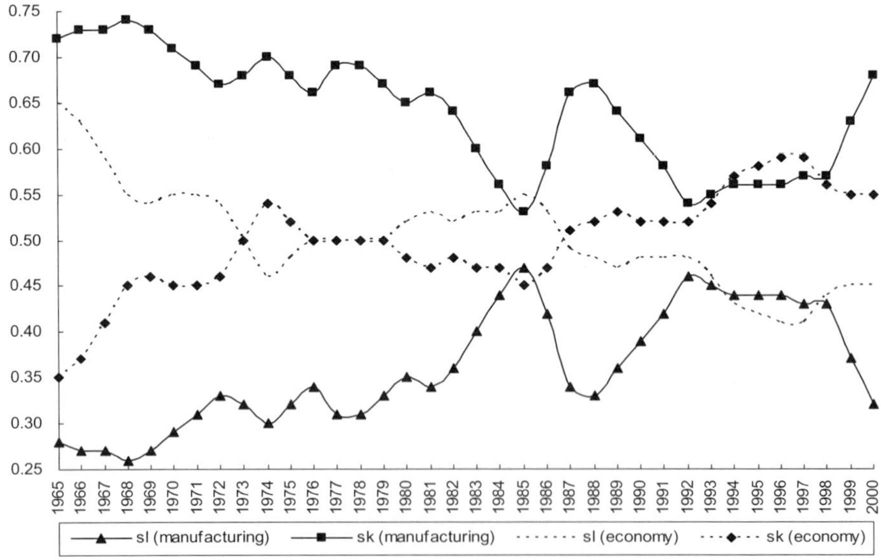

Fig. 6.1. Income shares of labor and capital (1965–2000).
Source: Author's calculations.

and (iv) transport equipment. The computation of the translog index of capital resembles that of labor. It is assumed here that the flow of capital services (K) is proportional to capital stock (KS) as proposed by Jorgenson *et al.* (1987, p. 267):

$$K(T) = c_K \cdot KS(T), \tag{6.18}$$

where the constant c_K transforms capital stock into flow of capital services. Then, similar to that of labor, the growth rate of the capital input can be written as the weighted sum of the changes either in its components (K_k) or in the stock of asset of type $k(KS_k(T))$:

$$\begin{aligned} \ln K(T) - \ln K(T-1) &= \sum sk_k(\ln K_k(T) - \ln K_k(T-1)) \\ &= \sum sk_k(\ln KS_k(T) - \ln KS_k(T-1)), \end{aligned} \tag{6.19}$$

where sk_k refers to the value shares of each type of capital asset in capital input. In order to compute indices of capital stock, sectoral capital stock is defined as the unweighted sum of its components (k):

$$KS = \sum_{k=1}^{n} KS_k. \tag{6.20}$$

There are n types of capital stock. Capital input data are available by industry and asset type. Then, as in the case of labor input, an index of quality for capital stock (KQ) can be calculated for capital as follows:

$$K = KQ \cdot KS. \tag{6.21}$$

Subsequently, the growth rate of the quality index of capital (KQ) can be written as the difference between the changes in the flow of capital services and capital stock as follows:

$$\begin{aligned} \ln KQ(T) - \ln KQ(T-1) = {} & [\ln K(T) - \ln K(T-1)] \\ & - [\ln KS(T) - \ln KS(T-1)]. \end{aligned} \tag{6.22}$$

KQ accounts for the change in the composition of sectoral capital stock. If all types of capital are growing at the same rate, then capital quality index does not change. Capital quality index rises if components of capital with higher flows grow more rapidly, and vice versa.

Finally, the share of capital input in total value-added is calculated as a residual by deducting the share of labor input from unity. This corresponds to the following ratio:

$$sk = \frac{compensation\ of\ capital + taxes \text{ on capital}}{total \text{ value-added}}. \tag{6.23}$$

It is assumed that total taxes on production are a sum of taxes on labor and capital. Taxes on capital can also be calculated if taxes on labor are already known.

6.1.3. *Translog index of productivity growth*

It is assumed that the production function is separable in n capital inputs and m labor inputs. Each of these functions is homogenous of degree one, like the aggregate production function. Then, the production function becomes homothetically separable. This means that it is possible to write the production function for output Q for a sector i as follows:

$$Q_i = f_i[I_i(K_i, L_i), t], \tag{6.24}$$

where I is a new function of aggregate inputs. f is homothetically separable if I is homogeneous of degree one. Here, Q is a function of aggregate input and technology. Under constant returns to scale, production function is homogenous of degree one in aggregate inputs. Productivity growth is, then, of Hicks-neutral form in this case. Subsequently, the following holds:

$$Q_i = A_i(t) \cdot I_i(K_i, L_i). \tag{6.25}$$

When productivity growth is Hicks-neutral, it is independent from capital and labor inputs and is dependent only on time t. Hence, productivity growth, s_t, is defined as follows:

$$s_{ti} = \frac{\partial \ln A_i(t)}{\partial t} = \frac{\Delta A_i}{A_i}. \tag{6.26}$$

Recall from (6.3) that output growth is equal to the sum of productivity growth and weighted growth rates of capital and labor inputs, where the weights are denoted as s_K and s_L, i.e., $\frac{\Delta Q_i}{Q_i} = \frac{\Delta A_i}{A_i} + \alpha_{Ki}\frac{\Delta K_i}{K_i} + \alpha_{Li}\frac{\Delta L_i}{L_i}$.[2]

---

[2]At the industry level, there are some restrictions for capital and labor. Aggregate output, aggregate capital, and aggregate labor inputs are calculated as industry summations, i.e., $Q = \sum_i Q_i, K = \sum_i K_i, L = \sum_i L_i$ and for changes in these inputs the following conditions hold: $\Delta Q = \sum_i \Delta Q_i, \Delta K = \sum_i KQ_i, \Delta L = \sum_i \Delta L_i$, where the operator Δ stands for change between two points in time. The restriction that real value-added of sub-industries add up to the aggregate real value-added in the manufacturing sector is difficult to verify. This is because the normalization of value-added is done using separate producer price indices. Generally, real value-added figures of sub-industries do not add up to real value-added of the manufacturing sector when they are calculated independently. To avoid inconsistency, real manufacturing value-added is calculated as the sum of the values of real value-added in sub-industries. This can be explained mathematically using the translog price functions (Kuroda *et al.*, 1996). For the production possibility frontier, a necessary condition for producer equilibrium is that the prices of output (p_Z) be expressed as a function of the sectoral prices of value-added, the prices of factor inputs, i.e., capital and labor, and time:

$$p_Z = R(p_{Q1}, p_{Q2}, \ldots, p_{QN}; p_{K1}, p_{K2}, \ldots, p_{Kn}; p_{L1}, p_{L2}, \ldots, p_{Lm}; T),$$

where it is assumed that there are N sectors, n types of capital, and m types of labor. p_Q, p_K, and p_L refer to prices of value-added, capital, and labor, respectively. Fixing the price of output to 1, one can obtain the price possibility frontier. Just like the value-added can be expressed as a function of capital and labor inputs and time, the price of value-added can be expressed as a function of the prices of capital, labor, and time:

$$p_Q = P(p_K, p_L, T),$$

this function, like its production counterpart, is homogenous of degree one for its components. Note that the prices of inputs are a function of their sub-components:

$$p_K = p_K(p_{K1}, p_{K2}, \ldots, p_{Kn}),$$
$$p_L = p_L(p_{L1}, p_{L2}, \ldots, p_{Lm}).$$

These translog price functions are also homogeneous of degree one. Under constant returns to scale, the values of capital and labor equal the sum of their subcomponents:

$$p_K \cdot K = \sum_k p_{Kk} \cdot K_k,$$
$$p_L \cdot L = \sum_l p_{Ll} \cdot L_l.$$

Like the value-added function, in order for an aggregate price function to exist, the sectoral prices of value-added must be identical up to a scalar value, c_P:

$$p_{Q,i} = p_{Q,i}(p_{K,i}, p_{L,i}, T)$$
$$= c_P \cdot P(p_K, p_L, T).$$

Prices of capital and labor are identical functions of the prices of the components of capital and labor respectively. If the prices of capital and labor are the same across sectors, then sectoral value-added prices $(p_{Q,i})$ are identical to the aggregate price of value-added (p_Q). Only in this case, aggregate value-added (i.e. $p_Q \cdot Q = \sum_i p_{Q,i} \cdot Q_i$) can be defined as the sum of sectoral amounts of value-added, $Q = \sum_i Q_i$.

The first term on the right-hand side refers to productivity growth, which is equivalent to s_t. In equilibrium, for any producer the following conditions hold:

$$sk_i = \frac{p_K \cdot K_i}{Q_i} = \frac{\partial \ln Q(K_i, L_i, t)}{\partial \ln K_i}, \quad (6.27)$$

$$sl_i = \frac{p_L \cdot L_i}{Q_i} = \frac{\partial \ln Q(K_i, L_i, t)}{\partial \ln L_i}. \quad (6.28)$$

where p_L and p_K refer to the prices of labor (remuneration) and capital (rental price), respectively. These conditions mean that, in producer equilibrium under the assumptions of constant returns to scale and perfect competition, the elasticity terms α_K and α_L are equal to the income shares of capital and labor (s_K and s_L).

Using the translog indices of capital and labor, the translog index of productivity growth is defined in the same way as in (6.3) using the translog expressions of the growth of capital and labor (i.e., Eqs. (6.10) and (6.19)) as follows:

$$\ln Q_i(T) - \ln Q_i(T-1) = \overline{sk_i}[\ln K_i(T) - \ln K_i(T-1)] + \overline{sl_i}[\ln L_i(T) - \ln L_i(T-1)] + \overline{s_{ti}}, \quad (6.29)$$

where K_i, L_i, s_{ti} and represent capital stock, labor hours, and translog index of productivity growth by industry. The income shares of capital and labor and the translog index of productivity are defined as Divisia indices[3] as

[3]Divisia indices are preferred because the data are in discrete time. The differentiation of the production function with respect to time requires that production be a continuous function of time. Therefore, Divisia indices are utilized to approximate income shares of inputs and translog indices of productivity. Divisia indices are computed as Törnqvist–Theil quantity indices, i.e., simple arithmetic average of the indices in the previous and current periods. It is important to note that Divisia indices are appropriate for translog production functions. Divisia indices are "exact" for the flexible functional form of translog production function. An "exact index number" is an index number that can be derived from a flexible aggregator. A "flexible aggregator" is a functional form that provides a second-order approximation to a twice differentiable homogeneous function, which is the translog production function here. See Diewert (1976) for details on the characteristics of exact index numbers. See also OECD (2001b, p. 88) for a mathematical explanation.

follows:

$$\overline{sk} = \frac{1}{2}(sk(T) + sk(T-1)), \tag{6.30}$$

$$\overline{sl} = \frac{1}{2}(sl(T) + sl(T-1)), \tag{6.31}$$

$$\overline{s_{ti}} = \frac{1}{2}(s_{ti}(T) + s_{ti}(T-1)). \tag{6.32}$$

Finally, the growth of output can be reformulated by rearranging (6.29) using the translog indices of capital and labor (i.e., Eqs. (6.12) and (6.19)):

$$\begin{aligned} \ln Q_i(T) - \ln Q_i(T-1) = \overline{sk_i} \sum \overline{s_{Kki}}[\ln K_{ki}(T) - \ln K_{ki}(T-1)] \\ + \overline{sl_i} \sum \overline{s_{Lli}}[\ln L_{li}(T) - \ln L_{li}(T-1)] + \overline{s_{ti}}. \end{aligned} \tag{6.33}$$

In rearranging (6.29) I made use of Eqs. (6.12) and (6.19) of the translog indices of growth in capital and labor inputs. The subcomponent shares of each input type in the respective total (sk_k) and (sl_l) are redefined as s_{Kk} and s_{Ll} in order to avoid confusion with the income shares of capital and labor at the aggregate level. These sub-component shares of capital and labor in total are also defined as Divisia indices as follows:

$$\overline{s_{Kki}} = \frac{1}{2}(s_{Kki}(T) + s_{Kki}(T-1)), \tag{6.34}$$

$$\overline{s_{Lli}} = \frac{1}{2}(s_{Lli}(T) + s_{Lli}(T-1)). \tag{6.35}$$

Translog index of productivity growth can be computed using Eq. (6.33) as follows:

$$\begin{aligned} \overline{s_{ti}} &= \ln Q_i(T) - \ln Q_i(T-1) \\ &\quad - \overline{sk_i} \cdot \sum sk_{ki}(\ln K_{ki}(T) - \ln K_{ki}(T-1)) \\ &\quad - \overline{sl_i} \cdot \sum sl_{li}(\ln L_{li}(T) - \ln L_{li}(T-1)). \end{aligned} \tag{6.36}$$

Finally, it is important to make clear what TFP growth measures. First, note the difference between embodied and disembodied technological change. Embodied technological change refers to technical knowledge embodied in installed machinery and equipment. Disembodied technical change arises from advances in research and development and innovational changes. The advantage of the translog index of productivity growth as the relevant measure of TFP growth is that it captures disembodied technological change better. In the standard growth accounting approach, qualitative changes in production factors are not taken into account. This generally produces higher estimates. Estimates of technical change disregarding such changes include incremental embodied technical change as part of TFP growth estimates. Translog production function approach generally reports lower TFP growth rates. TFP also reflects other factors such as spillover effects that arise from the use of capital and labor across industries and economies of scale. Any sort of measurement errors are also included in TFP growth as well. What TFP growth measures is more than an upgrading of technological level and updating of production process.

6.1.4. *Description of data*

TFP growth analysis is conducted only for manufacturing industries due to unavailability of consistent data on gross fixed assets for other sectors to construct capital stock.

Real value-added: The construction and source of real value-added by industries was explained in Section 5.1.1. The same real value-added values are employed in TFP growth analysis. The deflator used is the SMPI.

Employment and working hours: Labor input refers to total working hours by industries. The construction method and sources of employment was explained in Section 5.1.1. TFP growth analysis requires data also on qualitative characteristics of labor (i.e., age, sex, and education structure).

Education characteristics of labor are classified according to the highest educational qualification. These are classified into three groups: (i) "below high-school," comprising of no education or some education (below primary education), primary education, and secondary education, (ii) "high-school," which refers to upper secondary education, and (iii) "post secondary," which refers to tertiary education including polytechnics. This is the most consistent classification derived from different sources of data.

Age-specific employment and labor-income data are available only for nine major sectors but not for individual manufacturing industries. Therefore, age structure of labor is ignored and qualitative characteristics of labor are captured by cross-classifying labor by sex and educational attainment.

The abovementioned data are obtained from various sources. Main sources of data are the annual labor force surveys which have been conducted regularly since 1973. Labor-force surveys contain estimates of the government for labor-force with respect to qualitative characteristics of labor. For years prior to 1973, other data sources were used. The earliest data source on labor is *1966 Sample Household Survey*. This survey provides data on education, age, sex, and occupational status of the labor-force. Population censuses conducted in 1970, 1980, 1990, and 2000 also provide benchmark information for the characteristics of labor-force.

Working hours by education and sex are not available for all industries. Working hours by sex are available for nine major sectors only after 1980. Due to these problems, it is assumed that hours worked are same across sex and education groups and equal to industry or sector average for a given year.

Capital stock: Data on capital stocks are not available in official statistics and need to be estimated separately. The stock of capital in this study consists of four types of assets: (i) building and construction, (ii) plant and equipment, (iii) transport equipment, and (iv) office equipment. Land, consumer durables, and inventories are excluded. In Singapore statistics, *building* includes water and sewage systems, lifts, central cooling and ventilation equipment that are integral part of a building; *plant and equipment* includes power generating plant and cold storage equipment; *transport equipment* includes cranes, forklift equipment and durable containers besides company vehicles; and *office equipment* includes computers, word processors, calculating machines, cash registers, and other equipment.

First, data on gross fixed assets are collected for each type of asset. For manufacturing industries, data for capital are obtained from annual manufacturing surveys. Data for other sectors are not available and therefore those sectors other than manufacturing are excluded from TFP analysis. Capital formation data for the aggregate economy are obtained from the statistical yearbook and national accounts statistics. Consequently, capital stocks are estimated only for manufacturing industries and for the aggregate economy.[4]

[4]For some industries, data on fixed capital assets for several years were not available or were reported together with other industries. The data for textiles, wearing apparel, and leather products industries for the period 1959–1967 were published together under the title

As a result, TFP growth is computed only for these cases. Detailed data on three types of assets are available up to 1959 for all manufacturing industries and up to 1960 for the aggregate economy. Since 1991, data on fixed capital assets for manufacturing industries are reported for only two types of assets in aggregated form [(i) land, building, and structures, and (ii) machinery, office, and transportation equipment]. Also, for the aggregate economy the data for two types of assets, "plant and equipment" and "office equipment," are published in national account statistics together under one title, "machinery and equipment." Hence, capital assets for the aggregate economy are categorized into three asset types. Finally, price deflators for each type of capital asset are computed from national income accounts and the data in current prices are deflated using these deflators.

Estimation of the stock of capital: The stocks of capital for each industry are estimated using data on flows of capital formation according to the *perpetual inventory method* (PIM).[5] PIM is a widely used technique to calculate capital stock. The basic formula for the computation of capital stock is given as follows:

$$K(T) = K(T-1) + I(T) - \delta(T), \tag{6.37}$$

where $K(T)$ refers to estimated level of capital stock in period T, $K(T-1)$ to that of the previous period, I to additions to gross capital stock (investment), and d to depreciation. Equation (5.1) states that current period's capital stock

---

"textiles" with no decomposition and similarly for chemicals and petroleum industries under the title "chemicals" for the same period. A simple adjustment is made for these industries to compute capital stocks separately as follows: A quick look at the former industry group shows that the composition of capital assets across industries remained almost stable for the succeeding three years from 1967 on. Thus, it is assumed that the composition of capital assets was the same for the period 1959–1967 as 1967–1969 averages and the computed industry-group sum is redistributed among three industries using the shares of each industry in the average. For the latter, there is some variation although not much, but I again use the same method as in the former industry group to redistribute fixed assets between two industries.

[5]It is also possible to compute capital stock directly from the surveys of financial statement in the corporate sector. However, the figures in the balance sheets do not necessarily measure the economic value of capital stock adequately because the book values recorded in the balance sheets are highly influenced by tax considerations. Depreciation values in the balance sheets of firms do not aim at measuring the productive capacity of the assets and they are subject to accounting practices.

is composed of previous period's capital stock and additions to the previous year's stock of capital (investment) and is net of depreciation. To estimate capital stock using the PIM method, there is a need to choose a benchmark year, deflate investment data for each asset category to get real investment flow series, and determine depreciation rates for each type of asset. The benchmark year is chosen as 1959. Investment data deflated using relevant deflators are accumulated onto these initial values to compute capital stock series for each year.

One way to specify initial benchmark values of the stocks of capital assets, and the capital stock in total, is to take the values presented in a nation-wide wealth survey. However, Singapore has never conducted a national wealth survey. Therefore, the method in Young (1995) and Hsieh (2002) is used to specify benchmark values. In this method, benchmark capital stock for an asset is computed by dividing the initial value of relevant investment data by the sum of the depreciation rate and the average growth rate of investment for the first 10 years (1959–1968).

The formula to calculate the capital stock takes the following form:

$$K(T) = K(T-1) + \sum_{k} (1-\delta_k)\Delta K_k(T), \tag{6.38}$$

where δ_k refers to depreciation ratio for each asset of type k, where k is the building and structures, plant and equipment, and transport equipment. The term $\Delta K_k(T)$ refers to additions (investment) to existing stock of each type of asset. A summation of the additions to each type of capital assets in a given year produces total acquisition of fixed assets. Once the benchmark values are calculated, Eq. (6.38) yields capital stock in each year.

Depreciation rate: Depreciation rates that correspond to the economic value of assets are not readily available from official statistics and hence the values proposed by Jorgenson *et al.* (1987) are used: 0.0361 for building and structures, 0.1048 for plant and equipment, 0.2935 for transport equipment, and 0.2729 for office equipment. In national account statistics, the data for plant and equipment and office equipment for the entire economy are provided together. For these data, a joint rate of 0.1288 is applied. In the case of manufacturing industries, the classification of capital assets was reduced to two after 1991, and hence a weighted average of the above figures are calculated as 0.0361 for building and structures, and 0.1414 for machinery, office, and transportation equipment. In this calculation, the weighted averages of depreciation rates are used. The weights are calculated by averaging the relative shares of each asset type in total fixed assets for the five years preceding 1991.

Investment data must cover a sufficiently long period of time; at least it should cover the entire asset life of the longest-living asset. Capital asset data in this study covers a period over 40 years and it is reasonable to assume that capital assets lives are fully covered in the period of analysis.

Geometric depreciation is utilized in capital stock estimations.[6] An age-efficiency pattern that is geometrically declining is assumed for all assets.[7] In this pattern, age efficiency declines at a constant rate each year.

Finally, there is a need to investigate the robustness of capital stock series for each industry. This is checked by assuming that the benchmark year capital stock values were actually 100 percent higher than original estimates. Resulting capital stock growth rates are presented in Table 6.1. The results show that for almost all industries the differences are dismal. Hence, it can be safely argued that capital stock growth estimates computed by PIM are reliable and insensitive to the selection of benchmark values. Such small changes in capital stock growth changes do not lead to significantly large differences in TFP growth estimates.

Periodization: Periods of analyses are as explained in Section 5.1.1. However, we ignore the post-crisis sub-period (after 1998) in interpretations and rather focus on other sub-periods.

---

[6]Department of Statistics in Singapore (Singstat) also estimates capital stock and uses in its multifactor productivity growth estimates based on simple conventional growth accounting approach which are published in the statistical yearbook. However, its estimation method of capital stock is different than the one adopted in this study (see OECD, 2001a, pp. 97–98). Singstat assumes straight line depreciation (i.e., the market value of an asset declines at the same amount each year. In this method, if the service life of an asset is T years, then for each year of service deprecation amounts to $1/T$ times the initial asset value. Although the choice of straight-line or geometric depreciation is up to the researcher, for capital stock series where historical series of investment are not available but the benchmark year estimates are, geometric depreciation has practical advantages over straight-line depreciation. In addition, Singstat initiates its capital stock series from 1946 and assumes that capital stock prior to 1946 was zero. But, officially published statistics for gross fixed capital formation are available from 1959.

[7]For alternative patterns of retirement, see OECD (2001a, pp. 52–58).

Table 6.1. Sensitivity Analysis for Capital Stock Growth Rates (Unit: Percent).

	Capital Stock 100 % Higher (A)			Original Values (B)			Differencc (A–B)		
Industries	1965–1985	1986–2002	1965–2002	1965–1985	1986–2002	1965–2002	1965–1985	1986–2002	1965–2002
Food	8.37	4.74	6.83	9.58	4.89	7.50	−1.18	−0.05	−0.67
Tex	14.32	−1.06	7.39	14.39	−1.06	7.43	−0.07	0.00	−0.04
Wear	17.08	0.98	9.90	17.14	0.98	9.93	−0.06	0.00	−0.03
Leat	14.67	7.63	11.65	14.85	7.63	11.75	−0.18	0.00	−0.10
Wood	10.29	−1.22	4.98	10.53	−1.21	5.12	−0.24	−0.01	−0.14
Furn	17.78	−1.50	9.52	18.26	−1.50	9.81	−0.52	0.00	−0.29
Paper	17.48	5.54	12.28	17.43	5.55	12.83	−0.98	−0.01	−0.55
Pub	11.33	6.82	9.43	12.82	6.86	10.27	−1.50	−0.03	−0.85
Chem	17.68	10.85	14.64	17.86	10.85	14.73	−0.17	0.00	−0.10
Petr	20.73	2.80	12.59	20.85	2.80	12.66	−0.13	0.00	−0.07
Rub	26.16	7.98	18.04	25.23	7.98	17.52	0.93	0.00	0.52
Non-met	13.32	5.83	9.89	14.48	5.85	10.54	−1.15	−0.02	−0.65
Met	16.50	2.14	10.01	16.54	2.14	10.03	−0.04	0.00	−0.02
Fab-met	13.09	7.47	10.65	13.59	7.48	10.93	−0.50	−0.01	−0.28
Mach	25.26	6.42	16.81	26.50	6.42	17.49	−1.24	0.00	−0.68
Elec	29.74	13.44	22.92	30.46	13.44	23.26	−0.62	0.00	−0.34
Prec	15.65	7.53	11.41	15.65	7.53	11.41	0.00	0.00	0.00
Tran	14.58	5.20	10.31	14.90	5.21	10.49	−0.32	−0.01	−0.18
Oth-man	14.14	10.75	12.73	14.48	10.76	12.93	−0.35	0.00	−0.19
Manufac-turing	15.92	8.96	12.90	16.68	8.97	13.32	−0.76	−0.01	−0.42
Economy	13.82	6.98	10.91	14.06	6.98	11.05	−0.24	−0.01	−0.14

Source: Author's calculations.

6.2. TFP Growth Estimates

6.2.1. *Previous studies on total factor productivity growth and its sources*

TFP growth in Singapore attracted attention after two studies by Young (1992) and Kim and Lau (1994) that found "zero" TFP growth. In addition, based on the empirical findings of these two studies, Krugman (1994) criticized the rapid economic growth performance of Singapore by claiming that it was based on factor accumulation like in the former Soviet Union rather than TFP gains and further claimed that such high growth rates cannot be sustained. The Asian financial crisis in 1997 in Southeast Asia increased the interest in these studies.

There are various studies on TFP growth in Singapore. However, the findings of these studies are controversial; for the same period some studies find positive TFP growth rate while others find a negative one. The main reason for these differences is different methodologies employed. Furthermore, capital stock values are not available from official statistics and have to be estimated by researchers. Differing estimates of capital stock result in different capital and TFP growth rates. Previous studies on TFP growth in Singapore used one of the three approaches: (i) conventional growth accounting approach that computes TFP growth rate as Solow residual, (ii) econometric methods such as the stochastic frontier approach, and (iii) translog production function. A list of some previous TFP growth estimates in the past is presented in Table 6.2.

Those studies using the conventional growth accounting approach compute TFP growth as a residual by deducting weighted growth rates of capital and labor input from growth rate of real value-added, the weights being the respective shares of capital and labor in value-added. Their findings are rather optimistic compared to the results of other studies, producing generally positive TFP growth rates. In addition, various studies point to improvements in TFP performance for the aggregate economy after 1985. Among these studies, Thangavelu (2004) adjusts labor input for different skill levels and also employs capacity utilization rate for capital stock growth estimates. Hence, its findings are rather lower than others. Differing results of these studies are mainly due to construction of data and differing estimates of capital stock.

Econometric estimates of TFP growth are of two kinds. The stochastic frontier approach decomposes productivity growth into technical progress, technical efficiency change, scale economies, and allocative efficiency components. For this purpose, first a functional form of production function (such as Cobb–Douglas or translog) is specified and then the parameters

Table 6.2. Selected Previous TFP Growth Estimates of Singapore (Annual Averages in Percentage).

Source	Methodology	Time Period	Dimension	Finding (%)
Chen (1977)*	Conventional growth accounting	1957–1970	Aggregate economy	3.6
Ikemoto (1986)*	Conventional growth accounting	1970–1980	Aggregate economy	1.8
Elias (1990)*	Conventional growth accounting	1950–1987	Aggregate economy	1.8
World Bank (1993)	Conventional growth accounting	1960–1989	Aggregate economy	1.7
Kawai (1994)*	Conventional growth accounting	1970–1980	Aggregate economy	0.7
		1980–1990	Aggregate economy	1.6
Lindauer and Roemer (1994)*	Conventional growth accounting	1965–1990	Aggregate economy	3.6
Rao and Lee (1995)	Conventional growth accounting	1976–1984	Manufacturing	−0.4
		1987–1994	Manufacturing	3.2
Collins and Bosworth (1996)*	Conventional growth accounting	1960–1994	Aggregate economy	1.5
		1973–1984	Aggregate economy	1.0
		1984–1994	Aggregate economy	3.1
Marti (1996)*	Conventional growth accounting	1970–1990	Aggregate economy	1.4
Leung (1997)	Conventional growth accounting	1983–1993	Manufacturing	2.8
		1980–1985	Aggregate economy	−0.6
Wong and Sim (1997)	Conventional growth accounting	1985–1990	Aggregate economy	3.8

(*Continued*)

Table 6.2. (*Continued*)

Source	Methodology	Time Period	Dimension	Finding (%)
		1990–1998	Aggregate economy	1.2
		1970–1985	Aggregate economy	−2.1
Thangavelu (2004)	Conventional growth accounting	1986–1995	Aggregate economy	1.6
		1970–1995	Aggregate economy	−0.7
		1966–1972	Manufacturing	0.6
Tsao (1982)	Translog production function	1972–1980	Manufacturing	−0.9
Wong and Gan (1994)	Translog production function	1981–1990	Manufacturing	1.6
		1966–1990	Aggregate economy	−0.2
Young (1992 and 1995)	Translog production function	1970–1990	Manufacturing	−1.0
Bercuson (1995)	Translog production approach	1961–1991	Aggregate economy	1.8
Kim and Lau (1994)	Meta production function	1960–1990	Aggregate economy	0.0
Mahadevan and Kalirajan (2000)	Stochastic production frontier	1976–1984	Manufacturing	0.9
		1987–1994	Manufacturing	−0.5
Iwata *et al.* (2002)	Nonparametric derivative estimation	1960–1995	Aggregate economy	3.7
Sun (2002)	Stochastic coefficients production frontier analysis	1970–1997	Manufacturing	−0.8
Koh *et al.* (2004)	Stochastic frontier analysis	1975–1998	Manufacturing	1.8

*Cited from Felipe (1997).

of this function are estimated using the maximum likelihood estimation method.

As listed in Table 6.1 studies using the stochastic frontier approach produce different results for productivity growth. In addition to stochastic frontier approach, Kim and Lau (1994) estimated a so-called "meta-production function" by using panel data from East Asian and some developed countries. They found zero TFP growth for Singapore as well as for Korea and Taiwan. Another econometric approach is the non-parametric estimation by Iwata *et al.* (2002). This study makes no assumption on the competitive structure of the factor markets or the functional form of the production function. It uses a nonparametric derivative estimation technique to decompose output growth into its sources by estimating the output elasticities of capital and labor. This method produces the highest estimate for Singapore, at 3.7 percent level per annum for the 1960–1995 period, casting doubt on the findings of the previous approaches.

The translog approach takes into account the changes in the composition of capital and labor inputs and includes such changes in the growth rates of capital and labor inputs. The estimation of TFP growth rate in this approach is similar to the residual calculation in the conventional growth accounting approach. This study also utilizes this approach to estimate TFP growth rate. Translog production function can also be estimated by econometric methods. There are four other studies comparable to this study. Tsao (1982), the oldest of these, utilized translog price and production functions to estimate TFP growth for manufacturing industries for the periods 1966–1972 and 1972–1980. She found very low annual average manufacturing TFP growth rates, for these periods, 0.6 and −0.9 percent, respectively. Additional sensitivity analyses also did not change the fact that technical change in this period was almost zero. Tsao's study was later extended using the same methodology by Wong and Gan (1994). They found 1.6 percent TFP growth rate for the manufacturing sector for the period 1981–1990. Young (1992, 1995) estimated TFP growth rates using the translog production function approach for the aggregate economy and for the manufacturing sector for the 25-year period 1966–1990. He found zero annual average TFP growth rate for the aggregate economy and −1 percent TFP growth for the manufacturing sector. Moreover, he compares his results of TFP growth for the aggregate economy with those he found for Hong Kong (2.3 percent for period 1961–1991), Korea (1.7 percent for period

1960–1990), and Taiwan (2.6 percent for period 1961–1991) and concludes that TFP growth performance of Singapore was the worst among the newly developing Asian economies. The fourth study was conducted by an IMF staff team (Bercuson, 1995). This study estimates TFP growth for the aggregate economy for the period 1961–1991, but unlike the previous three studies, does not adjust factor inputs for quality changes. Both labor and capital are assumed to be of the same quality from 1960 to 1991. Thus, the results (1.8 percent for the period 1961–1991) are most likely to overestimate actual TFP growth as embodied technological change is included as part of the estimated TFP growth rate rather than advances in input quality.

6.2.2. *TFP growth estimates: Empirical findings*

TFP growth rates are estimated for each manufacturing industry and the aggregate economy. Capital stock data were modified to take into account capacity utilization rates. Capacity utilization rates generally fluctuate over time because of changes in demand conditions, seasonal variations, interruptions in the supply of intermediate products, or breakdown of machinery (OECD, 2001a, p. 74). Changes in capacity utilization rates, in turn, affect the flow of capital services. Capacity utilization rates can be calculated by applying econometric methods or by using a proxy for capacity utilization rates, such as horsepower equivalent of electricity use. But due to unavailability of reliable data for Singapore, capital stock series are detrended by dismantling the business cycle component of capital stocks using the Hodrick–Prescott filter.

TFP growth estimates are presented in Figure 6.2 and Table 6.3. In addition, the appendix displays translog indices of capital, labor, and productivity growth for each industry. These indices are set as 1 for the year 1985. The figures in the appendix present the estimates computed using real value-added values deflated by the SMPI. Figure 6.2 shows that TFP growth rates for manufacturing and the aggregate economy are very similar for the entire period. The figure also shows the improving trend in TFP growth rates in the post-1985 era. Table 6.3 presents in detail the TFP growth rates for each sub-period. Panels A and B present the findings for manufacturing industries using two different deflators for real value-added. Panel C compares the figures for the manufacturing sector and the aggregate economy.

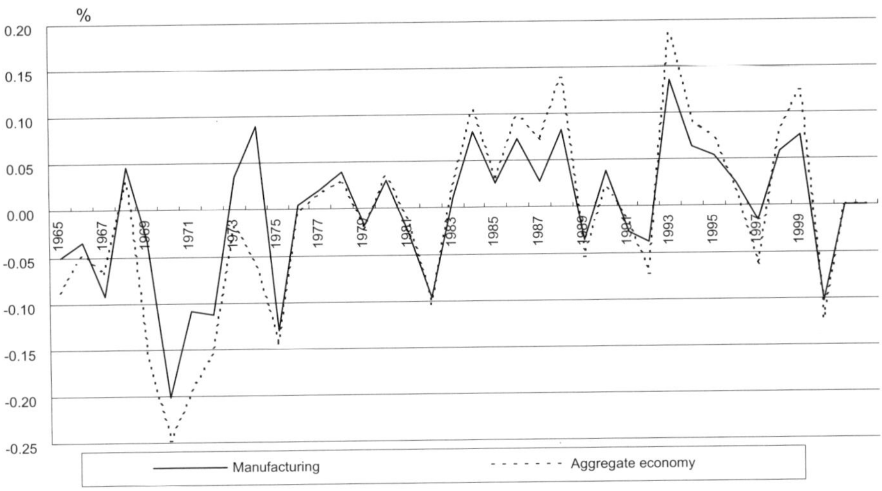

Fig. 6.2. TFP growth rate for manufacturing and the aggregate economy (1965–2000).
Source: Author's calculations.

Table 6.3. Average Annual TFP Growth rates by Industry and Period (Percent).

	1965–1978	1979–1985	1986–1997	1998–2002	1965–1985	1986–2002	1965–2002
A. Estimates based on real value-added computed by GDP deflator for the manufacturing sector							
Food	−2.0	−2.9	−0.6	−9.4	−2.3	−3.2	−2.7
Tex	−0.6	−2.3	3.5	−3.0	−1.2	1.6	0.1
Wear	−4.5	−3.7	−3.3	8.6	−4.2	0.2	−2.3
Leat	−8.8	−1.5	3.1	−7.0	−6.3	0.1	−3.5
Wood	−2.0	−6.4	2.2	−5.3	−3.5	0.0	−1.9
Furn	−8.2	4.2	−0.9	0.8	−4.0	−0.4	−2.4
Paper	−2.5	2.1	−1.4	−11.1	−1.0	−4.2	−2.4
Pub	−3.1	0.0	2.1	−9.0	−2.1	−1.2	−1.7
Chem	−0.9	−4.9	0.0	13.9	−2.3	4.1	0.6
Petr	−12.9	−10.9	0.4	6.8	−12.2	2.3	−5.7
Rub	−17.1	−3.1	0.6	−3.6	−12.4	−0.7	−7.2
Non-met	−3.9	−6.6	−0.5	−12.5	−4.8	−4.0	−4.5
Met	−12.7	−9.3	−3.9	−4.5	−11.6	−4.0	−8.2

(*Continued*)

Table 6.3. (*Continued*)

	1965–1978	1979–1985	1986–1997	1998–2002	1965–1985	1986–2002	1965–2002
Fab-met	−1.7	−3.4	0.1	−4.2	−2.2	−1.2	−1.8
Mach	−2.3	−6.8	−1.8	6.3	−3.8	0.6	−1.9
Elec	−7.2	−1.0	−0.6	−4.3	−5.1	−1.7	−3.6
Prec	−2.3	3.9	4.1	2.2	−0.2	3.6	1.5
Tran	0.5	−1.2	0.9	−4.8	−0.1	−0.8	−0.4
B. Estimates based on real value-added computed by SMPI							
Food	−1.9	0.9	0.8	−7.9	−1.0	−1.7	−1.3
Tex	0.2	2.6	5.7	0.2	1.0	4.1	2.4
Wear	−3.8	1.2	−1.2	11.8	−2.1	2.6	0.0
Leat	−8.0	3.4	5.2	−3.9	−4.2	2.5	−1.2
Wood	−1.3	−1.5	2.2	−5.4	−1.3	−0.1	−0.8
Furn	−7.4	9.1	−1.0	2.0	1.9	−0.1	−1.1
Paper	−1.8	7.0	−0.1	−11.1	1.2	−3.4	−0.9
Pub	−2.3	4.9	3.3	−7.7	0.1	0.1	0.1
Chem	0.0	−2.9	3.3	14.4	−1.0	6.5	2.4
Petr	−12.8	−16.2	8.1	−0.8	−13.9	5.5	−5.2
Rub	−16.1	−1.0	1.2	−3.5	−11.1	−0.2	−6.2
Non-met	−3.2	−1.7	0.4	−6.6	−2.7	−1.6	−2.2
Met	−12.0	−4.4	−1.7	−2.6	−9.4	−1.9	−6.1
Fab-met	−1.3	0.4	0.1	−0.9	−0.7	−0.2	−0.5
Mach	−2.0	−3.0	−1.1	6.5	−2.3	1.1	−0.8
Elec	−5.1	−0.4	5.1	−1.2	−3.5	3.2	−0.5
Prec	−1.9	7.7	5.5	2.2	1.3	4.5	2.8
Tran	0.9	2.6	0.1	−6.1	1.5	−1.7	0.0
C. Estimates for the manufacturing sector and the aggregate economy							
Manufacturing	−3.8	0.1	3.2	−3.0	−2.5	1.4	−0.8
Economy	−4.2	0.6	0.8	0.5	−2.6	0.7	−1.1

Source: Author's calculations.

Average TFP growth rate of the manufacturing sector in the post-1985 era (1.4 percent) surpassed that of the pre-1985 era (−2.5 percent). The same thing also holds for the aggregate economy (0.7 and −2.6 percent, respectively). These findings indicate a remarkable improvement in TFP growth performance between two periods from negative to moderately positive figures. One may argue that these positive figures are still low.[8] It is true that in international comparisons these figures are relatively low. However, the magnitude and the sign of the increase in TFP growth are remarkably high by any standard.

At the industry level, superior TFP growth performances of chemicals and precision equipment industries in the post-1985 period are noticeable. Electrical and electronic machinery industry also demonstrates a significant TFP growth rate. It is important to note that, among the figures for individual industries in Table 6.3, those in Panel B are much more reliable than those at Panel A since it deflates all industries' value-added series using the same deflator (manufacturing GDP deflator). Whichever the deflator used, Table 6.3 reveals that there is a general tendency for TFP growth performance of individual industries to improve from the pre-1985 period to the post-1985 period. This can also be observed from the indices of technical change by industries in Appendix Table A1.3. The large improvement in manufacturing TFP growth is led by TFP growth performances of chemicals, precision equipment, electrical and electronic machinery industries, disregarding the textiles industry. Abnormal TFP growth figures for the post-crisis years (1998–2002) are also noteworthy.

The remarkable improvement in the TFP growth rates in the post-1985 era is important in the sense that the government set as a priority in its industrial policies the upgrading of technology and gains in productivity via coordinated programs run by EDB, SPRING (PSB prior to 2002), and MTI. Of much interest is PSB, which was given a target of achieving an annual TFP growth rate of 2 percent at the onset of its establishment. This was a response to strong criticism by some influential studies that found zero TFP growth for Singapore over decades of rapid growth and criticized Singapore's growth which they found to result almost entirely from factor accumulation (Young, 1992; Kim and Lau, 1994).

[8]Wilson and Peebles (2005) argues that the official Singapore view towards the relatively low-TFP growth rates reflects the small indigenous manpower base and the lack of local industrial entrepreneurship but also the ignorance of these by the government. This seems to support the government's view that Singapore is not yet a developed country, as discussed in Wilson (2000). The government's view is such that there are strong reasons to believe that TFP growth will improve in the near future and expects past investments in education and infrastructure to bear fruits.

The finding that TFP growth rates improved in the post-1985 era relative to the pre-1985 era matches conclusions by various studies whose findings are presented in Section 6.2.1. What is of interest here is not the magnitude but the implications of those figures for different periods. The aim of the analysis in this chapter is not to calculate TFP growth rates and compare with other studies. TFP growth estimates are necessary in the forthcoming analysis which investigates the impact of resource reallocations of TFP growth.

6.2.3. *Sensitivity analysis for TFP growth estimates*

There is a need to check the robustness of TFP growth estimates. It is conducted in this section by first assuming that the benchmark capital stock rates were 100 percent higher than original estimates, and then by assuming that the share of labor in value-added was actually 0.1 percentage points higher than original labor share estimates.

The sensitivity analysis of TFP growth estimates are investigated using two different real value-added series for real value-added growth rates. It was found in Chapter 5 that using two different deflators produced two different real value-added series where the difference was not large. But such differences may lead to differing TFP growth rates up to 1 or 2 percentage points. TFP growth rates for individual manufacturing industries using two different series of real value-added are presented in Table 6.4. Panel A in Table 6.4 presents the results computed using real value-added series deflated by the manufacturing sector's GDP deflator. Panel B uses SMPI to deflate manufacturing value-added. Deflation of manufacturing value-added by the manufacturing GDP deflator brings down the original annual average manufacturing TFP growth rates in the amount of 2–3 percentage points. Finally, Panel C compares TFP growth rates when qualitative changes in capital and labor are not considered. This refers to the standard growth accounting approach. The standard growth accounting approach produces higher TFP growth rates by about 1 percentage point.

Sensitivity analysis in Table 6.4 also reviews the response of TFP growth estimates to different measures of output and input. First, the impact of doubling the capital stocks is checked. It was already argued that capital stock values are insensitive to benchmark capital stock values. The overall impact of doubling capital stocks on aggregate TFP growth is between 0 and

Table 6.4. Sensitivity Analysis for TFP Growth Rates (Unit: Percent).

	Aggregate Economy			Manufacturing Sector		
	Capital Benchmark 100 % Higher	Labor Share 0.1 Higher	Original Values	Capital Benchmark 100 % Higher	Labor Share 0.1 Higher	Original Values
A. Estimates based on manufacturing real value-added computed by manufacturing sector GDP deflator						
1965–1978	−4.1	−3.3	−4.2	−5.0	−4.2	−5.0
1979–1985	0.6	1.3	0.6	−2.9	−1.8	−2.9
1986–1997	0.8	1.3	0.8	0.8	1.8	1.1
1998–2002	0.5	1.2	0.5	−1.0	−2.5	−4.2
1965–1985	−2.5	−1.7	−2.6	−4.3	−3.4	−4.3
1986–2002	0.7	1.3	0.7	0.3	0.5	−0.4
1965–2002	−1.1	−0.4	−1.1	−2.2	−1.6	−2.6
B. Estimates based on manufacturing real value-added computed by SMPI						
1965–1978	−4.1	−3.3	−4.2	−3.8	−3.0	−3.8
1979–1985	0.6	1.3	0.6	0.1	1.2	0.1
1986–1997	0.8	1.3	0.8	2.9	3.9	3.2
1998–2002	0.5	1.2	0.5	0.2	−1.3	−3.0
1965–1985	−2.5	−1.7	−2.6	−2.5	−1.6	−2.5
1986–2002	0.7	1.3	0.7	2.1	2.3	1.4
1965–2002	−1.1	−0.4	−1.1	−0.4	0.2	−0.8

		Manufacturing Sector Only	
	Aggregate Economy	Value-added Deflated by GDP Deflator	Value-added Deflated by SMPI
C. Estimates based on capital and labor inputs measured by crude labor and capital inputs rather than translog indices			
1965–1978	−3.1	−4.9	−3.7
1979–1985	−0.3	−2.1	0.9
1986–1997	0.7	1.2	3.3
1998–2002	1.0	−0.6	0.6
1965–1985	−2.1	−3.9	−2.1
1986–2002	0.8	0.7	2.5
1965–2002	−0.8	−1.9	−0.1

−0.1 percentage points for the aggregate economy. For the manufacturing sector, the impact is strong for the post-1985 period whereas pre-1985 TFP growth rate is irresponsive to such a change. The only period where the responses are significant are the crisis and post-crisis period 1998–2002.

Next, the impact of increasing the share of labor in total value-added by 0.1 percentage points is checked (e.g., a rise from 0.33 to 0.43). The impact of an increase in labor share is generally greater than that of doubling benchmark capital stocks. TFP growth rates improve in the amount of 0.5–0.9 percentage points for the aggregate economy and around 1 percentage point for the manufacturing sector. If the actual income share of labor were 0.1 percentage points higher, TFP growth rate for the manufacturing sector for the whole period using the SMPI-deflated real value-added figures would turn from −0.8 to 0.2 percent.

6.3. The Impact of Resource Allocation on TFP Growth: Methodology

The portion of TFP growth not resulting from technical changes within sub-industries ("intra-industry technical change") was named "inter-industry technical change" by Massell (1961). The difference between aggregate TFP growth and output-weighted sectoral TFP growth rates is referred to as "reallocation effect" by Syrquin (1986). He notes that in the presence of significant sectoral differences in factor returns, structural change is important in determining the rate and pattern of growth. If structural changes are slow or bring about inefficient allocation of resources, then growth may be retarded. But, if they bring about more efficient allocation of resources, they contribute to growth. In Singapore, where the government actively monitors structural changes, the impact of government policies is important in this sense.

The impact of the reallocations of resources across industries on aggregate TFP growth rate can be investigated by decomposing TFP growth, following Massell (1961) and Timmer and Szirmai (2000). We start by taking the derivatives of the shares of each industry in total capital and labor, k_i and l_i, with respect to time. For k_i, the following holds:

$$\frac{dk_i}{dt} = \frac{\left(\frac{dK_i}{dt}K - \frac{dK}{dt}K_i\right)}{K^2}, \tag{6.39}$$

where the subscript i denotes industries and the terms without subscripts refer to economy aggregates. Divide both sides by k_i:

$$\frac{dk_i}{dt}\frac{1}{k_i} = \frac{dK_i}{dt}\frac{1}{K_i} - \frac{dK}{dt}\frac{1}{K}, \quad \text{or} \quad \frac{\Delta k_i}{k_i} = \frac{\Delta K_i}{K_i} - \frac{\Delta K}{K}. \tag{6.40}$$

Rearranging Eq. (6.40), we get:

$$\frac{\Delta K_i}{K_i} = \frac{\Delta k_i}{k_i} + \frac{\Delta K}{K}. \tag{6.41}$$

Similarly for sl_i:

$$\frac{\Delta L_i}{L_i} = \frac{\Delta l_i}{l_i} + \frac{\Delta L}{L}. \tag{6.42}$$

Next, we define the change in output as the sum of changes in output in individual industries, i.e., $\Delta Q = \sum_i \Delta Q_i$, then:

$$\frac{\Delta Q}{Q} = \sum_i \frac{\Delta Q_i}{Q} = \sum_i \frac{\Delta Q_i}{Q_i} \cdot \frac{Q_i}{Q}. \tag{6.43}$$

For convenience, we will denote the output share (Q_i/Q) of each industry by sq_i. Then, substituting (6.3), (6.41), and (6.42) into (6.43):

$$\frac{\Delta Q}{Q} = \sum_i sq_i \left[\frac{\Delta A_i}{A_i} + \alpha_{Ki}\left(\frac{\Delta K}{K} + \frac{\Delta k_i}{k_i}\right) + (1-\alpha_{Ki})\left(\frac{\Delta L}{L} + \frac{\Delta l_i}{l_i}\right)\right]. \tag{6.44}$$

Rearranging Eq. (6.44), we get:

$$\frac{\Delta Q}{Q} - \alpha_K \frac{\Delta K}{K} - (1-\alpha_K)\frac{\Delta L}{L} = \sum_i sq_i \left(\frac{\Delta A_i}{A_i} + \alpha_{Ki}\frac{\Delta k_i}{k_i} + (1-\alpha_{Ki})\frac{\Delta l_i}{l_i}\right). \tag{6.45}$$

By definition, reallocation effect is the portion of aggregate TFP growth not explained by the sum of TFP growth arising from within the industries:

$$RE = \frac{\Delta A}{A} - \sum_i q_i \frac{\Delta A_i}{A_i} = \sum_i q_i \alpha_{Ki} \frac{\Delta k_i}{k_i} + \sum_i q_i \alpha_{Li} \frac{\Delta l_i}{l_i}. \tag{6.46}$$

Equation (6.46) demonstrates the effects of changes in the shares (i.e., shifts) of capital and labor on aggregate TFP growth.[9] The right-hand side

[9]For a slightly different computation technique, see Kuroda *et al.* (1996).

of Eq. (6.46) includes two components of reallocation effect, the first term being capital reallocation effect and the second term being labor reallocation effect. Aggregate TFP growth is calculated, thus, as the sum of TFP growth arising from within individual industries and TFP growth resulting from reallocations of factors among industries.[10] Equation (6.46) implies that TFP growth within sectors have a direct effect on aggregate TFP growth.[11] On the other hand, the reallocations of resources during the course of industrialization have an indirect impact on aggregate TFP growth. This reallocation was stimulated largely by the government in Singapore. It is possible for such reallocations of resources, associated with interdependencies across related sectors, to improve aggregate TFP growth above an output-weighted average of TFP growth rates in individual industries. Interdependencies arise

[10]A different interpretation of reallocation effects is as follows (Syrquin, 1986). It can be shown using some algebraic manipulations that $\frac{\Delta LP}{LP} = \sum_i sq_i \cdot \frac{\Delta LP_i}{LP_i} + \sum_i sq_i \cdot \frac{\Delta l_i}{l_i}$. The second term on the right-hand side of this equation represents the impact of resource allocations on labor productivity in a framework where there is only production factor. Further elaboration shows that $\sum_i sq_i \cdot \frac{\Delta l_i}{l_i} = \frac{1}{Q}\sum_i \frac{\Delta L_i}{L_i}(LP_i - LP)\sum_i q_i \cdot \frac{\Delta l_i}{l_i} = \frac{1}{Q}\sum_i \frac{\Delta L_i}{L_i}(LP_i - LP)$, where the terms with no subscripts refer to aggregates. This equation shows that labor reallocation depends on differences of each sector's average labor productivity from the economy average. Labor productivity here refers to average product of existing labor. Syrquin (1986) prefers marginal product of labor to average product of labor in the previous equation. He adds a capital term to this equation and rewrites the total reallocation effect in marginal rather than average product terms as follows:

$$RE = \frac{1}{Q}\sum_i \frac{\Delta L_i}{L_i} \cdot (fL_i - fL) + \frac{1}{Q}\sum_i \frac{\Delta K_i}{K_i} \cdot (fK_i - fK),$$

where fL and fK refer to marginal product of labor and capital, respectively. This equation computes reallocation effects as the sum of the products of the growth rates of resources and the differences between sectoral marginal products and the average of all sectors. This implies that rising capital and labor shares of the industries that enjoy higher marginal products of inputs lead to positive reallocation effects and an improvement in disequilibrium (Syrquin, 1984). Reallocation effects sum to zero if marginal products are equal across sectors, i.e., in equilibrium. Disequilibrium exists when sectoral marginal products of capital and labor are higher in some sectors than others. Therefore, capital and labor may be shifting in order to adjust disequilibrium. Hence positive reallocation effects imply a move to improve disequilibrium in factor markets as well.

[11]Massell (1961) calls the intra-industry (within-industry) component of TFP growth as "innovation" in a narrow sense. He claims that reallocation effects are not innovational as they are concerned solely with changing input shares.

due to externalities among individual industries by which output and productivity growth stimulates output and productivity growth in other linked industries. In addition, the magnitude of reallocation effects sheds light on how structural adjustment was realized during selected periods.[12]

In TFP decomposition (Eq. (6.44)), TFP growth rate is calculated by using the translog indices of TFP growth. An important advantage of the translog production function over conventional growth accounting is the inclusion of quality changes in factor inputs.[13] If qualitative changes are not accounted for and production factors are treated as homogeneous across industries, reallocation effects will be overestimated (Timmer and Szirmai, 2000). To the extent that marginal productivities of factor inputs are higher due to their higher quality in some sectors than in others, they will be paid more. This will lead to a difference between the prices of capital and labor paid across sectors which then leads to shifts of factor inputs to those sectors where they are paid more. Then, reallocation effects will also include the changes in the quality of factor inputs. Therefore, total reallocation effects

[12]Note also that a positive reallocation effect may result even when the resources are optimally allocated before and after resource reallocation. Syrquin (1986) provides an explanation for this case using the example of a small country producing only two goods at fixed international prices. Under Rybczynski's theorem, with an increase in the amount of total capital input in equilibrium (i.e., marginal products are equal under across sectors), labor will be reallocated towards more capital-intensive production where labor productivity is already higher. In each sector, average and marginal products of labor remain constant and aggregate labor productivity increases in the amount of labor reallocation effect. Assuming that no resources are misallocated before and after the increase in capital, labor productivity increases are not a result of reallocation effects only. Labor productivity results from the accumulation of capital.

[13]Following the methodology in Jorgenson *et al.* (1987, Chap. 2), a decomposition of the translog index of technical change can be obtained as follows: The maximization problem of the producer's problem involves the maximization of aggregate output. Aggregate output is a proportion of value-added for all sectors. Output is maximized subject to the constraints given by the sectoral value-added functions and the availability of factor inputs. Aggregate output to be maximized (production possibilities function) for q number of sectors (or industries) can be written as $O(Q_1, Q_2, \ldots, Q_n; K_1, K_2, \ldots, K_n; L_1, L_2, \ldots, L_m; T)$. It is assumed that there are n types of capital and m types of labor. In this function, the share of value-added is found by:

$$so_i = \frac{p_{Qi} \cdot Q_i}{\sum_i p_{Qi} \cdot Q_i} = \frac{\partial \ln O}{\partial \ln Q_i},$$

where p_{Qi} denotes the price level of value-added. The Divisia share of value-added is then will contain an improvement in disequilibrium in factor markets and an improvement in input quality. In that case, the effects of structural change will be overestimated.

6.4. The Impact of Resource Allocation on TFP Growth: Empirical Findings

Before interpreting the results of the analysis there is a need to review TFP growth performances of promoted industries especially after 1985. TFP growth rates of promoted industries will be compared below with the economy and manufacturing averages and later the contributions by promoted industries to aggregate TFP growth will be investigated. TFP growth

---

found by the following approximation formula:

$$\overline{so_i} = \frac{1}{2}(so_i(T) + so_i(T-1)).$$

Multiplying the sectoral growth rates of productivity by sectoral value-added shares and deducting this value from aggregate productivity growth rate:

$$\begin{aligned}\overline{s_T} = & \left[\sum \frac{\overline{so_i}}{\overline{sq_i}} \cdot \overline{s_{Ti}}\right] + \left[[\ln Q(T) - \ln Q(T-1)] - \sum \overline{so_i}[\ln Q_i(T) - \ln Q_i(T-1)]\right] \\ & + \left[\sum \overline{so_i} \cdot \frac{\overline{s_{Ki}}}{sq_i} \sum \overline{s_{Kki}}[\ln K_{ki}(T) - \ln K_{ki}(T-1)]\right. \\ & \left. - \overline{s_K} \sum \overline{s_{Kk}}[\ln K_k(T) - \ln K_k(T-1)]\right] \\ & + \left[\sum \overline{so_i} \cdot \frac{\overline{sl_i}}{sq_i} \sum s_{Lli}[\ln L_{li}(T) - \ln L_{li}(T-1)]\right. \\ & \left. - \overline{s_L} \sum \overline{s_{Ll}}[\ln K_l(T) - \ln L_l(T-1)]\right],\end{aligned}$$

where so_i refers to the Divisia share of value-added. Note that value-added shares of sectors are derived from the maximization problem of gross output. Therefore, the weights reflect the output to value-added shares of each sector and hence their sum is larger than unity. The first term on the first line of the right-hand side of the equation above is a weighted sum of sectoral productivity growth rates and represents the intra-industry productivity growth effect. The other two terms represent the impacts of capital and labor allocations across sectors. This is a reinterpretation of Equations (6.45) and (6.46). Jorgenson *et al.* (1987, p. 66) touch upon the meaning and significance of reallocation effects, but they do not elaborate on the issue.

figures are calculated using the SMPI-deflated real value-added figures. The promoted industries for each period will be identified as follows:

(i) 1965–1978: textiles, wearing, petroleum and refined oil products, transport equipment;
(ii) 1979–1985: chemicals, petroleum and refined oil products, electrical and electronic machinery and equipment, transport equipment; and
(iii) post-1985: chemicals, electrical and electronic machinery and equipment (including IT services), precision equipment.

Among the promoted industries, only textiles and transport equipment industries in the period 1965–1978 and transport equipment industry in the period 1979–1985 exhibit TFP growth rates higher than the manufacturing average (Table 6.3). All other promoted industries had lower TFP growth rates. After 1985, however, promoted industries had higher TFP growth rates than manufacturing average. A simple conclusion that can be drawn from this finding, ignoring the reallocation effects for the time being, is that the selection of promoted industries was more effective in the post-1985 era than the pre-1985 era. An examination of reallocation effects provides more. It is also important to note that unlike the pre-1985 era which is characterized by negative TFP growth rates (which means that high growth was input-driven rather than productivity-driven, the post-1985 era is one with productivity-led growth. This is evident from very high intra-industry TFP growth effects resulting from promoted industries after 1985 (Table 6.5).

The results of the TFP decomposition exercise based on Eq. (6.46) for the aggregate economy and manufacturing sector are presented in Table 6.5. The sum of reallocation effects are small for the aggregate economy accounting for only 4.4 percent of TFP growth for the pre-1985 period and a relatively higher 10.6 percent for the post-1985 period. Reallocation effects are substantial only for the period 1979–1985. In the post-1985 era, reallocation effects are minimal and the contribution of labor reallocation is higher than that of capital reallocation. Note that, during the crisis period, aggregate TFP growth resulted almost entirely from TFP growth resulting from within industries.

The results of TFP decomposition in Table 6.5 show that reallocations of capital and labor across industries make up a substantial portion of manufacturing TFP growth, 67.0 and 50.3 percent for the pre-1985 and post-1985

Table 6.5. Results of TFP Decomposition for Singapore.

	1965–1978	1979–1985	1986–1997	1998–2002	1965–1985	1986–2002
A. Entire economy						
TFP growth rate	−4.22	0.61	0.82	0.50	−2.61	0.73
Intra-industry TFP growth	−5.44	0.14	0.71	0.49	−2.50	0.65
Capital reallocation effect	0.42	0.14	0.00	0.00	−0.01	0.00
Labor reallocation effect	0.79	0.32	0.11	0.01	−0.10	0.07
B. Manufacturing sector only						
TFP growth rate	−3.77	0.12	3.21	−1.78	−2.47	1.74
Intra-industry TFP growth	−0.70	0.08	1.48	−1.08	−0.82	0.87
Capital reallocation effect	−2.49	0.04	2.26	−0.36	−1.35	1.01
Labor reallocation effect	−0.58	0.01	−0.53	−0.34	−0.31	−0.13
C. Percentage contributions of its components to TFP growth (Aggregate economy)						
Intra-industry TFP growth	128.8	23.7	86.4	97.4	95.6	89.4
Capital reallocation effect	−10.0	23.0	0.6	0.0	0.4	0.4
Labor reallocation effect	−18.8	53.3	13.0	1.5	4.0	10.2
D. Percentage contributions of its components to TFP growth (Manufacturing only)						
Intra-industry TFP growth	18.5	64.5	46.0	61.0	33.0	49.7
Capital reallocation effect	66.0	30.0	70.4	20.1	54.6	57.9
Labor reallocation effect	15.5	5.5	−16.4	18.9	12.4	−7.6

(*Continued*)

Table 6.5. (*Continued*)

		1965–1978	1979–1985	1986–1997	1998–2002	1965–1985	1986–2002
E. Contributions							
Intra-industry TFP growth	Manufacturing	−0.78	0.39	0.38	0.31	−0.86	0.36
	Others	−4.66	−0.25	0.33	0.19	−1.64	0.29
Capital reallocation effect	Manufacturing	−2.79	0.18	0.58	0.10	−1.43	0.42
	Others	3.21	−0.04	−0.58	−0.10	1.42	−0.42
Labor reallocation effect	Manufacturing	−0.66	0.03	−0.14	0.09	−0.32	−0.06
	Others	1.45	0.29	0.24	−0.09	0.22	0.13

Note: Vertical sums of contributions are equal to the total economy values.
Source: Author's calculations.

Table 6.6. Industrial Contributions to Reallocation Effects in the Manufacturing Sector.

	Intra-industry TFP Growth (Percentage Points)						Capital Reallocation Effect (Percentage Points)						Labor Reallocation Effect (Percentage Points)					
	1965–1978	1979-1985	1986–1997	1998–2002	1965–1985	1986–2002	1965–1978	1979–1985	1986–1997	1998–2002	1965–1985	1986–2002	1965–1978	1979–1985	1986–1997	1998–2002	1965–1985	1986–2002
Food	0.03	−0.01	0.16	0.01	0.07	0.06	0.07	0.00	−0.16	−0.08	0.03	0.01	0.10	0.00	−0.02	−0.02	0.04	0.00
Tex	−0.05	0.00	0.03	0.00	−0.03	0.01	0.22	0.00	−0.04	0.00	0.08	−0.01	−0.03	0.00	−0.01	0.00	−0.01	0.00
Wear	−0.02	0.03	−0.02	0.00	−0.11	−0.01	0.01	0.00	−0.07	−0.02	0.00	0.00	−0.05	0.00	−0.03	0.00	−0.02	−0.01
Leat	0.00	0.00	0.01	0.00	0.00	0.00	0.00	0.00	0.00	0.01	0.00	−0.01	−0.01	0.00	0.00	0.00	0.00	0.00
Wood	−0.15	0.00	0.01	−0.01	−0.12	0.00	0.02	0.00	−0.02	0.00	0.00	0.00	−0.07	0.00	−0.01	0.00	−0.03	0.00
Furn	0.00	0.00	0.00	−0.01	−0.01	0.00	−0.08	0.00	−0.03	−0.01	−0.03	0.00	0.01	0.00	0.00	−0.01	0.00	0.00
Paper	−0.01	0.00	0.05	0.02	0.00	0.01	−0.06	0.00	−0.04	0.00	−0.07	−0.01	−0.01	0.00	0.00	0.00	−0.01	0.00
Pub	0.03	0.01	0.49	0.05	−0.03	0.19	0.08	0.00	−0.18	0.27	0.05	−0.28	0.00	0.00	0.03	−0.02	0.00	0.00
Chem	−0.11	0.05	−0.03	−0.54	−0.26	0.12	−0.29	−0.01	0.28	−3.98	0.01	3.40	0.01	0.00	0.03	−0.04	0.01	0.00
Petr	−0.15	−0.03	−1.13	−0.31	−0.01	−0.39	0.29	0.02	0.14	−0.08	−0.10	0.11	−0.03	0.00	−0.01	−0.01	−0.01	0.00
Rub	−0.10	0.00	0.05	0.00	−0.08	0.02	−0.72	0.00	0.01	−0.02	−0.29	0.02	0.05	0.00	0.02	0.01	0.01	0.00
Nonmet	−0.01	0.00	0.11	−0.07	0.00	0.06	0.25	0.00	−0.01	0.09	0.06	−0.08	0.03	0.00	0.04	0.00	0.02	0.01
Met	−0.08	0.00	0.16	0.00	−0.05	0.07	0.29	0.00	−0.07	−0.01	0.09	−0.01	−0.04	0.00	−0.01	−0.01	−0.01	0.00
Fabmet	−0.07	0.01	0.07	−0.14	−0.08	0.06	−0.71	0.01	0.23	−0.03	−0.39	0.09	0.00	0.00	0.00	0.00	−0.01	0.00
Mach	0.07	0.00	−0.04	−0.06	0.05	−0.01	−0.85	0.01	−0.04	−0.05	−0.46	0.03	−0.11	0.00	−0.09	−0.04	−0.04	−0.02
Elec	0.02	0.06	1.85	−0.14	−0.19	0.80	−1.17	−0.01	2.01	3.35	−0.25	−2.15	−0.28	0.00	−0.37	−0.13	−0.14	−0.08
Prec	0.00	0.00	0.17	−0.12	0.01	0.10	0.16	0.00	−0.02	0.10	0.04	−0.09	−0.05	0.00	−0.02	−0.02	−0.03	−0.01
Tran	−0.09	−0.01	−0.20	0.17	−0.02	−0.12	0.09	0.01	0.18	0.12	−0.09	−0.05	−0.11	0.00	−0.07	0.00	−0.06	−0.01
Total	−0.69	0.08	1.72	−1.13	−0.83	0.98	−2.40	0.03	2.15	−0.34	−1.31	0.96	−0.59	0.01	−0.53	−0.28	−0.29	−0.13

Notes: 1. Estimates are based on real value-added deflated by SMPI.
2. The figures refer to percentages of manufacturing TFP growth for the relevant period.
3. Bold figures refer to the relevant values of the promoted industries for the major sub-periods.

Source: Author's calculations.

periods, respectively. For the period 1980–1990, Wong and Gan (1994) also found contributions of reallocation effects to TFP growth over 60 percent. This characteristic of the manufacturing sector calls for a detailed decomposition of TFP growth at the industry level as presented in Table 6.6, where the column sums of industry contributions correspond to the manufacturing aggregates which are presented in Table 6.5. Capital reallocation effect stands out as it accounts for more than 50 percent of manufacturing TFP growth for both pre-1985 and post-1985 periods and labor reallocation effect is relatively unimportant, with negative contribution after 1985. This is a period where the labor market was gradually liberalized and there was a large shift of labor to service sectors.

Reallocation of capital towards the promoted industries paid off well in terms of contribution to manufacturing TFP growth in the pre-1985 era except the case of electrical and electronics machinery industry. This is most likely because this industry consisted mainly of assembly activities with not much technology transfer. Negative or very low TFP growth rates in promoted industries (intra-industry TFP growth effect) partially explain extremely low manufacturing TFP growth before 1985. It is interesting that the stimulation of producers to shift to higher value-added activities by the high wage policy (1979–1985) did not produce any TFP growth in manufacturing (0.08 percent) and the reallocations of labor and capital did not have a significant impact on manufacturing TFP growth.

After 1985, TFP growth resulted largely from the reallocations of resources. Here, we ignore the period 1998–2002 because of highly absurd numbers which result from the Asian financial crisis and other external shocks, e.g., the slump in world electronics markets. The results of the analysis in Table 6.5 reveal that both of the two most important promoted industries, electrical and electronics machinery and chemicals industries, exhibit highly positive capital reallocation effects while the former is dominant. In other words, capital reallocations toward promoted industries had a high payoff for manufacturing TFP growth. Note that negative labor reallocation effects of this period result mainly from electrical and electronics machinery industry, because of the release of some labor from restructuring electrical and electronics machinery industry to service sectors.

To sum up, the reallocations of resources in the manufacturing sector, stimulated by the industrial policies of the Singaporean government, worked generally in favor of aggregate TFP growth both before and after 1985, but much stronger in the post-1985 era. With the initially low TFP growth rates turning to positive after the 1985 recession, promoted industries contributed to TFP growth both by leading TFP growth rates and through their resource reallocation effects. To the extent that industrial diversification and changing industrial policies after 1985 that incorporated the opportunities of globalization and regionalization succeeded in raising manufacturing TFP growth performance, one can argue that such changes in industrial policies benefited the manufacturing sector and the economy.

Note that a dynamic adjustment mechanism that creates reallocation effects involves not only differences in marginal products of capital and labor but also changes in the sectoral demand structures (Massell, 1961). Here the analysis is purely supply-side and changes in demand are taken as exogenous. Certain sectors experienced sharp declines in demand for their products from the late 1970s to the 1980s, especially petroleum refining and transport equipment (i.e., shipbuilding and ship-repairing) industries whose output shares in manufacturing also declined steadily in this period. Note that capital reallocation effects involving these two declining industries are positive, most likely due to the fact that these industries faced a slump in world demand for their products. On the other hand, chemicals, precision equipment, and electrical and electronic machinery industries experienced high demand for their products. This led to an increase in real wages in these industries and to high rates of return to capital especially for the first two. Strong government involvement in the direction of investment capital (both foreign and local) into the areas designated by the government according to its industrial policies resulted in highly positive capital reallocation effects in the period 1986–1997.

6.5. TFP Growth: A Policy Discussion

The influence of industrial policies on TFP growth in the manufacturing sector was found to be different before and after 1985. Before 1985, aggregate TFP growth rate in the manufacturing sector was found to be negative. This figure turned to positive after 1985. Therefore, there is a very sharp difference between aggregate manufacturing TFP growth performances between these two periods. The impact of industrial policies on

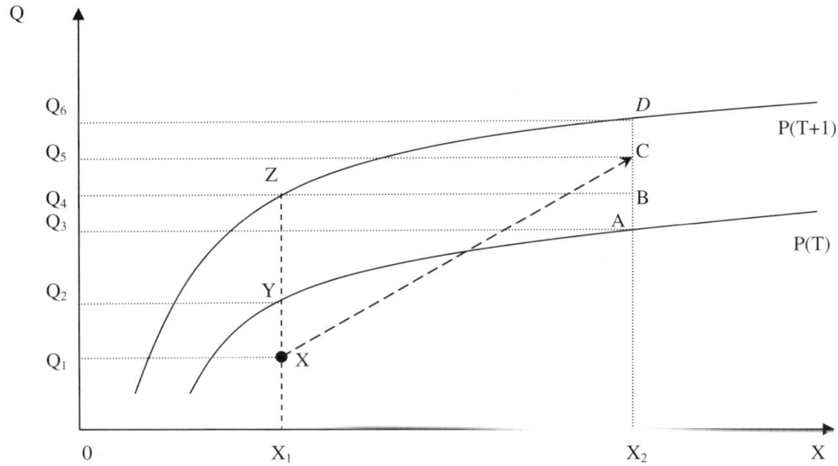

Fig. 6.3. Technical efficiency and technological change. *Source*: Adopted from Sun (2002).

aggregate manufacturing TFP growth rates runs through induced resource reallocations across manufacturing industries. Standard economic theory states that reallocations of resources increases efficiency in production if more productive resources are shifted to industries where productivity levels are higher.

To interpret the changes in TFP growth performance of manufacturing industries and the sources of output growth in Singapore, we will make use of the decomposition of output growth used in the stochastic production frontier approach.[14] Figure 6.3 portrays the sources of output growth. The vertical axis represents the level of output (Q) and the horizontal axis represents the level of inputs (X) used in production. The two curves refer to production frontiers which represent the maximum amount of output that can be obtained using a particular technology. A point below the production frontier points to inefficiency in production. Over time, production frontiers may shift for some reason (e.g., revolutionary changes in information technologies) from $P(T)$ at time T to $P(T+1)$ at time $T+1$. Each frontier represents production technology. An upper production curve means a higher level of production technology and movement along the same curve (such

[14]Aigner *et al.* (1977) and Battese and Coelli (1992) provide a description of the stochastic production frontier approach.

as from point Z to D) means the use of same technology but different combinations of outputs. Hence, output can also be increased with no changes in the level of technology but with accumulating the inputs used in production.

Figure 6.3 also presents a movement from a point such as X at time T and to a point such as C at time $T + 1$ (as shown by dashed arrow in the figure). This move can be decomposed into three components: change in technical efficiency of production, technological progress with initial input endowment, and output growth due to input accumulation.[15] The methodology used in this chapter first decomposed output growth into input accumulation (i.e., movement along the production frontier) and disembodied technological change, which is the sum of change in technical efficiency and technological progress in this case. Recall that technical efficiency refers to the distance from the production frontier whereas technological progress refers to the shift of the production frontier using the same amounts of inputs. In other words, the former refers to catching up with existing technologies and the latter refers to advancement in technology.

An estimation of these two sources of TFP growth, technical efficiency and technological progress, is not aimed in this section. Three previous studies have already investigated the extent of technical efficiency changes and technological progress in Singapore's manufacturing industries (Mahadevan and Kalirajan, 2000; Sun, 2002; Koh *et al.*, 2004). Their findings of TFP growth are not directly comparable to translog productivity growth indices computed in this study. However, they all emphasize substantial declines in technical efficiency before 1985, which led to inferior levels of technical efficiency changes. They also found moderately positive technological progress after 1985 while technical efficiency changes

[15] Output growth can be decomposed into its sources using the distances between the points in Figure 6.3 as follows:

$$Q_5 - Q_1 = XY + YZ + BC = XY + YZ + BD - CD = [XY - CD] + YZ + BD$$
$$= [(Q_2 - Q_1) - (Q_6 - Q_5)] + (Q_4 - Q_2) + (Q_6 - Q_4).$$

The first two terms in the last line are the distances of the production points from the production frontiers. The difference between these two terms refers to the change in technical efficiency. The third term is the shift in the production function over time from $P(T)$ to $P(T + 1)$, with the initial endowments of inputs (X_1). This refers to technological progress. Finally, the fourth term measures the change in output by a movement along the new production frontier $P(T + 1)$ from point Z to D. Noticeably, this represents an accumulation of inputs with the new technology.

remained very low. To put it the other way, the important role of technical efficiency changes before 1985 was replaced with technological progress in the post-1985 era. A common finding between this study and stochastic frontier studies is the significant improvement in technological progress after 1985, although the magnitudes are different.

It is necessary to pay attention to the decline in technical efficiency change after 1985. The level of technical efficiency can be improved through "software" aspects of productivity, i.e., learning-by-doing, upgrading of labor skills, on-the-job-training, etc. Small technical efficiency changes imply the failure of industries to make effective use of these means to improve overall efficiency, i.e., TFP growth. Young (1992) argues that rapid and continuous technology upgrading (which is represented here by technological progress component) is an important factor behind low TFP growth in Singapore's manufacturing sector. He argues that this is because although the new knowledge embedded in transferred technology cannot be absorbed within a short period of time, new technologies were consecutively introduced before previously transferred technology is absorbed fully. This argument points to the abovementioned findings of previous studies that technological progress coexisted with small or negative gains in technical efficiency changes in the post-1985 era.

An important policy implication of these findings is that policies focusing on improving the existing technologies can be the best candidates to stimulate TFP growth. This means the absorption of technologies by way of learning-by-doing and intra-firm productivity measures including labor training. In this sense, it appears that the launch of various policies by the government in the 1990s, which aimed at productivity enhancement is not contentious. Especially LIUP and various schemes designed for skills upgrading might be effective in the near future as a robust source of manufacturing TFP growth.

In short, the analysis in this chapter showed that industrial policies of the government before 1985 did not bring about technical efficiency or technological progress in Singapore manufacturing. In return, TFP growth was minus. In other words, allocative efficiency had priority in industrial policies over technical efficiency. After 1985, the importance of the absorption of technological advances by the labor force was still an important issue on which the government placed top priority. The external wing of the economy may also have been a deterministic factor behind positive GDP and TFP growth. Lower value-added manufacturing activities have been moved to lower cost countries such as Indonesia, Malaysia, and, recently, China. The remaining activities are the higher value-added manufacturing industries and other high value-added services such as finance, business, engineering, info-com, health, consultancy, education, and engineering services, among others. This restructuring surely leads to an increase in TFP growth.

CHAPTER 7

PRODUCTIVITY GROWTH AND RESOURCE ALLOCATION: AN INTERNATIONAL COMPARISON OF SINGAPORE WITH EAST ASIA

In this section, the impact of resource allocation on productivity growth in Singapore (both labor productivity and TFP) will be compared with the results for other countries. This will be done in two steps. First, Singapore will be compared with the other implementers of industrial countries in its region. As already discussed in Section 2, these countries are Japan, Korea, and Taiwan. Especially, the last two underwent a remarkable industrial transformation around the same time period as Singapore and metamorphosed from producers of traditional light industry products to producers of heavy industry and technologically sophisticated products. This transformation was associated with structural changes, i.e., changes in the composition of production and factor inputs (capital and labor) among industries.[1] Singapore is generally compared with Hong Kong for both are small cities and developed as free ports. However, due to insignificance of the manufacturing production in Hong Kong, we do not include it in the analysis here. The findings of similar other studies are then listed and compared with Singapore. Since we are dealing with industrial development in particular, the analysis is confined to only manufacturing industries rather than the aggregate economy.

[1]There is a long debate on the sources of economic growth in East Asia, specifically about whether it was due to accumulation of physical and human capitals and virtual insignificance of technological change or assimilation of new technologies that these countries maintained rapid growth rates. However, as pointed out by van Ark and Timmer (2003), there is another dimension of industrial development in these countries: "... the recent debate on the sources of growth in Asia has neglected the underlying dynamics of changes in productivity growth within sectors and related to this, the shift of resources from low to high-productivity sectors."

Most studies about industrial development in developing economies deal with structural change and productivity separately. Cross-country comparison of productivity with catching-up has recently been subject to many studies (e.g., Choi, 1990; Szirmai, 1993; OECD, 1996; Wagner and van Ark, 1996). It has been argued that the catch-up process of Asian economies stemmed from productivity growth of individual industries and the allocation of production factors from low- to high-productivity industries (e.g., Pilat, 1996; Wagner and van Ark, 1996). There is a need to examine the impact of structural changes in the manufacturing sectors of the East Asian economies on partial and total factor productivity growth.

7.1. Sources of Data and Periodization

In comparing Singapore with other countries, there is a need to ensure consistency in industrial classification. Manufacturing sector is divided into 15 industries as listed in Table 7.1. Based on this classification, changing output and employment shares of industries are presented in Table 7.2. Output refers to real value-added normalized by relevant producers' price indices. Table 7.2 reveals that the industries whose output shares were considerably higher were transport vehicles and electrical and electronic machinery industries along with food manufacturing industry in Japan, chemicals, basic machinery, electrical and electronic machinery, and transport equipment industries along with the traditional food and textiles industries in both Korea and Taiwan.

Periodization: For practical reasons, the industrial development experiences of the countries in question are categorized into distinctive periods. For Japan, the periods are 1960–1972 (high growth), 1973–1984 (from oil shock to the Plaza Accord which led to rapid appreciation of the yen and a relocation of industries towards overseas bases), 1985–1990 (bubble period), and 1991–2002 (recession). The periods in Korea are 1960–1970 (early export-orientation), 1971–1979 (Heavy and Chemical Industrialization Drive), 1980–1988 (structural adjustment), and 1989–1996 (technological sophistication and post-crisis). Finally, the periods in Taiwan are as follows: 1961–1972 (early export-orientation), 1973-1985 (science and technology

Table 7.1. Major Industry Groups.

Industry	Corresponding ISIC Categories	Major Industries Included
Food	3100, 311, 312, 3130, 3140	Food, beverages, and tobacco manufactures
Tex.	3200, 3210, 3220, 3230, 3240	Textiles, wearing apparel, leather and products, and footwear
Wood	3300, 3310, 3320	Wood, wood products, furniture, and fixtures
Pap.	3400, 3410, 3420	Paper, paper products, printing, and publishing
Chem.	3500, 3510, 3520, 3521, 3522, 3523, 2529	Industrial chemicals and other chemical products
Pet.	3530, 3540	Petroleum, petroleum refineries, coal products
Plas.	3550, 3560	Rubber and plastic products
Min.	3600, 3610, 3620, 3690	Non-metallic minerals, pottery, glass products
Bas. met.	3700, 3710, 3720	Basic metals, iron and steel, non-ferrous metals
Met. pr.	3800, 3810	Fabricated metal products (except machinery and equipment)
Mach.	3820, 3821, 3822, 3823, 3824, 3829	Non electrical (basic) machinery and equipment
Elec.	3825, 3830, 3831, 3832, 3833, 3839	Electrical appliances, electronic machinery, office equipment
Tran.	3840, 3841, 3842, 3843, 3844, 3845, 3849	Transport equipment (transport vehicles, shipbuilding and repair, etc.)
Prec.	3850	Professional equipment, optical equipment, precision equipment
Others	3900	Other manufacturing

promotion), 1986–1996 (restructuring and industrial hollowing out), and 1997–2002 (post-crisis).

What is of interest in the periodization of this type is the results for the intervals during which industrial policies that encouraged capacity creation and export promotion were actively implemented by the governments. These periods are roughly 1960–1984 for Japan, 1960–1988 for Korea, and

Table 7.2. Shares of Industries in Manufacturing Value-Added and Labor.

	Japan (1960–2002)				Korea (1960–2002)				Taiwan (1961–2002)			
	1960–1972	1973–1984	1985–1990	1991–2002	1960–1970	1971–1979	1980–1988	1989–2002	1961–1973	1974–1985	1986–1996	1997–2002
Value-added shares (percent)												
Food	17.7	15.6	14.2	12.0	15.8	18.0	14.7	9.0	24.6	12.5	9.5	6.0
Tex.	8.9	6.7	5.5	3.7	9.7	21.7	19.1	10.2	10.4	16.4	11.6	7.6
Wood	6.4	4.4	3.3	2.5	4.3	5.3	2.4	1.0	5.5	3.1	2.0	1.0
Pap.	4.3	3.4	3.7	3.6	3.7	4.3	5.2	4.8	7.6	5.4	3.7	1.9
Chem.	6.8	7.4	8.1	8.5	2.6	8.0	8.3	10.2	18.2	13.4	10.7	8.8
Pet.	8.8	7.6	3.9	3.7	9.9	9.7	2.8	2.9	8.0	5.9	5.2	6.0
Plas.	3.3	3.7	4.3	4.3	6.8	5.4	4.6	4.1	3.1	6.5	7.8	6.4
Min.	5.5	4.2	3.5	3.1	3.8	6.2	4.7	4.3	6.8	4.5	4.2	2.6
Bas. met	13.8	13.6	10.2	8.6	2.2	5.7	7.7	6.5	2.8	4.7	6.7	6.4
Met. pr.	4.6	5.1	5.0	4.9	1.4	2.3	4.2	4.3	2.4	4.0	6.3	7.8
Mach.	6.3	7.5	8.6	8.0	0.7	1.9	4.4	7.8	5.7	9.5	10.2	7.3
Elec.	3.8	6.9	13.1	19.7	2.3	6.0	11.4	20.2	3.2	8.5	15.4	27.5
Tran.	7.8	10.9	13.1	14.1	1.7	3.3	7.0	11.6	0.0	1.2	7.1	6.7
Prec.	1.0	1.3	1.5	1.3	0.1	0.5	1.0	1.0	0.0	0.3	1.1	0.9
Others	1.7	1.8	1.9	2.0	0.7	1.7	2.4	2.2	1.7	5.7	4.5	3.0

(*Continued*)

Table 7.2. (*Continued*)

	Japan (1960–2002)				Korea (1960–2002)				Taiwan (1961–2002)			
	1960–1972	1973–1984	1985–1990	1991–2002	1960–1970	1971–1979	1980–1988	1989–2002	1961–1973	1974–1985	1986–1996	1997–2002
Employment shares (percent)												
Food	14.0	14.6	15.1	14.8	9.5	11.4	8.5	7.2	13.4	6.8	5.3	4.5
Tex.	16.1	13.7	11.5	9.1	18.6	35.0	30.4	19.5	25.5	23.3	15.4	10.9
Wood	8.1	7.0	5.2	4.5	0.5	0.8	1.1	1.5	7.3	5.3	3.6	1.9
Pap.	5.0	4.9	5.6	6.2	3.9	5.1	4.6	5.5	5.2	3.7	4.6	5.0
Chem.	4.2	3.5	3.1	3.5	3.5	5.2	4.4	5.1	4.4	4.0	4.0	4.5
Pet.	0.4	0.5	0.4	0.3	0.8	1.2	0.7	0.6	1.3	1.2	1.2	1.2
Plas.	4.3	4.5	5.2	5.8	3.2	4.8	5.9	5.3	7.3	11.8	10.8	8.7
Min.	4.9	4.9	4.2	4.1	4.1	4.8	4.8	4.1	5.4	4.8	4.1	3.4
Bas. met	5.5	5.2	4.4	4.1	1.8	3.6	4.3	4.0	1.3	1.4	2.3	2.6
Met. pr.	7.5	7.7	7.5	8.2	2.7	4.2	4.7	6.2	7.5	8.4	11.8	13.9
Mach.	9.8	9.1	8.9	9.6	2.3	3.5	5.1	9.6	9.4	9.1	10.9	11.3
Elec.	9.5	11.8	16.0	16.6	2.3	9.4	12.8	15.7	7.4	14.5	17.9	21.3
Tran.	6.6	7.7	8.4	8.9	2.8	4.6	6.9	10.2	2.3	2.3	5.2	5.8
Prec.	1.9	2.1	1.9	1.8	0.4	1.2	1.6	1.6	0.3	0.6	1.0	1.0
Others	2.6	2.7	2.6	2.5	5.9	5.3	4.2	3.6	4.7	5.8	6.1	4.1

Source: Author's calculations.

1961–1985 for Taiwan. Industrial policies of these governments underwent significant changes after these periods towards more functional (i.e., emphasizing competitiveness rather than capacity creation) rather than the previous general-purpose industrial policies. In addition, due to the increasing competition from other developing countries, national industrialists were forced to move towards higher-value-added manufacturing with technology creation. As a result, national industries were restructured during 1980–1988 in Korea and during 1986–1996 in Taiwan. We are mostly interested in how resource shifts and reallocations during these periods affected the aggregate productivity growth performance of the manufacturing factor, which is the major determinant of long-run growth. In the case of Japan, the long recession during the 1990s led to a restructuring of national industries. However, the mechanism that led to the restructuring of national industries was not as in Korea and Taiwan. It resulted mainly due to the bubble burst which stimulated reallocation of resources in economic sectors.

Output: Output refers to real industrial value-added at constant prices in national currencies. Value-added data for Japanese industries are obtained from the *Japan Industrial Productivity Database 2006* (JIP 2006), which was compiled in collaboration between the Research Institute of Economy, Trade, and Industry and Hitotsubashi University and from various issues of the *Census of Manufactures* (*Kougyou Toukeihyou*). The details about construction sources of data in the JIP 2006 Database are available in Fukao *et al.* (2007). For Korea, real value-added figures are taken from various issues of the *Major Statistics of Korean Economy* and the *Report on Mining and Manufacturing Survey* (*Whole Country*). Value-added data are deflated by producer's price indices obtained from Korea Statistical Yearbook, and the *Long-term Data Series* of the Bank of Japan. Real value-added figures calculated at 1991 prices are obtained from Timmer (1998) and extended using the industrial value-added and wholesale price index data obtained from the Directorate General of Budget, Accounting and Statistics (DGBAS) *Statistical Yearbook* and various issues of the *Industry, Commerce and Service Census* published by the Republic of China National Statistics.

Labor: Employment data are obtained from various issues of industrial census for Japan, *Major Economic Statistics of Korean Economy* for Korea, and from Timmer (1998) and *Statistical Yearbook* for Taiwan. Labor input employed in TFP refers to total hours worked. These are calculated by multiplying monthly working hours by the factor 12 to obtain annual working hours per employee, and then multiplying by the number of workers. These data take into account only the actual working hours of the employees, including overtime but excluding recess. The sources for the actual working-hour data are *Annual Report on the Monthly Labor Survey – National Survey* for Japan, *Yearbook of Labor Statistics* for Korea. For Taiwan, working-hour data were not available, therefore labor input for Taiwanese industries reflect only the number of employees engaging in production.

To calculate labor shares in value-added, workers' remuneration data are obtained from the manufacturing censuses for Japan, from the *Yearbook of Labor Statistics* for Korea, and from the same abovementioned sources of employment data for Taiwan. These data include all payments made to employees including benefits. Total remuneration per employee is multiplied by number of workers and divided to value-added to calculate labor share in output. Subtracting this from unity, the share of capital is obtained.

Capital: Three types of tangible and reproducible assets are included capital stock estimations: (i) building and construction, (ii) plant and equipment, and (iii) transport equipment and others. Land, consumer durables, residential buildings and structures, and inventories, are excluded. To calculate capital stock the perpetual inventory method as shown in Eq. (6.38). It is assumed that the asset lives for each type of asset are asset-wise the same across countries. The data on capital stock therefore span enough number of years in order to cover the asset life of the longest-living asset.

Benchmark year capital stocks were available from other sources. The benchmark years are 1955 for Japan, 1968 for Korea, and 1961 for Taiwan. Real capital stock series at 1995 prices with benchmark values for Korean industries are obtained from Pyo (1998) and Pyo *et al.* (2006). These series are based on the results of the National Wealth Survey of 1968 and extend the benchmark figures using the industry-level fixed investment data. Real capital stock figures calculated at 1991 prices in Taiwan are obtained from Timmer (1998) and extended using the industrial data for gross fixed assets and the GDP deflators for fixed investments obtained from the national accounts published by the DGBAS and various issues of the *Industry, Commerce and Service Census*. For Japanese industries the benchmark values are obtained from the *National Wealth Survey* of 1955, whose results are also available in EPA (1967). Capital stock series are extended by adding net investment data to the benchmark values using Eq. (5.2). These data are compiled from the manufacturing censuses.

The deflators for capital assets are calculated from the national income accounts of each country. Finally, capital consumption allowance rates are adopted from Jorgenson and Sullivan (1981): 0.0361 for buildings, 0.1047 for machinery and equipment, and 0.2935 for transport equipment.

7.2. Industry-Level Productivity Performances

Table 7.3 presents labor productivity growth rates for the three periods. Labor productivity is measured as real value-added per employee. Labor productivity growth rates were particularly very high during high-growth (first period) and the bubble periods (second period) in Japan, during the Heavy and Chemical Industrialization Drive (second period) and technological sophistication periods (third period) in Korea, and the early export-orientation period in Taiwan. Productivity growth in Japan slowed down drastically after the burst of the bubble in the early 1990s. Productivity growth rates of Korean industries are the most impressive among the three countries. For the overall period, in average, labor productivity growth rates in the heavy and chemical industries for all countries tend to be higher than the primary and traditional industries.

7.3. The Impact of Structural Change on Labor Productivity

Aggregate labor productivity growth in the manufacturing sector is decomposed using Eq. (6.8). The results for Japan, Korea, and Taiwan are presented in Table 7.4. The results reveal that reallocation of labor across manufacturing industries was not important in explaining labor productivity gains for the past three decades in manufacturing sectors, accounting for small portions of labor productivity growth (3 percent in Singapore as it was found before, and a few percentage points in Japan, Korea, and Taiwan).

Table 7.3. Labor Productivity Growth Rates.

	Japan (1960–2002)					Korea (1960–2002)					Taiwan (1961–2002)				
	1960–1972	1973–1984	1985–1990	1991–2002	All	1960–1970	1971–1979	1980–1988	1989–2002	All	1961–1973	1974–1985	1986–1996	1997–2002	All
Food	11.9	0.7	2.9	1.0	4.5	9.1	13.0	6.5	7.1	8.6	4.6	8.1	5.1	0.9	5.2
Tex.	13.0	1.8	3.0	0.7	5.0	9.9	13.2	8.3	5.1	8.5	12.5	7.9	5.5	1.1	7.6
Wood	10.5	1.7	4.9	0.5	4.5	−4.6	12.0	−0.7	5.1	4.3	10.3	0.6	8.5	−3.7	5.0
Pap.	11.6	1.0	2.9	1.2	4.5	8.0	12.3	9.3	6.1	8.7	9.3	2.1	−2.3	1.1	2.9
Chem.	14.6	6.3	5.7	1.6	7.4	30.2	14.5	9.1	14.0	14.7	13.5	1.0	4.2	1.2	5.5
Pet.	12.1	−1.3	3.0	3.9	4.8	33.1	0.4	17.5	10.2	12.1	13.5	2.6	4.9	7.9	7.2
Plas.	14.9	2.9	3.8	1.3	6.2	9.5	12.2	6.9	8.5	9.1	20.0	4.5	10.5	0.3	10.0
Min.	12.2	0.4	5.1	1.7	5.0	27.0	10.2	8.0	9.1	11.1	3.9	5.2	7.8	−3.9	4.2
Bas. met	7.4	2.9	2.3	2.0	3.9	4.8	17.9	8.8	6.5	9.7	11.9	5.2	3.2	7.4	7.0
Met. pr.	14.6	3.1	4.1	0.5	6.0	5.1	15.6	14.0	4.7	9.8	11.9	4.5	9.0	1.3	7.4
Mach.	13.8	6.6	4.8	−0.3	6.6	5.9	24.2	10.7	11.6	13.9	19.0	6.6	3.2	2.3	8.7
Elec.	13.2	7.5	8.8	6.6	9.1	11.3	6.8	12.1	20.2	13.9	17.4	6.0	12.2	9.5	11.5
Tran.	13.4	3.9	8.4	1.8	6.8	16.6	14.4	12.0	12.9	13.4	24.2	1.8	2.2	3.9	8.8
Prec.	13.2	6.2	5.1	1.4	6.8	17.0	19.5	11.9	9.5	13.4	−6.2	0.6	1.9	7.4	0.1
Others	12.3	5.2	6.7	3.5	7.1	24.6	29.7	11.3	12.4	17.8	19.6	7.3	6.1	0.9	9.6

Source: Author's calculations.

Table 7.4. Shift-Share Analysis of Productivity Growth.

		Intra-Industry Productivity Growth	Static Shift Effects	Dynamic Shift Effects
Japan	1960–1972	102.6	−2.2	−0.4
	1973–1984	97.0	5.8	−2.7
	1985–1990	108.1	−7.7	−0.4
	1991–2002	88.0	12.2	−0.2
	Overall	98.3	2.4	−0.7
Korea	1960–1970	114.4	−4.7	−9.7
	1971–1979	117.9	−8.6	−9.3
	1980–1988	100.4	1.8	−2.2
	1989–2002	98.3	2.5	−0.8
	Overall	107.2	0.4	−7.6
Taiwan	1961–1973	124.9	−21.3	−3.6
	1974–1985	111.5	−5.1	−6.4
	1986–1996	82.9	17.2	−0.1
	1997–2002	93.4	5.5	1.1
	Overall	97.1	4.5	−1.6

Source: Author's calculations.

In Japan, labor productivity growth resulted almost entirely from intra-industry productivity growth during the first two periods (1960–1984), while shift effects summed to 12 percent of aggregate productivity growth during the 1990s recession, i.e., there was a reallocation of labor across industries due to restructuring of national industries. This positive figure for shift effects is almost entirely born by static shift effects, i.e., labor shifted to industries already enjoying higher productivity levels. Therefore, it can be asserted that there was a restructuring in the Japanese manufacturing sector during the lost decade of the 1990s in such a way that some high-productivity industries called for a shift of labor towards themselves. Table 7.5 shows that these industries are transport equipment, and to a lesser degree, food and chemicals industries, which are the major contributors to static-shift effects. During the previous periods, positive shift effects stemmed from chemicals, food, and electrical and electronic machinery and transport equipment industries. However, prior to the 1990s, these were cancelled out by negative shift effects arising generally from traditional manufacturing industries, such as textiles, wood, and paper.

During the Heavy and Chemical Industrialization Drive of the 1970s in Korea, the impact of labor shifts across industries on aggregate labor productivity growth was about −18 percent. During the following two periods, aggregate labor productivity growth resulted almost entirely from intra-industry effect. For the overall period, labor shifts worked against aggregate labor productivity. Positive shift effects arose mainly from electrical and electronic machinery and transport equipment industries whereas negative shift effects arose generally from textiles and food industries.

Finally in Taiwan, aggregate productivity growth resulted entirely from intra-industry productivity growth for the overall period. During the early export-orientation and the following science and technology promotion periods (1961–1985), shift effects were negative about one-tenth of aggregate productivity growth. The industrial composition of shift effects in Table 7.5 shows that during this period, the positive shift effect by the electrical and electronic machinery industry was more than offset by the negative shift effects by traditional industries, especially food and textiles. During the restructuring period (1986–1996), positive shift effects by electrical and electronic machinery and transport equipment industries was enough to keep the total shift effects at a positive level despite the counter figure observed in textiles. In this period, shift effects accounted for about 22 percent of aggregate productivity growth. After the Asian crisis (1997–2002), electrical and electronic machinery industry still reported a highly positive shift effect but this time it was trimmed largely by the negative shift effects by the traditional industries.

Overall, these findings shed some light to the pattern of industrial transformation in the East Asian countries from a productivity perspective. During the early export-orientation and high-growth periods, shift effects are generally negative. In Japan, the magnitude of this negative figure is smaller than in Korea and Taiwan. Following the restructuring efforts that came as a result of maturity levels reached after long periods of industrialization or as a result of large-scale shocks (recession in Japan and Asian crisis in Korea and Taiwan), shift effects turned positive, yet small as a fraction of aggregate productivity growth.

Table 7.5. The Impact of Labor Shifts on Aggregate Manufacturing Labor Productivity.

	Intra-Industry Productivity Growth (percent of total)					Static Shift Effects (percent of total)					Dynamic Shift Effects (percent of total)				
	1960–1972	1973–1984	1985–1990	1991–2002	All	1960–1972	1973–1984	1985–1990	1991–2002	All	1960–1972	1973–1984	1985–1990	1991–2002	All
Japan															
Food	**17.9**	3.9	**9.1**	3.3	**9.4**	−1.7	**8.1**	−6.3	6.0	1.4	−0.2	0.2	−0.3	0.0	−0.1
Tex.	**8.9**	4.3	3.6	0.9	4.7	−1.2	−4.0	−1.5	−5.9	−3.1	−0.2	−0.1	0.0	0.0	−0.1
Wood	5.2	2.7	3.5	0.5	3.0	−0.6	−3.9	−1.4	−2.0	−1.7	−0.1	−0.1	−0.1	0.0	−0.1
Pap.	4.3	1.3	2.4	1.7	2.6	−0.4	0.5	2.3	0.6	0.6	−0.1	0.1	0.0	0.0	0.0
Chem.	**7.7**	**16.2**	**9.8**	3.9	**8.4**	−0.9	−3.6	−1.0	4.7	0.3	−0.2	−0.7	−0.1	−0.3	−0.3
Pet.	**9.0**	**−7.0**	2.7	5.2	3.9	−0.1	4.8	−4.8	0.3	0.0	−0.1	−1.6	−0.2	−0.1	−0.4
Plas.	3.7	3.8	3.6	2.0	3.2	−0.1	1.8	1.6	1.7	1.1	0.0	0.2	0.1	0.0	0.0
Min.	5.2	0.5	3.8	1.7	3.1	0.4	−1.6	−1.1	−0.8	−0.6	0.0	−0.2	−0.1	−0.1	−0.1
Bas. met	**14.3**	**13.5**	5.2	6.9	**10.2**	−0.7	**−7.0**	−2.9	−1.9	−2.6	0.0	−0.6	−0.1	0.0	−0.2
Met. pr.	5.2	5.4	4.3	0.8	3.7	0.4	−1.7	2.2	0.8	0.5	0.1	−0.1	0.1	0.0	0.0
Mach.	6.1	**17.0**	**8.7**	0.1	6.7	0.5	−3.8	3.7	2.5	1.0	0.2	−0.4	0.3	0.1	0.1
Elec.	4.0	**16.5**	**24.1**	**46.3**	**22.7**	0.8	**9.8**	3.2	−1.3	2.2	0.2	0.6	0.2	0.1	0.2
Tran.	**8.4**	**13.1**	**23.1**	**11.0**	**12.8**	1.0	**7.3**	−2.0	**8.5**	3.8	0.1	0.1	−0.2	0.1	0.1
Prec.	1.0	2.8	1.6	0.6	1.3	0.1	−0.1	−0.1	−0.2	−0.1	0.0	0.0	0.0	0.0	0.0
Others	1.6	3.1	2.8	3.1	2.5	0.2	−0.7	0.2	−0.9	−0.3	0.0	−0.1	0.0	−0.1	0.0

(Continued)

Table 7.5. (*Continued*)

	Intra-Industry Productivity Growth (percent of total)					Static Shift Effects (percent of total)					Dynamic Shift Effects (percent of total)				
	1960–1970	1971–1979	1980–1988	1989–2002	All	1960–1970	1971–1979	1980–1988	1989–2002	All	1960–1970	1971–1979	1980–1988	1989–2002	All
Korea															
Food	8.1	**26.4**	**11.0**	6.1	**17.1**	1.8	**−8.1**	−3.7	−1.6	−0.4	−3.5	−2.5	−0.3	−0.4	−1.5
Tex.	8.2	**31.6**	**16.3**	4.3	**11.0**	**5.3**	−2.6	−5.0	−3.3	0.1	−1.0	0.6	−0.1	−0.3	−0.2
Wood	0.4	4.0	−0.7	0.4	−2.2	−0.4	−0.9	1.7	0.0	0.4	−1.3	−2.3	−0.3	−0.1	−3.0
Pap.	2.8	6.4	5.3	1.8	3.5	−1.1	−0.9	−0.2	1.3	−0.1	−0.9	−0.4	−0.1	−0.2	−0.2
Chem.	**13.5**	**14.0**	**8.8**	**11.6**	**15.2**	−0.1	−2.9	−0.4	−0.3	0.0	−0.5	−0.5	−0.3	−0.1	−1.1
Pet.	2.8	−5.6	5.2	1.7	**32.0**	0.5	**−9.7**	−0.2	−0.5	0.6	−1.6	−3.2	−1.3	−0.1	3.6
Plas.	3.4	4.1	4.6	2.5	8.2	−0.5	0.7	1.4	0.2	−0.3	−0.7	−1.8	−0.1	0.0	−3.8
Min.	4.0	6.6	4.5	2.8	**11.3**	1.9	−0.3	−0.9	−0.8	−0.1	−0.8	−0.3	−0.7	−0.1	−1.2
Bas. met	3.5	**8.4**	**7.3**	1.1	1.2	0.3	3.4	−1.0	−0.5	0.1	0.1	0.1	−0.3	0.0	0.2
Met. pr.	2.2	4.2	6.6	1.6	0.9	−1.3	0.9	−0.1	1.2	0.0	0.1	0.3	−0.1	0.0	−0.1
Mach.	8.7	4.7	5.4	**8.6**	0.5	−2.3	1.8	2.3	1.8	0.0	1.1	0.4	0.4	0.2	−0.1
Elec.	**42.1**	6.2	**13.3**	**42.1**	3.0	**−5.2**	**7.2**	**6.2**	2.6	0.1	−0.2	0.0	0.8	−0.2	−0.3
Tran.	**11.8**	3.6	**8.2**	**12.0**	3.1	−3.4	2.7	1.4	2.5	0.0	1.6	0.4	0.2	0.3	−0.2
Prec.	0.7	1.2	1.4	0.6	0.2	−0.2	0.3	0.4	0.0	0.0	0.0	0.0	0.1	0.0	0.0
Others	2.2	2.3	3.2	1.2	2.1	0.0	−0.2	−0.1	−0.1	0.0	−2.1	−0.1	−0.1	0.2	0.3

(*Continued*)

Table 7.5. (*Continued*)

	Intra-Industry Productivity Growth (percent of total)					Static Shift Effects (percent of total)					Dynamic Shift Effects (percent of total)				
	1961–1973	1974–1985	1986–1996	1997–2002	All	1961–1973	1974–1985	1986–1996	1997–2002	All	1961–1973	1974–1985	1986–1996	1997–2002	All
Taiwan															
Food	**10.3**	**18.6**	5.8	−0.4	**7.6**	**−13.7**	**−9.6**	−0.3	−3.0	−4.7	−0.7	−1.0	−0.1	0.3	−0.3
Tex.	**17.4**	**26.7**	**7.4**	2.1	**11.4**	0.8	**−7.7**	**−7.7**	**−5.6**	−5.9	0.2	−0.9	−0.4	0.0	−0.3
Wood	**7.5**	−1.4	2.2	−1.0	1.7	−1.1	−1.5	−1.7	−0.9	−1.4	−0.3	0.2	−0.1	0.0	−0.1
Pap.	**9.8**	1.8	−0.8	0.4	1.6	−3.9	0.4	1.6	0.2	0.2	−0.5	−0.3	0.0	0.0	−0.2
Chem.	**28.2**	1.1	**8.4**	3.2	**9.1**	−5.5	1.4	2.4	4.1	1.3	−1.7	−1.6	0.1	−0.2	−0.6
Pet.	**12.4**	3.5	1.3	**11.3**	5.6	−2.4	−1.7	3.1	−2.7	0.1	−0.7	−1.4	−0.7	−0.3	−0.7
Plas.	5.9	5.2	**8.2**	0.1	5.6	2.6	2.7	−3.4	0.3	−0.5	0.3	0.0	−0.2	0.1	0.0
Min.	3.5	4.1	3.1	−3.2	2.0	−1.8	−0.2	−0.5	−2.5	−1.1	−0.1	−0.1	0.0	0.1	0.0
Bas. met	5.5	5.3	3.7	**10.1**	5.6	−0.5	1.7	4.3	−0.1	2.1	−0.2	0.1	0.1	−0.2	0.0
Met. pr.	4.7	3.3	6.0	2.3	4.5	−0.4	2.7	2.5	2.6	2.1	−0.1	0.2	0.2	0.0	0.1
Mach.	**4.8**	**12.1**	**7.1**	4.4	**7.8**	−0.3	−0.3	5.1	−2.6	1.5	−0.2	−0.2	0.2	−0.1	0.0
Elec.	7.5	**10.6**	**25.8**	**54.9**	**25.9**	**5.0**	**3.8**	**5.5**	**21.7**	**8.6**	0.8	−0.2	0.8	1.7	0.8
Tran.	4.6	**13.3**	1.7	6.7	4.7	−0.4	0.2	**7.7**	−4.2	2.6	−0.2	−1.4	0.0	−0.2	−0.3
Prec.	−2.4	2.1	0.3	1.9	0.9	0.4	0.1	0.4	−0.3	0.2	−0.3	0.2	0.0	0.0	0.0
Others	5.1	5.1	2.6	0.6	3.0	0.0	3.0	−1.8	−1.6	−0.6	0.0	0.0	0.0	−0.1	0.0

Why were the shift effects negative during the periods when the governments actively implemented the industrial policies and export-oriented strategies and turn negative when the same governments eased the strictness in the implementation of industrial policies and initiated a restructuring across industries? During the former era of active industrial policies when there was a shift of workers towards the promoted industries under the export-oriented strategy and industrial policies, there was a need to enhance competitiveness of the industry by way of gains in productivity. The negative contribution of shift effects to aggregate productivity growth can be partially explained by the subsistence of tight labor market conditions in the three countries. Labor markets were tight in Japan for almost all periods. Tight labor markets in Korea and Taiwan are observed from the early and mid-1980s with technological sophistication. At this point, the responses of the governments to the tight labor market situation are important. The governments of Japan, Korea, and Taiwan stood relatively neutral. We know from Chapter 5 that, faced with the same problem, the government of Singapore opted for distorting the labor market and actively engaging in upgrading and improving the skills of labor. Singapore government placed a strong emphasis on higher value-added generation via skill upgrading and further automation. The large positive shift effects in Singapore after 1979 reflect these efforts. The negative shift effects observed in Japan and in Korea can be said to reflect the neutrality of the governments.

We can expect positive shift effects throughout the restructuring process because some labor may be released from less productive industries to more productive ones or from domestic-oriented industries to ones that are more exposed to international competition.[2] This may result in a revival of the employment share of the more productive industries that are more exposed to international competition and thus result in positive shift effects. This seems to be valid for Japan (see from Tables 7.2 and 7.3 that the labor share of the electrical and electronic machinery industry increased from the first two sub-periods to the last sub-period), Korea (the labor shares of metal products, basic machinery, and electrical and electronic machinery, and transport equipment industries increased from the first two sub-periods to

[2]Manufacturing employment declined steadily in Japan after the 1970s and during the 1990s in Korea. The decline in Korea is closely associated with restructuring via technological deepening.

the third sub-period), and Taiwan (the labor shares of plastic, metal products, and electrical and electronic machinery industries increased from the first two sub-periods to the third sub-period).

7.4. The Impact of Structural Changes on TFP Growth

The decomposition of TFP growth was introduced in Eqs. (6.45) and (6.46). In TFP growth estimations, labor input is represented by total working hours. The results of TFP growth estimations are presented in the second column of Table 7.6. Table 7.7 presents the decomposition results at the industry level. Overall TFP growth rates for Japan, Korea, and Taiwan are calculated as 1.6, 2.0, and 2.2 percent, respectively. Aggregate TFP growth rate for the overall period in Singapore computed in the previous chapter is far lower than these figures.

Table 7.6. TFP Growth and Reallocation Effects.

	Period	TFP Growth Rate	Intra-Industry TFP Growth	Capital Reallocation Effect	Labor Reallocation Effect
Japan	1960–1972	1.3	111.1	−9.0	−2.1
	1973–1984	2.0	117.7	−8.5	−9.2
	1985–1990	3.0	125.8	−9.0	−16.8
	1991–2002	1.2	93.3	2.4	4.4
	Overall	1.6	106.8	−4.7	−2.1
Korea	1960–1970	3.6	90.4	8.4	1.2
	1971–1979	−0.6	89.5	11.5	−1.0
	1980–1988	2.5	94.7	1.1	4.2
	1989–2002	4.5	95.5	0.8	3.6
	Overall	2.0	92.7	4.8	2.5
Taiwan	1961–1973	3.4	123.3	−4.5	−18.7
	1974–1985	0.9	144.2	−35.0	−9.2
	1986–1996	2.8	107.6	−2.8	−4.8
	1997–2002	1.9	96.7	−3.9	7.1
	Overall	2.3	117.2	−7.4	−9.8

Source: Author's calculations.

Table 7.7. TFP Growth Decomposition Results.

	Intra-Industry Productivity Growth (percent of total)					Static Shift Effects (percent of total)					Dynamic Shift Effects (percent of total)				
	1960–1972	1973–1984	1985–1990	1991–2002	All	1960–1972	1973–1984	1985–1990	1991–2002	All	1960–1972	1973–1984	1985–1990	1991–2002	All
Japan															
Food	0.4	1.0	−0.5	0.0	0.2	**0.9**	−0.1	0.2	0.0	0.2	0.0	**1.1**	**−0.7**	0.0	0.0
Tex.	0.0	−1.0	−0.1	−0.1	−0.1	0.5	0.1	0.1	−0.1	0.1	0.1	**−1.0**	−0.3	0.0	0.1
Wood	0.1	−0.7	−0.1	0.0	0.0	0.3	0.0	0.2	0.0	0.1	0.0	**−0.8**	−0.2	0.0	0.0
Pap.	0.1	0.0	0.5	0.0	0.1	0.3	0.0	0.1	0.0	0.1	0.0	0.0	0.4	0.0	0.0
Chem.	0.0	−0.4	0.1	0.0	0.1	0.4	**0.5**	**0.4**	0.0	**0.3**	0.1	**−0.9**	−0.3	0.0	0.0
Pet.	−0.4	−0.7	−0.8	0.0	−0.2	**−0.9**	−0.2	0.0	0.0	−0.3	0.0	−0.5	**−0.7**	0.0	0.0
Plas.	0.1	0.6	0.4	0.0	0.1	0.2	0.1	0.1	0.0	0.1	0.0	0.5	0.2	0.0	0.0
Min.	0.1	−0.4	0.0	0.0	0.0	0.2	0.0	0.2	0.0	0.1	0.0	−0.4	−0.2	0.0	0.0
Bas. met	−0.3	−1.2	−0.7	0.0	−0.1	**−1.4**	**0.3**	0.1	0.0	−0.2	−0.2	**−1.5**	−0.8	0.0	0.0
Met. pr.	0.2	−0.2	0.5	0.0	0.1	0.3	0.2	0.2	0.0	0.1	0.0	−0.4	0.3	0.0	0.0
Mach.	0.3	0.0	0.9	−0.2	0.2	0.3	**0.5**	**0.4**	−0.2	0.2	0.0	−0.5	**0.6**	0.0	0.0
Elec.	0.2	2.8	1.9	1.2	0.6	0.1	**0.5**	**0.9**	**1.2**	**0.6**	0.0	**2.2**	**1.0**	0.0	−0.1
Tran.	0.3	2.1	0.8	0.2	0.4	0.3	**0.3**	**0.9**	0.2	**0.3**	−0.1	**1.8**	−0.1	0.0	−0.1
Prec.	0.0	0.2	0.0	0.0	0.0	0.1	0.1	0.1	0.0	0.0	0.0	0.2	0.0	0.0	0.0
Others	0.1	−0.1	0.2	0.1	0.1	0.1	0.1	0.1	0.1	0.1	0.0	−0.1	0.1	0.0	0.0

(Continued)

Table 7.7. (*Continued*)

	Intra-Industry Productivity Growth (percent of total)					Static Shift Effects (percent of total)					Dynamic Shift Effects (percent of total)				
	1960–1970	1971–1979	1980–1988	1989–2002	All	1960–1970	1971–1979	1980–1988	1989–2002	All	1960–1970	1971–1979	1980–1988	1989–2002	All
Korea															
Food	**0.4**	−0.1	−0.1	−0.1	0.1	**0.4**	−0.1	0.0	0.0	0.1	−0.1	−0.0	−0.1	−0.1	0.0
Tex.	**0.4**	−0.2	0.2	−0.1	0.2	0.3	−0.1	**0.4**	0.3	**0.3**	0.1	−0.0	−0.2	−0.3	0.0
Wood	0.1	−0.0	0.0	−0.0	0.1	0.0	−0.0	0.0	−0.0	0.0	0.1	0.0	0.0	−0.0	0.0
Pap.	0.1	−0.0	0.2	0.1	0.1	0.1	−0.0	0.2	0.1	0.1	0.0	0.0	−0.1	0.1	0.0
Chem.	0.5	−0.1	0.2	**0.6**	0.2	**0.5**	−0.1	0.2	**0.4**	**0.2**	0.0	0.0	−0.0	0.2	0.0
Pet.	**1.5**	0.0	0.1	0.0	0.1	**1.2**	0.0	0.1	−0.0	0.1	0.2	−0.0	−0.0	0.0	0.0
Plas.	0.1	−0.0	0.2	0.1	0.1	0.1	−0.0	0.1	0.1	0.1	−0.1	0.0	0.1	0.0	0.0
Min.	0.2	−0.0	0.0	0.1	0.1	0.2	−0.0	0.0	0.1	0.1	0.0	0.0	−0.0	−0.1	0.0
Bas. met	0.1	−0.1	0.1	0.0	0.1	0.0	−0.0	−0.0	0.0	0.0	0.0	−0.0	0.1	−0.0	0.0
Met. pr.	0.0	−0.0	0.2	0.1	0.1	0.0	−0.0	0.2	0.0	0.1	0.0	0.0	−0.0	0.1	0.0
Mach.	0.0	−0.0	0.3	**0.5**	0.1	0.0	−0.0	0.2	0.4	0.1	0.0	−0.0	0.1	0.1	0.0
Elec.	0.1	−0.1	**0.7**	**2.2**	**0.5**	0.1	−0.1	**0.4**	**2.2**	**0.4**	0.0	−0.0	**0.3**	0.1	0.1
Tran.	0.1	−0.0	0.3	**0.7**	0.2	0.1	−0.0	0.2	**0.5**	0.1	0.0	−0.0	0.1	0.2	0.0
Prec.	0.0	−0.0	0.1	0.0	0.0	0.0	−0.0	0.1	0.0	0.0	0.0	0.0	−0.0	−0.0	0.0
Others	0.1	−0.0	0.1	0.1	0.0	0.1	−0.0	0.1	0.1	0.1	0.0	0.0	−0.0	−0.0	0.0

(*Continued*)

Table 7.7. (*Continued*)

	Intra-Industry Productivity Growth (percent of total)					Static Shift Effects (percent of total)					Dynamic Shift Effects (percent of total)				
	1961–1973	1974–1985	1986–1996	1997–2002	All	1961–1973	1974–1985	1986–1996	1997–2002	All	1961–1973	1974–1985	1986–1996	1997–2002	All
Taiwan															
Food	−1.1	0.0	0.0	−0.2	−0.4	0.0	0.4	0.1	−0.2	0.1	**−1.0**	−0.4	−0.1	−0.1	**−0.5**
Tex.	0.9	0.4	−0.3	−0.2	0.3	**0.8**	**0.7**	0.2	−0.1	**0.5**	0.1	−0.3	**−0.5**	−0.1	−0.2
Wood	0.2	−0.2	0.0	−0.1	0.0	0.3	−0.1	0.1	0.0	0.1	−0.1	−0.1	−0.1	0.0	−0.1
Pap.	0.0	−0.1	−0.1	0.0	−0.1	0.2	−0.1	−0.2	0.0	0.0	−0.2	0.0	0.1	0.0	0.0
Chem.	0.7	−0.7	0.0	0.0	0.0	**0.6**	**−0.7**	−0.1	−0.1	0.0	0.0	0.0	0.1	0.1	0.1
Pet.	0.3	−0.3	0.2	0.2	0.1	0.3	−0.2	0.0	0.3	0.0	0.0	−0.1	0.2	−0.1	0.0
Plas.	0.6	0.3	0.3	−0.1	0.3	**0.5**	0.2	**0.5**	−0.1	0.3	0.1	0.1	−0.2	0.0	0.0
Min.	−0.2	0.0	0.1	−0.2	−0.1	−0.2	−0.2	0.1	−0.2	−0.1	0.0	0.2	0.0	−0.1	0.0
Bas. met	0.2	0.2	0.2	0.3	0.2	0.1	0.1	0.0	0.3	0.1	0.0	0.1	0.2	0.0	0.1
Met. pr.	0.1	0.2	0.5	0.0	0.2	0.1	0.1	0.4	−0.1	0.2	0.0	0.1	0.0	0.0	0.1
Mach.	0.7	0.4	0.4	0.0	0.4	**0.8**	**0.5**	0.3	0.1	**0.5**	−0.2	−0.1	0.0	−0.2	−0.1
Elec.	0.7	0.3	1.6	2.5	1.1	0.4	0.3	**1.4**	**2.0**	**0.9**	0.3	0.0	0.2	**0.5**	0.2
Tran.	0.0	0.0	0.0	0.0	0.0	0.0	0.0	0.0	0.0	0.0	0.0	0.0	0.0	0.0	0.0
Prec.	0.0	0.0	0.0	0.0	0.0	0.0	0.0	0.0	0.0	0.0	0.0	0.0	0.0	0.0	0.0
Others	0.3	0.4	0.0	−0.1	0.2	0.3	0.3	0.1	0.0	0.2	0.0	0.1	−0.1	0.0	0.0

The results show that manufacturing TFP growth in Japan, Korea, and Taiwan resulted typically from intra-industry effect and reallocation effects are minimal. Reallocation effects are generally larger in size in Taiwan but with a negative sign. In Japan and Korea, reallocation effects are relatively small. In Japan, reallocation effects were small during the first period and negative by about 17 percent and a quarter of aggregate TFP growth during the 1970s and the 1980s. During the long recession of the 1990s, reallocation effects turn slightly positive but remain at a very low level. Factor markets in Japan were not distorted much in the post-1973 period and the reallocation of labor and capital across industries did not result in large changes in average product of both capital and labor. This reflects the working of factor markets in Japan in such a way to maintain equilibrium and the virtual non-existence of distortions in factor markets. Notice the large capital reallocation effect during this period until the 1990s. This is stimulated by the restructuring of Japanese industries in an era of deindustrialization and relocation of industries to overseas production sites where factor prices are lower.

In Korea, reallocation effects amount to a small positive figures for the 1970s and afterwards. During the HCI Drive of the 1970s, capital reallocation effects were positive about one-tenth of aggregate TFP growth. Positive capital reallocation effect during this period indicates that efforts to manipulate industrial structure as a bonus for TFP growth in Korea, i.e., capital's reallocation to the nurtured heavy and chemical industries where it could earn higher returns resulted in positive reallocation effect. Labor reallocation effect during the second third and fourth periods are positive, although its contribution to aggregate TFP growth is small. This finding can be interpreted as follows: industrial policies during these periods were successful in allocating labor to those areas where its marginal product was higher. This is most likely due to improvements in educational characteristics of labor and increasing technological deepening of Korean industries when high-technology industries were promoted and labor-intensive industries were replaced with capital-intensive ones.

In Taiwan, reallocation effects have been traditionally negative and between 8 and 44 percent of aggregate TFP growth until 1997. During the early expansion period (1960–1972), negative reallocation effects largely stemmed from labor reallocation affects and from capital reallocation effects during the technology promotion periods (1973–1985). Largely negative capital and labor reallocation effects under the industrial policies until the mid-1980s can be interpreted as the ongoing adjustment of the factor markets to the restructuring of the economy. The figures suggest that the response of the factor markets was slower than the restructuring that was being undertaken in national industries and this continued until the mid-1980s.

At the industry level, electrical and electronic machinery and transport equipment industries in Japan and Korea and the electrical and electronic machinery and transport equipment industry in Taiwan contribute relatively largely to aggregate TFP growth. Basic metals (iron and steel) and chemical industries in Japan, textiles and chemicals industries in Korea, and textiles, chemicals, and plastic industries are also important contributors to intra-industry TFP growth. Electrical and electronic machinery industry appears as an important industry in Japan with its highly positive influence on reallocation effects but the reallocation resources involving the basic metals and chemicals industries (and food and oil refining industries in some periods) run counter to the improvements introduced by these two industries. In Korea and Taiwan, the influences of individual industries to reallocation effects are of minor importance and no industry appears to have continuously influenced the reallocation effects largely either positive or negative.

To compare these results with similar other studies, Timmer and Szirmai (2000) found that factor reallocations constituted a very insignificant portion of labor productivity and TFP growth for Indonesia, Korea, India, and Taiwan, for the period 1963–1993. In addition, Kawai (1999) found higher contribution by reallocation effects for Japanese TFP growth in manufacturing, around 16 percent for the post-1970 period. The findings of those studies and this study can be reconciled with the explanation for industrial development in Harberger (1998) which differentiated between a "mushroom-process" (i.e., innovative activities in a particular industry improve productivity and cause a shift of resources from relatively low-productivity activities to itself), and a "yeast-process" (i.e., gains in productivity spreads across industries). The findings in this study reveal that the impact of structural changes in four Asian countries (Japan, Korea, Singapore, and Taiwan) on aggregate manufacturing level (i.e., the yeast process) in general is less significant than their impact at the industry level (i.e., mushroom process). Then, it seems safe to claim that industrial policies gave way to a mushroom-type industrial growth process.

In addition, Syrquin (1995) observed that the initial acceleration of the contribution of reallocation effects to TFP and output growth subsequently slows down as an economy industrializes. At the industrialized economy level, as represented by Japan in this study, the contribution of reallocation effects is thus expected to be minimal. This is partly explained by the "exhaustion of the shifts" (see Syrquin, 1995).

To sum up, during periods of heavy involvement by governments in capital reallocation in Singapore and in Korea (1970s), reallocation of resources acted as an additional facilitator of TFP growth. Labor was largely displaced during the course of technological sophistication due to the replacement of labor-intensive industries with capital-intensive ones. However, the Singapore government actively sought ways to improve the skills of the labor force and succeeded in enhancing the contribution of labor to TFP growth in the post-1985 period. Japanese government stood neutral and did not distort factor markets. This brought about a lack of significant contribution of resource shifts to TFP growth. However, the deep recession in the 1990s stimulated changes in the factor markets and the resulting shifts of factors ran counter to aggregate TFP growth.

CHAPTER 8

A CGE MODEL FOR THE SINGAPORE ECONOMY

Productivity analyses show that the Singapore economy, manufacturing sector in particular, is characterized by rising productivity growth especially after the mid-1980s. The forces that drive productivity up are various. Demand factors such as export demand in the world for some important manufacturing industries in Singapore were not mentioned in productivity analyses which were merely supply-side. Chapters 6 and 7 investigated the structural changes brought about by industrial development in a comparative perspective. The role of market mechanism and the interaction between various markets and relative prices are also deterministic in resource allocation. The impacts of industrial policies can be captured through a broader analysis that takes into account such factors. This chapter utilizes a computable general equilibrium (CGE) model which depicts the working of an economy from a Walrasian perspective. The CGE model presents the working of the economy and incorporates some country-specific features of Singapore. The model also helps us to understand the underlying mechanism of changes brought about by policy shocks.

Recently, there has been a large increase in the number of CGE models to evaluate economic policies. A CGE model describes the interactions between the behaviors of economic agents. These agents operate in an environment characterized by market equilibrium whereby the economic agents optimize their objectives. Due to the complications in CGE modeling not enough attention has been paid to CGE modeling in Singapore, although it is a useful tool for empirical research to analyze resource allocation in market economies and the impacts of specific policy changes. In this chapter, the aim is first to construct a CGE model for Singapore. Given the emphasis on industrial policies and on the performance of the promoted industries, the model focuses on the promoted industries and on the impacts of policy shocks on these industries and on general macroeconomic performance.

Subsequently, various policy experiments are also conducted. In Chapter 9, a comparison of the results from CGE models that sought the impact of industrial policies in Singapore with the other East Asian economies is also presented.

8.1. An Overview of CGE Modeling

From the beginning of the 1960s, applied CGE models have been widely used to evaluate economic policies in both developed and developing economies. Such models are successors of input–output and linear programming models of the 1950s. Applied CGE models introduced nonlinear programming techniques into their predecessors to enable much flexibility and incorporated substitutability in the formulation of demand, production, and trade relations.

Theoretical underpinnings of CGE models can be found in Arrow and Debreu (1954), which later became a tradition in CGE modeling. This tradition reformulates the Walrasian general equilibrium theory. This theory states that the sum of excess demands in all markets in an economy with given relative prices must be equal to zero. If there are n markets and $n - 1$ of them are in equilibrium with given behavior of consumers and producers, then the nth market has to be in equilibrium. In the Arrow–Debreu tradition, there are certain number of producers and consumers who have their preferences. The demands for the goods in markets are determined by prices. Producers operate with given technologies characterized by constant returns to scale and with the motive of profit maximization. The expenditures of each economic agent are bound by specific budget constraints, which state that their expenditures equal relevant incomes. The model then solves for relative prices and consequently the production levels and factor prices which clear all markets. What matters on the price side are the relative prices; all prices are calculated in equilibrium relative to a predetermined price index, i.e., the *numéraire*.

In analyzing the consequences of certain policies and exogenous shocks, multi-sector models have been used extensively. Not only these models are instrumental in measuring the impact on the economy, but also on individual sectors of the economy. Multi-sector CGE models designed for developing economies from the late 1970s have addressed different issues such as trade policies, environment, income distribution (e.g., Adelman and Robinson,

1978; Lysy and Taylor, 1980), and tax policies (e.g., Shoven and Whalley, 1984).

In static CGE models, economic agents that participate in economic transactions (producers and consumers) make their decisions within a given single period. The focus is on the allocation of resources based on optimal decisions of consumers and producers within a given period. In dynamic CGE models, the emphasis is on the dynamics toward a new steady state after a shock.[1] The dynamics of this move is characterized, for instance, by the accumulation of capital stock or labor supply. Intertemporal optimality is taken into consideration in a newer class of dynamic CGE models (e.g., Go, 1988). In this chapter, a recursive dynamic CGE model is used since it is capable enough to measure the impacts to the economy of policy changes of interest.

8.2. Previous General Equilibrium Models of Singapore

In the past there were a few attempts of CGE modeling of the Singapore economy. The remarkable ones are Chia (2000) and a series of CGE models based on the ORANI model[2] by Siriwardana (1991, 1997a,b, 2000). There are also other CGE models such as the applications of the Global Trade Analysis Project (GTAP)[3] Model (Siriwardana and Iddamalgoda, 2003) and Monetary Model of Singapore (MMS) in MAS (2000). Below, the main features and findings of these studies are briefly described.

Chia (2000) is the most original contribution among the models listed above. She constructs a CGE model with a nested production function

[1] Dynamic CGE models are of two types, multi-period and recursive dynamic (Keyzer, 1991). Multi-period models (e.g., Go, 1988; Devarajan and Go, 1998) follow the so-called Arrow–Debreu tradition where equilibrium is solved for the time horizon, i.e., the planning horizon of the agents in the model, under perfect foresight of the agents. The impact of the change that results from the altering of some parameters is interpreted as the new solution. In recursive dynamic models, optimization takes place in only one period and agents do not look ahead. Investment and consumption in the multi-period models are represented by dynamic equations whereas in the recursive dynamic models the dynamics of the model is represented by capital accumulation constraint and demographic changes that affect labor supply in the following periods.

[2] See Dixon *et al.* (1982) for a description of the ORANI model which is originally developed for the Australian economy.

[3] See Hertel and Tsigas (1997) for a comprehensive description of the GTAP model.

(output is a Leontief function of intermediate inputs and value-added at the top level and value-added is a Cobb–Douglas function of a composite of variable factors and sector specific capital at the bottom level; composite variable factor is a CES function of capital and labor). The model is designed as a multi-sector CGE model with eight household groups and 1983 as the base year to evaluate the tax system and its implication for income distribution in Singapore. For this purpose, a number of variables related to the tax system are incorporated into the model. The study finds small efficiency cost but significant redistribution in the existing tax system.

Siriwardana (1991) evaluates some of the policy options for Singapore after the 1985 recession, wage cost reductions, devaluation of the Singapore dollar, and increase in domestic absorption in particular, using the ORANI model. He found that 12 percent wage cut was the most attractive policy option for Singapore. Siriwardana (1997a) investigated the impact of exchange rate policy on the market power of Singapore in world market of manufactures using an 8-sector ORANI model. He found that under the ongoing strong currency regime, Singapore enjoyed some degree of market power in the world trade of manufactures. Siriwardana (1997b) illustrates some possible outcomes for the Singapore economy that emerge due to the increased world demand. The results of his study point out significant increases in real GDP and employment in Singapore due to world demand expansion, mainly through the manufacturing sector. Siriwardana (2000) examined the factors behind export growth and exchange rate misalignment.

Siriwardana and Iddamalgoda (2003) utilize the GTAP model to investigate the impact of Asian economic crisis on Singapore and investigates the consequences of various policy responses, in particular wage reduction, domestic demand stimulation, and exchange rate policies. They found that good macroeconomic fundamentals and sound macroeconomic policies made the economy less vulnerable to external shocks. But they also found that Singapore's policies should focus on improving competitiveness to enhance trade with other crisis-affected countries. Lowering wage costs works as an improving factor for competitiveness through depreciation of the real exchange rate. The stimulation of private consumption and government consumption expenditures are ineffective and lead only to moderate economic expansion.

The MMS is a 5-sector Keynesian short-run macroeconometric model of Singapore (MAS, 2000). It contains 241 equations, of which 38 are estimated, and the rest are identities. MAS (2000) simulates the effects of an electronics slowdown on the performance of the economy.

8.3. The Structure of the CGE Model of Singapore

The CGE model in this chapter is based on the standard static CGE models developed for policy analysis in developing economies by Dervis *et al.* (1982), Chenery *et al.* (1986), and International Food Policy Research Institute (Lofgren *et al.*, 2002).

The characteristics of the CGE model can be summarized as follows. All commodity and factor markets are characterized by perfect competition. The economy is a small open economy where the prices of tradables are determined by world prices and are not affected by domestic production and consumption decisions. Import prices are exogenous and the country does not have market power in exports. There are two factors of production, capital and labor. Labor is assumed to be mobile across sectors but sectoral capital stocks are fixed. This a short-run static model with foreign and domestic goods as imperfect substitutes (Armington assumption).

For the purposes of the study, the economy is divided into 11 production sectors each of which is assumed to produce a single representative output:

(i) industrial chemicals (CHE),
(ii) electrical and electronic machinery (ELE),
(iii) precision equipment (PRE),
(iv) declining manufacturing industries, i.e., transport equipment and oil refining (DEC),
(v) other manufacturing industries (MAN),
(vi) financial and business services (FIN),
(vii) info-communications services (INF),
(viii) education services (EDU),
(ix) engineering and environment services (ENV),
(x) consulting services (CON),
(xi) others, including construction, other services, agriculture, and utilities (OTH).

Table 8.1. Production Sectors in the CGE Model.

Name	Sector Codes in Input–Output Tables 1995
CHE	37–45
ELE	68–78, 84–91
PRE	98–99
DEC	36, 92–97
MAN	7–35, 46–67, 79–83, 100–105
FIN	128–134
INF	127, 135
EDU	145
ENV	136, 147
CON	137, 141
OTH	1–6, 106–126, 138–140, 142–144, 146, 148–156

The sectoral classification of the SAM follows the input–output classification. However, those industries emphasized in the government's recent reports as the promising or promoted industries are presented separately while the rest of the economic activities are aggregated into large groups. A description of these sectors with their abbreviations and input–output table sector codes are presented in Table 8.1. In the rest of the chapter these abbreviations will be used. CHE, ELE, PRE, FIN, INF, EDU, ENV, and CON were the promoted industries. DEC represents those industries promoted before the 1990s but declined afterwards, i.e., oil refining and transport equipment (mainly shipbuilding) industries. These two industries experienced large declines in their respective shares in total manufacturing output and labor.

The data used in the CGE model is organized in the form of a social accounting matrix (SAM) with 1995 as the benchmark year. The SAM is presented in Section 8.6. Table 8.2 presents mathematical formulations of the CGE model with a glossary.

Some explanations about the notation in model equations are necessary. Parameters are noted by small Roman and Greek characters. Prices are represented by small Roman characters. Both exogenous and endogenous variables are noted by capital letters in italics. The subscripts i and j represent the six sectors listed above.

Table 8.2. Model Equations and Glossary.

Prices

$p_{Ei}E_i = p_{Di}D_i + p_{Mi}M_i$
$p_{Qi}Q_i = p_{Xi}X_i + p_{Di}D_i$
$p_{MIi} = \sum_j a_{ji}p_i$
$p_{Qi}(1 - ts_i) = p_{MIi} + p_{VAi}$
$p_{Mi} = p^*_{Mi}(1 + t_{Mi})ER$
$p_{Xi} = p^*_{Xi}ER$
$PI = \sum_i \Omega_i P_i$

Production block

$Q_i = f(\overline{K_i}, L_i) = \alpha_{Qi}L_i^{\alpha_i}K_i^{1-\alpha_i}$
$L_\imath - \alpha_\imath Q_\imath p_{VA\imath}/w_\imath$
$k_i = (1 - \infty_i)Q_i p_{VAi}/r_i$
$MI_i = \sum_j a_{ij}Q_j$
$\Delta ST_i = str_i Q_j$

Imports and exports

$E_i = f(D_i, M_i) = \alpha_{Ei}[\beta_{Ei}D_i^{-\rho_{Ei}} + (1 - \beta_{Ei})M_i^{-\rho_{Ei}}]^{-\frac{1}{\rho_{Ei}}}$
$Q_i = f(X_i, D_i) = \alpha_{Ti}[\beta_{Ti}X_i^{-\rho_{Ti}} + (1 - \beta_{Ti})D_i^{-\rho_{Ti}}]^{\frac{1}{\rho_{Ti}}}$
$\frac{M_i}{D_i} = \left(\frac{\beta_{Ei}}{1 - \beta_{Ei}} \cdot \frac{p_{Di}}{p_{Mi}}\right)^{\frac{1}{1+\rho_{Ei}}}$
$\frac{X_i}{D_i} = \left(\frac{\beta_{Ti}}{1 - \beta_{Ti}} \cdot \frac{p_{Xi}}{p_{Di}}\right)^{\frac{1}{\rho_{Ti}-1}}$

Institutional incomes and expenditures

$p_iC_i = cs_i(1 - mps)YH(1 - t_H)$
$YH = \sum_i w_iL_i + TRN_{GH} + TRN_{FH} + ER \cdot TRN_{WH}$
$S_H = (1 - mps)YH(1 - t_H)$
$HHTAX = t_H YH$
$YG = ITAX + TAR + t_K YK + HHTAX + TRN_{WG} - SUB$
$ITAX = \sum_i ts_i p_i Q_i$
$TAR = \sum_i t_{Mi} p^*_{Mi} M_i ER$
$YK = \sum_i r_i K_i + KIN$
$S_G = YG - \left(\sum_i p_i G_i\right) - TRN_{GF} + TRN_{GH} - TRN_{GW}$
$G_i = gs \cdot G$

Savings and investment

$SAV = S_H + S_G + S_F + ER \cdot S_W$
$SAV = \sum_i I_i + DEP$
$\Delta ST_i = str_i Q_i$

(*Continued*)

Table 8.2. (*Continued*)

$DEP = \sum_i \delta_i K_i$

Market clearing conditions

$(MI_i + C_i + G_i + I_i + \Delta ST_i) - Q_i = 0$
$LS = \sum_i L_i$
$\sum_i p_{Mi} M_i + YL_W + YK_W + TRN_{FW} + TRN_{HW} + S_W =$
$\sum_i p_{Xi} X_i + REM + KIN + TRN_{WH} + TRN_{WG} + TRN_{KW}$

Glossary

Parameters and exogenous variables

α_i	Exponent parameter in Cobb–Douglas production function
α_{Ei}	Shift parameter in the CES Armington function
α_{Qi}	Shift parameter in Cobb–Douglas production function
α_{Ti}	Shift parameter in the CET function
β_{Ei}	Distribution parameter in the CES Armington function
β_{Ti}	Distribution parameter in the CET function
d_i	Depreciation rate of capital by sector
Ω_i	Sectoral shares in total output
ρ_{Ei}	Elasticity parameter in the CES Armington function
ρ_{Ti}	Exponent (elasticity) parameter in the CET function
a_{ij}	Input–output coefficients
cs_i	Shares of goods in household consumption
gl	Growth rate of total labor supply
gs_i	Shares of goods in total government expenditures
mps	Marginal propensity to save
str_i	Ratio of inventory investment to output
t_H	Taxes on household labor income
t_K	Taxes on capital income
t_{Mi}	Import tariff rate
ts_i	Indirect tax rate

Endogenous variables and prices

C_i	Total consumption by commodity
D_i	Domestic good production by sector
DEP	Total capital consumption allowances
E_i	Composite good supply by sector

(*Continued*)

Table 8.2. (*Continued*)

ER	Nominal exchange rate
G	Total government expenditures
G_i	Government consumption by commodity
$HHTAX$	Total taxes paid by households
I_i	Total investment by sector of destination
$ITAX$	Total indirect taxes
K_i	Capital stock by sector
KIN	Capital inflows
L_i	Labor demand by sector
LS	Labor supply
M_i	Imports by sector
MI_i	Consumption of intermediate inputs by sector
p_i	Price level of supply
p_{Ci}	Price of consumption
p_{Di}	Price of domestic goods
p_{Ei}	Price of composite output
p_{Ki}	Price of capital goods
p^*_{Mi}	World price of imports
p_{MIi}	Price of intermediate inputs
p_{Qi}	Price of gross output
p^*_{Xi}	World price of exports
P_{VAi}	Price of value-added
PI	Exogenous general price level
r_i	Rental rate of capital
$REMIT$	Remittances into the country
Q_i	Output supply by sector
S_F	Enterprise savings
S_G	Government savings
S_H	Household savings
SAV	Total savings
ST_i	Inventory investment (stocks)
SUB	Total subsidies provided to the firms
S_W	Foreign savings
TAR	Total tariff revenues of the government
TRN_{FH}	Enterprise transfers to households
TRN_{FW}	Enterprise transfers to the rest of the world
TRN_{GF}	Government transfers to enterprises
TRN_{GH}	Government transfers to households
TRN_{GW}	Government transfers to the rest of the world

(*Continued*)

Table 8.2. (*Continued*)

TRN_{HW}	Household transfers to the rest of the world
TRN_{WG}	Government transfers from the rest of the world
TRN_{WH}	Transfers the rest of the world to households
w_i	Wage rate by sector
X_i	Exports by sector
YG	Total government revenue
YH	Household income
YK	Capital income (gross operating surplus)
YK_W	Capital payments to the rest of the world
YL	Labor income (compensation of employees)
YL_W	Labor payments to the rest of the world

8.3.1. *Production and factors block*

Using the production functions to describe the underlying technology of production activities and profit maximization assumption of producers, it is possible to derive equations for production of output and demand for production factors. Firms engaging in production activities take prices as given and employ primary factors of production (capital and labor) and intermediate inputs to produce output. The technology underlying production maximizes profits subject to constant returns to scale, with unitary elasticity of substitution between capital and labor.

Firms produce output subject to a Cobb–Douglas production function where output is specified as a function of capital (K) and labor (L):

$$Q_i = f(\overline{K_i}, L_i) = \alpha_{Qi} L_i^{\alpha_i} K_i^{1-\alpha_i}, \tag{8.1}$$

where the parameters α_Q and α represent shift and exponent parameters in the Cobb–Douglas production function. The subscript i refers to sectors. Exponent parameters (e.g., output elasticities) of capital and labor (α and $1 - \alpha$) sum up to unity. Profit maximization condition is as follows:

$$L_i = \alpha_i Q_i p_{VAi} / w_i, \tag{8.2}$$

where w represents the average wage level of labor and p_{VA} refers to value-added price. The exponent parameter, α, represents the share of labor in total payments to production factors. In equilibrium, wage equals the marginal product of labor in each category. For sectoral capital stocks, a first order condition similar to Eq. (8.2) is set. Sectoral capital stocks sum to the economy's exogenously determined aggregate stock of capital.

In production, capital and labor are used with other intermediate commodities. Intermediate inputs make up a fixed proportion of gross output. The model does not distinguish between activities and commodities produced by activities. In other words, each activity produces one representative commodity.

Total intermediate input demand is formulated as follows:

$$MI_i = \min\left(\frac{Q_{ji}}{\alpha_{ji}}\right). \tag{8.3}$$

Substitution of intermediate inputs is not allowed. The fixed input output coefficients α_{ji} are obtained from the input–output tables and their sum is equal to unity:

$$\sum_j \alpha_{ij} = 1. \tag{8.4}$$

The composite material input used by firms in production is a function of intermediate inputs provided by other sectors. In this specification, intermediate inputs make up a fixed proportion of composite material input.

$$MI_i = \sum_j \alpha_{ij} Q_j. \tag{8.5}$$

Finally, the ratio of inventory investment (stocks) (ΔST) to output is defined as:

$$\Delta ST_i = str_i Q_j, \tag{8.6}$$

where *str* is a fixed coefficient that defines inventory investment as a fixed proportion of output. Figure 8.1 depicts the structure of output and inputs in the CGE model.

8.3.2. *Imports and exports*

In a small open economy, export is an activity that earns foreign exchange and makes imports of goods and services possible. SAM also places exports in "activities" column rather than "commodities" column. Imports can be financed partially by exports and foreign loans from the rest of the world.

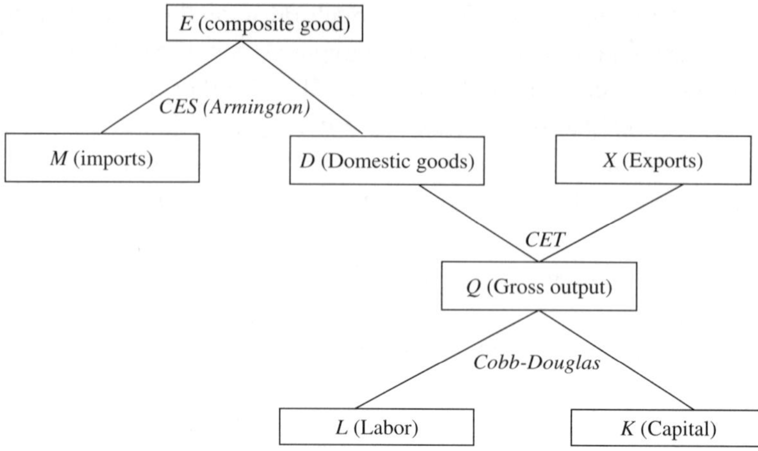

Fig. 8.1. Output structure of the CGE model.

Loans are disregarded because official statistics show that Singapore's foreign loans are nil since the late 1980s.

The model assumes that imports, exports, and domestic goods are imperfect substitutes. However, in the case of imports, differentiated products are allowed and this leads to the construction of a composite good consisting of both imported and domestic commodities. This composite good is then supplied to consumers. Finally, the model assumes that tariff rates are fixed simple ad-valorem rates that are unaffected by changes in import-quantities.

A constant-elasticity-of-scale (CES) Armington-type of substitution (as defined in Armington, 1969) is assumed between imported goods (M) and domestic goods (D) as imperfect substitutes:

$$E_i = f(D_i, M_i) = \alpha_{Ei}\left[\beta_{Ei} D_i^{-\rho_{Ei}} + (1-\beta_{Ei}) M_i^{-\rho_{Ei}}\right]^{-1/\rho_{Ei}}, \qquad (8.7)$$

where the parameters α_E, β_E, and ρ_E represent the shift parameter, share parameter, and the exponent (elasticity) parameter of the Armington CES function. E represents composite output. This applies to both final goods and intermediate commodities. Armington elasticities are different among sectors. Singapore has a small open economy and it is realistic to assume an infinitely elastic world supply with fixed prices. There are transaction costs involved with exports, imports, and domestic sales. These costs are defined in the input–output tables as a fixed portion of a unit of commodity. These costs include those related to wholesale and retail trades and transportation. Final goods (imported and domestic goods) are either final goods or intermediate goods to be used in the production of other goods. Demand for intermediate commodities is determined by production technology.

The model also assumes constant elasticity of transformation (CET) where producers can substitute between production for the domestic market and foreign market:

$$Q_i = f(X_i, D_i) = \alpha_{Ti}[\beta_{Ti} X_i^{-\rho_{Ti}} + (1 - \beta_{Ti}) D_i^{-\rho_{Ti}}]^{1/\rho_{Ti}}, \qquad (8.8)$$

where the parameters α_T, β_T, and ρ_T represent shift parameter, share parameter, and exponent (elasticity) parameter of the CET function. The elasticity parameter reflects the extent to which domestic producers are willing or able to shift between producing for domestic and foreign markets.

Optimal level of imports relative to domestic supply and the optimal level of exports relative to domestic goods are calculated using the prices and elasticities as expressed above:

$$\frac{M_i}{D_i} = \left(\frac{\beta_{Ei}}{1 - \beta_{Ei}} \cdot \frac{p_{Di}}{p_{Mi}}\right)^{1/1+\rho_{Ei}}, \qquad (8.9)$$

$$\frac{X_i}{D_i} = \left(\frac{\beta_{Ti}}{1 - \beta_{Ti}} \cdot \frac{p_{Xi}}{p_{Di}}\right)^{1/\rho_{Ti}-1}. \qquad (8.10)$$

8.3.3. *Prices block*

Prices of goods are specified in a similar manner as in the production block:

$$p_{Ei} E_i = p_{Di} D_i + p_{Mi} M_i, \qquad (8.11)$$

$$p_{Qi} Q_i = p_{Xi} X_i + p_{Di} D_i, \qquad (8.12)$$

where p_E, p_D, p_M, and p_X represent the prices of the composite output, domestic goods, imported goods, and exports, respectively. Composite output prices are determined by the prices of domestic and imported goods prices and output price is determined by domestic and exported goods prices.

The price of the composite material input is calculated as a weighted sum of its components:

$$p_{MIi} = \sum_j a_{ji} p_i. \tag{8.13}$$

Furthermore, the price of output is made of value-added (p_{VA}) and material input prices where value-added price is computed as a residual after deducting material input prices from output price, which is set at unity as other prices, i.e.:

$$p_{Qi}(1 - ts_i) = p_{MIi} + p_{VAi}. \tag{8.14}$$

Producers maximize their profits in the market where returns are higher. The returns are based on domestic and export prices (world prices multiplied by the exchange rate adjusted for taxes and subsidies). It is assumed that Singapore is a small country and therefore the demand for its products is perfectly elastic with fixed world prices. The prices for foreign trade, e.g., export prices (p_X) and import prices (p_M), are defined as:

$$p_{Mi} = p^*_{Mi}(1 + t_{Mi})ER \tag{8.15}$$

$$p_{Xi} = p^*_{Xi}ER. \tag{8.16}$$

The prices with an asterisk (*) are world prices and *ER* is the exchange rate defined as the price of US dollar in terms of Singapore dollar. A decrease in the value of *ER* means appreciation of the exchange rate. Singapore government does not impose any taxes on exports and does not provide any subsidies for exports. However, some goods are subject to import tariffs although these goods are very small in number and the tariff rates are very low, reflecting the government's free trade policy.

The links between the prices in the domestic and foreign sectors are depicted in Figure 8.2, which clearly shows that through interlinkages between domestic good and input prices and the world prices of imported and exported goods, a price change in world prices can be diffused into domestic prices.

8.3.4. *Demand block*

Social accounting matrix (SAM) defines three institutions: enterprises, government, and households. Since the focus of this paper is not distribution

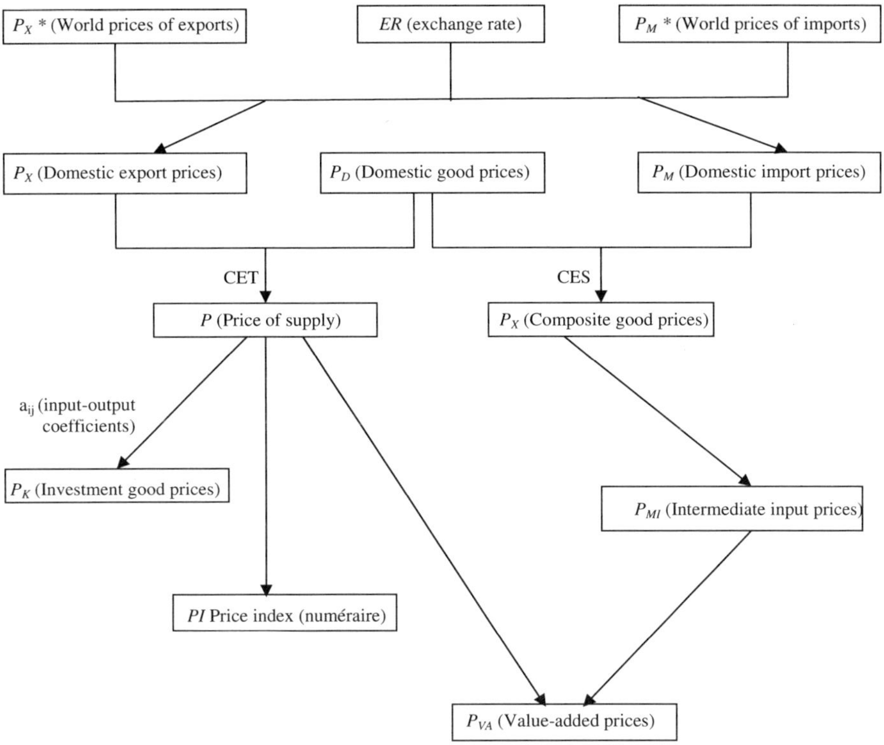

Fig. 8.2. Price mechanism of the CGE model.

of income, households are not disaggregated according to income levels. Institutions receive income and allocate it between consumption and saving and they face a budget constraint. Households and enterprises earn factor incomes for the services they provide and receive transfers from the government. The supply of capital is fixed for a given time-period and is immobile across sectors. It is assumed that labor is perfectly elastic for a given real wage rate. Factor incomes also include incoming and outgoing remittances. As households and firms own all factors of production, the sum of their disposable incomes roughly equals national income. Their disposable incomes consist of the returns to the services they provide and transfers from the rest of the world.

Firms use capital and labor for production, pay corporate taxes for the capital income that accrues to them, save some of their profits, and receive capital income. The payments of firms to the rest of the world in the form of transfers are included as part of their expenditures.

Households receive transfers from other institutions (government and enterprises), receive payments for the labor services they provide to enterprises, consume part of their income to purchase commodities, save a portion of their income, and pay income taxes and social security contributions to the government. The transfers between households and the rest of the world are included as part of their expenditures and incomes. Capital income of households is computed by deducting corporate savings, corporate taxes, capital consumption allowances, and changes in stocks.

Total household demand for consumption of good i (C_i) is defined as a share (cs) of total after-tax household income spent on consumption, as follows:

$$p_i C_i = cs_i(1 - mps)YH(1 - t_H), \tag{8.17}$$

where p, mps, YH, and t_H refer to consumption price, marginal propensity to save, household income, and taxes on household income, respectively. Household income is defined in SAM as follows:

$$YH = \sum_i w_i L_i + TRN_{GH} + TRN_{FH}, +ER \cdot TRN_{WH}, \tag{8.18}$$

where TRN_{GH}, TRN_{FH}, and TRN_{WH} represent government transfers to households, enterprise transfers to households, and transfers from the rest of the world to households, respectively. Households[4] save a certain amount of their incomes as follows:

$$S_H = (1 - mps)YH(1 - t_H), \tag{8.19}$$

[4]It has been discussed in Chapter 3 that Singapore has a central provident fund (CPF) system from which the mandatory savings can be withdrawn to finance housing, healthcare, and education. Compulsory savings are not model explicitly in the CGE model for two reasons. First, it is not a purpose of this study to measure the impact on income distribution or on different income groups. Second, although it has been argued by others that CPF was a major source the government utilizes in financing industrial policy; public investments were largely financed by CPF funds, it is also known that the government also utilized revenues from indirect and excise taxes in large amounts as well. For the purpose of exposition, the CGE model in the attached CD-ROM includes a social security equation. However, that equation has not been included in the baseline model here. Different variants of the model can be constructed using different equations. A model that emphasizes government accounts surely requires a social security payments account.

where S_H refers to household savings. Total household taxes (*HHTAX*) are computed by multiplying household tax rate (t_H) by household income (*YH*):

$$HHTAX = t_H YH. \tag{8.20}$$

Government income comes mainly from direct and indirect taxes and import tariffs. The government also receives income from its transactions with the rest of the world. It spends this income on its consumption and transfers to enterprises and households while saving part of it as government savings. In addition, it provides subsidies to enterprises which accrue as a cost item in its accounts. The difference between revenues and expenditures is the budget surplus. Using SAM balances, total government income (*YG*) is defined as follows:

$$YG = ITAX + TAR + t_K YK + HHTAX + TRN_{WG} - SUB, \tag{8.21}$$

$$ITAX = \sum_i ts_i p_i Q_i, \tag{8.22}$$

$$TAR = \sum_i t_{Mi} p^*_{Mi} M_i ER. \tag{8.23}$$

In these equations, TRN_{WG}, and *SUB* represent private consumption, investment demand, government spending, transfers from the rest of the world to the government, and government subsidies to firms, respectively. t_M, t_K, t_S, p_M, p, and *er* stand for import tariff rate, tax rate on capital income, indirect tax rate, price of imports, price of aggregate supply, and real exchange rate, respectively. Capital income that accrues to firms, i.e., gross operating surplus, is defined as follows:

$$YK = \sum_i r_i K_i + KIN, \tag{8.24}$$

where *r* represents rental rate of capital, *K* represents installed capital, and *KIN* refers to capital inflows to firms from the rest of the world.

Government savings is the excess of government revenues over its expenditures on public consumption and transfers to households and enterprises as follows:

$$S_G = YG - \left(\sum_i p_i G_i\right) - TRN_{GF} + TRN_{GH} - TRN_{GW}, \tag{8.25}$$

where TRN_{GW} refers to transfers from the government to the rest of the world. Government expenditure for a particular good is formulated as a portion (gs) of total government expenditures (G), as follows:

$$G_i = gs_i \cdot G. \tag{8.26}$$

8.3.5. *Savings–investment block*

Total savings (*SAV*) consist of government (S_G), enterprise (S_F), household (S_H), and foreign savings (S_W):

$$SAV = S_H + S_G + S_F + ER \cdot S_W. \tag{8.27}$$

Savings are used to finance investment. Government controls a large share of household savings by way of forced savings that accumulate in CPF. Additionally, there is an inflow of foreign capital from the rest of the world. It is assumed that the necessary adjustment in the interest rate takes place to ensure that savings equal investment in equilibrium. As an accounting identity, savings are equal to total investments inclusive of depreciation (*DEP*):

$$SAV = \sum_i I_i + DEP. \tag{8.28}$$

Total demand for investment is the sum of sectoral investment demands. Aggregate demand for investment (I) is the sum of the demands for investment by sector and the stock of inventories by sector as follows:

$$I = \sum_i (I_i^+ \rho_i \Delta ST_i). \tag{8.29}$$

Recall that the stock of inventories is calculated as follows:

$$\Delta ST_i = str_i Q_i. \tag{8.30}$$

Finally, depreciation of capital (*DEP*) is defined as a constant proportion (δ) of capital payments:

$$DEP = \sum_i \delta_i p_K K_i. \tag{8.31}$$

8.3.6. *Market clearing conditions and normalization*

The link between production and demand is the generation of factor incomes and the payment of these incomes to domestic institutions. There is a need to balance demand and supply for commodities and factors by some constraints.[5] These constraints are categorized into three equilibrium conditions: (i) balance in the demand and supply of all products, (ii) equilibrium of labor demand and labor supply, and (iii) equilibrium in the foreign exchange market.

Product market equilibrium: Equilibrium in the product markets requires that excess demand for commodities equal to zero. Aggregate demand (*AD*) for domestic production includes demands for intermediate inputs, private consumption, government consumption, and investment. Aggregate supply (Q) is measured by total output produced. Equilibrium is achieved through domestic and foreign prices and the changes in relative prices on production and employment that stimulate changes in institutional income and demand. Demand–supply equilibrium is defined as follows:

$$AD_i - Q_i = 0, \tag{8.32}$$

$$AD_i = MI_i + C_i + G_i + I_i + \Delta ST_i. \tag{8.33}$$

Labor market equilibrium: It is assumed that labor market is competitive and firms hire labor until marginal product of labor equals wage rate. Labor is supplied by consumers and fully employed by producers. Sectoral allocation of labor is determined endogenously according to wage distortion factors in each sector. Total payment to labor is an aggregation of sectoral payments to labor:

$$wL = \sum_i w_i L_i, \tag{8.34}$$

where w and L refer to wages and the number of workers by sector. For the labor markets to clear, labor demand should be equal to labor supply (*LS*), which is ensured by adjustments in flexible wage rates:

$$LS = \sum_i L_i. \tag{8.35}$$

The labor market closure adopted here is fixed aggregate labor supply with flexible real wages. This means that sectoral labor demands are adjusted

[5] See Ezaki (2007) for an overview of macroclosures in CGE models.

within the model in order to determine the levels of employment and real wages.[6]

Foreign exchange market equilibrium: In the foreign exchange market, equilibrium condition holds as follows:

$$p_{Mt}M_t + YL_W + YK_W + TRN_{FW} + TRN_{HW} + S_W$$
$$= p_{xt}X_t + REM + KIN + TRN_{WH} + TRN_{WG} + TRN_{KW}, \qquad (8.36)$$

where YL_W, YK_W, REM, TRN_{FW}, TRN_{HW}, TRN_{WH}, TRN_{WG}, and TRN_{KW} represent payments to foreigners' labor services, capital payments to foreigners, inward remittances, firms' transfers to the rest of the world, households' transfers to the rest of the world, transfers to households from the rest of the world, transfers to government from the rest of the world, and capital transfers to the rest of the world, respectively. Equation (8.36) shows that the balance in the current account is offset by flows in the capital account. Since *TRN* terms are generally kept exogenous in numerical solutions, it is not misguiding to aggregate them under one or two accounts.

CGE models usually require a balance between aggregate savings and aggregate investment. Marginal saving rates of domestic institutions are taken as fixed, and investment adjusts to attain saving–investment equality. Foreign savings in Singapore are negative, making the country net exporter of funds.

Price normalization: The CGE model computes relative prices of the system. There is a need to normalize prices. This is done by normalizing with the producer prices, i.e., the supply prices of goods are set exogenously, as follows:

$$PI = \sum_i \Omega_i P_i, \qquad (8.37)$$

where Ω is the share of each sector in total output, PI is the general price level (price index), and P is index of producer (supply) prices. This normalization rule implies a non-inflationary case. The choice of producer prices for price

[6]There are also other alternatives for labor market closure: (i) exogenously fixed sectoral labor demands with endogenous adjustments in real wages; (ii) exogenously fixed wages with endogenous adjustments in employment (i.e., infinitely elastic labor supply schedule); and (iii) exogenously fixed supply of labor with adjustments in real wages.

normalization has a strong implication. The system solves for the levels of other prices relative to this price index. In consequence, the resulting changes in wage rates, for instance, will be interpreted as relative changes in the cost of labor to the producers. Changes in real wages can also be checked by normalization with consumer prices rather than producer prices. The choice of consumer prices, as in many other studies, obviously does not match well with the purpose of this study.

8.4. Calibration of Model Parameters

With given parameters and SAM, the model must be able to replicate itself. Some parameters are provided from outside, such as the shares of labor and capital in production (distribution parameters in the production function), shift parameter of the production function, depreciation rates, government and household consumption shares of commodities, sectoral shares of investment by sector of destination, ratios of inventory investment to output, indirect tax rates, import tariff rates, income tax rate and tax rate of capital income (all these so far are calculated from the input–output table and SAM), and Armington and CET elasticity parameters which are provided exogenously. Using the data from the SAM and the behavioral equations of the CGE model, it is possible to compute the numerical values of the remaining parameters in the CGE model. Key parameters for each industry and some aggregates are presented in Table 8.3.

The distribution (β_{Ei} and β_{Ti}) and shift (α_{Ei} and α_{Ti}) parameters in trade aggregation functions (Armington and CET) are calibrated using the calculated elasticity parameters (ρ_{Ei} and ρ_{Ti}) and by rearranging the equations for optimal exports and imports (i.e., Eqs. (8.9) and (8.10)). Suppressing the sector subscript i, distribution parameters are computed as follows:

$$\beta_E = \left[\frac{p_M}{p_D}\left(\frac{M}{D}\right)^{1+\rho_E}\right] \Big/ \left[1 + \frac{p_{Mi}}{p_D}\left(\frac{M}{D}\right)^{1+\rho_E}\right], \tag{8.38}$$

$$\beta_T = 1 \Big/ \left[1 + \frac{p_D}{p_X}\left(\frac{X}{D}\right)^{\rho_T - 1}\right]. \tag{8.39}$$

Shift parameters can then be computed using the distribution and elasticity parameters rearranging the Armington and CET functions (Eqs. (8.7) and

Table 8.3. Values of Selected Benchmark Parameters and Variables.

	CHE	ELE	DEC	MAN	FIN	OTH	INF	EDU	ENV	CON	PRE
a_E	1.632	1.922	1.914	2.010	1.959	2.022	1.694	1.358	1.859	1.786	1.998
a_K	0.665	0.663	0.427	0.455	0.635	0.345	0.732	0.535	0.313	0.162	0.532
a_L	0.335	0.337	0.573	0.545	0.365	0.655	0.268	0.465	0.687	0.838	0.468
a_Q	2.742	4.375	3.475	0.796	0.941	0.450	1.077	0.523	0.425	0.293	1.469
a_T	2.181	2.014	2.097	2.000	2.190	2.149	2.128	5.705	2.011	2.025	2.026
β_E	0.225	0.392	0.610	0.540	0.390	0.429	0.283	0.152	0.359	0.322	0.464
β_T	0.646	0.458	0.392	0.508	0.649	0.633	0.624	0.926	0.537	0.555	0.443
ρ_E	2.0	2.0	2.0	2.0	2.0	2.0	2.0	2.0	2.0	2.0	2.0
ρ_T	2.0	2.0	2.0	2.0	2.0	2.0	2.0	2.0	2.0	2.0	2.0
C	0.735	3.363	3.594	6.839	4.669	27.185	0.657	0.675	0.007	0.019	0.009
D	10.042	44.956	7.991	16.786	34.543	81.104	3.612	0.808	1.788	1.314	0.778
G	0.000	0.000	0.000	0.000	0.000	9.237	0.000	0.000	0.000	0.000	0.000
I	0.101	2.854	1.455	5.224	4.523	27.767	0.011	0.002	0.002	0.009	0.047
L_S	12.7	138.6	40.3	172.4	253.4	998.7	25.4	9.1	27.1	15.3	9.2
M	0.849	18.637	19.630	23.109	14.154	45.735	0.561	0.026	0.559	0.296	0.583
MI	10.060	57.380	22.580	27.380	39.520	62.650	3.520	0.141	2.360	1.590	1.310
Q	13.055	108.04	27.289	32.568	44.625	108.31	4.924	0.813	3.114	2.157	2.004
t_S	0.045	0.001	0.001	0.001	0.050	0.022	0.002	0.040	0.002	0.003	0.002
VA	4.9	14.6	2.1	10.6	29.5	49.6	3.4	0.6	1.4	1.0	0.5
X	3.013	63.088	19.298	15.782	10.083	27.211	1.312	0.005	1.327	0.843	1.226

Source: Author's calculations.

(8.8)) as:

$$\alpha_E = E/[\beta_E M^{-\rho_E} + (1-\beta_E)D^{-\rho_E}]^{-1/\rho_E}, \quad (8.40)$$

$$\alpha_T = E/[\beta_T X^{\rho_E} + (1-\beta_T)D^{\rho_E}]^{-1/\rho_E}, \quad (8.41)$$

where the sector subscript i is again suppressed.

Finally, the shift parameter in the Cobb–Douglas production function, α_T, is calibrated using the calculated values of capital and labor, as follows:

$$\alpha_{Qi} = Q_i/(L_i^{\alpha_i} K_i^{1-\alpha_i}). \quad (8.42)$$

8.5. The Dynamic Module

In the dynamic model, the static model presented earlier is updated by factor accumulation. Updating equation for capital stock is as follows:

$$K_{i,t} = K_{i,t-1}(1-\delta) + I_{i,t}. \quad (8.43)$$

Capital stocks change with additions and depreciation. Sectoral capital stocks change across periods but are fixed within each period. There is accumulation of capital in each sector but no mobility across sectors.

Labor supply is updated exogenously by assuming a specific growth rate (gl):

$$LS_{t+1} = LS_t(1+gl). \quad (8.44)$$

In the current model the growth rate of the labor force is specified as 1 percent between two consecutive years. In every period, the model endogenously determines sectoral labor demands whose sum gives total labor supply. With all these features, the dynamic model is a recursive one.

The model is solved as a system of simultaneous equations using the General Algebraic Modeling System (GAMS) software and a non-linear solver (Conopt 3).[7]

8.6. 1995 Social Accounting Matrix for Singapore

A CGE model requires an economy-wide data set in the form of a social accounting matrix SAM for the base year. SAM is a square table that presents

---

[7]For an overview of GAMS, see Brooke *et al.* (1998).

the details of all transactions in an economy for a given year and incorporates economic agents into a consistent system where all transactions are recorded. SAM organizes vast amounts of data into a consistent system of accounts. Rows and columns of SAM represent various accounts. Each column in the SAM represents expenditures (payments) and each row represents receipts (income). Since total payments must equal total receipts, the sum of rows must be equal to the sum of columns. Ensuring this equality is a difficult task when preparing a SAM because a mixture of data from different data sources is used and there may be discrepancies. In order to construct a SAM, data from input–output tables, national income, external trade, household expenditures, and flow of funds statistics are necessary. In return, a balanced SAM offers a consistent and integrated dataset for CGE analysis. For this purpose, the SAM for Singapore is constructed for the year 1995. The reason 1995 is selected as base year was that there were published input–output tables for this year and 1995[8] seemed to be a "normal year," i.e., based on some criteria such as growth rates and the balance of payments, the economy was more or less on its long-run path. Therefore, policy experiments based on a CGE model using 1995 data are good approximations to deviations from long-run path. It can be argued that the immediate impact of the changes in industrial policies, most extensively from 1990 on, can be best understood by investigating the changes brought about by policies from the baseline. In this case, the baseline is represented by the year 1995.

Previous studies by Thomas and Bautista (1999) on Zimbabwe and by Thurlow (2003) on South Africa were used as references to construct the 1995 SAM. The chapter on SAM in Sadoulet and de Janvry (1995) was also used as a guide in constructing the SAM. Construction of a micro-SAM for Singapore involves three steps. First, an unbalanced macro-SAM is constructed. This table combines mainly the aggregated data from national accounts and allows the modeler to check consistency in micro-SAM accounts. Second, a micro-SAM is constructed by disaggregating the macro-SAM accounts. Finally, both micro- and macro-SAMs are balanced. Both SAMs are initially not balanced. As stated above, row sums must equal column sums in a balanced SAM. In balancing the unbalanced SAMs,

[8] *Singapore Input–Output Tables for 2000* have just been published by Singstat in 2006. Since we are specifically interested in 1995 as the base year, interested researchers may wish to prepare the SAM for 2000.

the cross-entropy method is employed. A description of the details of this method is not intended here but can be found in Robinson *et al.* (2000). Basically, this method creates a new set of coefficients to minimize the entropy distance between macro-SAM and the newly constructed micro-SAM.

8.6.1. *Macro-SAM*

The structure of the macro-SAM is depicted in Table 8.4. In this subsection, data sources and how the cell entries of macro- and micro-SAM are calculated are briefly explained. The macro-SAM is a representative of the total transactions in the economy. Therefore, most of its data come from national accounts and input–output tables. All values are expressed in current Singapore dollars.

Intermediate demand: Intermediate demand data are obtained from absorption (use) table published in *Singapore Input Output Tables 1995*. These are measured at basic values, e.g., producers' prices less commodity taxes. Purchaser's values itself is defined in input–output tables as the costs of goods and services in the market to the point of delivery to purchasers. This is equal to producers' prices inclusive of transaction costs, e.g., any cost incurred during the supply of good or service to the market such as transportation and trade margins.

Compensation of employees: Compensation data are obtained from the use table. Compensation data covers wages and salaries paid to employees in cash or in kind, employers' payments to pension funds and CPF, and other welfare payments.

Operating Surplus: Operating surplus refers to payments made to capital services. This is basically derived by deducting from gross output the sum of intermediate consumption at purchasers' prices, compensation of employees, and indirect taxes except commodity taxes. Note that consumption allowance of fixed capital is included in operating surplus. Therefore, this value refers to gross operating surplus. The data for operating surplus are obtained from the use table published in the input–output tables.

Table 8.4. The Structure of the Macro-SAM.

			Factors of Production		Institutions					
	Activities	Commodities	Labor	Capital	Enterprises	Households	Government	Capital Account	Rest of the World	Total
Activities		Domestic Sales							Exports	Production
Commodities	Intermediate demand					Household consumption	Government consumption	Investment		Domestic demand
Labor	Compensation of labor								Remittances	Total value-added
Capital	Operating surplus								Capital inflows	
Enterprises				Non-distributed profits			Government transfers to enterprises			Enterprise income
Households			Labor income	Dividends	Transfers		Government transfers to households		Transfers to households from the rest of the world	Household income
Government	Commodity taxes	Tariffs and indirect taxes			Taxes	Direct income taxes			Transfers to government from the rest of the world	Government income
Capital account					Enterprise savings	Household savings	Government savings		Capital transfers	Total savings
Rest of the world		Imports	Labor payments to the rest of the world	Outward capital payments	Enterprise transfers to the rest of the world	Household transfers to the rest of the world		Foreign savings		Foreign exchange earnings
Total	Production	Domestic supply	Labor outlay	Capital outlay	Enterprise income	Household income	Government income	Investment expenditures	Foreign exchange earnings	

Commodity taxes: Commodity taxes make up one part of indirect taxes levied as a proportion of the quantity produced. One such example is excise duty. These data are obtained from the use table. Import duties are also levied per unit of output but they are classified under taxes paid by the commodity account to the government in the macro-SAM.

Domestic sales: Domestic sales refer to trading of marketed commodities that arise from production activities. These data are calculated by deducting the value of exports from total activity output (column sum of the respective activity account) in the SAM.

Tariff and other indirect taxes: Both tariffs and other indirect taxes are paid per unit of domestic goods and imports sold in domestic markets. Customs duties (tariffs) are paid per unit of imports. There are very few commodities subject to tariffs in Singapore, e.g., tobacco, shirts, basic industrial chemicals, petroleum refining, and products related to repairing of ships, building construction, retail trade, restaurants, water transport, government services, and broadcasting and entertainment services. Sales taxes include general services tax (GST). These data are obtained from the supply table in input–output tables. Property taxes, business license fees, and stamp duties are included in indirect taxes on producers.

Imports: Import of goods and services is defined in input–output tables as all transfers of the ownership of goods and services from non-resident producers to Singapore residents. Imports are measured on cost-insurance-freight (c.i.f.) basis. Therefore, imports include all transport and insurance charges. Import data are obtained from the make table in input output tables.

Labor income: Labor income accruing to households refers to compensation of residents in return for the sale of their labor services. The data are obtained from national income accounts and labor-related data in the statistical yearbook.

Taxes on households and social security payments: Taxes on households refer to various taxes imposed on households by the government. Social security payments are paid by residents to the government. These data are obtained from the official statistical yearbook.

Transfers to the rest of the world: Factor transfers to the rest of the world refer to international transfers of capital profits and labor income. The data are computed from the balance of payments statistics, which are obtained from the statistical yearbook.

Dividends: Corporate dividends refer to indirect capital payments by firms to households. These payments include income from property and transfers to households. These data are obtained from an occasional paper of the Department of Statistics on financial statistics entitled *The Extent and Pattern of Foreign Investment Activities in Singapore*. The relevant data are presented in this document under the principal statistics section.

Retained corporate income: Retained corporate income that accrues to enterprises refers to gross operating surplus generated during production exclusive of taxes incurred during production and other costs including intermediate demand and compensation of employees. This value includes gross factor income arising from the use of capital inclusive of capital consumption allowance and received remittances of profits from the rest of the world. These data are not directly available from official statistics and hence were calculated as a residual item in order to balance the capital account.

Taxes on profits: Direct taxes on firms are obtained from statistical yearbook.

Household consumption: Household consumption consists of private consumption expenditure and income taxes. Household consumption demand for commodities is obtained from the use table in input–output tables. Private consumption expenditure is defined in input–output tables as final purchases of goods and services by households. This includes residents' expenditures abroad. Purchases by non-residents and tourists, foreign military personnel, and foreign diplomatic personnel are considered as part of exports and are not included under this item in the use tables.

Taxes paid by households and firms to government: Firms and households pay taxes to the government from the income they earn. These values are reflected in the government's tax accounts. These data are obtained from statistical yearbook.

Government transfers to households and firms: Current transfers to households from the government refer to social security payments. The data are computed from the statistical yearbook.

Current transfers abroad: Firms and households make transfers to the rest of the world in the form of factor payments. More specifically, firm transfers refer to remittance of profits and household transfers refer to remittance of income. Both values are computed at post-tax values. These data are calculated from the balance of payments accounts that are obtained from the statistical yearbook.

Household and corporate savings: Total savings of households is computed as the sum of the contributions to the CPF and the interest earned on CPF savings less the withdrawals from the CPF accounts due to retirement, death, and permanent leave from Singapore. Savings of firms are computed as a residual balancing item in the enterprises account. Firm savings refer to corporate savings and income from property. Note that the capital account reports savings of households, firms, government, and the rest of the world, which provide necessary funds for domestic investments. Data on household savings are obtained from the statistical yearbook.

Government consumption: Government consumption demand data are taken from the use table. These data refer to value of goods and services used by the government department and institutions.

Government savings: Government savings are calculated as the current account surplus of the consolidated government budget and the data are obtained from the public finance section of the statistical yearbook.

Exports: Exports of goods and services are defined in input–output tables as all transfers of the ownership of goods and services from Singapore residents to non-residents. Direct purchases of goods and services by tourists and other residents in Singapore are also treated as exports. Exports are measured on free-on-board (f.o.b.) basis and reflect the values of exports at the customs frontier. Exports data are obtained from the use table.

Transfers from the rest of the world: Transfers from the rest of the world to households, firms, and government are computed from the balance of payment statistics obtained from the statistical yearbook. A decomposition

Table 8.5. Macro-SAM for Singapore (Unit: Million Singapore Dollars).

	ACT	COM	FAC	ENT	HOU	GOV	CAP	ROW	Total
ACT	0.0	199504.8	0.0	0.0	0.0	0.0	0.0	143186.9	342691.7
COM	224662.8	0.0	0.0	0.0	47750.0	9237.0	41992.6	0.0	323642.5
FAC	106170.2	0.0	0.0	0.0	0.0	0.0	0.0	15239.9	121410.1
ENT	0.0	0.0	51560.5	0.0	0.0	981.0	0.0	−370.6	52170.9
HOU	0.0	0.0	52679.4	7781.0	0.0	828.1	0.0	0.0	61288.4
GOV	11858.7	1132.2	0.0	8468.8	2207.9	0.0	0.0	192.5	23860.0
CAP	0.0	0.0	0.0	36862.9	11330.5	13127.5	0.0	−20355.2	40965.8
ROW	0.0	123005.5	17170.3	−941.8	0.0	−313.6	−1026.9	0.0	137893.5
Total	342691.7	323642.5	121410.1	52170.9	61288.4	23860.0	40965.8	137893.5	

Notes: ACT: activities account; COM: commodities account; FAC: primary factors account; ENT: enterprises account; HOU: households account; GOV: government account; CAP: capital (saving-investment) account; ROW: rest of the world account.

		Activities											Commodities					
		CHE	ELE	DEC	MAN	FIN	OTH	INF	EDU	ENV	CON	PRE	CHE	ELE	DEC	MAN	FIN	OTH
Activities	CHE	0.00	0.00	0.00	0.00	0.00	0.00	0.00	0.00	0.00	0.00	0.00	10.04	0.00	0.00	0.00	0.00	0.00
	ELE	0.00	0.00	0.00	0.00	0.00	0.00	0.00	0.00	0.00	0.00	0.00	0.00	44.96	0.00	0.00	0.00	0.00
	DEC	0.00	0.00	0.00	0.00	0.00	0.00	0.00	0.00	0.00	0.00	0.00	0.00	0.00	7.99	0.00	0.00	0.00
	MAN	0.00	0.00	0.00	0.00	0.00	0.00	0.00	0.00	0.00	0.00	0.00	0.00	0.00	0.00	16.79	0.00	0.00
	FIN	0.00	0.00	0.00	0.00	0.00	0.00	0.00	0.00	0.00	0.00	0.00	0.00	0.00	0.00	0.00	34.54	0.00
	OTH	0.00	0.00	0.00	0.00	0.00	0.00	0.00	0.00	0.00	0.00	0.00	0.00	0.00	0.00	0.00	0.00	81.10
	INF	0.00	0.00	0.00	0.00	0.00	0.00	0.00	0.00	0.00	0.00	0.00	0.00	0.00	0.00	0.00	0.00	0.00
	EDU	0.00	0.00	0.00	0.00	0.00	0.00	0.00	0.00	0.00	0.00	0.00	0.00	0.00	0.00	0.00	0.00	0.00
	ENV	0.00	0.00	0.00	0.00	0.00	0.00	0.00	0.00	0.00	0.00	0.00	0.00	0.00	0.00	0.00	0.00	0.00
	CON	0.00	0.00	0.00	0.00	0.00	0.00	0.00	0.00	0.00	0.00	0.00	0.00	0.00	0.00	0.00	0.00	0.00
	PRE	0.00	0.00	0.00	0.00	0.00	0.00	0.00	0.00	0.00	0.00	0.00	0.00	0.00	0.00	0.00	0.00	0.00
Commodities	CHE	0.08	0.60	7.95	0.57	0.30	0.40	0.00	0.00	0.08	0.00	0.08	0.00	0.00	0.00	0.00	0.00	0.00
	ELE	0.02	53.60	0.39	1.68	0.47	0.63	0.31	0.02	0.07	0.03	0.16	0.00	0.00	0.00	0.00	0.00	0.00
	DEC	5.91	0.94	8.11	0.40	0.19	6.98	0.01	0.00	0.02	0.02	0.00	0.00	0.00	0.00	0.00	0.00	0.00
	MAN	0.19	8.04	2.06	9.80	1.64	5.42	0.06	0.02	0.36	0.04	0.20	0.00	0.00	0.00	0.00	0.00	0.00
	FIN	0.73	7.80	1.93	2.12	8.55	17.70	0.15	0.06	0.28	0.17	0.03	0.00	0.00	0.00	0.00	0.00	0.00
	OTH	1.19	21.38	4.47	7.09	2.94	23.03	0.75	0.07	0.16	0.69	0.88	0.00	0.00	0.00	0.00	0.00	0.00
	INF	0.03	0.25	0.07	0.15	0.63	1.96	0.24	0.00	0.10	0.08	0.01	0.00	0.00	0.00	0.00	0.00	0.00
	EDU	0.00	0.01	0.00	0.01	0.02	0.08	0.01	0.00	0.00	0.01	0.00	0.00	0.00	0.00	0.00	0.00	0.00
	ENV	0.04	0.20	0.03	0.07	0.18	1.19	0.02	0.00	0.61	0.02	0.00	0.00	0.00	0.00	0.00	0.00	0.00
	CON	0.02	0.21	0.13	0.04	0.25	0.81	0.02	0.01	0.04	0.06	0.00	0.00	0.00	0.00	0.00	0.00	0.00
	PRE	0.01	0.40	0.05	0.08	0.00	0.55	0.00	0.00	0.06	0.00	0.16	0.00	0.00	0.00	0.00	0.00	0.00
Factors	Labor	0.79	4.88	1.07	5.15	9.11	26.64	0.87	0.28	0.92	0.86	0.22	0.00	0.00	0.00	0.00	0.00	0.00
	Capital	2.90	9.09	0.87	4.67	18.12	16.11	2.44	0.34	0.42	0.17	0.26	0.00	0.00	0.00	0.00	0.00	0.00
Institutions	Households	0.00	0.00	0.00	0.00	0.00	0.00	0.00	0.00	0.00	0.00	0.00	0.00	0.00	0.00	0.00	0.00	0.00
	Enterprises	0.00	0.00	0.00	0.00	0.00	0.00	0.00	0.00	0.00	0.00	0.00	0.00	0.00	0.00	0.00	0.00	0.00
	Government	1.16	0.64	0.16	0.75	2.22	6.82	0.05	0.01	0.02	0.02	0.01	0.04	0.01	0.00	0.03	0.06	0.99
Rest of the world		0.00	0.00	0.00	0.00	0.00	0.00	0.00	0.00	0.00	0.00	0.00	0.81	18.63	19.63	23.08	14.09	44.75
Investment		0.00	0.00	0.00	0.00	0.00	0.00	0.00	0.00	0.00	0.00	0.00	0.00	0.00	0.00	0.00	0.00	0.00
Total		13.06	108.04	27.29	32.57	44.63	108.31	4.92	0.81	3.11	2.16	2.00	10.89	63.59	27.62	39.90	48.70	126.84

(*Continued*)

Table 8.6. (*Continued*)

		Commodities					Factors		Institutions			Rest of the		
		INF	EDU	ENV	CON	PRE	Labor	Capital	Households	Enterprises	Government	World	Investment	Total
Activities	CHE	0.00	0.00	0.00	0.00	0.00	0.00	0.00	0.00	0.00	0.00	3.01	0.00	13.06
	ELE	0.00	0.00	0.00	0.00	0.00	0.00	0.00	0.00	0.00	0.00	63.09	0.00	108.04
	PRE	0.00	0.00	0.00	0.00	0.00	0.00	0.00	0.00	0.00	0.00	19.30	0.00	27.29
	DEC	0.00	0.00	0.00	0.00	0.00	0.00	0.00	0.00	0.00	0.00	15.78	0.00	32.57
	MAN	0.00	0.00	0.00	0.00	0.00	0.00	0.00	0.00	0.00	0.00	10.08	0.00	44.63
	FIN	0.00	0.00	0.00	0.00	0.00	0.00	0.00	0.00	0.00	0.00	27.21	0.00	108.31
	INF	3.61	0.00	0.00	0.00	0.00	0.00	0.00	0.00	0.00	0.00	1.31	0.00	4.92
	EDU	0.00	0.81	0.00	0.00	0.00	0.00	0.00	0.00	0.00	0.00	0.01	0.00	0.81
	ENV	0.00	0.00	1.79	0.00	0.00	0.00	0.00	0.00	0.00	0.00	1.33	0.00	3.11
	CON	0.00	0.00	0.00	1.31	0.00	0.00	0.00	0.00	0.00	0.00	0.84	0.00	2.16
	OTH	0.00	0.00	0.00	0.00	0.78	0.00	0.00	0.00	0.00	0.00	1.23	0.00	2.00
Commodities	CHE	0.00	0.00	0.00	0.00	0.00	0.00	0.00	0.73	0.00	0.00	0.00	0.10	10.89
	ELE	0.00	0.00	0.00	0.00	0.00	0.00	0.00	3.36	0.00	0.00	0.00	2.85	63.59
	PRE	0.00	0.00	0.00	0.00	0.00	0.00	0.00	3.59	0.00	0.00	0.00	1.45	27.62
	DEC	0.00	0.00	0.00	0.00	0.00	0.00	0.00	6.84	0.00	0.00	0.00	5.22	39.90
	MAN	0.00	0.00	0.00	0.00	0.00	0.00	0.00	4.67	0.00	0.00	0.00	4.52	48.70
	FIN	0.00	0.00	0.00	0.00	0.00	0.00	0.00	27.19	0.00	9.24	0.00	27.77	126.84
	INF	0.00	0.00	0.00	0.00	0.00	0.00	0.00	0.66	0.00	0.00	0.00	0.01	4.17
	EDU	0.00	0.00	0.00	0.00	0.00	0.00	0.00	0.67	0.00	0.00	0.00	0.00	0.83
	ENV	0.00	0.00	0.00	0.00	0.00	0.00	0.00	0.01	0.00	0.00	0.00	0.00	2.35
	CON	0.00	0.00	0.00	0.00	0.00	0.00	0.00	0.02	0.00	0.00	0.00	0.01	1.61
	OTH	0.00	0.00	0.00	0.00	0.00	0.00	0.00	0.01	0.00	0.00	0.00	0.05	1.36
Factors	Labor	0.00	0.00	0.00	0.00	0.00	0.00	0.00	0.00	0.00	0.00	8.58	0.00	59.38
	Capital	0.00	0.00	0.00	0.00	0.00	0.00	0.00	0.00	0.00	0.00	6.66	0.00	62.03
Institutions	Households	0.00	0.00	0.00	0.00	0.00	52.68	0.00	0.00	7.78	0.83	0.00	0.00	61.29
	Enterprises	0.00	0.00	0.00	0.00	0.00	0.00	51.56	0.00	0.00	0.98	−0.37	0.00	52.17
	Government	0.00	0.00	0.00	0.00	0.00	0.00	0.00	2.21	8.47	0.00	0.19	0.00	23.86
Rest of the world		0.56	0.03	0.56	0.30	0.58	6.70	10.47	0.00	−0.94	−0.31	0.00	−1.03	137.89
Investment		0.00	0.00	0.00	0.00	0.00	0.00	0.00	11.33	36.86	13.13	−20.36	0.00	40.97
Total		4.17	0.83	2.35	1.61	1.36	59.38	62.03	61.29	52.17	23.86	137.89	40.97	

of transfers is not available but transfers involving the government are separately reported. I assume that household transfers are negligibly small and attribute all transfers other than government transfers to enterprises.

Capital transfer: Capital transfer refers to the balance on the current account, e.g., the excess of receipts from abroad over expenditures abroad. These data are obtained from the balance of payments statistics published in the statistical yearbook.

Investment: Investment demand refers to additions to stocks of fixed assets. Investment demand data for each commodity are obtained from the use table. These values include expenditures made by households on new residential dwellings, acquisitions of machinery and equipment by producers, capital repairs and improvement, and changes in inventories. Changes in inventories refer to raw materials, work-in-progress on construction of residential and non-residential buildings, and finished goods. Investment demand data are obtained from the use table in input–output tables.

Balanced SAM is estimated using the GAMS software. Table 8.5 presents the balanced macro-SAM of Singapore for 1995.

8.6.2. *Micro-SAM*

Table 8.6 presents the micro-SAM for 1995, which is a 30 × 30 matrix consisting of Eleven production and commodity groups, 3 institutional accounts (households, enterprises), 2 factors of production (capital and labor), an investment-saving account, and an account for the rest of the world. Eleven sectors in the CGE analysis were presented in Table 8.1.

Since the aim of the CGE model is not an evaluation of the impact on income distribution, no disaggregation among households is intended. Therefore, all households are represented in one household account. Finally, it should be noted that capital expenditures and government income are not included in the government account. They are considered as part of gross capital formation. Income tax consists of individual income taxes and corporate taxes including tax on property.

CHAPTER 9

POLICY EXPERIMENTS FOR JAPAN, KOREA, AND SINGAPORE

Quantifying the changes in economic variables of interest such as prices, exchange rate, output, and resource demands resulting from exogenous shocks or policy changes is important in applied CGE modeling. Policy experiments help the modeler understand the direction and magnitude of the changes brought about by such shocks. These are important tools in drawing policy lessons and conclusions for a given economy. This chapter examines the results of policy experiments for Singapore with the CGE model and overviews the results of similar other studies for the Japanese and Korean industrial policies.

9.1. The Structure of the Singapore Economy in 1995

Table 9.1 presents the structure of the economy in the base year (1995).[1] Promoted industries, i.e., "winners," are CHE, ELE, PRE, FIN, INF, EDU, CON, and ENV. It is important to note that FIN was emphasized by the government as an engine of growth after the mid-1980s. The promoted industries make up more than half of intermediate input demand, a large portion of which is imported, total exports, value-added, and domestic sales.

Petroleum refining and transport equipment industries (DEC) received government support before 1985, but failed to maintain this support after 1985 due to worsening prospects of world demand for these industries. Consequently, its importance declined steadily. In 1995, its share in employment declined to a mere 2 percent of total labor force (about 8 percent of manufacturing employment) and its share in total value-added in the economy to about 4 percent (about 13 percent of manufacturing value-added). However,

[1] Soon and Tan (1993) and Huff (2000) also provide excellent reviews of the economy.

Table 9.1. Structure of the Economy in 1995, Percentage Sectoral Shares in Total.

	CHE	ELE	PRE	DEC	MAN	FIN	INF	EDU	ENV	CON	OTH
Composite output	3.8	31.1	0.6	7.9	9.4	12.9	1.4	0.2	0.9	0.6	31.2
Consumption	1.5	7.0	0.0	7.5	14.3	9.8	1.4	1.4	0.0	0.0	56.9
Domestic sales	4.9	22.1	0.4	3.9	8.2	17.0	1.8	0.4	0.9	0.6	39.8
Exports	2.1	44.1	0.9	13.5	11.0	7.0	0.9	0.0	0.9	0.6	19.0
Gross output	3.3	19.4	0.4	8.4	12.2	14.9	1.3	0.3	0.7	0.5	38.7
Gross profits	5.2	16.4	0.5	1.6	8.4	32.7	4.4	0.6	0.8	0.3	29.1
Imports	0.7	15.1	0.5	16.0	18.8	11.5	0.5	0.0	0.5	0.2	36.4
Indirect taxes	9.7	5.4	0.1	1.4	6.3	18.7	0.4	0.1	0.1	0.1	57.5
Intermediate inputs	3.6	40.8	0.7	11.0	9.6	6.6	0.7	0.1	0.8	0.5	25.7
Investment	0.2	6.8	0.1	3.5	12.4	10.8	0.0	0.0	0.0	0.0	66.1
Labor	0.7	8.1	0.5	2.4	10.1	14.9	1.5	0.5	1.6	0.9	58.7
Labor cost	1.6	9.6	0.4	2.1	10.1	17.9	1.7	0.6	1.8	1.7	52.4
Value-added	4.1	12.4	1.8	9.0	25.0	42.0	2.8	0.5	1.1	0.9	0.4

Note: Industry abbreviations are explained in the text.
Source: Author's calculations using the values from the SAM.

it still accounts for about 14 percent of total exports and 16 percent of total imports.

Remaining services sectors (OTH) pay a large portion of indirect taxes as they produce four-tenth of total output and domestic sales and their share in consumption is much higher since their output is produced mostly for the domestic market. They employ a large portion of total labor force and account for half of total payments to labor.

The economy of Singapore is highly dependent on international trade of resources and goods. A large portion of material inputs and output in each sector are imported and exported. For this reason, it is difficult to classify production activities strictly as tradable or non-tradable. The CGE model does not specify separate trade aggregation functions by categorizing production sectors as tradable and non-tradable, but rather treats each sector as tradable. Finally, intersectoral input–output relations need to be emphasized. Table 9.2 presents the condensed input–output coefficients for six sectors prepared using the *Singapore Input–Output Tables 1995*. DEC, ELE,

Table 9.2. Input–Output Coefficients.

	CHE	ELE	PRE	DEC	MAN	FIN	INF	EDU	ENV	CON	OTH
CHE	0.006	0.006	0.291	0.017	0.007	0.004	0.000	0.002	0.024	0.000	0.041
ELE	0.001	0.496	0.014	0.052	0.011	0.006	0.064	0.022	0.021	0.013	0.079
PRE	0.452	0.009	0.297	0.012	0.004	0.064	0.002	0.002	0.006	0.008	0.002
DEC	0.015	0.074	0.075	0.301	0.037	0.050	0.012	0.022	0.116	0.020	0.099
MAN	0.056	0.072	0.071	0.065	0.192	0.163	0.030	0.077	0.090	0.077	0.014
FIN	0.091	0.198	0.164	0.218	0.066	0.213	0.153	0.083	0.052	0.321	0.437
INF	0.003	0.002	0.002	0.004	0.014	0.018	0.049	0.005	0.031	0.037	0.003
EDU	0.000	0.000	0.000	0.000	0.001	0.001	0.002	0.005	0.001	0.004	0.000
ENV	0.003	0.002	0.001	0.002	0.004	0.011	0.004	0.005	0.194	0.008	0.001
CON	0.001	0.002	0.005	0.001	0.006	0.007	0.004	0.007	0.013	0.028	0.002
OTH	0.000	0.004	0.002	0.002	0.000	0.005	0.000	0.000	0.018	0.001	0.078

Source: *Singapore Input–Output Tables, 1995.*

and PRE provide most of the inputs they demand by themselves. CHE has strong input relations with PRE, and FIN has strong input relations with ELE, DEC, CON, OTH, and itself.

9.2. Base-Run

Base-run results are expected to be very close to SAM figures since the parameters used in the CGE model are derived from the SAM. However, the CGE model assumes that markets are in equilibrium and the changes in relative prices of goods and factors lead to this equilibrium. Therefore, base-run results differ slightly from SAM values. First, the model fixes the base year prices at unity and recalculates relative prices and other variables using behavioral equations.

In the base-run, some variables (total labor supply and total capital stock within periods, factor price distortion factors, and marginal saving rate) are set as exogenous. All other variables are allowed to adjust to their equilibrium levels. Base-run results are used as benchmark values to compare the results from simulations. Each exogenous shock given to the model result in relative price changes to which the economic agents respond. Total labor supply and total capital stock is fixed within periods, but is updated each period using accumulation equations. Sectoral factor demands, however, are not fixed. Therefore, general equilibrium of the economy results in intersectoral reallocation of factors according to sectoral factor demands and factor prices. An index of producer prices is set as the numéraire and other prices are expressed relative to this index. Responding to the changes in relative prices, factors are reallocated when a shock is given. To maximize profits, producers change their demand for factors in policy shocks.

A modeler can choose between fixed and flexible exchange rate in CGE modeling. The choice of the exchange regime is related to the preference of the modeler for balance of payments equilibrium in the model. If a flexible exchange rate is assumed, then the model computes the real exchange rate level that endogenously maintains the balance of payments equilibrium. On the other hand, the flexible exchange rate allows for fluctuations in the balance of payments. Since the early 1980s, the Monetary Authority of Singapore has implemented a managed floating exchange rate policy in which the weighted value of Singapore dollar *vis-à-vis* the currencies of major trading partners is left to fluctuate within an undisclosed range. Both the range and the basket of currencies are updated with respect to changes in the economy. Exchange rate has an effect on other prices in the model (see Figure 9.2). Fixed exchange rate enables balance of payments adjustment. In the present model, the exchange rate is fixed to isolate the effect of the exchange rate on relative prices. The changes in relative prices are, therefore, direct effects.[2]

The results of the baseline (benchmark) solution are summarized for major variables of interest in Table 9.3. A 20-year horizon is chosen for all simulations. The figures in Table 9.3 represent the values of each item in long-run equilibrium, i.e., after 20 years. The figures are therefore representative of the long-run growth path of the economy. Each value in Table 9.3 refers to the ratio of the terminal year value for the relevant variable or scalar to its value at the benchmark solution, which replicates the SAM. Implied average annual growth rates for the variables of interest are presented in Table 9.4. The long-run growth path of the economy demonstrates a tendency for total output, consumption, and exports to grow by

[2]This means that the difference in relative price changes for a specific price variable in an experiment results from the real exchange rate. Denoting the relative price change for the flexible exchange rate case as ΔP_f and as ΔP_x for the fixed exchange rate case, the indirect effect of the real exchange rate on the relative price change is $\Delta P_f - \Delta P_x$.

Table 9.3. Baseline Summary Results for the Terminal Year (Base Year = 1.00).

	CHE	ELE	PRE	DEC	MAN	FIN	INF	EDU	CON	ENV	OTH	All
C	3.42	2.61	2.15	3.31	2.51	2.54	3.58	4.11	2.41	2.05	2.42	2.61
I	1.18	1.01	0.96	1.04	0.97	1.14	1.27	1.00	0.67	1.00	0.93	0.97
K	5.19	4.35	3.33	8.81	4.27	4.99	6.75	8.20	5.50	3.99	5.00	4.98
L	2.07	1.01	0.72	2.08	1.00	1.23	1.51	1.85	1.20	0.86	1.24	1.22
M	2.56	2.66	2.51	3.21	2.78	2.04	2.31	4.35	5.11	3.35	2.95	2.81
Q	3.81	2.55	1.63	3.85	1.94	2.99	4.52	4.10	1.53	1.39	2.01	2.54
X	4.78	2.52	1.44	3.96	1.68	3.74	6.25	4.00	0.74	0.87	1.56	2.57
Prices												
P	0.89	1.01	1.06	0.99	1.07	0.90	0.85	1.03	1.44	1.26	1.13	
Pc	0.87	1.01	1.08	0.99	1.05	0.90	0.80	1.03	1.46	1.28	1.10	
Pd	0.86	1.01	1.15	0.95	1.13	0.86	0.78	1.03	1.62	1.40	1.17	

Notes: C: consumption; I: investment; K: capital; L: employment; M: imports; Q: output; X: exports; P: supply (composite output) prices; Pc: consumption price level; Pd: domestic prices.

Table 9.4. Baseline Results at Terminal Year, Average Percentage Annual Growth Rates.

	CHE	ELE	PRE	DEC	MAN	FIN	INF	EDU	CON	ENV	OTH	All
C	6.2	4.8	3.8	6.0	4.6	4.7	6.4	7.1	4.4	3.6	4.4	4.8
I	0.8	0.1	−0.2	0.2	−0.1	0.7	1.2	0.0	−2.0	0.0	−0.4	−0.2
K	8.2	7.3	6.0	10.9	7.3	8.0	9.6	10.5	8.5	6.9	8.0	8.0
L	3.6	0.1	−1.6	3.7	0.0	1.0	2.1	3.1	0.9	−0.8	1.1	1.0
M	4.7	4.9	4.6	5.8	5.1	3.6	4.2	7.3	8.2	6.0	5.4	5.2
Q	6.7	4.7	2.4	6.7	3.3	5.5	7.5	7.1	2.1	1.6	3.5	4.7
X	7.8	4.6	1.8	6.9	2.6	6.6	9.2	6.9	−1.5	−0.7	2.2	4.7
Prices												
P	−0.6	0.0	0.3	−0.1	0.4	−0.6	−0.8	0.1	1.8	1.2	0.6	
Pc	−0.7	0.0	0.4	−0.1	0.3	−0.5	−1.1	0.1	1.9	1.2	0.5	
Pd	−0.8	0.1	0.7	−0.3	0.6	−0.8	−1.2	0.1	2.4	1.7	0.8	

Notes: C: consumption; I: investment; K: capital; L: employment; M: imports; Q: output; X: exports; P: supply (composite output) prices; Pc: consumption price level; Pd: domestic prices.

Table 9.5. Baseline Macroeconomic Results.

	Relative to SAM	Average Annual Growth Rate (Percent)
Total private consumption	4.56	7.6
Total private savings	2.75	5.1
Real GDP	2.55	4.7
Government savings	2.89	5.3
Government investments	3.07	5.6
Real wage level	2.38	4.3
Real rental rate of capital	0.51	−3.3

4.7–4.8 percent. The growth rate of imports is larger (5.2 percent). Changes in the price levels and output-related variables are various for individual sectors as presented in Tables 9.3 and 9.4. The largest increases in output are experienced in CHE, DEC, FIN, INF, and EDU. The long-run growth path of the economy demonstrates a GDP growth potential of the economy by 4.7 percent.

Some results for selected macroeconomic variables are summarized in Table 9.5. The importance of private investments (including both domestic and foreign investments) is clear from the presented results. It is important to note also that the growth rate of public investments is larger than the growth rate of the economy because the primary budget balance of the government is in a surplus which rises throughout the period of analysis. Real wages rise and the real rental rate of capital decreases by 3.3 percent each year, indicating the diminishing returns to accumulated capital as a result of high rates of capital accumulation.

It is clear from the baseline solution that the benchmark solution depicts the working of the Singapore economy very realistically. In the simulation experiments discussed in the following sections, the results of each simulation are summarized relative to the initial base-year values. Average annual growth rates are also presented separately. By presenting the results this way, we can capture the real impacts on individual sectors and the economy. Therefore the results are indicative of the long-run effects of given shocks to the economic variables. In what follows, the deviations of growth rates from the benchmark solution are especially emphasized to detect the long-run impact better.

9.3. Policy Experiments

Three policy experiments are run using the CGE model. The first experiment is designed to investigate the effects of an exogenous price shock (10 percent increase in the world export prices of ELE). The second experiment investigates the consequences of exogenous TFP growth by 2 percent in each sector. Finally, a counterfactual simulation experiment (Simulation 3) examines the results for different variations of labor and capital market restrictions. One of the variations is perfect mobility in both factor markets, which measures the impact on the economy of abolishing all distortions in factor markets and replacing it with perfect competition in factor markets.

9.3.1. *Simulation 1: 10 percent increase in the world price of electrical and electronic machinery and equipment*

We start with an exogenous shock in the form of 10 percent increase in the world price of ELE, the most important export industry. International economic theory assumes that such a change in a small country leads to a decline in the terms of trade and a worsening of the country's welfare. This is established by 0.5 percentage point lower average annual real GDP growth rate (4.2 percent) with respect to the base run (4.7 percent).

Some of the results relative to the base-year values are summarized in Table 9.6. In addition, Table 9.7 presents the average annual growth rates for the variables of interest by sector. Due to the rise in world price, the growth rate of the exports of ELE is larger (5.5 percent) compared to the long-run growth path of the benchmark solution. The amount of total exports do not change much at the terminal year compared to the base-run path. This is possible only when exports by other sectors are substituted with ELE exports. In fact, this is what happens: the growth rates of exports by all other sectors are reduced. Export growth rate by 5.5 percent as opposed to 10 percent increase in the world prices implies low supply price elasticity of ELE.

Table 9.6. Simulation 1: Summary Results (Base = 1.000).

	CHE	ELE	PRE	DEC	MAN	FIN	INF	EDU	CON	ENV	OTH	All
C	2.839	2.988	2.249	2.917	2.551	2.559	3.538	4.121	2.386	2.061	2.464	2.65
I	1.178	1.039	0.957	1.045	0.985	1.148	1.273	2.000	0.667	1.000	0.936	0.98
K	4.234	5.109	3.361	6.790	4.210	4.914	6.523	8.185	5.359	3.940	4.992	4.98
L	1.695	1.196	0.732	1.607	0.991	1.219	1.463	1.857	1.173	0.849	1.245	1.22
M	2.204	3.008	2.672	2.905	2.856	2.111	2.371	4.462	5.145	3.428	3.053	2.88
Q	3.117	3.000	1.647	2.972	1.914	2.955	4.368	4.107	1.501	1.374	2.010	2.58
X	3.804	3.013	1.433	2.984	1.633	3.594	5.903	3.800	0.708	0.847	1.527	2.61
Prices												
P	0.905	1.008	1.072	0.998	1.082	0.907	0.860	1.042	1.456	1.273	1.147	
Pc	0.881	1.003	1.090	0.998	1.058	0.908	0.819	1.041	1.469	1.290	1.113	
Pd	0.873	1.005	1.168	0.993	1.150	0.875	0.796	1.043	1.642	1.418	1.189	

See notes in Table 9.3.

Table 9.7. Simulation 1: Average Annual Percentage Growth Rates.

	CHE	ELE	PRE	DEC	MAN	FIN	INF	EDU	CON	ENV	OTH	All
C	5.2	5.5	4.1	5.4	4.7	4.7	6.3	7.1	4.3	3.6	4.5	4.9
I	0.8	0.2	−0.2	0.2	−0.1	0.7	1.2	3.5	−2.0	0.0	−0.3	−0.1
K	7.2	8.2	6.1	9.6	7.2	8.0	9.4	10.5	8.4	6.9	8.0	8.0
L	2.6	0.9	−1.6	2.4	0.0	1.0	1.9	3.1	0.8	−0.8	1.1	1.0
M	4.0	5.5	4.9	5.3	5.2	3.7	4.3	7.5	8.2	6.2	5.6	5.3
MI	5.2	5.4	4.1	5.0	4.4	4.5	4.4	4.2	4.4	3.6	4.6	4.8
Q	5.7	5.5	2.5	5.4	3.2	5.4	7.4	7.1	2.0	1.6	3.5	4.7
X	6.7	5.5	1.8	5.5	2.5	6.4	8.9	6.7	−1.7	−0.8	2.1	4.8
Prices												
P	−0.5	0.0	0.3	0.0	0.4	−0.5	−0.8	0.2	1.9	1.2	0.7	
Pc	−0.6	0.0	0.4	0.0	0.3	−0.5	−1.0	0.2	1.9	1.3	0.5	
Pd	−0.7	0.0	0.8	0.0	0.7	−0.7	−1.1	0.2	2.5	1.7	0.9	

See notes in Table 9.3.

Comparing the levels and the implied average annual growth rates of output, exports, consumption, and production factors capital and labor (Tables 9.6 and 9.7) with relevant figures for the long-run path (Tables 9.3 and 9.4), it is easily seen that the economy aggregates are minimally

Table 9.8. Simulation 1: Macroeconomic Results.

	Relative to Base Run	Average Annual Growth Rate (Percent)
Total private consumption	4.58	7.6
Total private savings	3.86	6.8
Real GDP	2.57	4.7
Government savings	2.90	5.3
Government investments	2.98	5.5
Real wage level	2.41	4.4
Real rental rate of capital	0.52	−3.3

influenced whereas the impact on individual sectors are higher for CHE and DEC than others. Average growth rates for these variables are reduced by 0.7–1.4 percentage points for CHE and DEC. For ELE, output, consumption, and factor demand all increase by 0.8–0.9 percent. The impact of the increase in world prices of ELE exports on prices is negligible. There is not much change in the levels and therefore, in the growth rates of the prices in the long run. Finally, the figures in Table 9.8 indicate that macro balances are not affected much from the exogenous price shock.

9.3.2. *Simulation 2: 2 percent TFP growth*

During the course of industrial development, an important development that was experienced by Singapore after the transformation of industrial policies around 1985–1990 was the increase in TFP growth rates. This was examined using a partial equilibrium analysis in Chapter 6. Such a drastic change in the economy cannot be ignored in economic analysis. The increase in TFP growth rate implies efficiency improvement and a better functioning of the markets. It was seen before in productivity analysis that the TFP growth in Singapore was realized together with the strong hand of the government in economic decision-making. The model is used to quantify the impact of exogenous TFP growth in each sector annually by 2 percent. For this purpose, 11 simulations are run. The results are summarized in Tables 9.9 and 9.10. Implied average annual growth rates are presented in Tables 9.11 and 9.12.

Table 9.9. Simulation 2: Summary Results (Base Year = 1.00).

	CHE	ELE	PRE	DEC	MAN	FIN	INF	EDU	CON	ENV	OTH	All
2 percent TFP growth in CHE												
C	8.98	1.74	2.22	7.46	2.93	3.01	4.49	4.71	3.16	2.32	2.83	3.28
I	1.79	1.22	1.19	1.41	1.24	1.45	1.55	2.00	0.89	1.00	1.17	1.22
K	11.28	2.52	3.25	30.17	4.86	6.07	8.55	10.27	7.86	4.77	6.17	6.18
L	3.66	0.48	0.58	5.80	0.93	1.22	1.56	1.89	1.40	0.84	1.25	1.27
M	5.01	2.13	2.80	6.78	3.42	2.58	3.14	5.46	7.81	4.25	3.75	3.81
Q	11.50	1.37	1.45	11.72	1.97	3.38	5.41	4.68	1.85	1.44	2.17	3.20
X	17.54	1.20	1.18	12.66	1.57	3.97	7.12	4.00	0.74	0.79	1.50	3.43
2 percent TFP growth in ELE												
C	2.04	5.26	3.06	2.53	3.18	3.08	4.10	4.53	2.74	2.37	3.04	3.42
I	1.40	1.37	1.15	1.27	1.21	1.37	1.45	2.00	0.89	1.00	1.12	1.18
K	3.02	6.81	3.98	3.86	4.68	5.62	7.19	9.63	6.23	4.49	6.05	5.78
L	1.03	1.36	0.74	0.78	0.94	1.19	1.37	1.86	1.16	0.82	1.28	1.22
M	1.85	5.00	4.09	2.79	3.84	2.93	3.24	5.81	6.89	4.63	4.28	3.90
Q	2.11	5.61	1.81	1.54	1.95	3.19	4.61	4.49	1.59	1.40	2.19	3.33
X	2.28	5.77	1.39	1.36	1.45	3.35	5.56	3.60	0.62	0.71	1.38	3.51
2 percent TFP growth in PRE												
C	3.39	2.63	2.29	3.28	2.52	2.54	3.59	4.12	2.41	2.06	2.43	2.61
I	1.18	1.02	1.09	1.04	0.98	1.14	1.27	1.00	0.67	1.00	0.93	0.97
K	5.14	4.37	3.76	8.68	4.28	4.99	6.76	8.22	5.50	4.01	5.02	4.99
L	2.04	1.02	0.81	2.04	1.00	1.23	1.50	1.85	1.19	0.86	1.24	1.22
M	2.54	2.68	2.08	3.19	2.79	2.05	2.32	4.38	5.13	3.35	2.97	2.82
Q	3.77	2.56	2.73	3.78	1.94	2.99	4.51	4.11	1.53	1.39	2.01	2.54
X	4.71	2.53	2.90	3.89	1.68	3.72	6.23	4.00	0.73	0.88	1.56	2.58
2 percent TFP growth in DEC												
C	8.57	1.78	2.18	6.89	2.86	2.93	4.43	4.59	3.08	2.26	2.75	3.17
I	1.49	1.17	1.15	1.35	1.19	1.40	1.55	2.00	0.78	1.00	1.12	1.17
K	14.00	2.61	3.21	19.41	4.78	5.95	8.52	9.99	7.66	4.64	6.03	6.08
L	4.58	0.50	0.57	3.76	0.92	1.21	1.56	1.85	1.37	0.82	1.23	1.22
M	6.29	2.13	2.74	6.21	3.32	2.47	3.02	5.27	7.49	4.09	3.61	3.64
Q	9.64	1.42	1.43	11.25	1.95	3.32	5.40	4.56	1.81	1.41	2.13	3.09
X	12.25	1.26	1.17	12.22	1.56	3.95	7.21	4.00	0.74	0.79	1.49	3.28
2 percent TFP growth in MAN												
C	3.13	2.56	2.24	3.13	3.19	2.63	3.71	4.30	2.42	2.11	2.57	2.73
I	1.27	1.10	1.04	1.13	1.20	1.24	1.36	2.00	0.78	1.00	1.00	1.06

(Continued)

Table 9.9. (*Continued*)

	CHE	ELE	PRE	DEC	MAN	FIN	INF	EDU	CON	ENV	OTH	All
K	4.81	4.23	3.44	7.81	6.58	5.17	6.94	8.90	5.67	4.21	5.39	5.31
L	1.75	0.90	0.68	1.69	1.41	1.17	1.42	1.84	1.13	0.83	1.22	1.22
M	2.45	2.70	2.67	3.11	2.85	2.20	2.54	4.81	5.56	3.61	3.28	2.96
Q	3.43	2.40	1.61	3.24	4.23	3.01	4.53	4.27	1.47	1.38	2.04	2.66
X	4.17	2.32	1.39	3.27	4.77	3.61	6.05	3.80	0.64	0.82	1.49	2.69
2 percent TFP growth in FIN												
C	2.64	1.87	1.73	2.80	2.47	3.34	3.73	4.52	2.74	2.18	2.47	2.54
I	1.41	1.21	1.13	1.28	1.19	1.97	1.36	2.00	0.89	1.00	1.13	1.24
K	3.87	2.78	2.24	6.01	3.68	7.75	6.20	9.01	5.90	3.94	4.88	5.40
L	1.52	0.64	0.48	1.39	0.85	1.88	1.36	2.00	1.27	0.83	1.19	1.22
M	2.17	2.09	2.23	2.84	2.90	1.43	3.05	5.62	6.61	4.00	3.19	2.72
Q	2.83	1.62	1.09	2.60	1.65	6.87	4.13	4.48	1.62	1.36	1.94	2.56
X	3.31	1.51	0.87	2.56	1.31	13.32	4.86	3.60	0.67	0.75	1.39	2.49
2 percent TFP growth in INF												
C	2.74	2.18	1.89	2.84	2.33	2.41	5.62	4.38	2.42	2.10	2.41	2.44
I	1.21	1.03	0.98	1.08	1.01	1.18	2.55	2.00	0.78	1.00	0.97	1.01
K	4.04	3.30	2.78	6.56	3.78	4.60	21.68	8.58	5.38	3.99	4.84	5.15
L	1.66	0.79	0.62	1.59	0.91	1.17	4.99	2.00	1.21	0.88	1.24	1.22
M	2.13	2.37	2.25	2.82	2.62	1.99	0.94	4.81	5.11	3.42	2.96	2.66
Q	3.00	1.96	1.38	2.91	1.74	2.79	21.71	4.36	1.54	1.42	1.98	2.44
X	3.65	1.85	1.20	2.93	1.48	3.39	47.95	4.00	0.74	0.89	1.52	2.44
2 percent TFP growth in EDU												
C	3.42	2.62	2.16	3.31	2.51	2.54	3.59	5.36	2.43	2.06	2.42	2.62
I	1.18	1.01	0.96	1.04	0.97	1.14	1.27	2.00	0.67	1.00	0.93	0.97
K	5.19	4.36	3.34	8.81	4.28	5.00	6.78	7.35	5.54	4.00	5.01	4.99
L	2.06	1.01	0.72	2.07	1.00	1.23	1.51	1.66	1.20	0.86	1.24	1.22
M	2.56	2.67	2.51	3.21	2.78	2.04	2.31	3.19	5.14	3.36	2.96	2.81
Q	3.81	2.55	1.63	3.84	1.94	3.00	4.53	5.46	1.54	1.39	2.01	2.54
X	4.77	2.52	1.44	3.95	1.68	3.75	6.28	9.40	0.74	0.87	1.56	2.57
2 percent TFP growth in CON												
C	3.51	2.60	2.16	3.37	2.52	2.56	3.61	4.15	2.46	2.07	2.44	2.63
I	1.19	1.02	0.96	1.05	0.98	1.16	1.27	2.00	0.89	1.00	0.94	0.98
K	5.34	4.33	3.33	9.13	4.29	5.04	6.83	8.31	4.83	4.04	5.05	5.02
L	2.11	1.00	0.71	2.13	0.99	1.23	1.51	1.86	1.04	0.86	1.24	1.22
M	2.63	2.66	2.52	3.26	2.80	2.05	2.34	4.38	3.41	3.38	2.98	2.83

(*Continued*)

Table 9.9. (*Continued*)

	CHE	ELE	PRE	DEC	MAN	FIN	INF	EDU	CON	ENV	OTH	All
Q	3.91	2.53	1.62	3.97	1.93	3.01	4.55	4.14	1.99	1.40	2.02	2.55
X	4.90	2.49	1.43	4.09	1.67	3.76	6.29	4.00	1.51	0.88	1.56	2.59
2 percent TFP growth in ENV												
C	3.40	2.61	2.19	3.30	2.52	2.55	3.60	4.13	2.44	2.29	2.43	2.61
I	1.19	1.02	0.96	1.05	0.98	1.15	1.27	2.00	0.67	2.00	0.93	0.97
K	5.17	4.34	3.39	8.75	4.29	5.01	6.80	8.25	5.57	4.45	5.04	5.00
L	2.05	1.01	0.73	2.05	1.00	1.23	1.51	1.85	1.21	0.95	1.24	1.22
M	2.55	2.66	2.56	3.20	2.79	2.05	2.33	4.38	5.18	2.30	2.96	2.81
Q	3.79	2.54	1.65	3.81	1.94	3.00	4.54	4.12	1.54	2.29	2.01	2.54
X	4.75	2.51	1.46	3.91	1.68	3.74	6.28	4.00	0.74	2.28	1.56	2.57
2 percent TFP growth in OTH												
C	3.05	2.87	2.68	3.34	2.78	2.95	4.11	4.39	2.92	2.62	2.97	2.97
I	1.35	1.22	1.17	1.23	1.15	1.26	1.36	2.00	0.78	1.00	1.24	1.23
K	4.48	4.80	4.42	7.39	4.35	5.14	7.07	8.79	6.41	4.69	5.13	5.12
L	1.74	1.09	0.93	1.70	0.99	1.24	1.54	1.94	1.36	0.98	1.24	1.22
M	2.52	2.93	3.03	3.37	3.19	2.80	3.16	5.54	6.86	4.92	2.93	3.05
Q	3.26	2.79	2.14	3.18	1.94	3.06	4.70	4.35	1.75	1.60	3.01	2.87
X	3.79	2.75	1.94	3.15	1.59	3.23	5.78	3.60	0.74	0.86	3.05	2.78

See notes in Table 9.3.

Due to linkages among sectors, TFP growth in one sector is expected to impact on other industries as well. TFP shocks affect the TFP-improving industry more strongly than the rest of and in positive direction in almost all cases. Comparing implied average annual growth rates (Table 9.11) with those in Table 9.4, it is easy to see that sectoral TFP growth results in equivalent movements in endogenous variables. TFP growth in PRE, EDU, CON, and ENV lead to deviations from long-run growth rates only in themselves, whereas the impact of CHE, ELE, DEC, FIN, INF, and OTH and, to a small extent, in MAN is widespread. TFP growth in all sectors increase the growth rate of that sector's output and exports between 1 and 5 percentage points. The largest improvements are in CHE, DEC, FIN, and INF. Total output growth increases by 1.1–1.3 percentage points when TFP grows by 2 percent in CHE, ELE, and DEC. It is important to note that these are also large export industries and much of

Table 9.10. Simulation 2: Summary Results for Prices (Base Year = 1.00).

	CHE	ELE	PRE	DEC	MAN	FIN	INF	EDU	CON	ENV	OTH	All
2 percent TFP growth in CHE												
P	0.81	1.07	1.11	0.96	1.12	0.92	0.87	1.08	1.58	1.35	1.20	
Pc	0.75	1.10	1.13	0.95	1.08	0.93	0.84	1.08	1.57	1.35	1.15	
Pd	0.73	1.15	1.24	0.86	1.22	0.90	0.82	1.08	1.80	1.52	1.26	
2 percent TFP growth in ELE												
P	0.96	0.99	1.14	1.07	1.16	0.98	0.91	1.14	1.60	1.40	1.26	
Pc	0.95	0.98	1.16	1.05	1.10	0.98	0.89	1.13	1.59	1.40	1.19	
Pd	0.95	0.97	1.31	1.20	1.28	0.97	0.87	1.14	1.83	1.60	1.33	
2 percent TFP growth in PRE												
P	0.89	1.01	0.97	0.99	1.07	0.90	0.85	1.03	1.44	1.26	1.14	
Pc	0.87	1.01	0.95	0.99	1.05	0.90	0.81	1.03	1.46	1.28	1.11	
Pd	0.86	1.01	0.92	0.95	1.14	0.86	0.78	1.03	1.63	1.40	1.17	
2 percent TFP growth in DEC												
P	0.89	1.06	1.10	0.96	1.12	0.92	0.87	1.07	1.57	1.34	1.20	
Pc	0.86	1.10	1.12	0.95	1.08	0.92	0.83	1.07	1.56	1.35	1.15	
Pd	0.85	1.14	1.24	0.84	1.21	0.89	0.81	1.07	1.79	1.51	1.25	
2 percent TFP growth in MAN												
P	0.91	1.02	1.08	1.00	0.94	0.91	0.87	1.06	1.51	1.29	1.17	
Pc	0.88	1.03	1.09	1.00	0.95	0.92	0.83	1.06	1.52	1.31	1.13	
Pd	0.88	1.04	1.18	0.99	0.88	0.88	0.81	1.06	1.72	1.45	1.22	
2 percent TFP growth in FIN												
P	0.93	1.04	1.12	1.01	1.12	0.72	0.92	1.12	1.56	1.35	1.18	
Pc	0.91	1.06	1.14	1.01	1.08	0.65	0.90	1.12	1.55	1.35	1.14	
Pd	0.90	1.09	1.27	1.03	1.22	0.57	0.89	1.12	1.77	1.52	1.23	
2 percent TFP growth in INF												
P	0.91	1.03	1.07	1.00	1.08	0.91	0.67	1.05	1.44	1.26	1.14	
Pc	0.88	1.04	1.09	1.00	1.06	0.91	0.41	1.05	1.45	1.28	1.11	
Pd	0.87	1.06	1.17	0.99	1.15	0.88	0.37	1.05	1.62	1.40	1.18	
2 percent TFP growth in EDU												
P	0.89	1.01	1.06	0.99	1.07	0.90	0.85	0.77	1.44	1.26	1.13	
Pc	0.87	1.01	1.08	0.99	1.05	0.90	0.80	0.77	1.46	1.28	1.10	
Pd	0.86	1.01	1.15	0.95	1.13	0.86	0.78	0.77	1.62	1.40	1.17	

(*Continued*)

Table 9.10. (*Continued*)

	CHE	ELE	PRE	DEC	MAN	FIN	INF	EDU	CON	ENV	OTH	All
2 percent TFP growth in CON												
P	0.89	1.01	1.06	0.98	1.08	0.90	0.85	1.03	1.15	1.26	1.14	
Pc	0.87	1.01	1.08	0.98	1.05	0.90	0.80	1.03	1.18	1.28	1.11	
Pd	0.86	1.02	1.15	0.95	1.14	0.86	0.78	1.03	1.23	1.40	1.18	
2 percent TFP growth in ENV												
P	0.89	1.01	1.06	0.99	1.07	0.90	0.85	1.03	1.44	1.00	1.13	
Pc	0.87	1.01	1.08	0.99	1.05	0.90	0.81	1.03	1.46	1.00	1.10	
Pd	0.86	1.02	1.15	0.95	1.14	0.86	0.78	1.03	1.63	1.00	1.17	
2 percent TFP growth in OTH												
P	0.93	1.01	1.05	1.01	1.11	0.97	0.90	1.13	1.54	1.37	0.99	
Pc	0.91	1.01	1.06	1.01	1.07	0.98	0.88	1.12	1.54	1.37	0.99	
Pd	0.90	1.02	1.12	1.02	1.19	0.97	0.86	1.13	1.75	1.55	0.99	

Notes: P: supply (composite output) prices; Pc: consumption price level; Pd: domestic prices.

this increase in output growth stems from the increases in export growth rates. In all other cases, output and export growth rates are relatively unaffected.

In the case of resource allocation, it is easy to see from the figures in Tables 9.4 and 9.11 that capital and labor growth rates are increased remarkably in the range of between 1.4 and 5.8 percentage points in CHE, ELE, DEC, MAN, FIN, and INF. The largest increases are in FIN, however. This finding reflects the large growth potential in this sector. In the remaining sectors, resource accumulation process does not seem to be affected much.

The impact on output, exports, and imports on manufacturing activities are much stronger than on relative prices. TFP growth in a sector affects the price levels in that sector much more than the prices in other sectors (see Tables 9.10 and 9.12). In all industries, TFP growth reduces supply prices, domestic prices, and consumption price levels, as expected. The largest price reductions are observed in FIN, INF, EDU, CON, and ENV. These are all services-related sectors. Manufacturing sectors (CHE, ELE, PRE, DEC, and MAN) exhibit lower price declines.

The impact of TFP shocks on real GDP is presented in Table 9.13. With TFP growth in a sector, GDP growth rate naturally increases in all

Table 9.11. Simulation 2: Average Annual Percentage Growth Rates.

	CHE	ELE	PRE	DEC	MAN	FIN	INF	EDU	CON	ENV	OTH	All
2 percent TFP growth in CHE												
C	11.0	2.8	4.0	10.0	5.4	5.5	7.5	7.7	5.8	4.2	5.2	5.9
I	2.9	1.0	0.9	1.7	1.1	1.9	2.2	3.5	−0.6	0.0	0.8	1.0
K	12.1	4.6	5.9	17.0	7.9	9.0	10.7	11.6	10.3	7.8	9.1	9.1
L	6.5	−3.7	−2.8	8.8	−0.4	1.0	2.2	3.2	1.7	−0.9	1.1	1.2
M	8.1	3.8	5.1	9.6	6.1	4.7	5.7	8.5	10.3	7.2	6.6	6.7
Q	12.2	1.6	1.8	12.3	3.4	6.1	8.4	7.7	3.1	1.8	3.9	5.8
X	14.3	0.9	0.8	12.7	2.2	6.9	9.8	6.9	−1.5	−1.2	2.0	6.2
2 percent TFP growth in ELE												
C	3.6	8.3	5.6	4.6	5.8	5.6	7.1	7.6	5.0	4.3	5.6	6.1
I	1.7	1.6	0.7	1.2	1.0	1.6	1.9	3.5	−0.6	0.0	0.6	0.8
K	5.5	9.6	6.9	6.8	7.7	8.6	9.9	11.3	9.1	7.5	9.0	8.8
L	0.1	1.5	−1.5	−1.2	−0.3	0.9	1.6	3.1	0.7	−1.0	1.3	1.0
M	3.1	8.0	7.0	5.1	6.7	5.4	5.9	8.8	9.6	7.7	7.3	6.8
Q	3.7	8.6	3.0	2.2	3.3	5.8	7.6	7.5	2.3	1.7	3.9	6.0
X	4.1	8.8	1.6	1.5	1.9	6.1	8.6	6.4	−2.4	−1.7	1.6	6.3
2 percent TFP growth in PRE												
C	6.1	4.8	4.2	5.9	4.6	4.7	6.4	7.1	4.4	3.6	4.4	4.8
I	0.8	0.1	0.4	0.2	−0.1	0.7	1.2	0.0	−2.0	0.0	−0.4	−0.2
K	8.2	7.4	6.6	10.8	7.3	8.0	9.6	10.5	8.5	6.9	8.1	8.0
L	3.6	0.1	−1.0	3.6	0.0	1.0	2.0	3.1	0.9	−0.8	1.1	1.0
M	4.7	4.9	3.7	5.8	5.1	3.6	4.2	7.4	8.2	6.0	5.4	5.2
Q	6.6	4.7	5.0	6.6	3.3	5.5	7.5	7.1	2.1	1.6	3.5	4.7
X	7.8	4.6	5.3	6.8	2.6	6.6	9.2	6.9	−1.5	−0.7	2.2	4.7
2 percent TFP growth in DEC												
C	10.7	2.9	3.9	9.7	5.3	5.4	7.4	7.6	5.6	4.1	5.1	5.8
I	2.0	0.8	0.7	1.5	0.9	1.7	2.2	3.5	−1.3	0.0	0.6	0.8
K	13.2	4.8	5.8	14.8	7.8	8.9	10.7	11.5	10.2	7.7	9.0	9.0
L	7.6	−3.5	−2.8	6.6	−0.4	0.9	2.2	3.1	1.6	−1.0	1.0	1.0
M	9.2	3.8	5.0	9.1	6.0	4.5	5.5	8.3	10.1	7.0	6.4	6.5
Q	11.3	1.8	1.8	12.1	3.3	6.0	8.4	7.6	3.0	1.7	3.8	5.6
X	12.5	1.2	0.8	12.5	2.2	6.9	9.9	6.9	−1.5	−1.2	2.0	5.9
2 percent TFP growth in MAN												
C	5.7	4.7	4.0	5.7	5.8	4.8	6.6	7.3	4.4	3.7	4.7	5.0
I	1.2	0.5	0.2	0.6	0.9	1.1	1.6	3.5	−1.3	0.0	0.0	0.3

(*Continued*)

Table 9.11. (*Continued*)

	CHE	ELE	PRE	DEC	MAN	FIN	INF	EDU	CON	ENV	OTH	All
K	7.9	7.2	6.2	10.3	9.4	8.2	9.7	10.9	8.7	7.2	8.4	8.3
L	2.8	−0.5	−1.9	2.6	1.7	0.8	1.8	3.0	0.6	−1.0	1.0	1.0
M	4.5	5.0	4.9	5.7	5.2	3.9	4.7	7.9	8.6	6.4	5.9	5.4
Q	6.2	4.4	2.4	5.9	7.2	5.5	7.6	7.3	1.9	1.6	3.6	4.9
X	7.1	4.2	1.7	5.9	7.8	6.4	9.0	6.7	−2.2	−1.0	2.0	5.0
2 percent TFP growth in FIN												
C	4.9	3.1	2.7	5.1	4.5	6.0	6.6	7.5	5.0	3.9	4.5	4.7
I	1.7	1.0	0.6	1.2	0.9	3.4	1.6	3.5	−0.6	0.0	0.6	1.1
K	6.8	5.1	4.0	9.0	6.5	10.2	9.1	11.0	8.9	6.9	7.9	8.4
L	2.1	−2.2	−3.7	1.7	−0.8	3.2	1.5	3.5	1.2	−0.9	0.9	1.0
M	3.9	3.7	4.0	5.2	5.3	1.8	5.6	8.6	9.4	6.9	5.8	5.0
Q	5.2	2.4	0.4	4.8	2.5	9.6	7.1	7.5	2.4	1.5	3.3	4.7
X	6.0	2.0	−0.7	4.7	1.3	12.9	7.9	6.4	−2.0	−1.5	1.6	4.6
2 percent TFP growth in INF												
C	5.0	3.9	3.2	5.2	4.2	4.4	8.6	7.4	4.4	3.7	4.4	4.5
I	0.9	0.1	−0.1	0.4	0.1	0.8	4.7	3.5	−1.3	0.0	−0.2	0.0
K	7.0	6.0	5.1	9.4	6.7	7.6	15.4	10.7	8.4	6.9	7.9	8.2
L	2.5	−1.2	−2.4	2.3	−0.5	0.8	8.0	3.5	0.9	−0.6	1.1	1.0
M	3.8	4.3	4.1	5.2	4.8	3.4	−0.3	7.9	8.2	6.1	5.4	4.9
Q	5.5	3.4	1.6	5.3	2.8	5.1	15.4	7.4	2.2	1.7	3.4	4.5
X	6.5	3.1	0.9	5.4	2.0	6.1	19.4	6.9	−1.5	−0.6	2.1	4.5
2 percent TFP growth in EDU												
C	6.1	4.8	3.8	6.0	4.6	4.7	6.4	8.4	4.4	3.6	4.4	4.8
I	0.8	0.1	−0.2	0.2	−0.1	0.7	1.2	3.5	−2.0	0.0	−0.4	−0.2
K	8.2	7.4	6.0	10.9	7.3	8.1	9.6	10.0	8.6	6.9	8.1	8.0
L	3.6	0.1	−1.6	3.6	0.0	1.0	2.1	2.5	0.9	−0.8	1.1	1.0
M	4.7	4.9	4.6	5.8	5.1	3.6	4.2	5.8	8.2	6.1	5.4	5.2
Q	6.7	4.7	2.4	6.7	3.3	5.5	7.6	8.5	2.2	1.6	3.5	4.7
X	7.8	4.6	1.8	6.9	2.6	6.6	9.2	11.2	−1.5	−0.7	2.2	4.7
2 percent TFP growth in CON												
C	6.3	4.8	3.8	6.1	4.6	4.7	6.4	7.1	4.5	3.6	4.5	4.8
I	0.9	0.1	−0.2	0.3	−0.1	0.7	1.2	3.5	−0.6	0.0	−0.3	−0.1
K	8.4	7.3	6.0	11.1	7.3	8.1	9.6	10.6	7.9	7.0	8.1	8.1
L	3.7	0.0	−1.7	3.8	0.0	1.0	2.1	3.1	0.2	−0.8	1.1	1.0
M	4.8	4.9	4.6	5.9	5.1	3.6	4.2	7.4	6.1	6.1	5.5	5.2

(*Continued*)

Table 9.11. (*Continued*)

	CHE	ELE	PRE	DEC	MAN	FIN	INF	EDU	CON	ENV	OTH	All
Q	6.8	4.6	2.4	6.9	3.3	5.5	7.6	7.1	3.4	1.7	3.5	4.7
X	7.9	4.6	1.8	7.0	2.6	6.6	9.2	6.9	2.1	−0.6	2.2	4.8
2 percent TFP growth in ENV												
C	6.1	4.8	3.9	6.0	4.6	4.7	6.4	7.1	4.5	4.1	4.4	4.8
I	0.9	0.1	−0.2	0.2	−0.1	0.7	1.2	3.5	−2.0	3.5	−0.3	−0.1
K	8.2	7.3	6.1	10.8	7.3	8.1	9.6	10.5	8.6	7.5	8.1	8.1
L	3.6	0.0	−1.6	3.6	0.0	1.0	2.1	3.1	0.9	−0.3	1.1	1.0
M	4.7	4.9	4.7	5.8	5.1	3.6	4.2	7.4	8.2	4.2	5.4	5.2
Q	6.7	4.7	2.5	6.7	3.3	5.5	7.6	7.1	2.2	4.1	3.5	4.7
X	7.8	4.6	1.9	6.8	2.6	6.6	9.2	6.9	−1.5	4.1	2.2	4.7
2 percent TFP growth in OTH												
C	5.6	5.3	4.9	6.0	5.1	5.4	7.1	7.4	5.4	4.8	5.4	5.4
I	1.5	1.0	0.8	1.0	0.7	1.2	1.6	3.5	−1.3	0.0	1.1	1.0
K	7.5	7.8	7.4	10.0	7.3	8.2	9.8	10.9	9.3	7.7	8.2	8.2
L	2.8	0.4	−0.3	2.6	0.0	1.1	2.2	3.3	1.5	−0.1	1.1	1.0
M	4.6	5.4	5.5	6.1	5.8	5.1	5.8	8.6	9.6	8.0	5.4	5.6
Q	5.9	5.1	3.8	5.8	3.3	5.6	7.7	7.4	2.8	2.4	5.5	5.3
X	6.7	5.1	3.3	5.7	2.3	5.9	8.8	6.4	−1.5	−0.8	5.6	5.1

See notes in Table 9.3.

simulations. GDP growth rates are improved by about 0.6–0.9 percentage points with TFP growth in CHE, DEC, ELE, FIN, and OTH. What is of interest here is that the TFP improvement in EDU, CON, ENV, and PRE does not lead to any significant gain in the growth rate of the economy.

Results for some endogenous macroeconomic variables are presented in Table 9.14. TFP growth in PRE, EDU, CON, and ENV result in no significant changes in macro balances and factor balances compared with the base-run long-run growth path. In all other cases, private consumption and savings grow between 0.3 and 0.9 percentage points faster than the benchmark long-run path. Government savings and public investments grow faster than benchmark long-run growth path. The rise in the growth rate is faster for TFP growth in CHE, ELE, and DEC. The large expansion in output within and across individual sectors that result from TFP growth lead to increasing demand for labor and hence rising real wages. The increase

Table 9.12. Simulation 2: Average Annual Percentage Growth Rates for Prices.

	CHE	ELE	PRE	DEC	MAN	FIN	INF	EDU	CON	ENV	OTH
2 percent TFP growth in CHE											
P	−1.1	0.3	0.5	−0.2	0.6	−0.4	−0.7	0.4	2.3	1.5	0.9
Pc	−1.5	0.5	0.6	−0.2	0.4	−0.4	−0.9	0.4	2.3	1.5	0.7
Pd	−1.6	0.7	1.1	−0.8	1.0	−0.5	−1.0	0.4	3.0	2.1	1.2
2 percent TFP growth in ELE											
P	−0.2	−0.1	0.7	0.3	0.7	−0.1	−0.5	0.6	2.4	1.7	1.2
Pc	−0.2	−0.1	0.7	0.2	0.5	−0.1	−0.6	0.6	2.3	1.7	0.9
Pd	−0.3	−0.2	1.4	0.9	1.2	−0.2	−0.7	0.6	3.0	2.3	1.4
2 percent TFP growth in PRE											
P	−0.6	0.0	−0.1	−0.1	0.4	−0.5	−0.8	0.2	1.8	1.2	0.6
Pc	−0.7	0.0	−0.2	−0.1	0.3	−0.5	−1.1	0.1	1.9	1.2	0.5
Pd	−0.8	0.1	−0.4	−0.2	0.6	−0.7	−1.2	0.2	2.4	1.7	0.8
2 percent TFP growth in DEC											
P	−0.6	0.3	0.5	−0.2	0.5	−0.4	−0.7	0.3	2.2	1.5	0.9
Pc	−0.8	0.5	0.6	−0.3	0.4	−0.4	−0.9	0.3	2.2	1.5	0.7
Pd	−0.8	0.7	1.1	−0.8	0.9	−0.6	−1.1	0.3	2.9	2.1	1.1
2 percent TFP growth in MAN											
P	−0.5	0.1	0.4	0.0	-0.3	−0.5	−0.7	0.3	2.1	1.3	0.8
Pc	−0.6	0.1	0.4	0.0	-0.3	−0.4	−0.9	0.3	2.1	1.3	0.6
Pd	−0.7	0.2	0.8	−0.1	-0.6	−0.6	−1.1	0.3	2.7	1.9	1.0
2 percent TFP growth in FIN											
P	−0.4	0.2	0.6	0.0	0.6	−1.7	−0.4	0.6	2.2	1.5	0.8
Pc	−0.5	0.3	0.6	0.0	0.4	−2.1	−0.5	0.5	2.2	1.5	0.6
Pd	−0.5	0.4	1.2	0.1	1.0	−2.8	−0.6	0.6	2.9	2.1	1.0
2 percent TFP growth in INF											
P	−0.5	0.1	0.4	0.0	0.4	−0.5	−2.0	0.2	1.8	1.2	0.7
Pc	−0.6	0.2	0.4	0.0	0.3	−0.5	−4.5	0.2	1.9	1.2	0.5
Pd	−0.7	0.3	0.8	0.0	0.7	−0.7	−4.9	0.2	2.4	1.7	0.8
2 percent TFP growth in EDU											
P	−0.6	0.0	0.3	−0.1	0.4	−0.6	−0.8	-1.3	1.8	1.2	0.6
Pc	−0.7	0.0	0.4	−0.1	0.3	−0.5	−1.1	-1.3	1.9	1.2	0.5
Pd	−0.8	0.1	0.7	−0.3	0.6	−0.8	−1.2	-1.3	2.4	1.7	0.8

(Continued)

Table 9.12. (*Continued*)

	CHE	ELE	PRE	DEC	MAN	FIN	INF	EDU	CON	ENV	OTH
2 percent TFP growth in CON											
P	−0.6	0.0	0.3	−0.1	0.4	−0.6	−0.8	0.1	0.7	1.2	0.6
Pc	−0.7	0.1	0.4	−0.1	0.3	−0.5	−1.1	0.1	0.8	1.2	0.5
Pd	−0.8	0.1	0.7	−0.3	0.6	−0.8	−1.2	0.1	1.0	1.7	0.8
2 percent TFP growth in ENV											
P	−0.6	0.0	0.3	−0.1	0.4	−0.5	−0.8	0.2	1.8	0.0	0.6
Pc	−0.7	0.1	0.4	−0.1	0.3	−0.5	−1.1	0.2	1.9	0.0	0.5
Pd	−0.8	0.1	0.7	−0.3	0.6	−0.7	−1.2	0.2	2.4	0.0	0.8
2 percent TFP growth in OTH											
P	−0.4	0.0	0.2	0.0	0.5	−0.1	−0.5	0.6	2.1	1.6	0.0
Pc	−0.5	0.1	0.3	0.0	0.3	−0.1	−0.7	0.6	2.1	1.6	0.0
Pd	−0.5	0.1	0.6	0.1	0.9	−0.2	−0.8	0.6	2.8	2.2	−0.1

Notes: P: supply (composite output) prices; Pc: consumption price level; Pd: domestic prices.

in the growth rate of real wage is higher in the case of TFP growth by 0.7–1.0 percentage points than without TFP growth. Real rental rate of capital in individual sectors, on the other hand, declines to about half of its level after 20 years due to rapid accumulation of capital (see Table 9.11).

9.3.3. *Simulation 3: Impacts of restricting factor mobility*

The baseline model and the following two simulation exercises correspond to the working of a Walrasian free market economy. To accommodate the realistic market perspectives, four different versions of the base model are used to examine the impact of different restrictions of capital and labor mobility. In this experiment, different variations of capital and labor mobility are examined. The effect of removing the distortions in the factor markets is influenced largely by the underlying assumptions of the CGE model about mobility in the factor markets and the existence of factor distortions. Factor mobility can be restricted in the model by fixing the sectoral capital stocks and labor supply. Factor market distortions are induced by fixing the total supply of factors and keeping the sectoral levels of factor demand flexible. In this case, intersectoral factor reallocations will be

Table 9.13. Simulation 2: Changes in GDP.

	GDP Level		GDP Growth Rate (Percent)	
	Relative to Base Year (Base = 1.00)	Deviation from the Long-run Path	Relative to Base Year (Base = 1.00)	Deviation from the Long-run Path
TFP growth in CHE	3.01	0.46	5.51	0.83
TFP growth in CON	2.57	0.02	4.72	0.04
TFP growth in DEC	2.92	0.37	5.36	0.68
TFP growth in EDU	2.56	0.01	4.71	0.02
TFP growth in ELE	2.91	0.35	5.34	0.65
TFP growth in ENV	2.57	0.01	4.71	0.03
TFP growth in FIN	3.00	0.45	5.50	0.81
TFP growth in INF	2.65	0.10	4.88	0.19
TFP growth in MAN	2.72	0.17	5.01	0.32
TFP growth in OTH	3.04	0.48	5.55	0.87
TFP growth in PRE	2.56	0.00	4.70	0.01

realized according to the adjustments in factor prices. Factors will migrate from sectors with lower return to those with higher returns. Five simulations are specified as follows:

(i) In Simulation 3-A, there is perfect mobility of the labor market with fixed wages and total capital stock is immobile. Wages are exogenous and labor reallocation is realized endogenously in each sector. Aggregate capital supply is also set exogenous but distortions in the capital market are maintained. Then, capital is reallocated among sectors on the basis of adjustment in real returns to capital.

Table 9.14. Simulation 2: Macroeconomic Results.

	Cp	Sp	Sg	Ig	W	r
TFP growth in CHE						
Relative to base run	5.32	3.32	3.77	5.50	2.79	0.49
Average growth rate	8.4	6.0	6.6	8.5	5.1	−3.6
TFP growth in ELE						
Relative to base run	5.16	3.31	3.58	4.36	2.88	0.53
Average growth rate	8.2	6.0	6.4	7.4	5.3	−3.2
TFP growth in PRE						
Relative to base run	4.57	2.76	2.89	3.08	2.39	0.51
Average growth rate	7.6	5.1	5.3	5.6	4.4	−3.3
TFP growth in DEC						
Relative to base run	5.16	3.21	3.67	5.48	2.75	0.49
Average growth rate	8.2	5.8	6.5	8.5	5.1	−3.6
TFP growth in MAN						
Relative to base run	4.88	2.95	3.09	3.24	2.59	0.51
Average growth rate	7.9	5.4	5.6	5.9	4.7	−3.4
TFP growth in FIN						
Relative to base run	5.46	3.25	3.09	1.65	2.70	0.58
Average growth rate	8.5	5.9	5.6	2.5	5.0	−2.8
TFP growth in INF						
Relative to base run	4.58	2.86	2.81	2.03	2.40	0.51
Average growth rate	7.6	5.2	5.2	3.5	4.4	−3.3
TFP growth in EDU						
Relative to base run	4.58	2.75	2.89	3.08	2.38	0.51
Average growth rate	7.6	5.1	5.3	5.6	4.3	−3.3
TFP growth in CON						
Relative to base run	4.59	2.77	2.91	3.10	2.40	0.51
Average growth rate	7.6	5.1	5.3	5.7	4.4	−3.3
TFP growth in ENV						
Relative to base run	4.58	2.77	2.90	3.04	2.40	0.51
Average growth rate	7.6	5.1	5.3	5.6	4.4	−3.3
TFP growth in OTH						
Relative to base run	5.42	3.14	3.26	3.32	2.71	0.57
Average growth rate	8.4	5.7	5.9	6.0	5.0	−2.8

Notes: Cp: total private consumption; Sp: total private savings; Sg: government savings; Ig: government investments; W: real wage level; r: real rental rate of capital.

(ii) Simulation 3-B is similar to Simulation 3-A on the labor market side, but sectoral capital stocks are fixed. The fixity of sectoral capital stocks indicates short-run adjustment by way of real return adjustments.

(iii) In Simulation 3-C, total labor supply is exogenous with flexible wages and there is perfect mobility for sectoral capital stocks. The distortions in the labor market are maintained and the model reallocates labor among sectors by way of wages. Intersectoral movements of capital are also allowed. Full mobility in the capital market implies long-run adjustment in the capital market.

(iv) Simulation 3-D is similar to Simulation 3-C on the labor market side but there is no mobility for sectoral capital stocks. Therefore, total labor supply is exogenous and labor is reallocated among sectors based on the basis of wage distortions.

(v) Simulation 3-E is a counterfactual experiment where there is perfect mobility in the labor market with flexible wages and perfect mobility for total capital supply. All distortions in factor markets are removed and sectoral demands of factors are left to the working of the market. This simulation examines the impact of the abolishment of factor market restrictions. Wherever the distortions remain, the level of such distortions can be interpreted as autonomous deviations from the average marginal products of production factors.

The five experiments above investigate the results for five different closure rules. In this experiment, we give the model a minor shock and examine the consequences. For this purpose, TFP growth rate of ELE only is raised by 0.5 percent. In the baseline case, TFP growth rates for all sectors are set as 0 percent and the results obtained from simulation 3 are compared with the baseline solution. The results of the experiments are reported in Table 9.15.

In this simulation exercise we are interested not in the quantitative impacts of TFP growth but rather in the differences in results resulting from different types of closures. Different closures have different implications for factor price adjustment and intersectoral allocation of factors. Distortion factors are defined as the ratio of sectoral wages and real rental rates to the economy-wide averages. Fixing the average wage in the economy with perfectly mobile labor in Simulations 3-A and 3-B results in large adjustments in wages. Labor demand in CHE and EDU increases between 10 and 33 percent regardless of capital mobility. With fixed capital and flexible labor,

Table 9.15. Simulation 3: Summary Results (Base = 1.0).

		3-A	3-B	3-C	3-D	3-E
Macroeconomic results						
Average real wage level		1.00	1.00	1.20	0.43	1.37
Real rental rate		0.93	1.20	1.00	1.08	1.12
Real GDP		0.98	0.82	0.89	1.03	0.993
Sectoral results						
Labor demand	CHE	1.11	1.26	1.11	2.52	1.10
	ELE	0.69	1.46	0.97	1.10	0.85
	PRE	0.98	0.88	1.00	1.09	0.99
	DEC	0.78	0.90	1.10	2.63	1.02
	MAN	0.82	0.56	1.04	1.57	0.91
	FIN	0.74	0.86	1.00	1.23	1.01
	INF	0.94	0.26	0.87	0.75	0.89
	EDU	1.33	1.22	1.02	3.96	1.03
	CON	0.98	0.53	0.61	3.08	0.65
	ENV	0.93	0.61	1.01	0.97	0.98
	OTH	1.01	0.47	1.00	0.69	1.00
Capital	CHE	0.96	1.00	1.27	1.00	0.89
	ELE	0.99	1.00	1.38	1.00	0.89
	PRE	1.15	1.00	1.14	1.00	0.85
	DEC	1.40	1.00	1.15	1.00	0.92
	MAN	1.01	1.00	1.01	1.00	1.00
	FIN	0.97	1.00	0.99	1.00	0.86
	INF	1.32	1.00	0.90	1.00	0.97
	EDU	1.66	1.00	1.80	1.00	1.94
	CON	1.05	1.00	0.98	1.00	1.00
	ENV	1.04	1.00	1.01	1.00	1.00
	OTH	0.95	1.00	0.24	1.00	1.05
Real wage distortion factor	CHE	1.48	0.92	1.07	3.23	1.14
	ELE	1.44	0.73	0.89	2.04	0.86
	PRE	1.09	0.78	0.55	1.56	0.74
	DEC	1.83	1.69	1.11	0.00	0.88
	MAN	1.25	1.47	0.78	1.71	0.84
	FIN	1.40	1.08	0.81	2.04	0.75
	INF	1.36	4.14	1.03	4.25	1.07
	EDU	1.22	1.22	1.24	0.97	1.16

(*Continued*)

Table 9.15. (*Continued*)

		3-A	3-B	3-C	3-D	3-E
	CON	1.02	1.49	1.10	0.94	1.19
	ENV	1.04	1.16	0.71	2.15	0.71
	OTH	1.01	1.93	0.83	3.74	0.74
Real rental rate distortion factor	CHE	1.00	0.52	0.63	1.82	0.95
	ELE	1.00	0.82	0.71	0.86	0.95
	PRE	1.00	0.57	0.59	0.70	1.06
	DEC	1.00	1.16	1.18	0.00	1.11
	MAN	1.00	0.63	0.90	1.02	0.88
	FIN	1.00	0.67	0.88	0.91	0.96
	INF	1.00	0.85	1.19	1.27	1.18
	EDU	1.00	1.18	0.82	1.51	0.73
	CON	1.00	0.65	0.83	1.19	0.96
	ENV	1.00	0.59	0.88	0.87	0.87
	OTH	1.00	0.66	3.66	0.93	0.76

demand for labor in ELE rises by 46 percent. Restricting capital mobility raises average real return while maintaining capital market distortions lead to a deterioration in average real return.

Introducing flexible wages with labor market distortions in Simulations 3-C and 3-D, labor is reallocated among sectors. When there is mobility in the capital market, average wage level increases by 20 percent and when there is no mobility in the capital market, average wage level is more than halved. The latter case in wage changes is of more interest here. When sectoral capital stocks are fixed, labor is expected to move from low- to high-wage sectors. As the large decline in the average wage level shows, this does not occur. Labor is reallocated mainly from low- to high-capital-intensity sectors and this increases labor productivity, hence leading to output gain. At the sectoral level, labor is driven out of OTH and INF and mainly towards manufacturing sectors. The rise in GDP by 3 percent means that there is an expansion of output and therefore, the induced reallocations labor produce welfare gain. When the distortions in the capital market are removed, there is a migration of labor out of INF and CON. The increase in labor demand in other sectors is larger with fixed capital. It is important to note that when capital market distortions in sectors are removed in Simulation 3-C, a large migration of capital occurs from OTH to manufacturing sectors hence leading to a decline in rate of return in these sectors. This reflects the capital-intensive character of manufacturing sectors. Also, with flexible wages and labor market distortions, real return to capital declines by more than 10 percent in ELE, FIN, and PRE and increases remarkably in INF. Immobility in the capital market increases real return to capital in CHE, EDU, and CON while mobility decreases real returns in DEC and OTH.

Macroeconomic changes are less severe than the sectoral results. It is noteworthy that restricting the mobility of sectoral capital (3-B and 3-D) results in negative changes in real GDP. When mobility in the capital market is restricted and wages are flexible in the labor market, there is a GDP gain in the amount of 3 percent while fixed wages reduce real GDP by 18 percent. In the case of flexible wages when labor market distortions are maintained and capital is mobile, real GDP declines by 11 percent.

The results of the counterfactual Simulation 3-E have strong implications for development policies. After all the distortions are removed, average wage and real rental rate both rise by 37 and 12 percent, respectively. Real GDP level does not change much. This finding is instructive for the impact of a removal of all distortions in the economy. There is no welfare gain from removing the distortions in factor markets. The distortions even produce a slight gain in real GDP by 0.7 percentage points. Therefore, there is no empirical support for the proposition that removing the distortions in the Singapore economy would bring welfare gains. On the contrary, there is an important role for government intervention in Singapore. To put differently, the empirical results reveal that industrial policies have a positive impact on output growth.

9.3.4. *Summary of results*

So far in this chapter, some policy experiments for Singapore are conducted using a CGE model. These simulations are useful in understanding the consequences of the economic structure and resource allocation which are products of the industrial policies of the government. These policies were explained previously in Chapter 3. The external wing of the economy is very large in Singapore and the country is completely integrated with global commodity and financial markets. At the start, the first experiment examined the impact of an external price shock for the country's most important export sector, i.e., a 10 percent rise in the world export prices of ELE. Quantitative analysis results showed that export structure favors ELE at the expense of other sectors. Macro balances and real GDP, on the other hand, are unaffected.

The second simulation examined the impacts of sector-wise 2 percent TFP growth rate by each sector. Among the sectors promoted by the government, PRE, EDU, CON, and ENV do not offer much benefit to the rest by improving efficiency internally but the impacts of CHE, ELE, DEC, FIN, INF, and OTH are widespread. We are particularly interested in CHE, ELE, FIN, and INF as the four most important promoted sectors in the economy with explicit government commitment in their development. TFP growth in these sectors increases the growth rate of that sector's output and exports largely and long-run GDP growth is improved by 0.6–0.9 percentage points. The conclusion of this simulation is that major promoted industries serve the economy in a way that the improvements in their efficiencies benefit the economy significantly. This finding indicates the government's success in effective industry selection and promotion.

Finally, some variations of the model are used to examine the impact of differing levels and types of factor market distortions on economic performance. It was also found that restrictions on capital mobility across sectors affect the economy more strongly than labor market restrictions. This is expected when one considers large dependence of the Singapore economy to investments in large amounts to achieve high growth rates. Counterfactual experiment that abolished all types of factor market distortions demonstrated that real GDP gain is nil. Quantitative analyses provide empirical support for the effectiveness of the widely criticized interventions of the government in the economy. It cannot be said from this conclusion that there is more space for government action in the economy, but it can be safely argued that there is no harm in government intervention.

The findings of these simulations point to the fact that the economy needs high performances of the promoted sectors at least to maintain the long-run potential growth rate. Induced changes in real wages and labor market flexibility were also found to be deterministic in sectoral factor demands. Real wages are generally subject to large changes during economic downturns. Therefore, labor market flexibility can absorb such a shock partially. The changes in the labor market towards more flexibility during the 1990s can therefore be said to have contributed to the high performance of the economy.

9.4. CGE Evaluation of Industrial Policies in Japan and Korea

Apart from theoretical studies, numerous quantitative studies in the past have sought to contribute to the discussion about strategic trade policies.[3] However, there are only few studies that specifically examined the role of industrial policies as described in this book using the CGE modeling approach and included the policy instruments of industrial policies such as quantitative and price barriers to trade, export subsidies, depreciation allowances, low-cost credits, and government loans.

The results for the CGE exercises on Singapore in this chapter are comparable to the results of similar other studies for Japan and Korea. The basis for the comparisons is the CGE models developed by Lee (1988) and Ezaki (1994) for Japan and the model constructed by Kwon and Paik (1995) for Korea. The results of selected simulations in these studies are summarized in the following sections.

9.4.1. *Japan*

The outstanding characteristics of the model in Lee (1988) (see also Lee, 1993) are that it is a multi-sectoral model where the industries subject to industrial policies are identified by scale economies and Cournot-type imperfect competition. The model is calibrated to 1960 data and quantifies the impact of Japanese government's industrial policies and industrial targeting in the 1960s. In its large part, the model shares the common properties of standard CGE models such as the one adopted here for Singapore in output, input, price, and factor demand blocks. The novelty of Lee's model is the incorporation of scale economies and imperfect competition. This is done by adding the ratio of average cost to marginal cost

[3]An early review of CGE studies for trade policy analysis can be found in de Melo (1988).

as a measure of scale economies and separately estimating sectoral cost functions. Non-manufacturing sectors are assumed to be perfectly competitive with constant returns to scale and in all manufacturing sectors there are economies of scale. In these manufacturing sectors, market equilibrium is represented by oligopolistic Cournot competition where firms enjoy a markup over marginal cost. The model is a static one.

Policy instruments impact on the economy through their effect on costs in the model. For instance, export subsidies reduce export prices and increase export demand. Expansion of output then raises factor prices and therefore, export subsidies have an impact on costs and competitiveness. Public loans and depreciation allowances result in changes in costs via their effect on the user cost of capital. Public loans usually bear lower interest rates and therefore, they lower the cost of capital. Similarly, depreciation allowances have a direct impact on the user cost of capital. Due to its cost-reducing and productivity-improving effect, Lee also added research and development (R&D) subsidies in cost functions.

Policy experiments are specified as exogenous changes in the above-mentioned policy instruments. Lee takes the averages of actual changes in each policy instrument for the period 1960–1965 in each sector and employs them in policy simulations. The results are summarized in Table 9.16. The results show that different industries benefited from different instruments of industrial policy. Output in steel, nonferrous metal, electric machinery, and transport equipment industries were affected the largest by changes in export subsidies. Public loans had the largest impact on agriculture, food processing, textiles, and chemicals and depreciation allowances on the rest of the production sectors. An interesting finding is that tariff protection had a contractionary effect in all industries. Changes in marginal cost of the targeted sectors induced by public loans contribute to the development of heavy industries in the 1960s. The effect of the changes in policy instruments on macroeconomic variables are presented at the bottom panel of Table 9.16. It is easily seen that exports are affected the largest and mainly from the changes in export subsidies. Investment is affected positively from the changes in public credits and accelerated depreciation allowances. Welfare has also been increased largely as real GDP is also improved significantly.

A counterfactual experiment is also conducted by assuming perfect competition for all sectors. The results will not be presented here but can be

Table 9.16. Effects of Industrial Policies on Output, Marginal Cost, and Trade in Japan (Baseline = 1.000).

	Agriculture					Metal Products				
	TR	XS	AD	PL	RD	TR	XS	AD	PL	RD
Q	0.996	1.013	1.019	1.031	1.000	0.994	1.029	1.031	1.023	1.001
MC	0.996	1.014	1.016	0.997	1.000	1.003	0.985	0.984	0.993	1.000
X	1.004	1.014	0.984	1.003	1.000	0.994	1.090	1.039	1.017	1.001
M	0.975	1.028	1.036	1.028	1.001	0.791	1.004	1.009	1.015	1.000
	Food					Non-Electrical Machinery				
Q	0.992	1.017	1.023	1.030	1.001	0.992	1.039	1.039	1.031	1.001
MC	0.999	1.009	1.007	0.997	1.000	1.003	0.987	0.981	0.989	0.999
X	1.004	0.999	0.977	1.009	0.999	0.995	1.156	1.032	1.018	1.001
M	1.106	1.026	1.031	1.028	1.001	0.966	1.015	1.020	1.021	1.000
	Textiles					Electrical Machinery				
Q	0.995	1.013	1.020	1.021	1.000	0.992	1.034	1.033	1.025	1.001
MC	0.999	1.008	1.005	1.000	1.000	1.002	0.994	0.992	0.998	0.999
X	1.002	0.982	0.989	1.000	0.999	0.995	1.098	1.024	1.006	1.002
M	0.968	1.022	1.028	1.024	1.001	0.959	1.019	1.026	1.026	1.000

(*Continued*)

Table 9.16. (*Continued*)

	Wood and Paper					Transport Equipment				
	TR	XS	AD	PL	RD	TR	XS	AD	PL	RD
Q	0.994	1.017	1.023	1.021	1.001	0.992	1.110	1.046	1.031	1.001
MC	0.999	1.008	1.005	1.001	1.000	1.003	0.968	0.978	0.992	1.000
X	1.005	0.968	0.980	0.996	0.999	0.989	1.500	1.075	1.028	1.000
M	0.992	1.019	1.025	1.022	1.001	0.919	1.010	1.019	1.023	1.001
	Chemicals					Precision Equipment				
Q	0.993	1.025	1.028	1.028	1.001	0.998	1.021	1.027	1.021	1.001
MC	1.003	0.997	0.992	0.989	1.000	1.000	1.004	0.999	1.002	1.000
X	0.992	1.053	1.022	1.029	1.000	1.000	1.015	0.988	0.999	0.999
M	1.001	1.017	1.016	1.011	1.001	0.868	1.024	1.036	1.027	1.001
	Petroleum					Other Manufacturing				
Q	0.990	1.032	1.037	1.028	1.001	0.995	1.024	1.028	1.025	1.001
MC	1.014	0.995	0.984	0.992	1.000	0.999	1.008	1.005	1.000	1.000
X	0.963	1.015	1.044	1.023	1.000	1.005	1.006	0.995	1.000	1.000
M	0.988	1.033	1.036	1.027	1.000	0.872	1.342	1.035	1.026	1.001

(*Continued*)

Table 9.16. (*Continued*)

	Non-Metallic Minerals					Transport and Communications				
	TR	XS	AD	PL	RD	TR	XS	AD	PL	RD
Q	0.994	1.017	1.021	1.019	1.001	0.994	1.020	1.028	1.025	1.001
MC	1.002	1.004	1.003	1.001	1.000	0.999	1.007	1.005	1.000	1.000
X	0.997	0.994	0.958	0.999	1.000	1.005	0.993	0.995	1.000	1.000
M	0.955	1.026	1.028	1.022	1.000	0.872	1.029	1.035	1.026	1.001
	Steel					Utilities				
Q	0.984	1.099	1.076	1.041	1.001	0.991	1.032	1.035	1.035	1.001
MC	1.017	0.925	0.935	1.001	1.000	1.005	0.993	0.991	0.980	1.000
X	0.962	1.250	1.171	0.999	1.000	—	—	—	—	—
M	1.006	1.020	1.013	1.022	1.000	—	—	—	—	—
	Non-Ferrous Metals					Services				
Q	0.991	1.054	1.042	1.027	1.002	0.994	1.011	1.019	1.018	1.001
MC	1.009	0.980	0.982	0.988	0.999	0.996	1.013	1.013	1.013	1.000
X	0.979	1.047	1.043	1.028	1.002	1.004	0.988	0.987	0.987	1.000
M	0.995	1.051	1.039	1.025	1.002	1.207	1.024	1.032	1.032	1.001

(*Continued*)

Table 9.16. (*Continued*)

	Aggregate Variables									
	TR	XS	AD	PL	RD	TR	XS	AD	PL	RD
Real GDP	0.993	1.021	1.021	1.022	1.001					
Consumption	0.995	1.014	1.018	1.019	1.000					
Investment	0.987	1.010	1.032	1.039	1.001					
Exports	0.993	1.123	1.036	1.019	1.001					
Imports	0.992	1.031	1.034	1.025	1.001					

Notes: Simulation descriptions: TR: change in tariff rates; XS: change in export subsidies; AD: ratio of accelerated depreciation allowances; PL: subsidy equivalent of public credits; RD: change in R&D subsidies. Q: output; MC: marginal cost; X: exports; M: imports.

Source: Rearranged from Lee (1993).

found in Lee (1993). Changes induced by the industrial policies are much smaller in the perfect-competition version of the model. This is due to the removal of the scale economies assumption which then has no effect on marginal costs. As a result, changes in output, marginal cost, exports, and imports are smaller than one-fourth of the changes in the scale-economies-version. The implication of this finding is that if all production sectors were perfectly competitive, industrial policies would not have the desired effects. Especially, real GDP gain is less than half of that under industrial policies.

In sum, Lee's study asserts that there is an important role for government intervention in the form of industrial policies when there are some industries possessing the characteristics of scale economies and oligopolistic competition. Lee found empirical evidence for the positive and important role of industrial targeting on the expansion of output and exports and improvement in competitiveness. One important point that needs to be emphasized in Lee's study is that industrial policies are effective when there are scale economies and oligopolistic market structure. Quantitative results obtained support the historical observations in Japan.

Ezaki (1994) also constructed a CGE model for Japan. His model depicts the Japanese economy hypothetically as a free-market economy by taking the base year as 1960 and investigates the effects of government intervention around 1960 with an emphasis on trade liberalization efforts of the time. The results will not be presented here but the findings are noteworthy. Ezaki concluded that trade liberalization requires liberalization in factor markets, especially in capital market. He emphasizes that the working of the capital market is the key for successful trade liberalization, e.g., industries with higher returns to capital attract more capital.

9.4.2. *Korea*

Paik (1991) and Kwon and Paik (1995) examine the impact of the industrial-financial policy of Korean government. Paik and Kwon define the industrial-financial policy in Korea as the government's policy centered on low-interest policy loans for the purpose of promoting economic development and industrialization (Paik, 1991, p. 28). The core model to evaluate the industrial-financial policy describes the supply-side, demand-side, international sector, and price normalization. Kwon and Paik's model is built on a previous model developed by de Melo (1977) to quantify the distortions in the factor markets and it shares most of the features of the one used in this book as well. On the demand side, Paik prefers a Stone–Geary utility function which defines linear consumption demands in prices and expenditures. The model also incorporates rural–urban wage differences but the primary emphasis of the model is on factor distortions, which are defined by distortions of factor returns across industries relative to the economy average as in this study. Paik separately estimates factor scale parameters outside the model and injects them into the model. The borrowing rates of various financial institutions involved in the distribution of policy loans are also explicitly stated. The model is calibrated to 1978 data.

Paik runs some static simulations for different alternatives combining different factor mobility and existence/removal of distortions. These experiments are similar to Simulation 3 in Section 9.3.3. Some of the results regarding sectoral levels of output, capital, and employment are summarized in Tables 9.17 and 9.18. With fixed exchange rate and removal of labor market distortions, there are large increases about 5–6 percent in welfare when capital is mobile and capital market distortions are removed. Fixity of capital results in a 2 percent gain in welfare. The welfare gain is a result of the increase in consumption and imports due to a reallocation of resources. The reallocation of resources also induces a shift of resources out of heavy and chemical industries. Changes in GDP are less than 1 percent whether capital is fixed or mobile. This is due to the fact that reallocations of factors across sectors stimulate changes in output and positive output change in some sectors can be offset by negative changes in some others. When distortions are completely removed in the capital market, GDP increases by 3 percent. Therefore, it can be argued that strict controls on the allocation of capital under the industrial policies of the Korean government at the peak of its industrial policies during the late 1970s were not as destructive as claimed by the opponents of Korean industrial policies. The results should be interpreted with caution, however. The removal of capital market distortions in the model triggers a shift of capital from capital-intensive heavy industries to the less capital-intensive light industries. When capital is fixed, labor migrates into heavy industries and when the distortions in the capital

Table 9.17. Effects of Removing Factor Market Distortions in Korea (Baseline = 1.000).

	Generated Value-Added			Production Workers			Capital Stock		Generated Output		
	F	M	D-F	F	M	D-F	M	D-F	F	M	D-F
Agriculture	0.998	0.998	0.998	1.156	1.148	1.147	0.910	0.997	1.083	1.015	0.997
Mining	1.005	0.998	0.985	1.162	1.219	1.049	0.950	0.812	1.059	1.076	0.947
Food	0.993	0.984	0.996	0.695	0.588	0.750	0.646	1.091	0.881	0.678	0.957
Beverage	1.004	1.004	1.015	0.397	0.308	0.603	0.642	1.895	0.904	0.627	1.558
Tobacco	1.004	0.999	1.005	0.341	0.261	0.390	0.647	1.238	0.918	0.636	1.106
Textiles	0.989	0.984	0.982	0.476	0.352	0.437	0.512	0.812	0.739	0.478	0.650
Leather	0.979	0.981	0.995	0.945	0.915	1.177	0.820	1.412	0.997	0.902	1.292
Wood	0.978	0.978	0.984	0.813	0.726	0.719	0.702	0.719	0.905	0.741	0.749
Paper	0.996	0.983	0.974	1.980	1.941	1.275	0.841	1.395	1.018	0.928	1.286
Printing	1.020	1.012	1.014	0.976	0.927	1.206	0.774	1.684	0.900	0.808	1.188
Chemicals	1.004	0.991	0.995	1.382	1.453	1.438	0.986	1.049	1.106	1.119	1.165
Petroleum	1.006	0.998	0.990	1.629	1.574	2.368	0.866	1.772	1.046	0.937	1.694
Rubber	0.983	0.977	0.981	1.076	1.099	1.010	0.908	0.844	1.059	1.038	0.971
Non-met.	1.009	0.990	0.979	1.319	1.372	1.012	0.982	0.625	1.109	1.119	0.802
Metals	1.006	0.983	0.970	1.472	1.443	0.819	0.902	0.363	1.078	1.008	0.498
Fab-met	0.998	0.985	0.981	1.360	1.475	1.720	1.036	1.637	1.144	1.211	1.575
Machinery	0.991	0.988	0.978	1.142	1.101	0.846	0.831	0.552	1.009	0.908	0.676
Appliances	0.994	0.991	1.002	0.538	0.419	0.477	0.600	0.753	0.850	0.586	0.699
Transport Eq.	0.990	0.987	0.995	1.589	1.793	1.371	1.081	0.707	1.160	1.269	0.943
Precision	0.995	0.992	0.990	1.065	1.114	1.193	0.945	1.255	1.065	1.072	1.239

(*Continued*)

Table 9.17. (*Continued*)

	Generated Value-Added			Production Workers			Capital Stock		Generated Output		
	F	M	D-F	F	M	D-F	M	D-F	F	M	D-F
Other man.	0.977	0.978	0.972	0.465	0.346	0.390	0.518	0.662	0.754	0.490	0.581
Utilities	0.625	0.921	1.193	2.161	3.375	4.068	0.889	0.805	1.061	1.084	1.064
Construction	0.997	0.993	1.005	0.860	0.721	0.890	0.599	0.988	0.777	0.585	0.790
Commerce	1.131	1.114	0.946	1.432	1.527	1.308	1.047	1.340	1.007	1.056	1.117
Tran-Comm	0.898	1.001	0.950	1.393	1.732	1.620	1.007	1.113	1.048	1.138	1.179
Fin-Bus	1.228	1.168	1.539	1.468	1.702	1.985	1.229	1.011	1.022	1.210	1.127
Others	0.733	0.723	0.736	1.388	1.621	1.596	0.779	0.940	1.078	1.212	1.232

Notes: F: capital fixed; M: capital mobile; D-F: distortion-free capital market. Non-met: non-metallic minerals; Fab-met: fabricated metal products; Eq: equipment; Other man: other manufacturing industries; Tran-Comm: transport and communication services; Fin-Bus: financial and business services.

Source: Rearranged from Kwon and Paik (1995).

Table 9.18. Effects of Removing Factor Market Distortions in Korea (Baseline = 1.000).

	Factor Mobility	Distortions in Factor Markets	Welfare Index	GDP	Wage of Production Workers	Rate of Return to Capital
Experiment 1	L: mobile K: fixed	L: removed K: maintained	1.021	1.004	0.996	1.005
Experiment 2	L: mobile K: mobile	L: removed K: maintained	1.057	1.000	0.913	1.124
Experiment 3	L: mobile K: mobile	L: removed K:removed	1.055	1.032	0.953	1.014

Notes: L: labor; K: capital.
Source: Rearranged from Kwon and Paik (1995).

market are also removed, the structural changes are reversed. Overall, it is clear that the welfare effects of removing factor price distortions depend on the assumptions about factor mobility and distortions. Kwon and Paik also add intertemporal capital accumulation into the model and find that capital market distortions bring about more rapid capital accumulation and shift of capital towards promoted industries.

In sum, Paik (1991) concludes that welfare costs of factor price distortions were not significant in the Korean economy. His findings suggest that the efficiency loss argument due to factor price distortions alone is not empirically supported. Therefore, there is empirical evidence from the Korean experience for how an economy can grow in spite of factor market distortions.

9.5. A Summary of the Results from the CGE Analyses of Industrial Policies in East Asia

In this chapter, the consequences of industrial policies in Singapore, Japan, and Korea are assessed comparatively. The focus has been placed on Singapore and the results from previous quantitative analyses for Japan and Korea are also provided. The results of the Singapore model favored industry targeting in Singapore due to their significantly positive contribution to economic performance. Moreover, it was found that the government's strong hand in the economy was found to produce no adverse effects on the economy. Similar studies for Japan and Korea have found that there was plenty of room for government intervention in industrial development and that the instruments the governments used were functional in enhancing growth and development. Considering that the economies in question realized a remarkable industrial transformation, it can be argued in light of the quantitative findings here that government intervention had a positive impact on this success. In other words, industrial policies helped these economies achieve the targets of industrialization.

The findings of the quantitative analyses also point to the differences in the targets and instruments of industrial policies which were explained in detail in Chapter 2. For Japan, the government's policy of restricting competition and creating oligopolistic industries that were characterized by scale economies was found to be effective and the policy instruments helped achieve competitiveness. In Korea, the emphasis was on policy finance and the allocation of capital and quantitative findings also support the stance of the Korean government in its aim of achieving growth. Therefore, differing characteristics of industrial policies in Japan and Korea seem to have produced favorable results for the respective economies.

It is important to note that the dynamic efficiency gains from resource allocation induced by factor market distortions are important. The results of the CGE analyses for Japan, Korea, and Singapore all point to the importance of distortions in factor markets for economic growth and industrial development. It was already argued in earlier chapters that factor markets were distorted deliberately by the intervening governments in order to stimulate factor accumulation favoring the targeted industries. It appears from the quantitative analyses here that especially when exports are important, factor market distortions can induce gains from the resource allocation they lead to, and any adverse effect that leads to allocative inefficiency due to such resource allocations can be offset by these gains. The gains from the distortions are various ranging from technology transfer in early development stages in Japan and in early and middle stages in Korea and Taiwan and throughout the development history of Singapore. Especially in Singapore, the attempt of the government to facilitate technology transfer to domestic firms has proven to be helpful. In summary, CGE models of Japan, Korea, and Singapore provide evidence for the positive role of industrial policies in economic development.

CHAPTER 10

CONCLUSION

The trade-off between free market economy with minimal government involvement and one with interventions in markets is an important problem in economic development, which has important political, economic, and social consequences. The experience of the East Asian economies shows that development via rapid industrialization can be facilitated by state apparatus. Any government policy aims to enhance the welfare of citizens. As indicated in the Introduction, the purpose of this study was to provide a quantitative evaluation of industrial policies in the four East Asian countries which have been subject to academic scrutiny from both economic and political science perspectives. The main contribution of this book to the debate is two-fold: (i) the description of industrial policies and emphasizing the differences of Singapore with respect to the other three and (ii) quantifying the impacts of industrial policies on the respective economies. In the latter case, a major contribution was the CGE model of the Singapore economy. Empirical results from the standard models and easy-to-interpret productivity analyses have been used to quantify the impacts of various policies in different periods.

The current state of development economics is characterized by disharmony between empirical studies and generalizations from these studies and singling out of "marginal" studies that are difficult to use in generalizations. In the context of this book, the experience of Singapore has long been seen as a "special case," which does not seem to be appropriate for any sort of generalization. It is the opinion of the author of this book that what applies to all developing countries is also amenable to Singapore despite its small size, and that there are lessons to be learned from the Singapore experience as well.[1] The first lesson is that there are benefits from intervention

[1] In a recent work, Chia (2005) argues that "...Singapore's export-led and FDI-led industrialization has lost its uniqueness as countries in the East Asian region, including PRC, followed

in markets. Behind the success of this intervention, there are a number of reasons that are discussed in this book and elsewhere (e.g., Lim *et al.*, 1988, pp. 61–66; Soon and Tan, 1993; Huff, 2000; Wong, 2001). The most important of these reasons are strong public–private cooperation (deliberate councils), stable politics which allowed the implementation of major in the medium- and long-run, a free trade and free enterprise policy[2] (e.g., creation of an environment where private firms can operate freely), a friendly attitude towards foreign investment, an efficient and well-working economic bureaucracy, pragmatism in economic decision-making, and quick response to changing world market conditions.

This book analyzes three other countries to make it possible for readers to compare the specific conditions in each country and to demonstrate the peculiarities concerning the industrial policies in each economy. The punch line of this study is that the success of industrial transformation in Japan, Korea, and Taiwan lies in capital accumulation process favoring industrial targeting, labor mobilization and reallocation, and government activism. Starting from the early 1980s, majority of the works published in the fields of development economics have emphasized the necessity to ensure the working of free markets to achieve development as opposed to government intervention. It was seen in this book that in Japan, Korea, and Taiwan, free markets and government interventionism have been substitutes for each other to some extent though not completely. However, for Singapore they were rather complementary. The role of the government especially after the late 1980s in Singapore was such that under government monitoring of the markets, industrial development and gains from trade could be facilitated. A pragmatic government such as the one in Singapore can internalize the

suit. However, countries should also learn from the experiences of the Republic of Korea and Taipei, China in fostering a dynamic and vibrant domestic entrepreneurship. Other characteristics of the Singapore development experience are worthy of study by other developing economies – the vision, competence and probity of its political leadership and bureaucracy; promote economic efficiency through exposures to global competition; emphasis on human resource development and infrastructure development to support the private sector; consistency and coherence of its FDI policies; maintaining social cohesion through its ethnic and language policies, and ensuring the welfare of workers through policies to promote full employment, provision of social safety net through the Central Provident Fund, provision of public housing, quality education and healthcare at affordable cost."

[2]Lim *et al.* (1988, p. 61) argues that production was realized by free enterprises but distribution was done by the government on a socialistic basis in Singapore.

opportunities of globalization in the financial and commodity markets and sustain economic growth for long periods.

Main conclusions drawn from the analyses are presented in the following sections.

Industrial Policies in Asia: At the start, to promote economic growth, the governments in Japan, Korea, Singapore, and Taiwan implemented interventionist policies to achieve high-growth rates and to realize a transformation from their initial industrial backwardness to an industrial structure similar to that of the advanced nations. The interventions took the forms of import protection, tax concessions to collaborating firms, provision of public funds as loans, and a wide range of direct subsidies mainly for investments and production for exports. As the countries were short of foreign exchange at the beginning of industrial development, the governments took some measures to nurture several manufacturing industries with export potential under an export promotion strategy. With increased degrees of development achieved by these industries, the degree of government support was reduced from the early 1970s in Japan and from the late 1980s in Korea and Taiwan. Finally, after achieving maturity in economic structure, previous interest in government intervention and industrial policies was turned into economic diversity and competitiveness.

Today, the economic environment is considerably different from that of the 1960s and 1970s. Since the late 1980s, there are only few opportunities left to exploit scale economies, which was a primary objective of industrial policies in achieving industrial and economic development. The outset of the Asian financial crisis in 1997 even demonstrated that the East Asian countries, especially Korea, Singapore, and Taiwan, were fragile against financial globalization and the interest in industrial policies was also turned to financial matters. Japan faced the criticism much earlier than the other three and had to undertake significant liberalization in its financial market. However, the tradition of protectionism still remains in Japan in different forms, most visibly in agriculture. For all the four countries in this study, it has become clear during the past decade that industrial policies lost their appeal as instruments to achieve competitiveness in global markets. This does not mean, however, that market failures do not exist any more. Industrial policies will still be appropriate tools to fix market failures, but their importance as an instrument to achieve higher national welfare have been deteriorated.

Uniqueness of Singapore: Among the four East Asian countries under question in this book, Singapore is a unique case where the government did not reduce its presence in the economy even after the late 1980s when industrial policies were highly degraded. On the contrary, high level of government intervention was maintained. The instruments employed by the government were also different in Singapore. The biggest difference was in trade policies. Singapore adopted a free trade regime throughout its industrial development whereas the other countries exercised different trade policies in different periods, starting with import substitution, followed by limited liberalization of imports and export promotion, and finally substantially large liberalization in the end. The extent to which industrial policies in Singapore contributed to competitiveness and industrial and economic growth is still a controversial topic. In a comprehensive list of studies, it is asserted that the government's interventions have had a very important impact on industrial development and creation of dynamic comparative advantages while some influential studies such as Young (1992) argued that the strong hand of the government in the economy impacted negatively on the economy by way of inability to ensure efficiency improvements. Recent studies generally contend that the primary reason behind Singapore's success is that the government provided superior infrastructure facilities and a well-working institutional environment for the markets.

The book found support for the effectiveness of Singapore's industrial policies by way of adapting the policies according to changing global and regional economic environment. Industry targeting was especially successful and the opportunities brought about by regionalization and global integration of financial and commodity markets were successfully internalized.

Empirical results confirm that the policy mix in Singapore, where heavy dependence on FDI is mixed with government intervention in product and factor markets, what might seem like a paradox for many developing countries, can actually be a rational strategy for industrial development if effectively implemented. This finding opposes the arguments by Young (1992) and the likes which state that Singapore is a victim of its industrial policies which lead to the development of the sectors that have lower productivity. The empirical findings of this book may have some further implications that might be important for policymakers.

Review of Empirical Results: The debate on the industrial policies in Asia focuses mainly on whether such policies have contributed positively to economic development and whether the economies could have performed better if governments intervened less in the markets. This issue suffers from a controversy in assessment. In the case of industrial policies in Singapore, local economists argue that industrial policies facilitated fast growth and industrialization (e.g., Lim *et al.*, 1988; Wong, 2001). On the other hand, some popular studies found almost zero TFP growth and criticized the governments of Korea, Singapore, and Taiwan for their strong involvement in the economy (e.g., Krugman, 1994; Young, 1992).[3] For this purpose, first a simple analysis of productivity and resource allocation is conducted to demonstrate the impact of industrial policies in different periods in the use of resources. This was followed by a CGE analysis.

From a supply-side perspective, the consequences of resource allocation can be examined using a partial equilibrium analysis. For this purpose, trends in labor productivity and TFP growth and their components are investigated first. The decomposition exercises demonstrated that during the periods of industrial development characterized by strong government intervention, reallocation of resources facilitated gains in productivity in Korea and Singapore. The government in Japan was neutral in factor markets and therefore, factor reallocations were ineffective in bringing productivity gains. The reallocations of resources across manufacturing industries accounted for half of aggregate TFP improvement in Singapore after 1985 and much of this came from the reallocation of capital. It may then be argued that, contrary to general perception of the accumulation process and its impact on productivity growth in Singapore, the industrial policies of the Singapore government assisted in efficient accumulation of capital, which in turn contributed significantly to productivity and hence economic growth.

[3]Noland and Pack (2003) critically assesses industrial policies in Japan, Korea, and Taiwan. Based on some empirical analyses including input–output and econometric studies, they find little support for industrial policies as major sources of growth.

The productivity analyses provide evidence on the efficacy of industrial policies in improving productivity growth.

Partial equilibrium analysis is purely a supply-side one and does not take into account the demand side of the economy. CGE analysis allows for a better assessment of policies and their impact on the economy and its sectors. CGE analyses of Japan and Korea have demonstrated that government intervention in industrial development and the instruments the governments used have had a positive and important effect on economic growth and industrial development. The results of the Singapore model favored industry targeting in Singapore due to their significantly positive contribution to economic performance. In Japan, Korea, and Singapore, the interventions of the government and the distortions in the product and factor markets it was involved in was found to have a significant and positive impact on welfare. Only in Korea, the welfare effect was negative but very small. By any means, it can be argued based on the quantitative findings of the CGE analyses that industrial policies are instrumental in achieving the targets of industrialization and improving the national welfare.

Limitations: There were data limitations in analyses. For instance, data for the number of foreign workers and payments made for their labor services with their industrial compositions in Singapore are not available in official statistics. Therefore, it was not possible to decompose labor into domestic and foreign components in the Singapore SAM. Furthermore, data on incentives provided to foreign enterprises were also not available. The government generally negotiates such incentives at the enterprise level and such information is generally not disclosed. The lack of these data does not allow for capturing the relations between the government and foreign enterprises better. Finally, price statistics in Singapore are yet inadequate. Some bias may be thought to exist in the TFP estimations due to the supply chain of MNCs that involves a number of countries. In this case, adjustments in export and import prices become necessary. Future line of research should address this issue.

BIBLIOGRAPHY

Adelman, Irma and Sherman Robinson (1978) *Income Distribution Policy in Developing Countries: A Case Study of Korea*, Oxford: World Bank, Oxford University Press.

Aigner, Dennis, C. A. Knox Lovell and Peter Schmidt (1977) Formulation and Estimation of Stochastic Frontier Models, *Journal of Econometrics*, vol. 6, pp. 21–37.

Akamatsu, Kaname (1962) A Historical Pattern of Economic Growth in Developing Countries, *Developing Economies*, vol. 1, pp. 3–25.

Amsden, Alice H. (1989) *Asia's Next Giant: South Korea and Late Industrialization*, New York: Oxford University Press.

Amsden, Alice H. (1991) Diffusion of Development: The Late Industrializing Model and Greater East Asia, *American Economic Review*, vol. 81, no. 2, pp. 282–286.

Amsden, Alice H. (2001) *The Rise of "the Rest": Challenges to the West from Late-Industrializing Economies*, Oxford: Oxford University Press.

Aoki, Masahiko (1998) Unintended Fit: Organizational Evolution and Government Design of Institutions in Japan, in Masahiko Aoki, Hyung-Ki Kim and Masahiro Okuno-Fujiwara (eds.), *The Role of Government in East Asian Economic Development*, Oxford: Clarendon Press, pp. 233–253.

Armington, Paul S. (1969) A Theory of Demand for Products Distinguished by Place of Production, *International Monetary Fund Staff Papers*, vol. 16, no. 1, pp. 159–176.

Arrow, Kenneth J., Hollis B. Chenery, B. S. Minhas and Robert M. Solow (1961) Capital-Labor Substitution and Economic Efficiency, *Review of Economics and Statistics*, vol. 43, no. 3, pp. 225–250.

Arrow, Kenneth J. and Gerrard Debreu (1954) Existence of an Equilibrium for a Competitive Economy, *Econometrica*, vol. 22, no. 3, pp. 265–290.

Asher, Mukul G. (1989) An Economic Perspective, in Ian Thynne and Mohamed Ariff (eds.), *Privatisation: Singapore's Experience in Perspective*, Singapore: Longman, pp. 159–182.

Battese, George E. and Tim Coelli (1992) Frontier Production Functions, Technical Efficiency and Panel Data: With Application to Paddy Farmers in India, *Journal of Productivity Analysis*, vol. 3, pp. 153–169.

Beebe, Jack and Jane Haltmaier (1980) An Intersectoral Analysis of the Secular Productivity Slowdown, *Federal Reserve Bank of San Francisco Economic Review*, Fall 1980, pp. 7–28.

Bercuson, Kenneth (ed.) (1995) Singapore: A Case Study in Rapid Development, International Monetary Fund, Occasional Paper, No. 119.

Bhattacharya, Amarenda and Johannes F. Linn (1988) *Trade and Industrial Policies in the Developing Countries of East Asia*, World Bank Discussion Papers, no. 27.

Brooke, Anthony, David Kendrick, Alexander Meeraus and Ramesh Raman (1998) *GAMS: A User's Guide*, GAMS Development Corporation.

Campbell, Kathleen M., Donald J. Campbell and Audrey Chia (2003) Regionalization: Policy Issues for Singapore, in Linda Low and Douglas Johnston (eds.), *Singapore Inc.: Public Policy Options in the Third Millennium*, Singapore: Eastern University Press, pp. 113–130.

Carling, Robert G. (1995) Labor Market Policies, in Kenneth Bercuson (ed.), *Singapore: A Case study in Rapid Development*, Washington DC: International Monetary Fund Occasional Paper No. 119, pp. 29–33.

Chang, Ha-Joon (2000) The Political Economy of Industrial Policy in Korea, in Robert Ash and Anne Booth (eds.), *The Economies of Asia: 1950-1998, Volume III – The Four Tigers*, New York: Routledge, pp. 265–299.

Chang, Ha-Joon (2006) Industrial Policies in East Asia – Lessons for Europe, *EIB Papers*, vol. 11, no. 2, pp. 106–132.

Chen, Edward K.Y. (1977) Factor Inputs, Total Factor Productivity, and Economic Growth: The Asian Case, *Developing Economies*, vol. 15, no. 1, pp. 121–143.

Chenery, Hollis B., Jeffrey Lewis, Jaime de Melo and Sherman Robinson (1986) Alternative Routes to Development, in Hollis B. Chenery, Sherman Robinson, and Moshe Syrquin (eds.), *Industrialization and Growth: A Comparative Study*, New York: Oxford University Press, Chapter 11.

Chenery, Hollis B., Sherman Robinson and Moshe Syrquin (1986) *Industrialization and Growth: A Comparative Study*, New York: Oxford University Press.

Chia, Ngee Choon (2000) Using a Computable General Equilibrium (CGE) Model to Evaluate the Singapore Tax System, in Guillermo Perry, John Whalley, and Gary McMahon (eds.), *Fiscal Reform and Structural Change in Developing Countries Volume 1*, Great Britain: Macmillan Press, pp. 142–170.

Chia, Siow Yue (1971) Growth and Pattern of Industrialization, in You Poh Seng and Lim Chong Yah (eds.), *The Singapore Economy*, Singapore: Eastern University Press, pp. 224–245.

Chia, Siow Yue (1985) The Role of Foreign Trade and Investment in the Development of Singapore, in Walter Galenson (ed.), *Foreign Trade and Investment: Economic Development in the Newly Industrializing Asian Countries*, Madison, Wisconsin: University of Wisconsin Press, pp. 259–297.

Chia, Siow Yue (1997) Singapore: Advanced Production Base and Smart Hub of the Electronics Industry, in Wendy Dobson and Siow Yue Chia (eds.), *Multinationals and East Asian Integration*, International Development Research Center, pp. 31–61.

Chia, Siow Yue (2005) The Singapore Model of Industrial Policy: Past Evolution and Current Thinking, paper presented at the ADB-Latin America conference "Competing in the 21st Century: Revisiting the Role of Government in Latin America and Asia," Buenos Aires, 28–29 November 2005.

Chiu, Stephen W. K., K. C. Ho and Tai-lok Lui (1997) *City States in the Global Economy: Industrial Restructuring in Hong Kong and Singapore*, Boulder, Colorado: Westview Press.

Cho, Yoon Je (1998) Government Intervention, Rent Distribution, and Economic Development in Korea, in Masahiko Aoki, Hyung-Ki Kim and Masahiro Okuno-Fujiwara (eds.), *The Role of Government in East Asian Economic Development*, Oxford: Clarendon Press, pp. 208–232.

Choi, Jeong Pyo (1990) Factor Demand and Production Technology in Korean and Taiwanese Manufacturing, in Jene K. Kwon (ed.), *Korean Economic Development*, Greenwood Press, pp. 167–181.

Chong, Li-Choy and Mark Goh (1992) SME Development in Singapore: Intra-industry Cooperation among the SMEs, *Public Enterprise*, vol. 12, nos. 1–2, pp. 41–48.

Christensen, Lauritz R., Dale W. Jorgenson and Lawrence J. Lau (1973) Transcendental Logarithmic Production Frontiers, *Review of Economics and Statistics*, vol. 55, no. 1, pp. 28–45.

Collins, Susan M. and Barry P. Bosworth (1996) Economic Growth in East Asia: Accumulation versus Assimilation, *Brookings Papers on Economic Activity*, vol. 2, pp. 135–203.

Committee on Singapore's Competitiveness (CSC) (1998) *Report on Domestic Businesses*, Reference No: Pr/51/98.

De Melo, Jaime (1977) Distortions in the Factor Market: Some General Equilibrium Estimates, *Review of Economics and Statistics*, vol. 59, pp. 398–405.

De Melo, Jaime (1988) Computable General Equilibrium Models for Trade Policy Analysis in Developing Countries: A Survey, *Journal of Policy Modeling*, vol. 10, no. 4, pp. 469–503.

Dervis, Kemal, Jaime de Melo and Sherman Robinson (1982) *General Equilibrium Models for Development Policy*, New York: Cambridge University Press.

Devarajan, Shantayan and Delfin Sia Go (1998) The Simplest Dynamic General Equilibrium Model of an Open Economy, *Journal of Policy Modeling*, vol. 29, no. 6, pp. 677–714.

Deyo, Frederic C. (1981) *Dependent Development and Industrial Order: An Asian Case Study*, New York: Praeger.

DGBAS (Directorate General of Budget, Accounting and Statistics, Executive Yuan, the Republic of China) (2001) *Quarterly National Income Statistics in Taiwan Area, the Republic of China (1961–2000).*

Diewert, W. E. (1976) Exact and Superlative Index Numbers, *Journal of Econometrics*, vol. 4, no. 2, pp. 115–145.

Dixon, Peter B., B. R. Parmenter, John Sutton and D. P. Vincent (1982) *ORANI: A Multisectoral Model of the Australian Economy*, Contributions to Economic Analysis, no. 142, Amsterdam: North Holland Publishing Company.

Elias, V. J. (1990) The Role of Total Factor Productivity on Economic Growth, paper prepared for the *1991 World Development Report*, Washington, DC: World Bank.

Entrepreneurship and Internationalization Subcommittee – EISC (2002) *Report of the Entrepreneurship and Internationalization Subcommittee,* accessed in March 2004 from http://www.mti.gov.sg/public/ERC/frm_ERC_Default.asp?sid=121.

Enterprise Promotion Centres (1991) *Government Development Assistance Programmes – A Guide for Entrepreneurs*, Singapore: Craft Print.

EPA (Economic Planning Agency) (1967) *Waga Kuni Sangyo Kozo to Keizai Yosoku* [Industrial Structure and an Economic Forecast of Our Nation], published by Economic Planning Agency, Tsusan Shiryo Chosakai (in Japanese).

EPC (Economic Planning Committee, Ministry of Trade and Industry, Republic of Singapore) (1991) *Strategic Economic Plan – Towards a Developed Nation*, SNP Publishers.

ESCAP (Economic and Social Council for Asia-Pacific) (1995) Singapore, in *Expansion of Manufactured Exports by SMEs in ESCAP, Volume II: National Studies*, ESCAP Studies in Trade and Investment, New York: United Nations, pp. 146–162.

Ezaki, Mitsuo (1994) Shijo to Seifu Kainyu: Waga Kuni Sangyo Seisaku no CGE (Tabumon Ippan Kinko Bunseki) [Market and Government Intervention: A Multi-sector CGE Analysis of Japan's Industrial Policy], *Forum of International Development Studies*, vol. 1, pp. 65–85 (in Japanese).

Fagerberg, Jan (2000) Technological Progress, Structural Change and Productivity Growth: A Comparative Study, *Structural Change and Economic Dynamics*, vol. 11, pp. 393–411.

Felipe, Jesus (1997) Total Factor Productivity in Asia: A Critical Survey, Asian Development Bank (ADB), *EDRC Report Series,* no. 65.

Frey, Bruno S., Werner W. Pommerehne, Friedrich Schneider and Guy Gilbert (1987) Consensus and Dissension among Economists: An Empirical Inquiry, *American Economic Review*, vol. 74, no. 5, pp. 986–994.

Fukao, Kyoji, Sumio Hamagata, Tomohiko Inui, Keiko Ito, Hyeog Ug Kwon, Tatsuji Makino, Tsutomu Miyagawa, Yasuo Nakanishi, Joji Tokui (2007) *Estimation Procedures and TFP Analysis of the JIP Database 2006*, RIETI Discussion Paper Series, No. 07-E-003.

Go, Delfin S. (1988) *Growth and Adjustment in the Philippines: A Dynamic General Equilibrium Analysis*, Ph.D. Dissertation, Cambridge, MA: Harvard University.

Goh, Keng Swee (1976) A Socialist Economy That Works, in C. V. Devan Nair (ed.), *Socialism That Works – The Singapore Way*, Singapore: Federal Publications, pp. 77–85.

Haggard, Stephan (1999) An External View of Singapore's Developed Status, in Linda Low (ed.), *Singapore: Toward Developed Status*, Oxford: Oxford University Press, pp. 345–375.

Harberger, Arnold C. (1998) A Vision of the Growth Process, *American Economic Review*, vol. 88, no. 1, pp. 1–32.

Hattori, Tomio and Yukihito Sato (1997) A Comparative Study of Development Mechanisms in Korea and Taiwan: Introductory Analysis, *Developing Economies*, vol. 35, no. 4, pp. 341–357.

Hellman, Thomas, Kevin Murdock and Joseph Stiglitz (1998) Financial Restraint: Towards a New Paradigm, in Masahiko Aoki, Hyung-ki Kim, and Masahiro Okuno-Fujiwara (eds.), *The Role of the Government in East-Asian Economic Development: A Comparative Institutional Analysis*, Oxford: Oxford University Press, pp. 163–208.

Hertel, Thomas W. and Marinos E. Tsigas (1997) Structure of GTAP, in Thomas W. Hertel (ed.), *Global Trade Analysis: Modeling and Applications*, New York: Cambridge University Press, pp. 13–73.

Hobday, Mike (1995) East Asian Latecomer Firms: Learning the Technology of Electronics, *World Development*, vol. 23, no. 7, pp. 1171–1193.

Hodrick, R.J. and E.C. Prescott (1997) Postwar US Business Cycles: An Empirical Investigation, *Journal of Money, Credit and Banking*, vol. 29, pp. 1–16.

Hong, Sung G. (1997) *The Political Economy of Industrial Policy in East Asia: The Semiconductor Industry and South Korea*, Cheltenham: Edward Elgar.

Hsieh, Chang-Tai (2002) What Explains the Industrial Revolution in East Asia? Evidence from Factor Markets, *American Economic Review*, vol. 92, no. 3, pp. 502–526.

Huff, W. G. (1994) *The Economic Growth of Singapore: Trade and Development in the Twentieth Century*, Cambridge University Press.

Huff, W. G. (2000) What is the Singapore Model of Economic Development, in Robert Ash and Anne Booth (eds.), *The Economies of Asia: 1950–1998, Volume III – The Four Tigers*, Routledge, pp. 105–134.

Hughes, Helen (1969) From Entrepôt Trade to Manufacturing, in Helen Hughes and Poh Seng You (eds.), *Foreign Investment and Industrialization in Singapore*, Madison: The University of Wisconsin Press, pp. 1–45.

Ikemoto, Y. (1986) Technical Progress and the Level of Technology in Asian Countries, *Developing Economies*, vol. 24, no. 4, pp. 368–390.

Inoue, Ryuichiro, Hirohisa Kohama, and Shujiro Urata (eds.) (1993) *Industrial Policy in East Asia*, JETRO.

Ito, Takatoshi (2001) Growth, Crisis, and the Future of Economic Recovery in East Asia, in Joseph E. Stiglitz and Shahid Yusuf (eds.), *Rethinking the East Asia Miracle*, Oxford University Press, pp. 55–94.

Itoh, Motoshige, Kazuharu Kiyono, Masahiro Okuno-Fujiwara, and Kotaro Suzumura (1988) *Sangyou Seisaku no Keizai Bunseki* (Economic Analysis of Industrial Policy), Tokyo University Press (in Japanese).

Itoh, Motoshige, Kazuharu Kiyono, Masahiro Okuno-Fujiwara, and Kotaro Suzumura (1991) *Economic Analysis of Industrial Policy*, New York: Academy Press.

Iwata, Shigeru, Mohsin Khan and Hiroshi Murao (2002) Sources of Economic Growth in East Asia: A Nonparametric Assessment, *IMF Working Paper*, No. 02/13.

Jalava, Jukka, S. Heikkinen and R. Hjerppe (2002) Technology and Structural Change: Productivity in the Finnish Manufacturing Industries, 1925–2000, paper presented at *XIII Economic History Congress*, Buenos Aires, 28 June 2002.

Johnson, Chalmers A. (1982) *MITI and the Japanese Miracle: The Growth of Industrial Policy, 1925–1975*, Stanford: Stanford University Press.

Jones, Leroy P. And Il Sakong (1980) *Government, Business, and Entrepreneurship in Economic Development: The Korean Case*, Harvard East Asian Monographs, Cambridge, MA: Harvard University Asia Center.

Jorgenson, Dale W., Barbara Fraumeni and Frank M. Gollop (1987) *Productivity and U.S. Economic Growth*, Cambridge, MA: Harvard University Press.

Jorgenson, Dale W. and M. Sullivan (1981) Inflation and Corporate Capital Recovery, in Charles Hulten (ed.), *Depreciation, Inflation, and the Taxation of Income from Capital*, Urban Institute.

Kaldor, Nicholas (1963) *Essays on Economics Stability and Growth*, London: Gerald Duckworth & Co.

Kaldor, Nicholas (1966). *Causes of the Slow Rate of Economic Growth of the United Kingdom*, An Inaugural Lecture, Cambridge: Cambridge University Press.

Kang, Chul Kyu (1989) *Industrial Policy in Korea: Review and Perspective*, Seoul: Korea Institute for Economics and Technology.

Kato, Kozo, Tsutomu Shibata, Koichiro Fukui, Aichiro Mogi, Yuichiro Miyawa, Yoshikazu Niwa, Nobuhiro Ichikawa and Masahiro Furuta (1994) *Policy-Based Finance: The Experience of Postwar Japan*, World Bank Discussion Papers, No. 221.

Kawai, Hiroki (1994) International Comparative Analysis of Economic Growth, *Developing Economies*, vol. 32, no. 4, pp. 373–397.

Kawai, Hiroki (1999) Productivity Growth and Structural Change in Japanese Economy: Resource Reallocation and Firm Dynamics, Paper presented at *Pacific Economic Outlook – Structure Meeting*, Osaka, September 13–14, 1999.

Keyzer, Michiel A. (1991) On the Approximation of Infinite Horizon Allocations, in Henk Don, Theo van de Klundert, Jarig van Sinderen (eds.), *Applied General Equilibrium*, Leiden: Kluwer Academic Publishers.

Kim, Eun Mee (1997) *Big Business, Strong State: Collusion and Conflict in South Korean Economic Development, 1960–1990*, Albany: State University of New York Press.

Kim, Hyung-ki and Jun Ma (1998) The Role of Government in Acquiring Technological Capability: The Case of the Petrochemical Industry in East Asia, in Masahiko Aoki, Hyung-Ki Kim and Masahiro Okuno-Fujiwara (eds.), *The Role of Government in East Asian Economic Development*, Oxford: Clarendon Press, pp. 101–133.

Kim, Jong-il and Lawrence Lau (1994) The Sources of Economic Growth of the East Asian Newly Industrializing Countries, *Journal of the Japanese an International Economies*, vol. 8, pp. 235–271.

Koh, Soo-Wei, Shahidur Rahman and G. K. Randolph Tan (2001) Consistently Defined Price and Volume Relatives for Singapore Manufacturing Industries: 1975–1998, *SABRE Center Working Paper*, Singapore: Nanyang Technological University, Singapore.

Koh, Soo-Wei, Shahidur Rahman and Randolph G. K. Tan (2004) Stochastic Frontier Analysis of Singapore Manufacturing Industries, *Singapore Economic Review*, vol. 49, no. 1, pp. 85–103.

Krause, Lawrence B. (1987) The Government as an Entrepreneur, in Lawrence B. Krause, Koh Ai Tee, and Lee (Tsao) Yuan (eds.), *The Singapore Economy Reconsidered*, Singapore: Institute of Southeast Asian Studies, pp. 107–127.

Krueger, Anne O. (1980) Trade Policy as an Input to Development, *American Economic Review*, vol. 70, no. 2, pp. 288–292.

Krugman, Paul (1994) The Myth of Asia Miracle, *Foreign Affairs*, vol. 73, no. 6, pp. 62–78.

Kuchiki, Akifumi (2003) *Changing Industrialization Policy of East Asia under Globalization*, Nagoya University Graduate School of International Development, Discussion Paper No. 113.

Kumar, Sree (1998) Johor-Singapore-Riau Growth Triangle: A Model of Subregional Cooperation, in Myo Thant, Min Thang, and Hiroshi Kakazu (eds.), *Growth Triangles in Asia – A New Approach to Regional Economic Cooperation*, Hong Kong: Oxford University Press, pp. 187–229.

Kumar, Sree and Lee Tsao Yuan (1991) A Singapore Perspective, in Lee Tsao Yuan (ed.), *Growth Triangle: The Johor-Singapore-Riau Experience*, Singapore: Institute of Southeast Asian Studies, pp. 1–36.

Kuroda, Masahiro (1984) *Jissho Keizaigaku Nyumon* [Introduction to Applied Economics], Tokyo: Nihon Hyoronsha (in Japanese).

Kuroda, Masahiro, Kazuyuki Motohashi and Kazushige Shimpo (1996) Issues on the International Comparison of Productivity: Theory and Measurement, in *OECD Proceedings, Industry Productivity: International Comparison and Measurement Issues*, Paris: OECD, pp. 49–95.

Kwon, Jene and Hoon Paik (1995) Factor Price Distortions, Resource Allocation, and Growth: A Computable General Equilibrium Analysis, *Review of Economics and Statistics*, vol. 77, no. 4, pp. 664–676.

Kwong, Kai-Sun (ed.) (2001) *Industrial Development in Singapore, Taiwan, and South Korea*, World Scientific.

Laeven, Luc (2002) Financial Constraints on Investments and Credit Policy in Korea, *Journal of Asian Economics*, vol. 13, no. 2, pp. 251–269.

Lee, Chung H., Keun Lee and Kang-koo Lee (2000) Chaebol, Financial Liberalization, and Economic Crisis: Transformation of Quasi-Internal Organization in Korea, Seoul National University, Institute of Economic Research, Discussion Paper, No. 31, Seoul, Korea.

Lee, Hiro Hakuyu (1988) *Imperfect Competition, Industrial Policy, and Japanese International Competitiveness*, Ph.D. Dissertation, Berkeley: University of California.

Lee, Hiro (1993) General Equilibrium Evaluation of Industrial Policy in Japan, *Journal of Asian Economics*, vol. 4, no. 1, pp. 25–40.

Lee, Kyu Uck (1998) *Competition Policy, Deregulation and Economic Development: The Korean Experience*, Korea Institute for Industrial Economics and Trade.

Lee, Kyu Uck and Dong Gull Lee (1996) *Competition Policies, Trade and Foreign Direct Investment in the Asia Pacific Region: Special Reference to Korea*, Seoul: Korea Institute for Industrial Economics and Trade.

Lee, Tsao Yuan (1987) The Government in the Labor Market, in Lawrence B. Krause, Koh Ai Tee, and Lee (Tsao) Yuan (eds.), *The Singapore Economy Reconsidered*, Singapore: Institute of Southeast Asian Studies, pp. 174–216.

Lee, Tsao Yuan and Linda Low (1990) *Local Entrepreneurship in Singapore – Private and State*, the Institute of Policy Studies, Singapore: Times Academic Press.

Lee, William K. Mun (1997) Foreign Investment, Industrial Restructuring and Dependent Development in Singapore, *Journal of Contemporary Asia*, vol. 27, no. 1, pp. 58–70.

Leipziger, Danny M. and Peter A. Petri (1993) Korean Industrial Policy: Legacies of the Past and Directions for the Future, World Bank Discussion Papers, No. 197.

Leung, Hing-Man (1997) Total Factor Productivity Growth in Singapore's Manufacturing Industries, *Applied Economics Letters*, vol. 4, no. 8, pp. 525–528.

Li, K. T. (1976) *The Experience of Dynamic Economic Growth on Taiwan*, Taipei: Mei Ya Publications.

Li, Kuo-ting (1988) *The Evolution of Policy behind Taiwan's Development Success*, New Haven: Yale University Press.

Lim, Chong Yah and associates (1988) *Policy Options for the Singapore Economy*, Singapore: McGraw Hill.

Lim, Chong Yah and Chee-Tong Lee (2002) An Examination of Labor Productivity Growth and Structural Changes in the Singapore Labor Force, *Asian Economic Journal*, vol. 16, no. 3, pp. 267–283.

Lim, Linda (1983) Chinese Business, Multinationals and the State Manufacturing for Export in Malaysia and Singapore, in Linda Lim and L. A. P. Gosling (eds.), *The Chinese in Southeast Asia, vol. 1, Ethnicity and Economic Activity*, Singapore: Maruzen Asia, pp. 245–274.

Lim, Linda and Pang Eng Fong (1991) *Foreign Direct Investment and Industrialization in Malaysia, Singapore, Taiwan, and Thailand*, Organization for Economic and Cooperative Development (OECD), Paris, France.

Lin, Ming-ji (2002) Republic of China, in Asian Productivity Organization, *SMEs in Competitive Markets*, Tokyo: Asian Productivity Organization, pp. 29–50.

Lindauer, D. L. and M. Roemer (1994) Legacies and Opportunities, in D. L. Lindauer and M. Roemer (eds.), *Asia and Africa: Legacies and Opportunities in Development*, International Center for Economic Growth and Harvard Institute for International Development.

Liu, Paul C., Yin-Chuan Liu and Hui-Lin Wu (1993) The Manufacturing Enterprise and Management in Taiwan, in *Economic and Social Development in East Asia: Policies, Management and Population*, University Research Center, Nihon University, pp. 439–487.

LIUP Centre (1997) *LIUP News* (newsletter published by the LIUP Center), July 1997.

Lofgren, Hans, Rebecca Lee Harris and Sherman Robinson (2002) *A Standard Computable General Equilibrium (CGE) Model in GAMS*, Microcomputers in Policy Research 5, Washington, DC: International Food Policy Research Institute.

Low, Linda (1988) Privatization in Singapore, in Paul Cook and Colin Kirkpatrick (eds.), *Privatization in Less Developed Countries*, Brighton: Wheatsheaf Books, pp. 259–280.

Lysy, Frank J. and Lance Taylor (1980) A Computable General Equilibrium Model for the Functional Distribution of Income: Experiments for Brazil, 1959–71, in Lance Taylor, Admar L. Bacha, Eliana A. Cardoso, and Frank Lysy (eds.), *Models of Growth and Distribution for Brazil*, Oxford: Oxford University Press.

Mahadevan, Renuka and Kali Kalirajan (2000) Singapore's Manufacturing Sector's TFP Growth: A Decomposition Analysis, *Journal of Comparative Economics*, vol. 28, no. 4, pp. 828–839.

Marti, C. (1996) *Is There an East Asian Miracle?*, Union Bank of Switzerland Economic Research Working Paper, Zurich.

MAS (Monetary Authority of Singapore) (2000) Special Feature on the MMS Model of the Singapore Economy: Simulating the Electronics Slowdown, *MAS ED Quarterly Bulletin*, December 2000, pp. 53–62.

Massell, B. F. (1961) A Disaggregated View of Technical Change, *Journal of Political Economy*, vol. 69, pp. 547–557.

Meaney, Constance Squires (1994) State Policy and the Development of Taiwan's Semiconductor Industry, in Joel D. Aberbach, David Dollar, Kenneth L. Sokoloff (eds.) *The Role of the State in Taiwan's Development*, New York: East Gate, pp. 170–192.

Meier, Gerald M. (ed.) (1984) *Leading Issues in Economic Development*, New York: Oxford University Press.

MTI (Ministry of Trade and Industry, Republic of Singapore) (1986) *The Singapore Economy: New Directions*, Report of the Economic Committee, February 1986.

MTI (Ministry of Trade and Industry, Republic of Singapore) (1998) *The Report of the Committee on Singapore's Competitiveness*, November 1998.

MTI (Ministry of Trade and Industry, Republic of Singapore) (2001) Singapore's Productivity Performance, *Economic Survey of Singapore, First Quarter 2001*, pp. 40–48.

MTI (Ministry of Trade and Industry, Republic of Singapore) (2003) *New Challenges, Fresh Goals – Towards a Dynamic Global City*, Report of the Economic Review Committee, February 2003.

MTI (Ministry of Trade and Industry, Republic of Singapore) *Economic Survey of Singapore, various years.*

Myers, Ramon (1990) The Economic Development of the Republic of China on Taiwan, in Lawrence J. Lau (ed.), *Models of Development – A Comparative Study of Economic Growth in South Korea and Taiwan*, International Center for Economic Growth, pp. 17–64.

Naidu, G. (1998) Johor-Singapore-Riau Growth Triangle: Progress and Prospects, in Myo Thant, Min Thang, and Hiroshi Kakazu (eds.), *Growth Triangles in Asia – A New Approach to Regional Economic Cooperation*, Hong Kong: Oxford University Press, pp. 231–255.

Noland, Marcus and Howard Pack (2003) Industrial Policy in an Era of Globalization: Lessons from Asia, Washington, DC: Institute of International Economics.

Noland, Marcus and Howard Pack (2005) The East Asian Industrial Policy Experience: Implications for the Middle East, Washington, DC: Institute of International Economics, Working Paper Series, No. WP 05–14.

Normal, Paul (1999) Putting Iterative Proportional Fitting on the Researcher's Desk, Working Paper No. 99/3, Leads: School of Geography, University of Leeds.

OECD (1996) Industry Productivity: International Comparison and Measurement Issues.

OECD (2001a) *Measuring Capital – OECD Manual: Measurement of Capital Stocks, Consumption of Fixed Capital, and Capital Services.*

OECD (2001b) *Measuring Productivity – OECD Manual: Measurement of Aggregate and Industry-Level Productivity Growth.*

Okazaki, Tetsuji and Masahiro Okuno-Fujiwara (1999) Japan's Present-Day Economic System and Its Historical Origins, in Tetsuji Okazaki and Masahiro Okuno-Fujiwara (eds.), *The Japanese Economic System and Its Historical Origins*, translated by Susan Herbert, Oxford University Press, pp. 1–37.

Osada, Hiroshi (1993) *Import Liberalization of Japan in the 1960s and its Impacts on Manufacturing Industries*, Nagoya University Graduate School of International Development, Discussion Paper, No. 5.

Pack, Howard (1988) Industrialization and Trade, in Hollis Chenery and T. N. Srinivasan (eds.), *Handbook of Development Economics*, Elsevier Science Publishers, pp. 333–380.

Pack, Howard (2000) Industrial Policy: Growth Elixir or Poison? *World Bank Research Observer*, vol. 15, no. 1, pp. 47–67.

Pack, Howard (2001) Technological Change and Growth in East Asia: Macro versus Micro Perspectives, in Joseph E. Stiglitz and Shahid Yusuf (eds.), *Rethinking the East Asia Miracle*, Oxford University Press, pp. 95–142.

Paik, Hoon (1991) *Industrial-Financial Policy, Resource Allocation, and Growth: A Computable General Equilibrium Analysis of Korea*, PhD Dissertation, Northern Illinois University.

Pang, Eng Fong (2000) Staying Global and Going Regional – Singapore's Inward and Outward Direct Investment, in Robert Ash and Anne Booth (eds.), *The Economies of Asia: 1950–1998, Volume III – The Four Tigers*, Routledge, pp. 497–510.

Park, Sung-Joon (1999) Sources of Economic Growth and the Role of Industrial Policy in Korea, Korea Economic Research Institute, Research Paper No. 17.

Peebles, Gavin and Peter Wilson (2002) *Economic Growth and Development in Singapore: Past and Future*, Cheltenham, UK: Edward Elgar.

Pilat, Dirk (1996) Labour Productivity Levels in OECD Countries: Estimates for Manufacturing and Selected Service Sectors, OECD Economics Department Working Paper No. 169.

PSDC (Public Sector Divestment Committee) (1987) Report of the Public Sector Divestment Committee, 21 February 1987.

Pyo, Hak-Kil (1998) *Estimates of Fixed Reproducible Tangible Assets in the Republic of Korea, 1953–1996*, Korea Development Institute.

Pyo, Hak-Kil, Geun-Hee Rhee and Bongchan Ha (2006) *Growth Accounting and Productivity Analysis by 33 Industrial Sectors in Korea (1984-2002)*, Hi-Stat

Discussion Paper Series No. D06-171, Institute of Economic Research, Hitotsubashi University.

Ranis, Gustav (2000) Another Look at the East Asian Miracle, in Robert Ash and Anne Booth (eds.), *The Economies of Asia: 1950–1998, Volume III — The Four Tigers*, Routledge, pp. 300–326.

Rao, Bhanoji V. V. and M. K. Ramakrishnan (1980) *Income Inequality in Singapore: Impact of Economic Growth and Structural Change 1966–1975*, Singapore: Singapore University Press.

Rao, Bhanoji V. V. and Christopher Lee (1995) Sources of Growth in Singapore Economy and its Manufacturing and Service Sectors, *Singapore Economic Review*, vol. 38, no. 2, pp. 231–251.

Regnier, Philippe (1987) *Singapore: City-state in South East Asia*, translated from French by Christopher Hurst, Honolulu: University of Hawaii Press.

Rieber, William J. (1996) Aspects of Singapore in the International Economy, in Basant K. Kapur, Euston T. E. Quah, and Hoon Hian Teck (eds.), *Development, Trade and the Asia-Pacific: Essays in Honour of Professor Lim Chong Yah*, Singapore: Prentice Hall, pp. 36-51.

Robinson, Sherman, Andrea Cattaneo and Moataz el-Said (2000) Updating and Estimating a Social Accounting Matrix Using Cross Entropy Methods, TMD Discussion Papers, No. 58, Washington, DC: International Food Policy Research Institute (IFPRI).

Rodan, Garry (1989) *The Political Economy of Singapore's Industrialization: National State and International Capital*, Hong Kong: Macmillan Press.

Rodan, Garry (1998) Singapore: Economic Diversification and Social Divisions, in Garry Rodan, Kevin Hewison and Richard Robison (eds.), *The Political Economy of Southeast Asia: An Introduction*, Oxford University Press, pp. 148–178.

Rodrik, Dani, Gene Grossman, Victor Norman (1995) Getting Interventions Right: How South Korea and Taiwan Grew Rich, *Economic Policy*, vol. 10, no. 20, pp. 53–107.

Sadoulet, Elisabeth and Alain de Janvry (1995) *Quantitative Development Policy Analysis*, Johns Hopkins University Press.

Sakong, Il (1993) *Korea in the World Economy*, Washington, DC: Institute for International Economics.

Salter, W. E. G. (1960) *Productivity and Technical Change*, University of Cambridge Department of Applied Economics Monographs, Cambridge: Cambridge University Press.

Shen, Xiaofang (2000) Linking Local Suppliers to Multinationals: How Can Governments Play a Useful Role? *Transition Newsletter*, World Bank Development Economics Research Group, vol. 11, nos. 3–4, pp. 14–15.

Shin, Jang-Sup (1996) *The Economics of the Latecomers: Catching-up, Technology Transfer and Institutions in Germany, Japan, and South Korea*, New York: Routledge.

Shinohara, Miyohei (1982) *Industrial Growth, Trade and Dynamic Patterns in the Japanese Economy*, Tokyo: University of Tokyo Press.

Shoven, John B. and John Whalley (1984) Applied General-Equilibrium Models of Taxation and International Trade: An Introduction and Survey, *Journal of Economic Literature*, vol. 22, no. 3, pp. 1007–1051.

SICC (Singapore International Chamber of Commerce) (2003) *The Investor's Guide to Singapore*, 2003 edition, Singapore: Continental Press.

SILS (The Society of International Law, Singapore) (1995) *Privatization in Singapore: Policy and Impact on Labor Relations*, SILS Information Series, No. 5.

Singapore Department of Statistics *Yearbook of Statistics*, various years.

Singstat (Singapore Department of Statistics) (2003) *Singapore's Balance of Payments: Methodological Improvements and New Reporting Format for the Services Account*, Information Paper on Economic Statistics.

Siriwardana, Mahinda (1991) *A General Equilibrium Appraisal of Some Policy Options for Singapore*, Occasional Working Papers in Economic Development, University of New England, Armidale, Faculty of Economic Studies (Australia), Paper No. 45.

Siriwardana, Mahinda (1997a) Exchange Rate Policy and Market Power: A General Equilibrium Analysis for Singapore, *ASEAN Economic Bulletin*, July 1997, pp. 57–79.

Siriwardana, Mahinda (1997b) *The Impact of the World Economic Recovery on a Small Open Economy: The Case of Singapore*, UNE Working Papers in Economics, No. 41, University of New England, Armidale, Faculty of Economic Studies (Australia).

Siriwardana, Mahinda (2000) A General Equilibrium Explanation of the Growth in Singapore's Exports, *Journal of the Asia Pacific Economy*, vol. 5, no. 3, pp. 303–335.

Siriwardana, Mahinda and Anoma Iddamalgoda (2003) *Effects of the Asian Economic Crisis on Singapore and Its Policy Responses: A General Equilibrium Analysis*, UNEAC Asia Papers, No. 6.

Smith, Heather (2000) Taiwan's Industrial Policy in the 1980s, in Robert Ash and Anne Booth (eds.), *The Economies of Asia: 1950–1998, Volume III – The Four Tigers*, Routledge, pp. 407–441.

Soon, Teck-Wong and C. Suan Tan (1993) *The Lessons of East Asia — Singapore: Public Policy and Economic Development*, Washington, DC: World Bank.

Stern, Joseph J., Ji-Hong Kim, Dwight H. Perkins and Jung-Ho Yoo (1995) *Industrialization and the State: The Korean Heavy and Chemical Industry Drive*, Cambridge, MA: Harvard Institute for International Development.

Stiglitz, Joseph E. (1989) Markets and Development, NBER Working Paper Series, Working Paper No. 2961.

Sun, Chia-Hung (2002). Productivity Growth in Singapore's Manufacturing Industries: Evidence from Stochastic Coefficients Analysis, paper presented at the *Econometric Society Australasian Meeting ESAM02*, Queensland University of Technology, Brisbane, Australia, July 7–10, 2002.

Syrquin, Moshe (1984) Resource Reallocation and Productivity Growth, in Moshe Syrquin, Lance Taylor, and Larry E. Westphal (eds.), *Economic Structure and Performance – Essays in Honor of Hollis B. Chenery*, Orlando, Florida: Academic Press, pp. 75–101.

Syrquin, Moshe (1986) Productivity Growth and Factor Reallocation, in Hollis Chenery, Sherman Robinson, and Moshe Syrquin (eds.), *Industrialization and Growth: A Comparative Study*, published for the World Bank by Oxford University Press, pp. 229–262.

Syrquin, Moshe (1995) Patterns of Structural Change, in H. Chenery and T.N. Srinivasan (eds.), *Handbook of Development Economics, Volume 1*, Elsevier, pp. 203–273.

Szirmai, Adam (1993) Comparative Productivity in Manufacturing: A Case Study for Indonesia, in A. Szirmai, B. van Ark, and D. Pilat (eds.), *Explaining Economic Growth: Essays in Honor of Angus Maddison*, North Holland, pp. 217–240.

Tan, Augustine H. H. (1999) Official Efforts to Attract FDI: Case of Singapore's EDB, paper presented at the *EWC/KDI Conference on Industrial Globalization in 21st Century: Impact and Consequences for East Asia and Korea*, 2–3 August 1999.

Tan, Kong Yam. (1996) The ASEAN Free Trade Area: A Singapore Perspective, in Basant K. Kapur, Euston T. E. Quah, and Hoon Hian Teck (eds.), *Development, Trade and the Asia-Pacific: Essays in Honour of Professor Lim Chong Yah*, Singapore: Prentice Hall, pp. 52–63.

Teranishi, Juro (2002) The Main Bank System, in Tetsuji Okazaki and Masahiro Okuno-Fujiwara (eds.), *The Japanese Economic System and Its Historical Origins*, Oxford University Press, pp. 63–96.

Thangavelu, Shandre Mugan (2004) Singapore, in Asian Productivity Organization, *Total Factor Productivity Growth: Survey Report*, pp. 280–296.

Thant, M. and M. Tang (1998) Growth Triangles: Conceptual and Operational Considerations, in M. Thant, M. Tang, and H. Kakazu. (eds.), *Growth Triangles in Asia: A New Approach to Regional Economic Cooperation*, Oxford: Oxford University Press, pp. 23–48.

Thomas, Marcelle and Romeo M. Bautista (1999) *A 1991 Social Accounting Matrix (SAM) for Zimbabwe*, Washington, DC: International Food Policy Research Institute.

Thurlow, James (2003) *A Dynamic Computable General Equilibrium (CGE) Model for South Africa: Extending the Static IFPRI Model*, Washington, DC: International Food Policy Research Institute.

Thynne, Ian (1989) The Administrative State in Transition, in Ian Thynne and Mohamed Ariff (eds.), *Privatisation: Singapore's Experience in Perspective*, Singapore: Longman, pp. 19–58.

Timmer, Marcel P. (1998) *Catch Up Patterns in Newly Industrializing Economies: An International Comparison of Manufacturing Productivity in Taiwan, 1961–1993*, Research Memorandum No. GD-40, University of Groningen, Groningen Growth and Development Center.

Timmer, Marcel P. and A. Szirmai (2000) Productivity Growth in Asian Manufacturing: The Structural Bonus Hypothesis Examined. *Structural Change and Economic Dynamics* vol. 11, pp. 371–392.

Tsao, Lee Yuan (1982) *Growth and Productivity in Singapore: A Supply Side Analysis*, PhD Dissertation, Cambridge, MA: Harvard University.

Tsay, Chin-lung (1995) Taiwan: Labor Shortage, in Won Bae Kim and Gordon L. Clark (eds.), *Asian NIEs and the Global Economy: Industrial Restructuring and Corporate Strategy in the 1990s*, Johns Hopkins University Press, pp. 197–216.

Urata, Shujiro (2001) Emergence of an FDI-Trade Nexus and Economic Growth in East Asia, in Joseph E. Stiglitz and Shahid Yusuf (eds.), *Rethinking the East Asia Miracle*, Oxford University Press, pp. 409–459.

Van Ark, Bart and Marcel P. Timmer (2003) Asia's Productivity Performance and Potential: The Contribution of Sectors and Structural Change, paper presented at *RIETI-KEIO Conference on Japanese Economy: Leading East Asia in the 21st Century?* Tokyo, 30 May 2003.

Vernon, Raymond (1966) International Investment and International Trade in the Product Cycle, *Quarterly Journal of Economics*, vol. 80, pp. 190–207.

Voyvoda, Ebru and A. Erinc Yeldan (1999) Patterns of Productivity Growth and the Wage Cycle in Turkish Manufacturing, paper presented at the *METU Economic Research Conference III*, Ankara, September, 1999.

Wade, Robert (1990) Governing the Market – Economic Theory and the Role of Government in East Asian Industrialization, Princeton University Press.

Wade, Robert (1992) East Asia's Economic Success, Conflicting Perspectives, Partial Insights, Shaky Evidence, *World Politics*, vol. 44, no. 2, pp. 270–320.

Wagner, Karin and Bart van Ark (eds.) (1996) *International Productivity Differences: Measurement and Explanations*, Contributions to Economic Analysis No. 233, Elsevier.

Wilson, Peter (2000) The Dilemma of a More Advanced Developing Country: Conflicting Views on the Development Strategy of Singapore, *Developing Economies*, vol. 38, no. 1, pp. 105–134.

Wilson, Peter and Gavin Peebles (2005) Don't Frighten the Horses – the Political Economy of Singapore's Foreign Exchange Regime since 1981, Department of Economics, National University of Singapore, Singapore Center for Applied and Policy Economics, Working Paper, No. 2005/06.

Wolf, Charles (1988) *Markets or Governments: Choosing between Imperfect Alternatives*, Cambridge, MA: MIT Press.

Wong, Fot-Chyi and Weng Beng Gan (1994) Total Factor Productivity Growth in Singapore Manufacturing Industries During the 1980s, *Journal of Asian Economics*, vol. 5, no. 2, pp. 177–196.

Wong, Poh-Kam (1996a) From NIE to developed economy: Singapore's industrial policy to the year 2000, *Journal of Asian Business*, vol. 12, no. 3, pp. 65–85.

Wong, Poh-Kam (1996b) Senshinkoku Keizaika no Tame no Nekusuto Rappu Senryaku wo Kakageru Shingaporu, (Singapore Carrying Out the Next Lap Strategy to Achieve the Status of Developed Economy) in *Ajia Shoku no Sangyou Senryaku: Ajia no Jizokuteki Kaihatsu wo Tasu Shinsangyouseisaku* (Industrial Strategies in Asian Countries: New Industrial Policies Supplementing Sustainable Development in Asia), Nomura Research Institute, pp. 101–120 (in Japanese).

Wong, Poh-Kam (2000) Riding the Waves: Technological Change, Competing US-Japan Production Networks and the Growth of Singapore's Electronics

Industry, in M. Borrus, S. Haggard and D. Ernst (eds.), *International Production Networks in Asia: Rivalry or Riches?* London: Routledge, pp. 176–197.

Wong, Poh-Kam (2001) The Role of State in Singapore's Industrial Development, in Poh-Kam Wong and Chee-Yuen Ng (eds.), *Industrial Policy, Innovation and Economic Growth: The Experience of Japan and the East Asian NIEs*, Singapore University Press, pp. 503–579.

Wong, Poh-Kam, Phang Sock Yang, Yong Jong-Say and Chng Meng-Kng (1998) Development of Internationally Competitive Indigenous Manufacturing Firms in Singapore, in Takahashi Kazuo (ed.), *Asia's Development Experiments – How Internationally Competitive National Manufacturing Firms Have Developed in Asia*, FASID, pp. 372–453.

Wong, Soon Teck and Soon Beng Sim (1997) Total Factor Productivity Growth in Singapore: Methodology and Trends, paper presented at the OECD *Capital Stock Conference, Agenda Item VII*, 10–14 March 1997, Canberra, Australia.

World Bank (1993) *The East Asian Miracle: Economic Growth and Public Policy*, published for the World Bank by Oxford University Press.

Wu, Rong-I and Ming-Shen Tseng (1998) The Development of the Information Industry in Taiwan, in Kazuo Takahashi (ed.), *Asia's Development Experiences: How Internationally Competitive Manufacturing Firms Developed in Asia*, FASID, pp. 76–124.

Yeung, Henry Wai-Chung (1998) The Political Economy of Transnational Corporations: A Study of the Regionalization of Singaporean Firms, *Political Geography*, vol. 17, no. 4, pp. 389–416.

Young, Alwyn (1992) A Tale of Two Cities: Factor Accumulation and Technical Change in Hong Kong and Singapore, in *NBER Macroeconomics Annual 1992*, National Bureau of Economic Research, MIT Press, pp. 13–54.

Young, Alwyn (1995) The Tyranny of Numbers: Confronting the Statistical Realities of the East Asian Growth Experience, *Quarterly Journal of Economics*, vol. 110, no. 3, pp. 641–68.

Yue, Chia Siow Yue, Nick J. Freeman, *et al.* (2001) *Growth and Development of the IT Industry in Bangalore and Singapore: A Comparative Study*, New Delhi: Sterling Publishers.

Yusuf, Shahid (2001) The East Asian Miracle at the Millenium, in Joseph E. Stiglitz and Shahid Yusuf (eds.), *Rethinking the East Asia Miracle*, Oxford University Press, pp. 1–53.

APPENDIX

TRANSLOG INDICES OF CAPITAL, LABOR, AND PRODUCTIVITY GROWTH BY INDUSTRIES

Aggregate economy

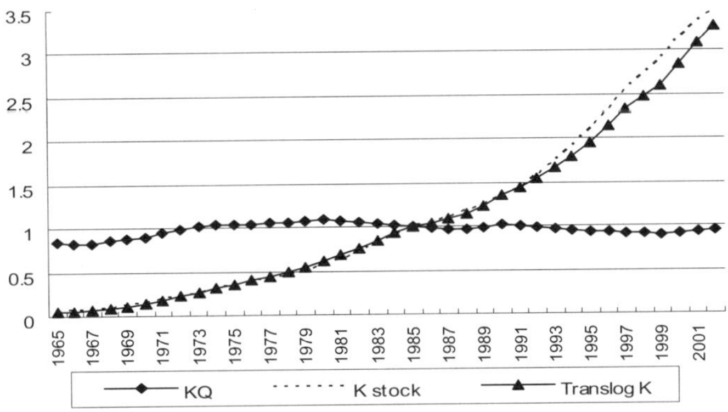

Manufacturing sector

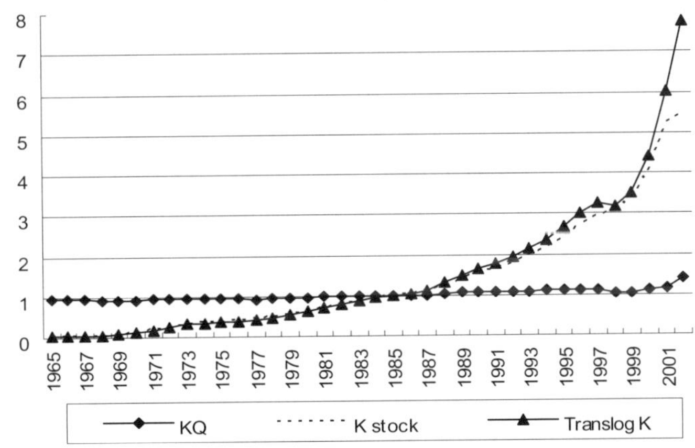

Fig. A.1. Translog indices by industry; Trans-log indices of capital by industry (1985 = 1.0).

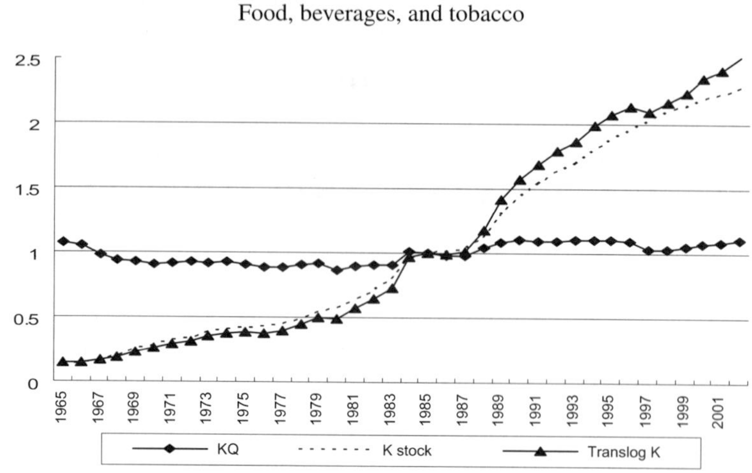

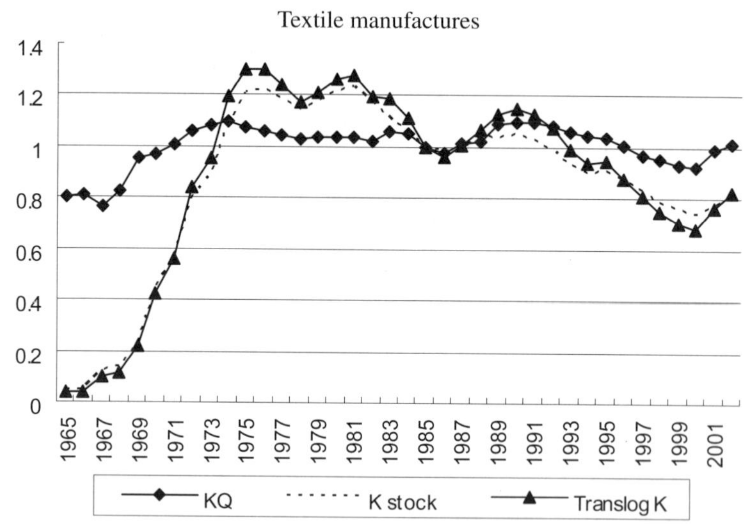

Fig. A.1. (*Continued*)

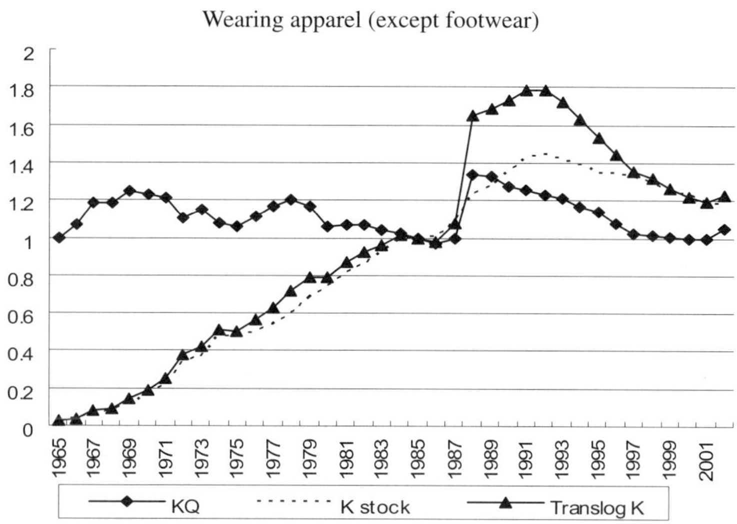

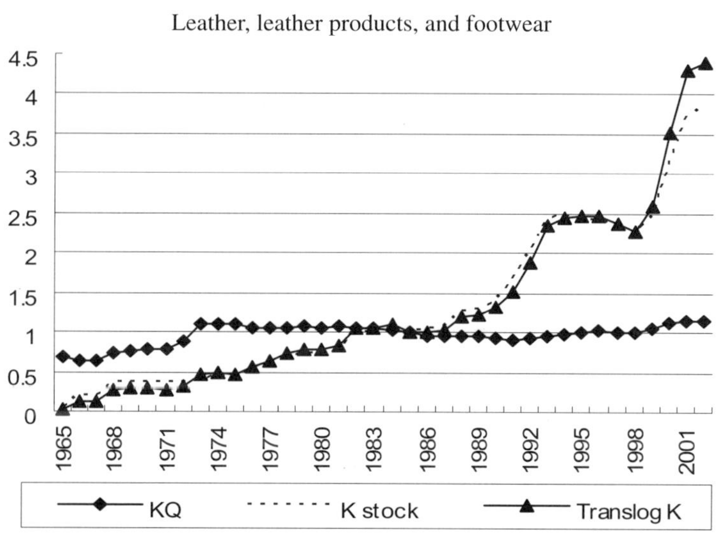

Fig. A.1. (*Continued*)

Wood and wood products

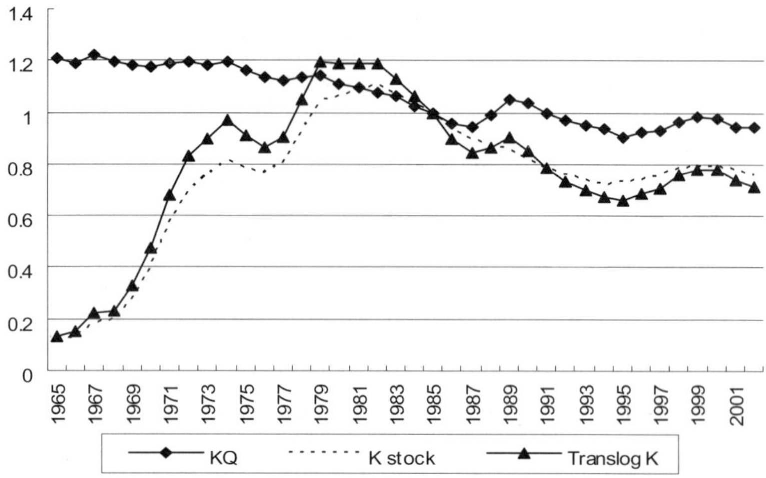

Furniture and fixtures (excl. metal furniture)

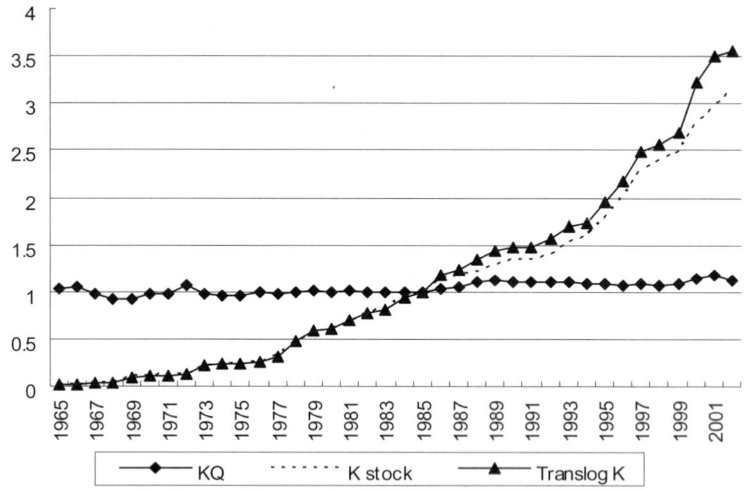

Fig. A.1. *(Continued)*

Paper and paper products

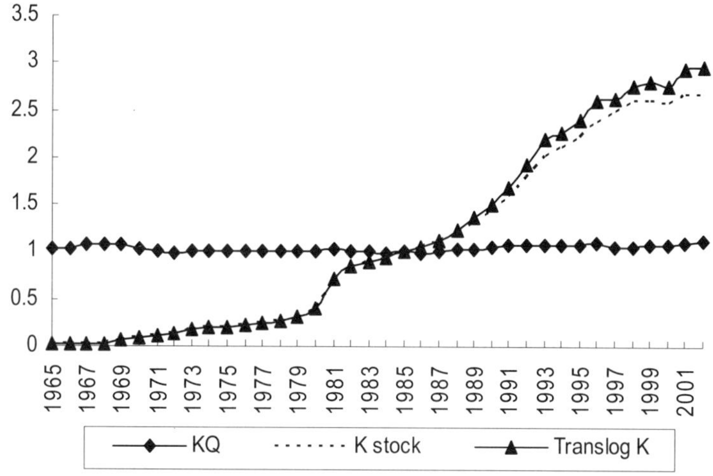

Publishing and printing

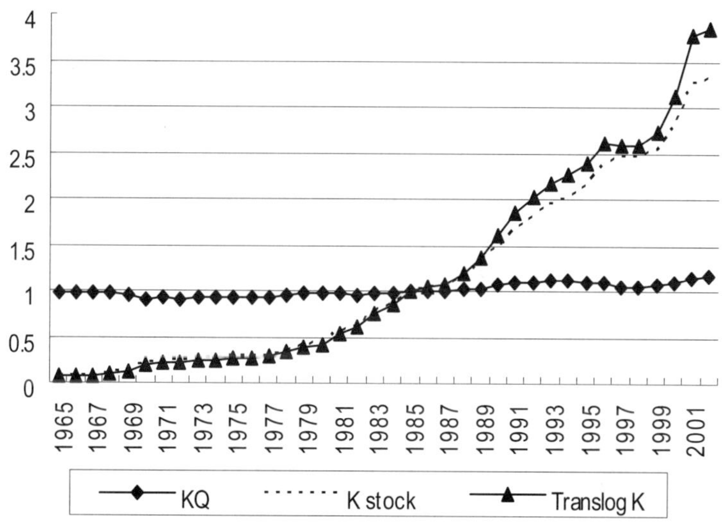

Fig. A.1. (*Continued*)

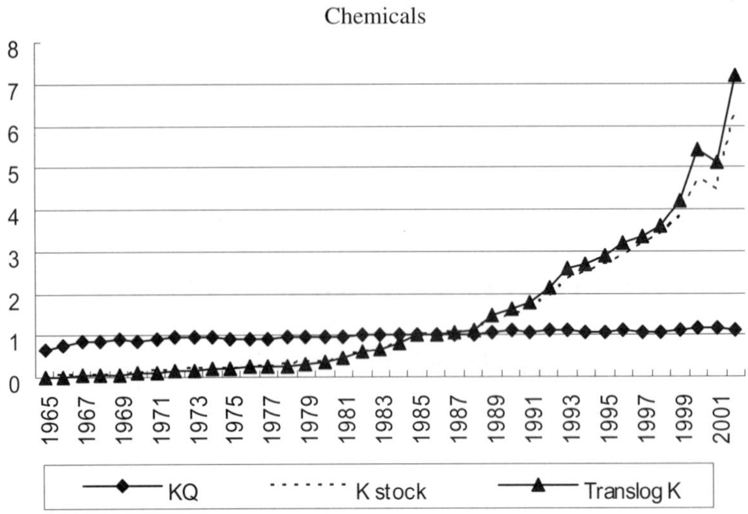

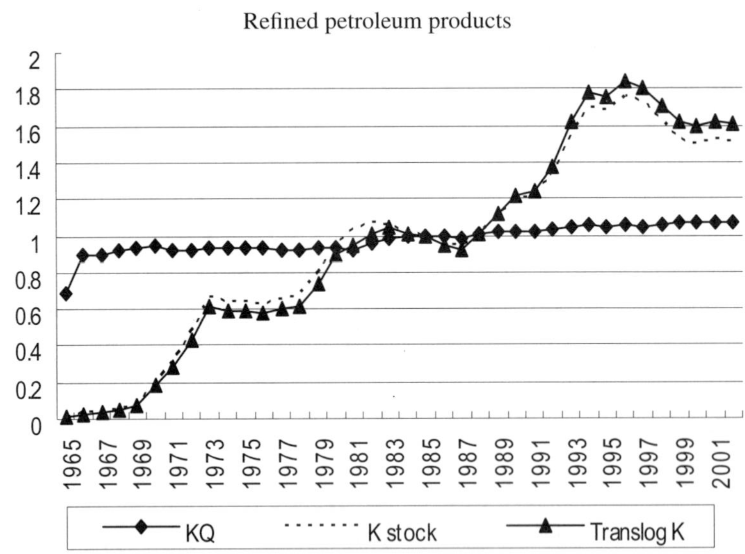

Fig. A.1. (*Continued*)

Rubber and plastic products

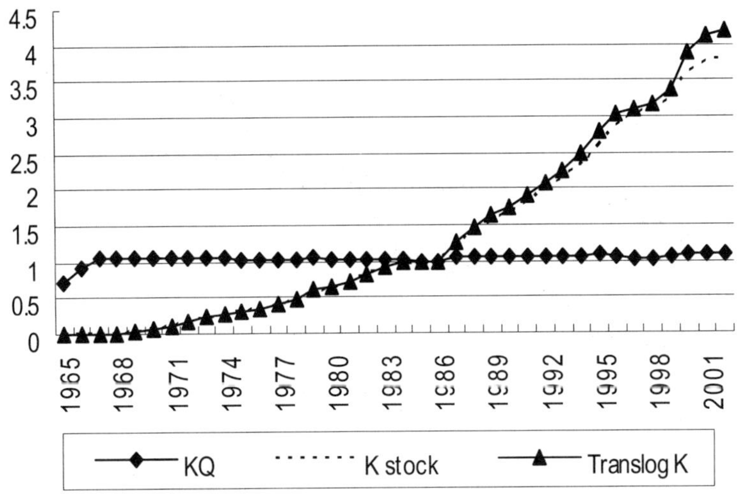

Non-metallic minerals

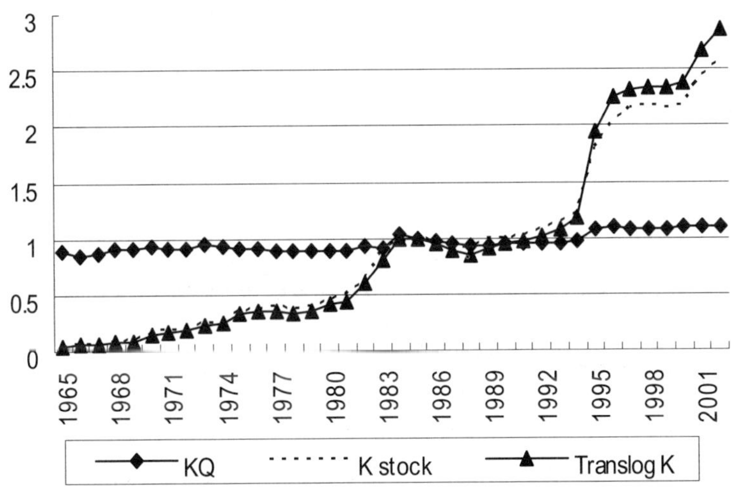

Fig. A.1. (*Continued*)

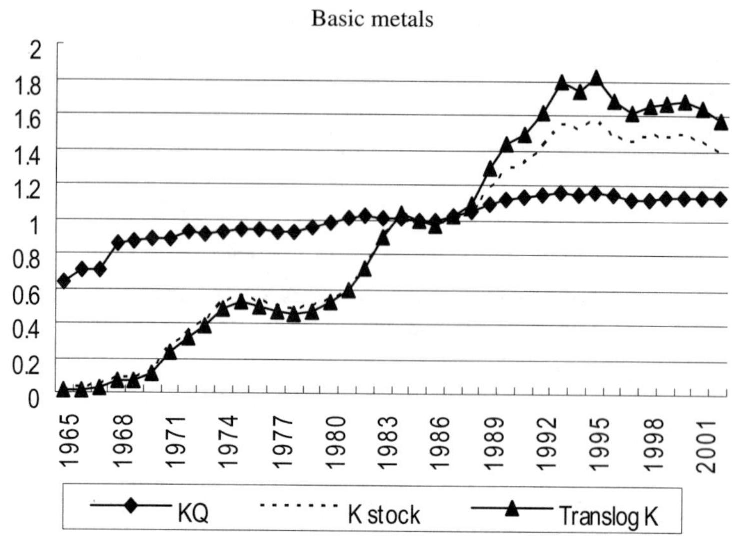

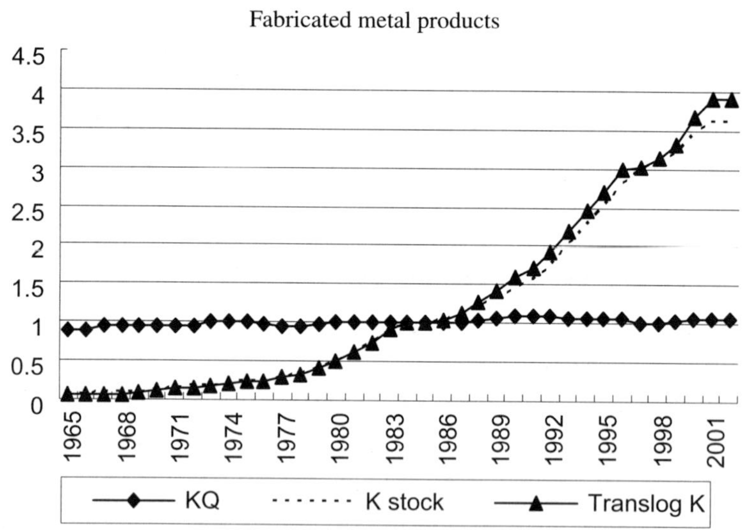

Fig. A.1. (*Continued*)

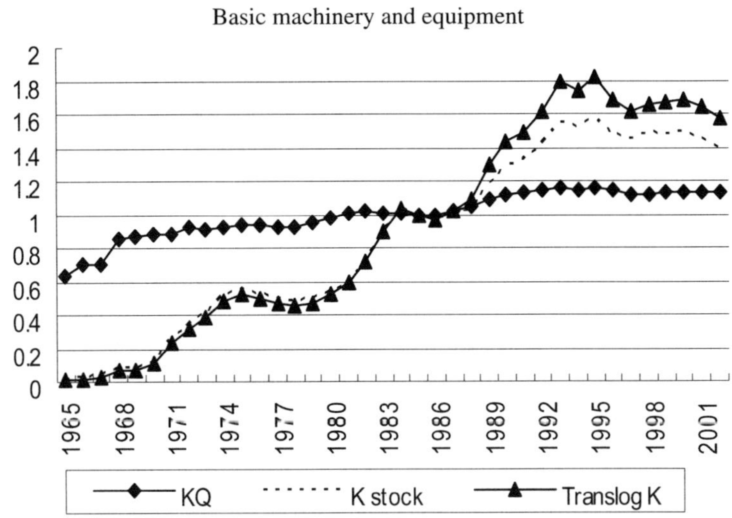

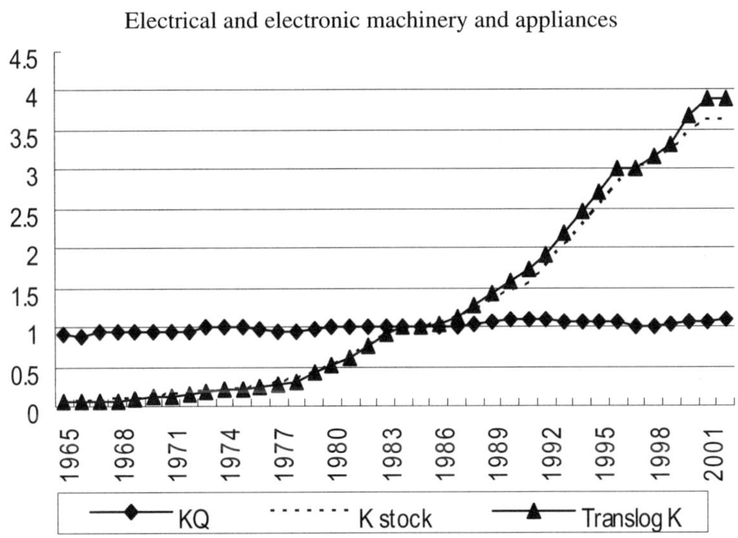

Fig. A.1. *(Continued)*

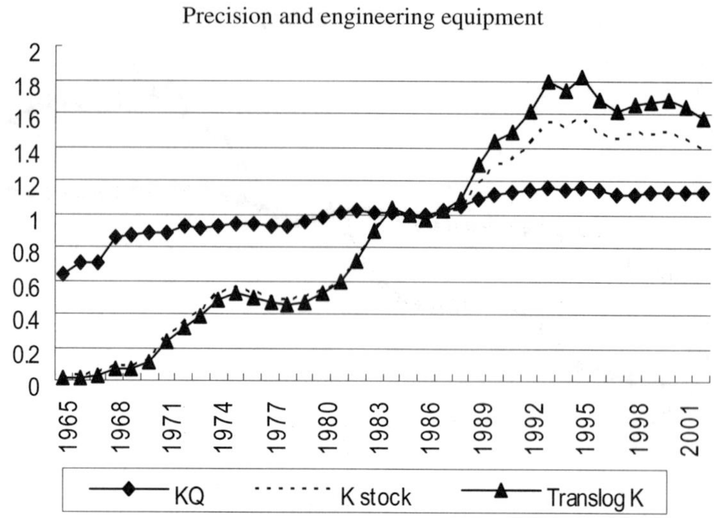

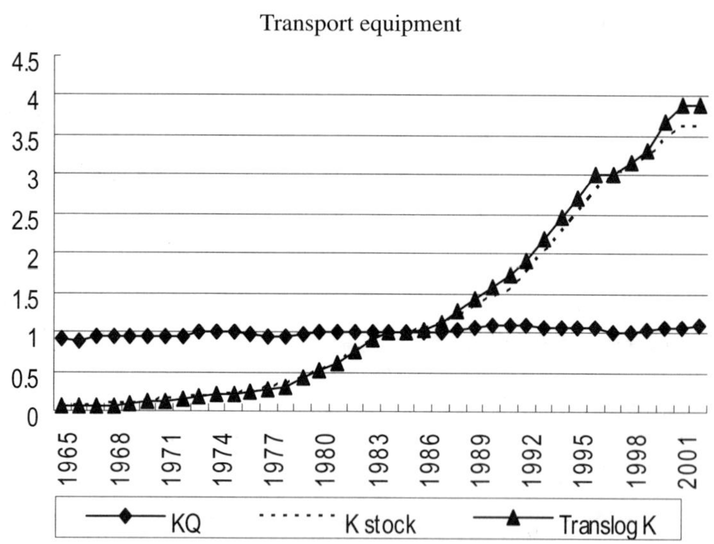

Fig. A.1. (*Continued*)

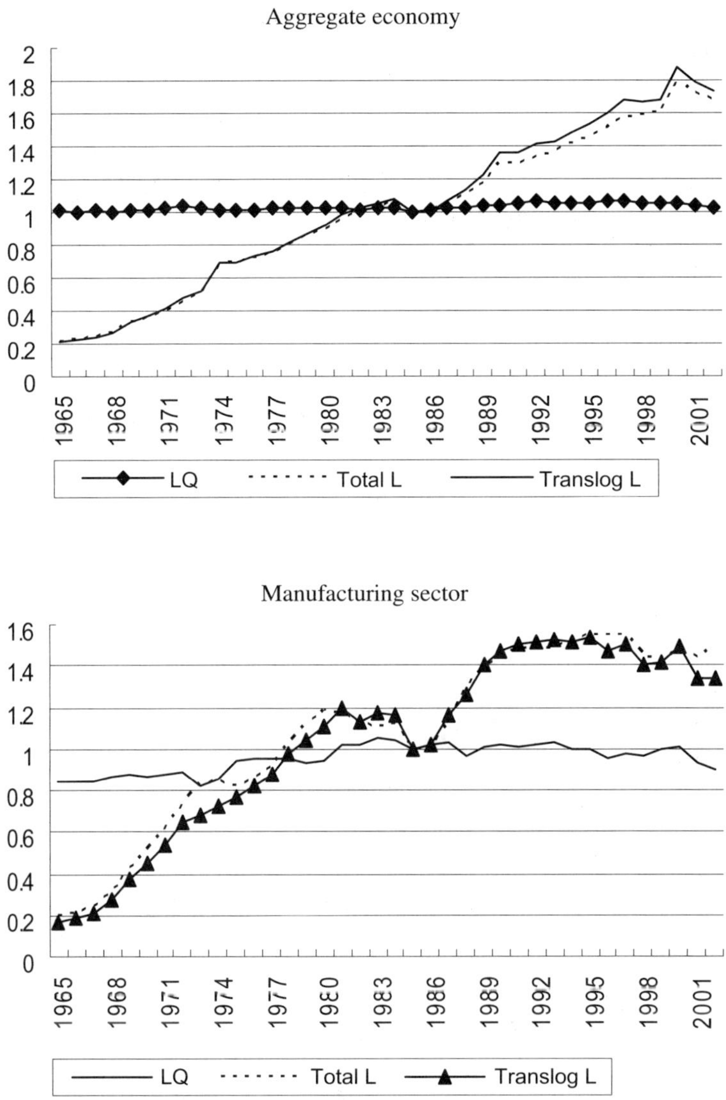

Fig. A.2. Translog indices of labor by industry (1985 = 1.0).

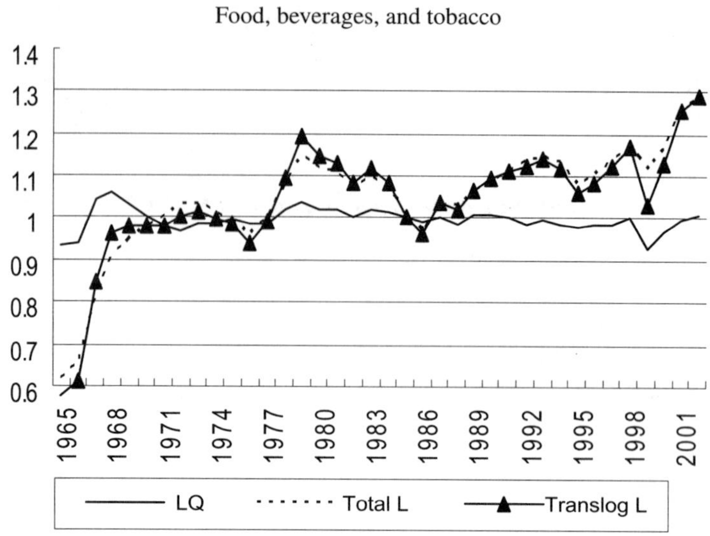

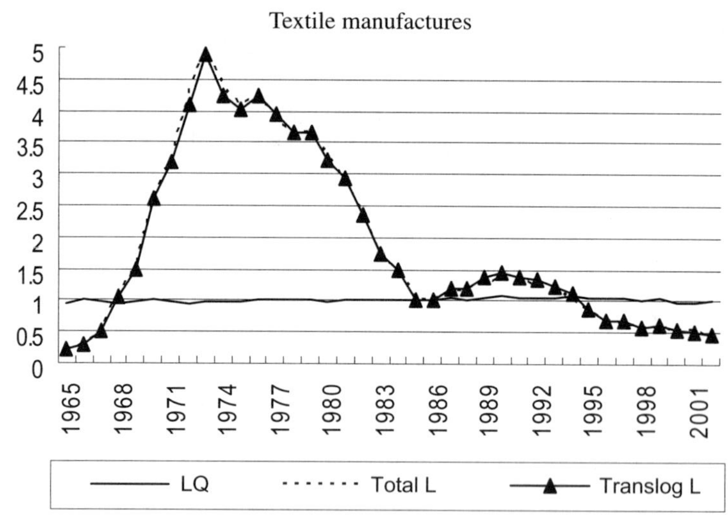

Fig. A.2. (*Continued*)

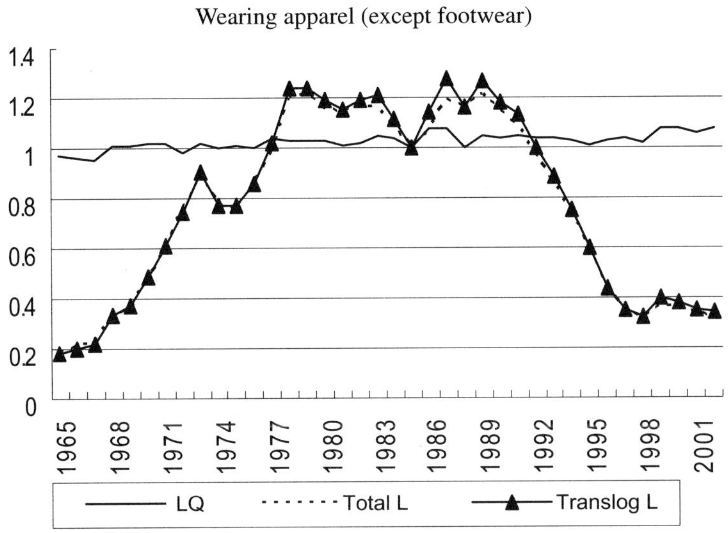

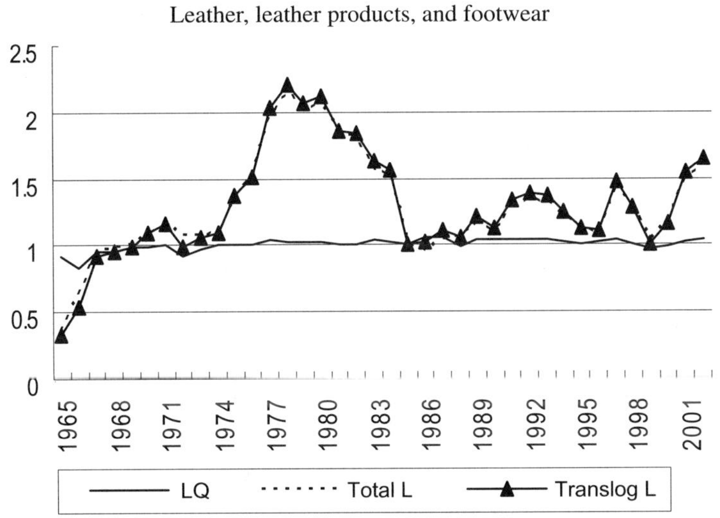

Fig. A.2. (*Continued*)

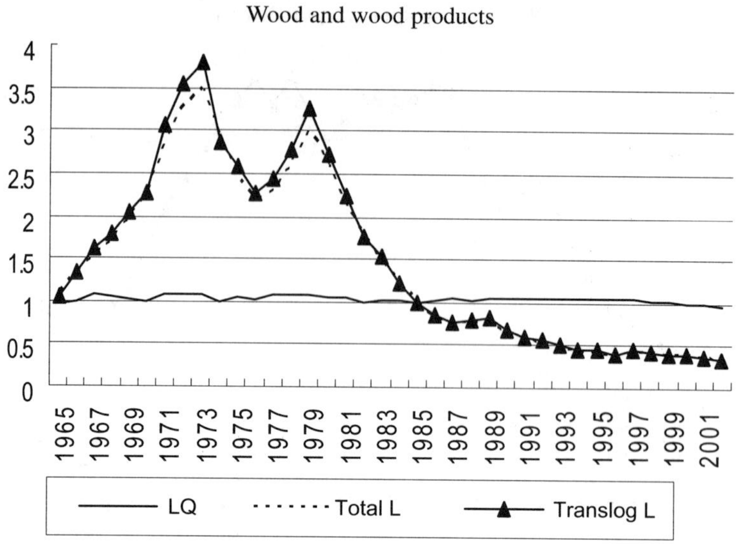

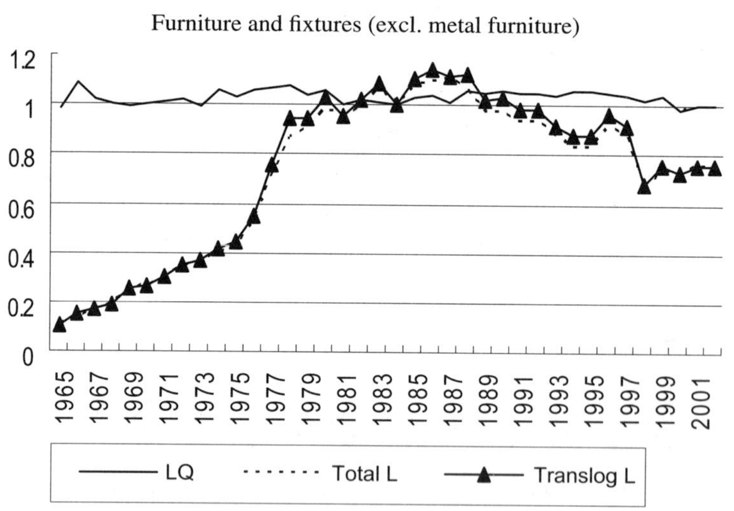

Fig. A.2. (*Continued*)

Paper and paper products

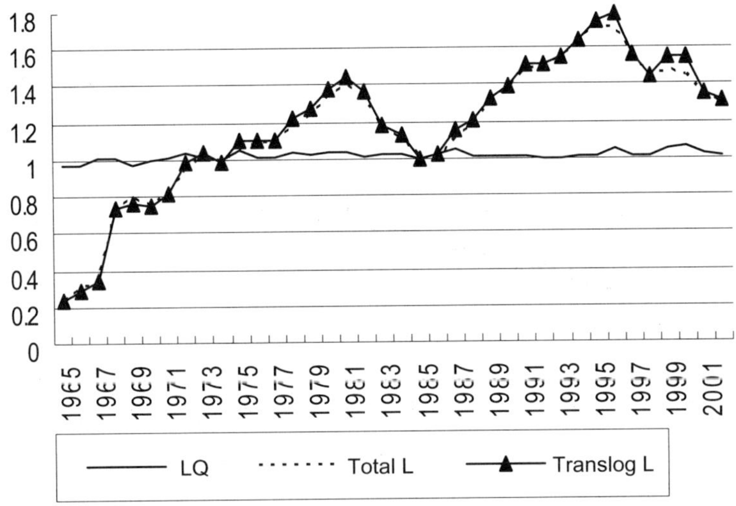

Publishing and printing

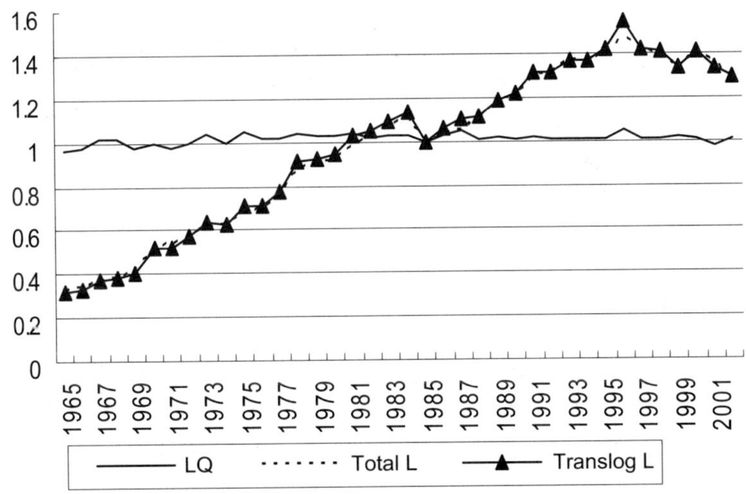

Fig. A.2. *(Continued)*

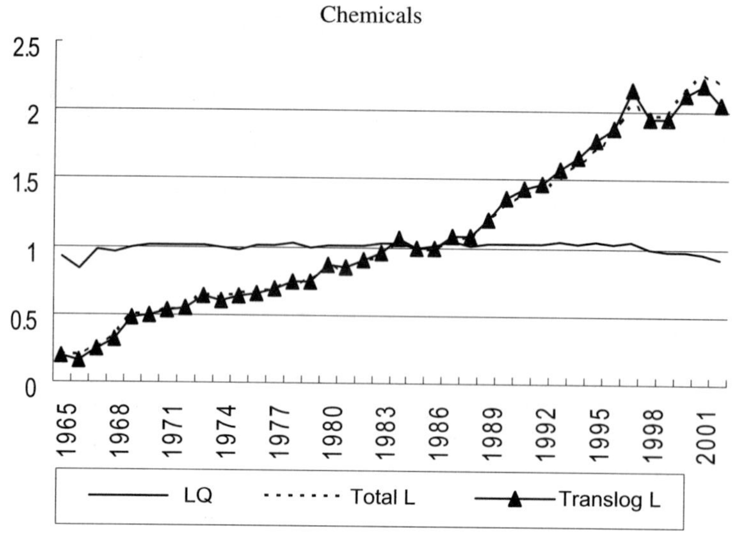

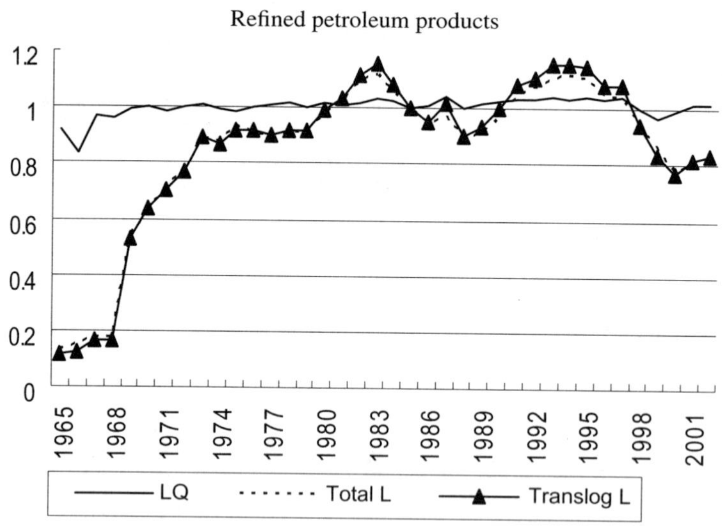

Fig. A.2. (*Continued*)

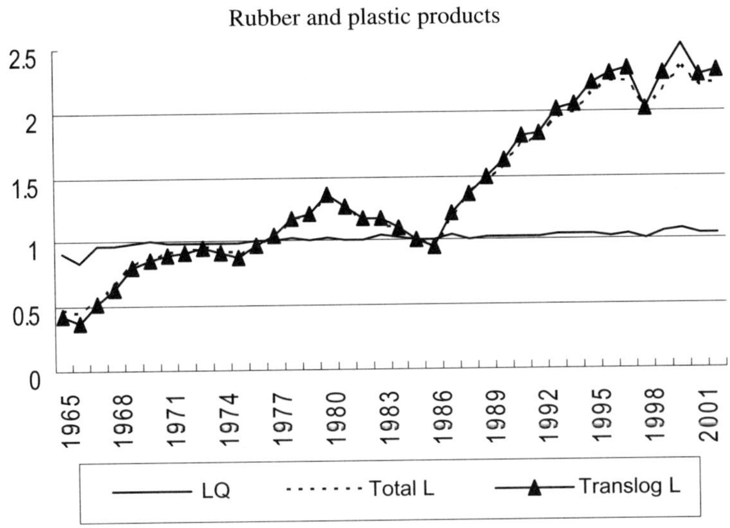

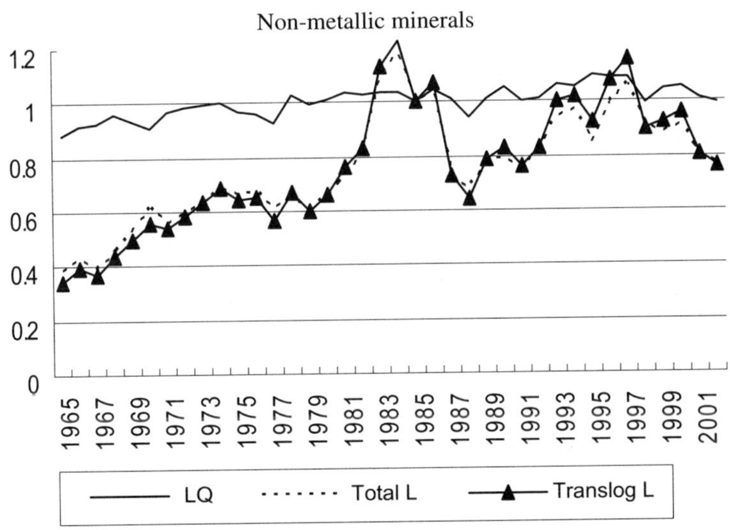

Fig. A.2. *(Continued)*

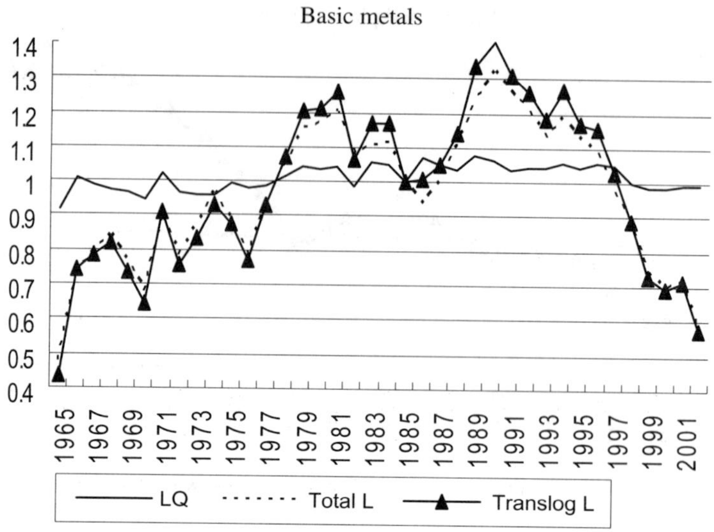

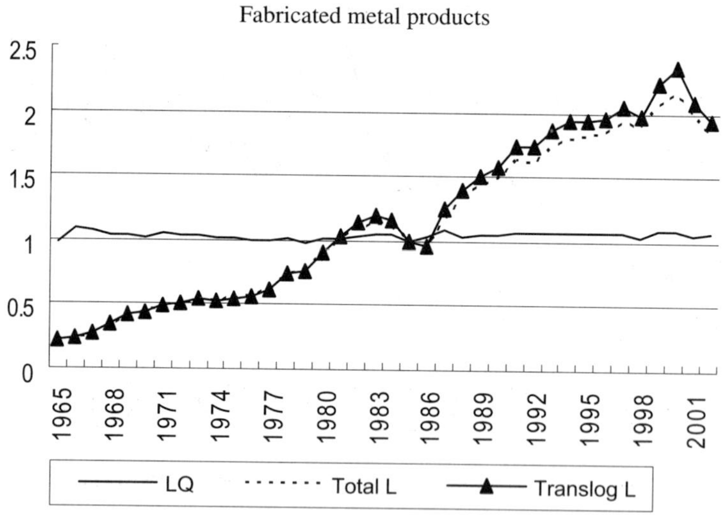

Fig. A.2. (*Continued*)

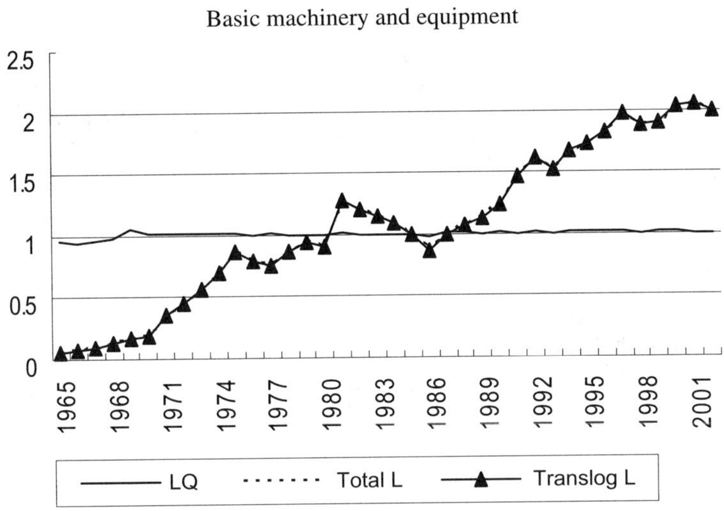

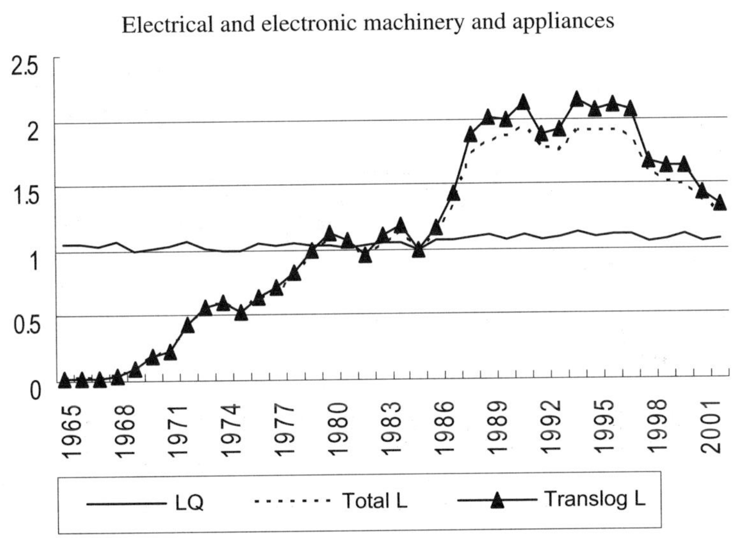

Fig. A.2. (*Continued*)

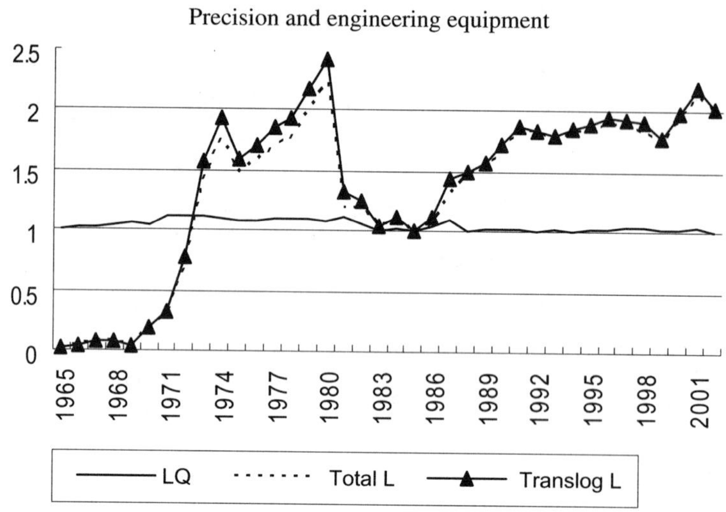

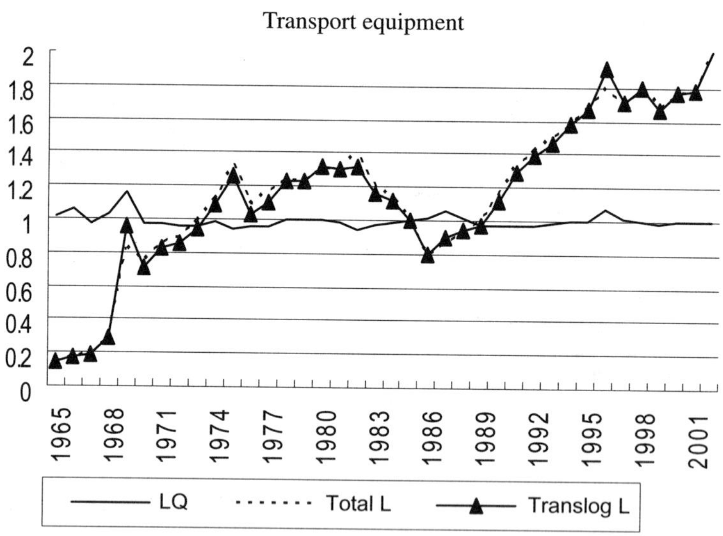

Fig. A.2. *(Continued)*

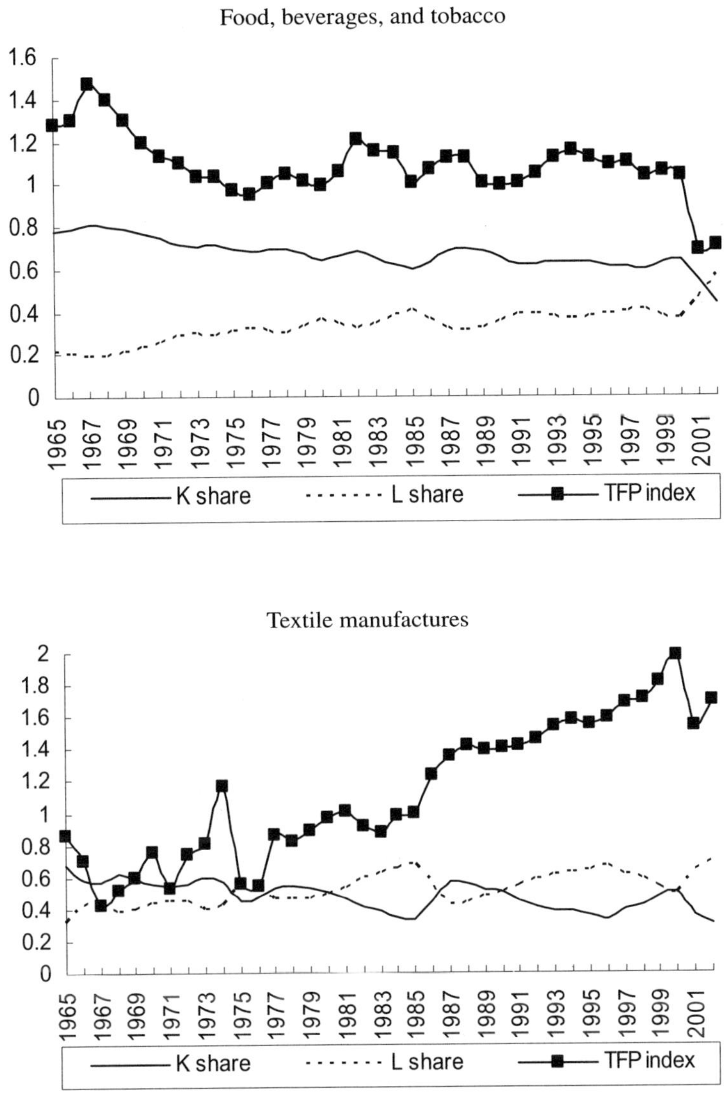

Fig. A.3. Translog index of productivity growth by industry (1985 = 1.0).

Wearing apparel (except footwear)

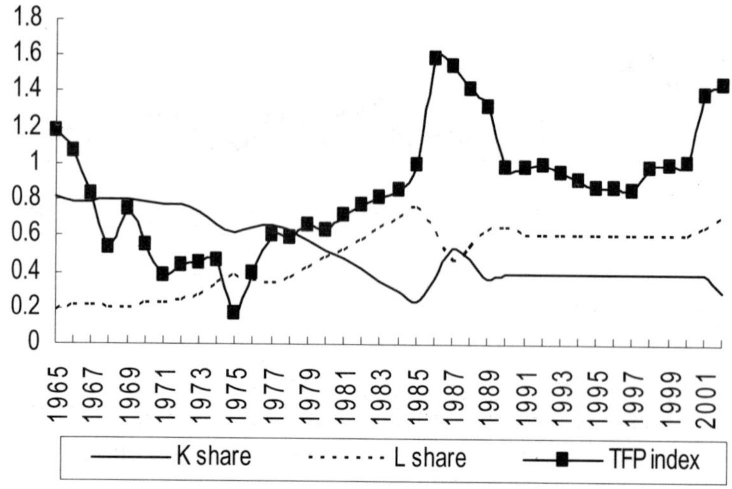

Leather, leather products, and footwear

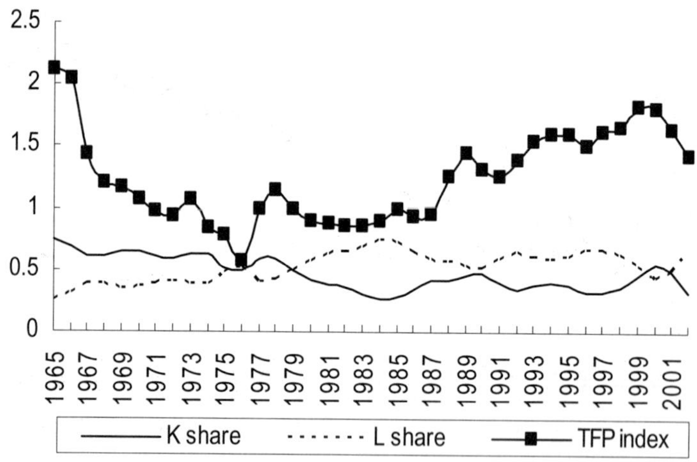

Fig. A.3. (*Continued*)

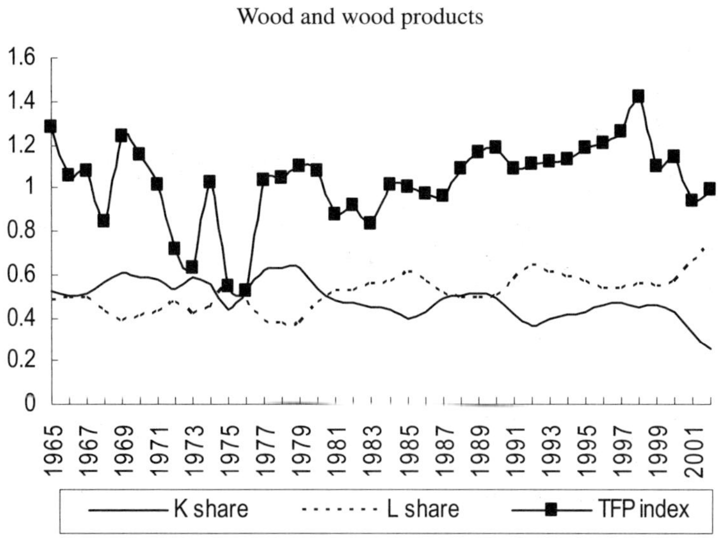

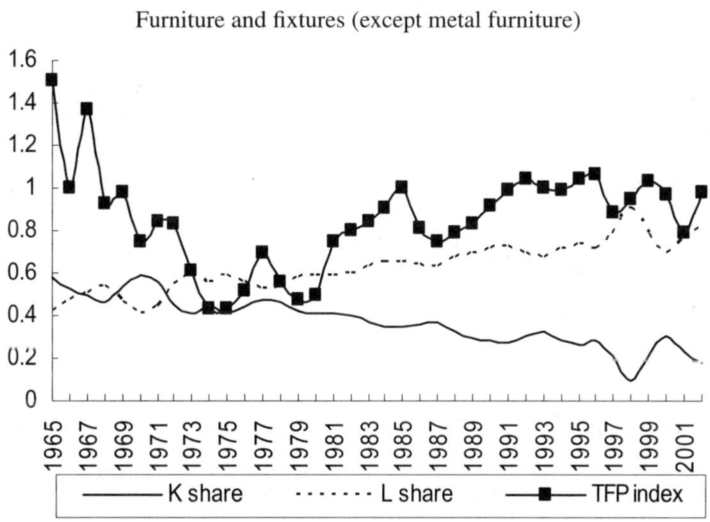

Fig. A.3. (*Continued*)

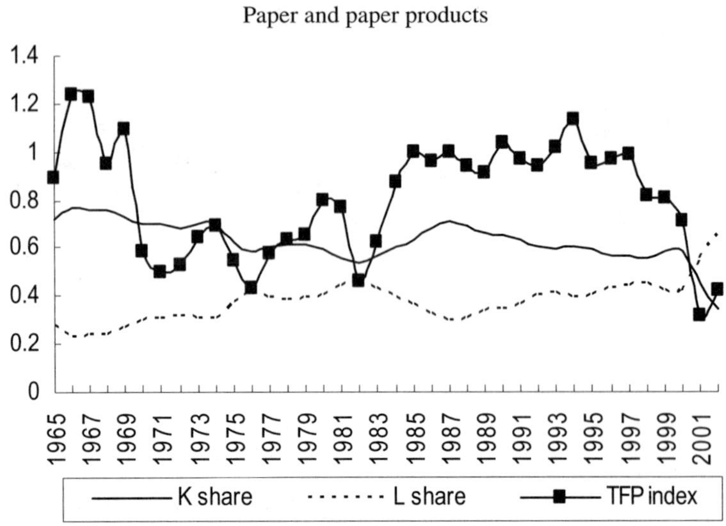

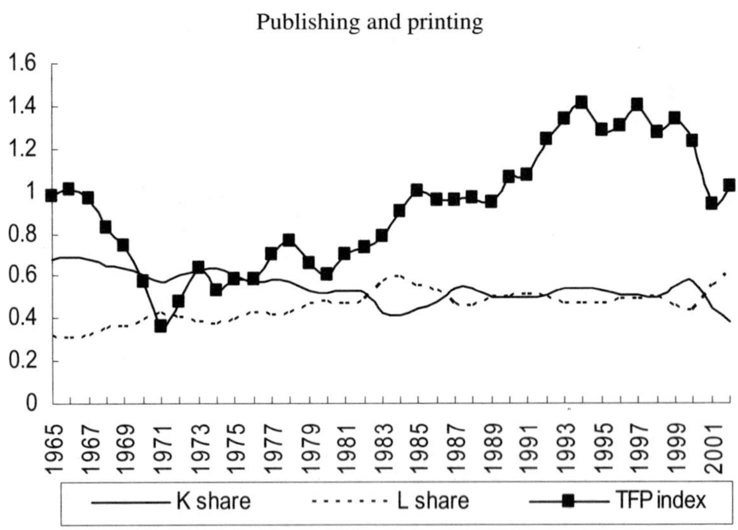

Fig. A.3. (*Continued*)

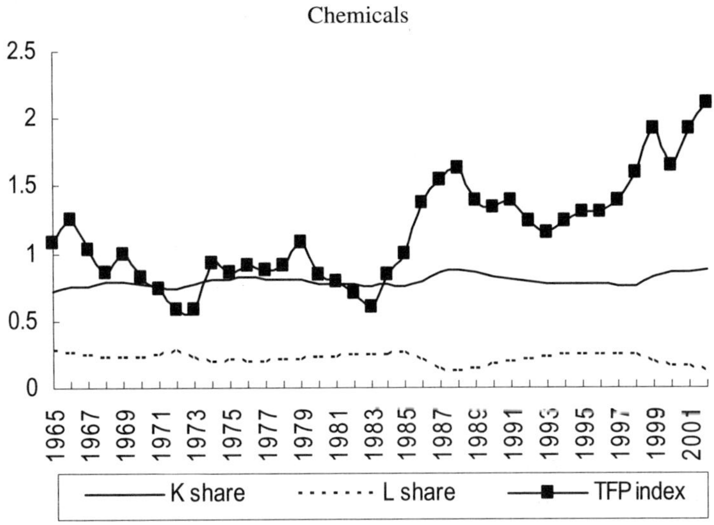

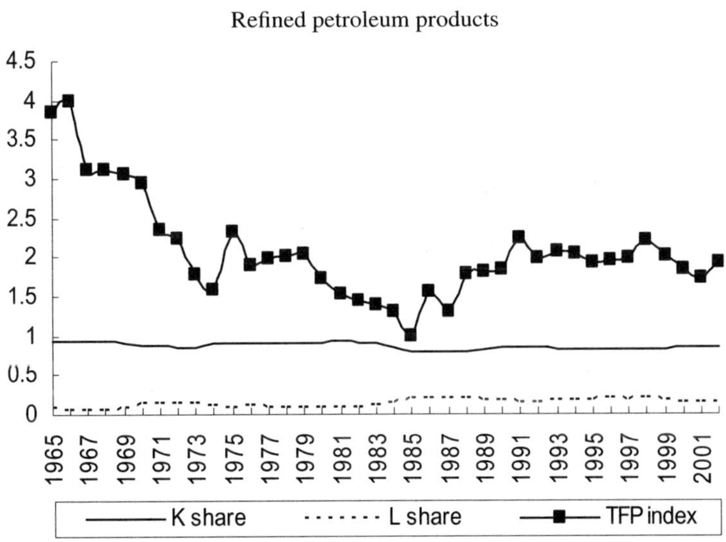

Fig. A.3. (*Continued*)

Rubber and plastic products

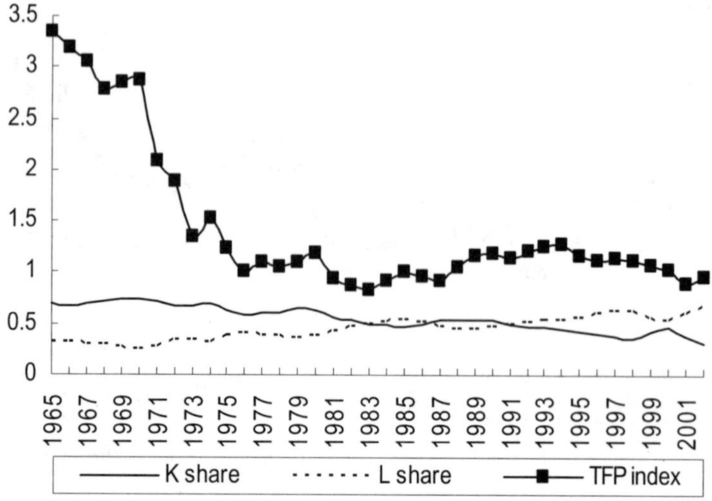

Non-metallic minerals

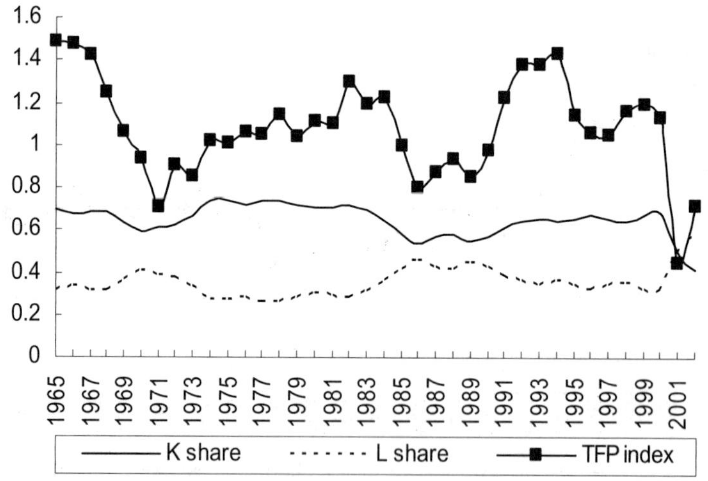

Fig. A.3. (*Continued*)

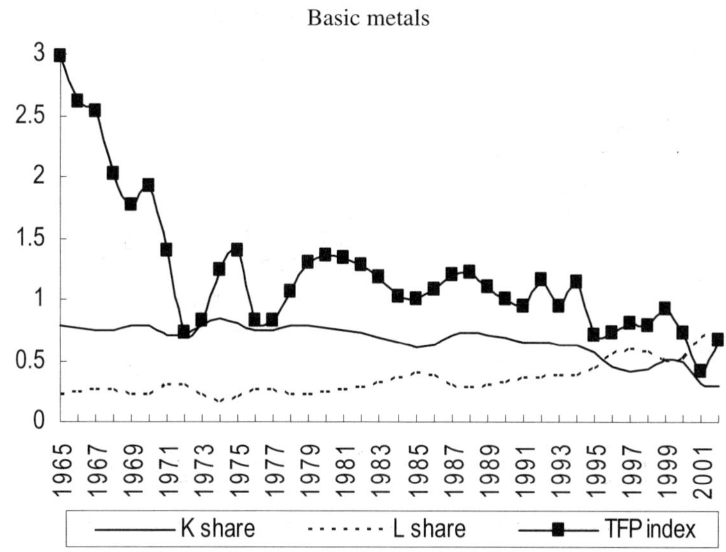

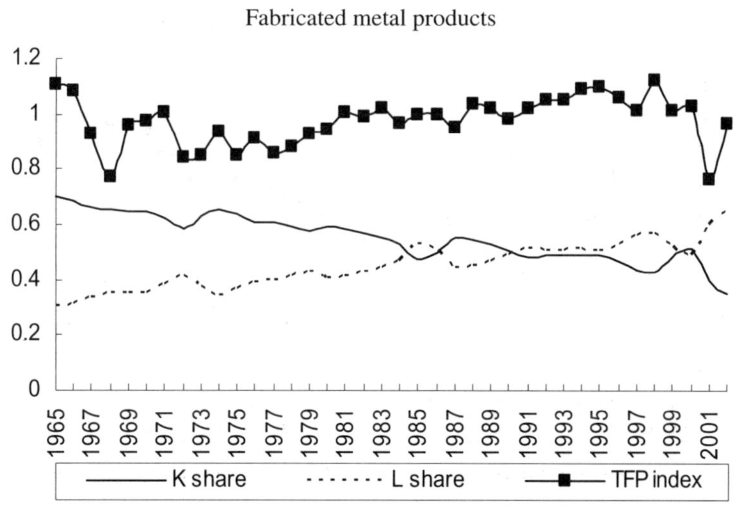

Fig. A.3. *(Continued)*

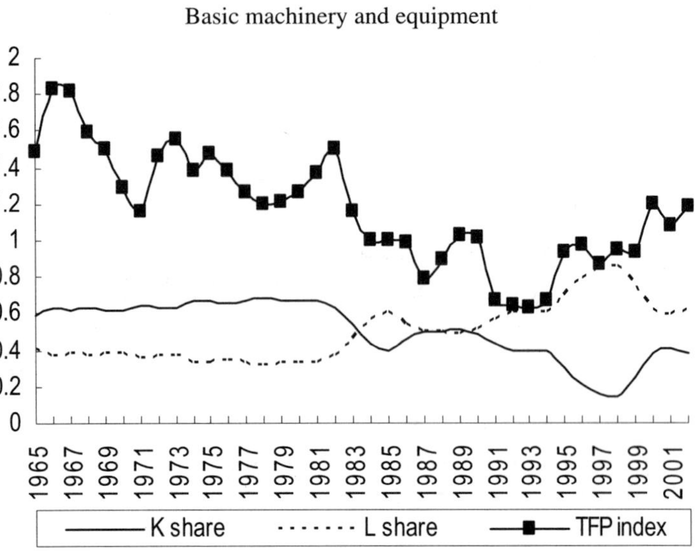

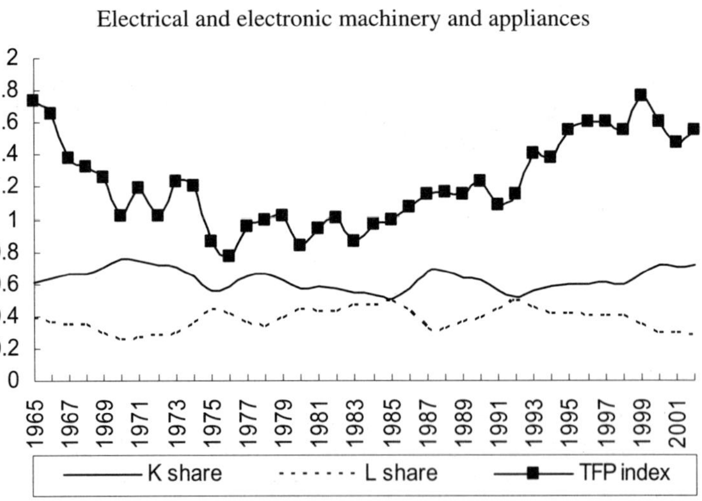

Fig. A.3. (*Continued*)

Precision and engineering equipment

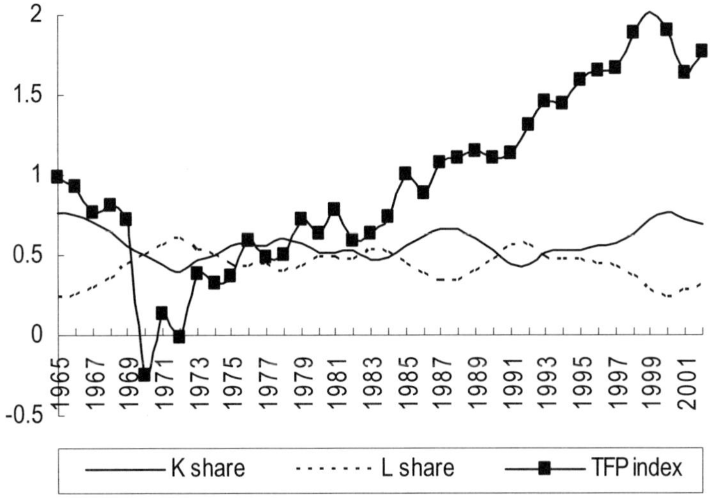

Transport equipment

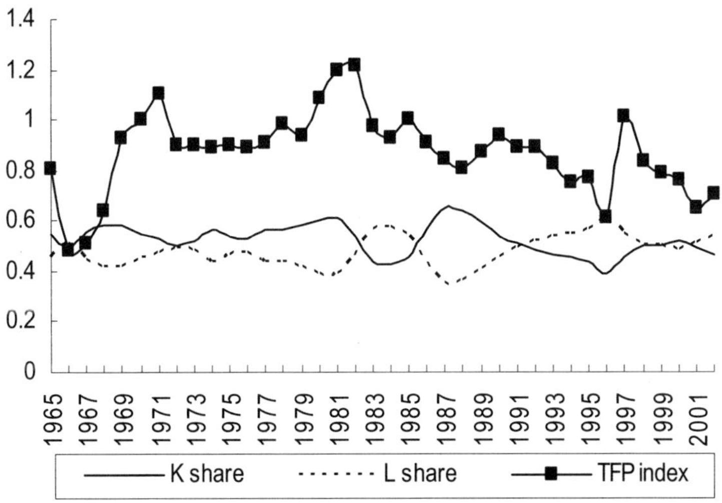

Fig. A.3. (*Continued*)

Index